SOMETHING ABOUT THE AUTHOR®

Something about
the Author *was named
an "**Outstanding
Reference Source,**"
the highest honor given
by the American
Library Association
Reference and Adult
Services Division.*

ISSN 0276-816X

SOMETHING ABOUT THE AUTHOR®

**Facts and Pictures about Authors
and Illustrators of Books for Young People**

volume 123

GALE GROUP

THOMSON LEARNING

Detroit • New York • San Diego • San Francisco
Boston • New Haven, Conn. • Waterville, Maine
London • Munich

STAFF

Scot Peacock, *Managing Editor, Literature Product*
Mark W. Scott, *Publisher, Literature Product*

Frank Castronova, *Senior Editor;* Katy Balcer, Sara L. Constantakis, Kristen A. Dorsch, Lisa Kumar, Thomas McMahon, Colleen Laine Tavor, *Editors;* Alana Joli Foster, Shayla Hawkins, Motoko Fujishiro Huthwaite, Arlene M. Johnson, Jennifer Kilian, Michelle Poole, Thomas Wiloch, *Associate Editors;* Madeline Harris, Maikue Vang, *Assistant Editors;* Anna Marie Dahn, Judith L. Pyko, *Administrative Support;* Joshua Kondek, Mary Ruby, *Technical Training Specialists*

Alan Hedblad, Joyce Nakamura, *Managing Editors*
Susan M. Trosky, *Literature Content Coordinator*

Victoria B. Cariappa, *Research Manager;* Tracie A. Richardson, *Project Coordinator;* Maureen Emeric, Barbara McNeil, Gary J. Oudersluys, Cheryl L. Warnock, *Research Specialists;* Sarah Genik, Ron Morelli, Tamara C. Nott, *Research Associates;* Nicodemus Ford, *Research Assistant;* Michelle Campbell, *Administrative Assistant*

Maria L. Franklin, *Permissions Manager;* Margaret Chamberlain, *Permissions Associate*

Mary Beth Trimper, *Manager, Composition and Prepress;* Dorothy Maki, *Manufacturing Manager;* Stacy Melson, *Buyer*

Barbara J. Yarrow, *Manager, Imaging and Multimedia Content;* Randy Bassett, *Imaging Supervisor;* Robert Duncan, Dan Newell, *Imaging Specialists;* Pamela A. Reed, *Imaging Coordinator;* Dean Dauphinais, *Senior Editor;* Robyn V. Young, *Project Manager;* Kelly A. Quin, *Editor*

Library of Congress Catalog Card Number 72-27107

ISBN 0-7876-4711-X
ISSN 0276-816X

Printed in the United States of America

10 9 8 7 6 5 4 3 2 1

Contents

Authors in Forthcoming Volumes vii
Introduction ix
Acknowledgments xiii
Illustrations Index 203
Author Index 229

Authors in Forthcoming Volumes

Below are some of the authors and illustrators that will be featured in upcoming volumes of *SATA*. These include new entries on the swiftly rising stars of the field, as well as completely revised and updated entries (indicated with *) on some of the most notable and best-loved creators of books for children.

Roberta Angeletti: Italian author Angeletti is the illustrator of more than twelve children's books, including Italian translations of *Alice in Wonderland* and *Pinocchio*. Angeletti's writings include the "Journey Through Time" series, which has been published simultaneously in English, French, and Italian. Two books in the series are *Nefertari, Princess of Egypt* and *The Cave Painter of Lascaux*.

Carmel Bird: A native of Australia and a former high school teacher, Bird writes and edits novels and short stories for children. Bird's titles include *The White Garden*, *Red Shoes*, and *Not Now Jack—I'm Writing a Novel*. Bird's critically acclaimed book, *The Bluebird Café,* is set in Tasmania, where she currently resides. Bird has been awarded six Australia Council grants.

Don Carter: Carter is an illustrator whose unique three-dimensional drawings have appeared in numerous children's books, as well as in *Sesame Street* and *Nick Jr.* magazines. Carter's own children's book titles include *Get to Work, Trucks!* and *Heaven's All-Star Jazz Band*. In 2000, Carter received the Original 2000 award from the Society of Illustrators.

*Jean Craighead George: Newbery Medal-winner George has made nature the center of her fiction and nonfiction in a writing career that has lasted more than fifty years. George has written over 100 books for children, including *Julie of the Wolves*, *River Rats, Inc.,* and *Frightful's Mountain*, which the *New York Times* listed as a Notable Children's Book in 1999.

Keiko Kasza: Born and raised in Japan, Kasza brings her childhood influences to the books she both writes and illustrates for young children. Kasza's acclaimed titles include *The Wolf's Chicken Stew*, *Grandpa Toad's Secrets*, and *Don't Laugh, Joe!*, which was designated as a Charlotte Zolotow Honor Book by the Cooperative Children's Book Center in 1998.

*Jim Murphy: Murphy pens both fiction and nonfiction titles for children and young adults. Murphy has published over twenty books, including *The Long Road to Gettysburg*, *Dinosaur for a Day*, and *Into the Deep Forest with Henry David Thoreau*. In addition to his numerous other citations and awards, Murphy received a Newbery Medal Honor Book designation in 1996 for *The Great Fire*.

Celia Rees: Rees is an English writer famous for her frightening and graphic horror novels for teenagers. Her titles include *Blood Sinister, Soul Taker,* and *Witch Child*. Rees is also the author of the popular "H.A.U.N.T.S." ghost story series for younger children.

*Robert Alan Silverstein: With his parents, Silverstein has coauthored more than forty science books for children. Silverstein writes proficiently in numerous scientific genres, as evidenced by his titles which include *Cystic Fibrosis*, *The Skeletal System*, *Plants*, and *Overcoming Acne: The How and Why of Healthy Skin Care*. Silverstein has also published over thirty children's and adult e-books under the pen names Robert Alan and Lyndon de Robertis.

*Brian Wildsmith: An English author and illustrator of fiction, poetry, and concept books for children, Wildsmith is considered by many critics to be one of the most accomplished artists in juvenile literature. Wildsmith also illustrates his own books, which include *ABC*, *The Seven Ravens*, and *Brian Wildsmith's Amazing World of Words*. Wildsmith's art is held in such high esteem that in 1994 the Brian Wildsmith Museum of Art opened in Izu, Japan.

*Lisa Yount: Yount is a prolific author who specializes in making scientific issues understandable to young readers. Among her books are *Black Scientists*, *Medical Technology,* and *Physician-Assisted Suicide and Euthanasia,* which in 2001 was given the "Not Ready for Newbery" award by the Pennsylvania School Librarians Association.

Introduction

Something about the Author (*SATA*) is an ongoing reference series that examines the lives and works of authors and illustrators of books for children. *SATA* includes not only well-known writers and artists but also less prominent individuals whose works are just coming to be recognized. This series is often the only readily available information source on emerging authors and illustrators. You'll find *SATA* informative and entertaining, whether you are a student, a librarian, an English teacher, a parent, or simply an adult who enjoys children's literature.

What's Inside SATA

SATA provides detailed information about authors and illustrators who span the full time range of children's literature, from early figures like John Newbery and L. Frank Baum to contemporary figures like Judy Blume and Richard Peck. Authors in the series represent primarily English-speaking countries, particularly the United States, Canada, and the United Kingdom. Also included, however, are authors from around the world whose works are available in English translation. The writings represented in *SATA* include those created intentionally for children and young adults as well as those written for a general audience and known to interest younger readers. These writings cover the entire spectrum of children's literature, including picture books, humor, folk and fairy tales, animal stories, mystery and adventure, science fiction and fantasy, historical fiction, poetry and nonsense verse, drama, biography, and nonfiction.

Obituaries are also included in *SATA* and are intended not only as death notices but also as concise overviews of people's lives and work. Additionally, each edition features newly revised and updated entries for a selection of *SATA* listees who remain of interest to today's readers and who have been active enough to require extensive revisions of their earlier biographies.

New Autobiography Feature

Beginning with Volume 103, *SATA* features three or more specially commissioned autobiographical essays in each volume. These unique essays, averaging about ten thousand words in length and illustrated with an abundance of personal photos, present an entertaining and informative first-person perspective on the lives and careers of prominent authors and illustrators profiled in *SATA*.

Two Convenient Indexes

In response to suggestions from librarians, *SATA* indexes no longer appear in every volume but are included in alternate (odd-numbered) volumes of the series, beginning with Volume 57.

SATA continues to include two indexes that cumulate with each alternate volume: the Illustrations Index, arranged by the name of the illustrator, gives the number of the volume and page where the illustrator's work appears in the current volume as well as all preceding volumes in the series; the Author Index gives the number of the volume in which a person's biographical sketch, autobiographical essay, or obituary appears in the current volume as well as all preceding volumes in the series.

These indexes also include references to authors and illustrators who appear in Gale's *Yesterday's Authors of Books for Children*, *Children's Literature Review*, and *Something about the Author Autobiography Series*.

Easy-to-Use Entry Format

Whether you're already familiar with the *SATA* series or just getting acquainted, you will want to be aware of the kind of information that an entry provides. In every *SATA* entry the editors attempt to give as complete a picture of the person's life and work as possible. A typical entry in *SATA* includes the following clearly labeled information sections:

- *PERSONAL:* date and place of birth and death, parents' names and occupations, name of spouse, date of marriage, names of children, educational institutions attended, degrees received, religious and political affiliations, hobbies and other interests.

- *ADDRESSES:* complete home, office, electronic mail, and agent addresses, whenever available.

- *CAREER:* name of employer, position, and dates for each career post; art exhibitions; military service; memberships and offices held in professional and civic organizations.

- *AWARDS, HONORS:* literary and professional awards received.

- *WRITINGS:* title-by-title chronological bibliography of books written and/or illustrated, listed by genre when known; lists of other notable publications, such as plays, screenplays, and periodical contributions.

- *ADAPTATIONS:* a list of films, television programs, plays, CD-ROMs, recordings, and other media presentations that have been adapted from the author's work.

- *WORK IN PROGRESS:* description of projects in progress.

- *SIDELIGHTS:* a biographical portrait of the author or illustrator's development, either directly from the biographee—and often written specifically for the *SATA* entry—or gathered from diaries, letters, interviews, or other published sources.

- *BIOGRAPHICAL AND CRITICAL SOURCES:* cites sources quoted in "Sidelights" along with references for further reading.

- *EXTENSIVE ILLUSTRATIONS:* photographs, movie stills, book illustrations, and other interesting visual materials supplement the text.

How a SATA Entry Is Compiled

A *SATA* entry progresses through a series of steps. If the biographee is living, the *SATA* editors try to secure information directly from him or her through a questionnaire. From the information that the biographee supplies, the editors prepare an entry, filling in any essential missing details with research and/or telephone interviews. If possible, the author or illustrator is sent a copy of the entry to check for accuracy and completeness.

If the biographee is deceased or cannot be reached by questionnaire, the *SATA* editors examine a wide variety of published sources to gather information for an entry. Biographical and bibliographic sources are consulted, as are book reviews, feature articles, published interviews, and material sometimes obtained from the biographee's family, publishers, agent, or other associates.

Entries that have not been verified by the biographees or their representatives are marked with an asterisk (*).

Contact the Editor

We encourage our readers to examine the entire *SATA* series. Please write and tell us if we can make *SATA* even more helpful to you. Give your comments and suggestions to the editor:

BY MAIL: Editor, *Something about the Author,* The Gale Group, 27500 Drake Rd., Farmington Hills, MI 48331-3535.

BY TELEPHONE: (800) 877-GALE

BY FAX: (248) 699-8054

Something about the Author Product Advisory Board

The editors of *Something about the Author* are dedicated to maintaining a high standard of excellence by publishing comprehensive, accurate, and highly readable entries on a wide array of writers for children and young adults. In addition to the quality of the content, the editors take pride in the graphic design of the series, which is intended to be orderly yet inviting, allowing readers to utilize the pages of *SATA* easily and with efficiency. Despite the longevity of the *SATA* print series, and the success of its format, we are mindful that the vitality of a literary reference product is dependent on its ability to serve its users over time. As literature, and attitudes about literature, constantly evolve, so do the reference needs of students, teachers, scholars, journalists, researchers, and book club members. To be certain that we continue to keep pace with the expectations of our customers, the editors of *SATA* listen carefully to their comments regarding the value, utility, and quality of the series. Librarians, who have firsthand knowledge of the needs of library users, are a valuable resource for us. The *Something about the Author* Product Advisory Board, made up of school, public, and academic librarians, is a forum to promote focused feedback about *SATA* on a regular basis. The five-member advisory board includes the following individuals, whom the editors wish to thank for sharing their expertise:

- **Eva M. Davis,** Teen Services Librarian, Plymouth District Library, Plymouth, Michigan

- **Joan B. Eisenberg,** Lower School Librarian, Milton Academy, Milton, Massachusetts

- **Francisca Goldsmith,** Teen Services Librarian, Berkeley Public Library, Berkeley, California

- **Monica F. Irlbacher,** Young Adult Librarian, Middletown Thrall Library, Middletown, New York

- **Caryn Sipos,** Librarian--Young Adult Services, King County Library System, Washington

Acknowledgments

Grateful acknowledgment is made to the following publishers, authors, and artists whose works appear in this volume.

ALLEN, PAMELA. Allen, Pamela, illustrator. From illustrations in her *A Lion in the Night.* G. P. Putnam's Sons, 1985. Copyright © 1985 by Pamela Allen. Reproduced by permission of The Putnam Publishing Group. / Allen, Pamela, illustrator. From an illustration in her *Mr. Archimedes' Bath.* Angus & Robertson, 1980. Copyright © Pamela Allen 1980. Reproduced by permission of HarperCollins Publishers Australia. / Allen, Pamela, photograph by Jim Allen. Reproduced by permission of Pamela Allen.

BLUMBERG, RHODA. Morgan, Mary, illustrator. From a cover of *Bloomers!,* by Rhoda Blumberg. Aladdin Paperbacks, 1996. Illustrations copyright © 1993 by Mary Morgan. Reproduced by permission of Simon & Schuster Macmillan. / Buxton, John, illustrator. From a jacket of *What's the Deal? Jefferson, Napoleon, and the Louisiana Purchase,* by Rhonda Blumberg. National Geographic Society, 1998. Jacket copyright © 1998 National Geographic Society. Reproduced by permission of the illustrator. / Blumberg, Rhoda, photograph. Reproduced by permission of Rhoda Blumberg.

BRADBURY, RAY. Diamond, Donna, illustrator. From a cover of *Fahrenheit 451,* by Ray Bradbury. Ballantine, 1991. Reproduced by permission of Random House, Inc. / Bradbury, Ray. From a cover of his *The Illustrated Man.* Bantam Books, 1967. Copyright © 1951 by Ray Bradbury. Reproduced by permission of Bantam Books, a division of Random House, Inc. / Bradbury, Ray, photograph. The Library of Congress.

CATTELL, JAMES. Cattell, James, photograph. Reproduced by permission.

CUMMINGS, PHIL. Cummings, Phil, photograph. Reproduced by permission.

DALE, KIM. Dale, Kim, photograph. Reproduced by permission.

DE GOLDI, KATHLEEN DOMENICA. De Goldi, Kathleen Domenica, photograph. Reproduced by permission.

DEFORD, DEBORAH H. Mock, Paul, illustrator. From a cover of *An Enemy Among Them,* by Deborah H. DeFord and Harry S. Stout. Houghton Mifflin Company, 1987. Cover artwork © 1987 by Paul Mock. Reproduced by permission of Houghton Mifflin Company.

FEINBERG, BARBARA SILBERDICK. Feinberg, Barbara Silberdick, photograph. Reproduced by permission.

FIGLER, JEANIE. Figler, Jeanie, photograph. Reproduced by permission.

FREEDMAN, RUSSELL. Freedman, Russell. From a cover of his *Lincoln: A Photobiography.* Clarion Books, 1987. Reproduced by permission of Houghton Mifflin Company. / Freedman, Russell. From a jacket of his *Babe Didrikson Zaharias: The Making of a Champion.* Clarion Books, 1999. Copyright © 1999 by Russell Freedman. (Center, top right, bottom left cover photos by UPI/Corbis Bettman; top left photo from Babe Didrikson Zaharias Collection, Special Collections, Mary and John Gray Library, Lamar University,Beaumont, Texas; bottom right photo by AP/World Wide Photographs.) Reproduced by permission of Houston Mifflin Company. / Trumbull, John, illustrator. From a jacket of *Give Me Liberty! The Story of the Declaration of Independence,* by Russell Freedman. Holiday House, 2000. Jacket painting *The Death of General Warren at the Battle of Bunker's Hill, 17 June 1775* by John Trumbull. Reproduced by permission of Yale University Art Gallery. / Freedman, Russell, looking forward, books on shelves in background, photograph. Reproduced by permission.

GARANT, ANDRE J. Garant, Andre J., photograph. Reproduced by permission. / Garant, Andre J. From a cover of his *Slap Shot.* 1st Books Library, 2000. Copyright © 2000 Andre J. Garant. Reproduced by permission of 1st Books Library.

GHERMAN, BEVERLY. Rockwell, Norman, illustrator. From a cover of *Norman Rockwell: Storyteller with a Brush,* by Beverly Gherman. Atheneum, 2000. Cover illustration *Soda Jerk* by Norman Rockwell. Reproduced by permission of Columbia Museum of Art, Ohio and the Norman Rockwell Estate.

GOLDBERG, JAN. Goldberg, Jan, photograph. Reproduced by permission.

HALE, BRUCE. Hale, Bruce, photograph by Brian Reed. Reproduced by permission of Mr. Hale.

HALVORSON, MARILYN. Halvorson, Marilyn, photograph. Reproduced by permission.

HAMILTON, VIRGINIA (ESTHER). Hamilton, Virginia, sitting in front of computer monitor, smiling directly at camera, photograph. Reproduced by permission.

HARVEY, ROLAND. Harvey, Roland, illustrator. From an illustration in *My Place in Space,* by Robin and Sally Hirst. Orchard, 1992. Illustration copyright © 1988 by The Five Miles Press. Airbrushed astronomical painting copyright © 1988 by Joe Levine. Reproduced by permission of Orchard Books.

HERNANDEZ, NATALIE NELSON. Hernandez, Natalie Nelson, photograph. Reproduced by permission.

HOGROGIAN, NONNY. Hogrogian, Nonny, illustrator. From a jacket of *The Animal,* by David Kherdian. Jacket illustration by Nonny Hogrogian. Reproduced by permission of Nonny Hogrogian. / Hogrogian, Nonny, all photographs reproduced by permission of the author.

HURD, (JOHN) THACHER. Hurd, Thacher. From an illustration in his *Axle the Freeway Cat.* Reproduced by permission of Hurd Thacher. / Hurd, Thacher, illustrator. From an illustration in his *Mystery on the Docks.* Reproduced by permission of Thacher Hurd. / Hurd, Thacher. From an illustration in his *Art Dog.* Reproduced by permission of Thacher Hurd. / Hurd, Thacher, with his wife Olivia at their Peaceable Kingdom Press, photograph by John Blaustein. Reproduced by permission of Thacher Hurd / Hurd, Thacher, wearing denim shirt, in studio, photograph by Steve Fisch. Reproduced by permission of Thacher Hurd. / All other photographs reproduced bypermission of the author.

JOHNSON, ART. Johnson, Art. From a cover of his *Famous Problems and Their Mathematicians.* Libraries Unlimited, Inc., 1999. Copyright © 1999 Libraries Unlimited. (800) 237-6124 or www.lu.com. Reproduced by permission. / Johnson, Art, photograph. Reproduced by permission.

KIRSHNER, DAVID S. Kirshner, David S., photograph. Reproduced by permission.

KRUPP, E.C. Krupp, E. C., photograph. Reproduced by permission.

LANINO, DEBORAH. Lanino, Deborah, photograph. Reproduced by permission.

MATHABANE, MARK. Mathabane, Mark. From a cover of *Kaffir Boy: An Autobiography.* Touchstone, 1986. Cover photographs: (boy) © Fred House/Tony Stone Images, (landscape) © Kirsty McLaren/tony Stone Images. Reproduced by permission of Getty Stone Images. / Mathabane, Mark. From a cover of *Miriam's Song: A Memoir,* by Miriam Mathabane. Retold by Mark Mathabane. Simon & Schuster, 2000. Copyright © 2000 by Mark Mathabane. Jacket photographs (top) by Allan Penn/Nonstock, (bottom) by Gail Mathabane. Reproduced by permission of Nonstock and Getty Stone Images. / Mathabane, Mark, photograph. www.mathabane.com. Reproduced by permission of Gail Mathabane.

MEDEARIS, ANGELA SHELF. Byrd, Samuel, illustrator. From an illustration in*Dancing With the Indians,* by Angela Shelf Medearis. Holiday House, 1991. Illustration copyright © 1991 by Samuel Byrd. Reproduced by permission of Holiday House, Inc. / Johnson, Larry, illustrator. From a jacket of *Daisy and the Doll,* by Angela and Michael Medearis. Vermont Folklife Center, 2000. Reproduced by permission. / Ward, John, illustrator. From a jacket of *Poppa's New Pants,* by Angela Medearis. Holiday House, 1995. Jacket illustration copyright © 1995 by John Ward. Reproduced by permission of Holiday House, Inc. / Vitale, Stefano, illustrator. From an illustration in *Too Much Talk,* by Angela Shelf Medearis. Candlewick Press, 1997. Illustration copyright © 1995 by Stefano Vitale. Reproduced by permission of the publisher Candlewick Press, Inc., Cambridge, MA. / Medearis, Angela Shelf, photograph. Reproduced by permission of Angela Shelf Medearis.

OUTCALT, TODD. Outcalt, Todd, photograph. Reproduced by permission.

PARK, BARBARA. Brunkus, Denise, illustrator. From an illustration in *Junie B. Jones Is a Beauty Shop Guy,* by Barbara Park. Random House, 1998. Illustration copyright © 1998 by Denise Brunkus. Reproduced by permission of Random House Children's Books, a division of Random House, Inc. / Walker, Jeff, illustrator. From a cover of *Skinny-Bones,* by Barbara Park. Random House, 1982. Cover art copyright © 1997 by Jeff Walker. Reproduced by permission of Alfred A. Knopf Children's Books, a division of Random House, Inc. / Colin, Paul, illustrator. From a jacket of *The Graduation of Jake Moon,* by Barbara Park. Atheneum, 2000. Jacket illustration copyright © 2000 by Paul Colin. Reprinted with the permission of Atheneum Publisher, an imprint of Simon & Schuster Publishing. / Park, Barbara, photograph.Reproduced by permission.

POLACCO, PATRICIA. Polacco, Patricia. From a cover of her *My Rotten Redheaded Older Brother.* Aladdin Paperbacks, 1994. Copyright © 1994 by Patricia Polacco. Reproduced by permission of Simon & Schuster Books for Young Readers, an imprint of Simon & Schuster Children's Publishing Division. / Polacco, Patricia, illustrator. From an illustration in *Chicken Sunday,* by Patricia Polacco. Philomel Books, 1992. Copyright © 1992 by Babushka, Inc. Reproduced by permission of Philomel Books, an imprint of Penguin Putnam Books for Young Readers, a division of Penguin Putnam,

SOMETHING ABOUT THE AUTHOR

ABDELSAYED, Cindy 1962-

Personal

Born December 29, 1962; married Nader Abdelsayed (a physician), May 28, 1988; children: Amy, Steven. *Education:* University of Massachusetts at Amherst, B.S.N., 1985.

Addresses

Home—Las Vegas, NV. *E-mail*—NAbdel612@aol.com.

Career

Registered nurse; worked as a pediatric nurse in Los Angeles, CA, 1985-92.

Writings

Connection to the Heart (stories), Press-Tige Publishing (Catskill, NY), 1999.

Sidelights

Cindy Abdelsayed told *SATA:* "My children's book, *Connection to the Heart,* will always be very dear to me. It contains two stories of a little girl named Sylvia. In the first story, she deals with the death of her mother with the help of her favorite toy, a cat named Penny-Kitty. The plush toy acts as a conduit, sending warm and supportive thoughts from her mother's spirit in heaven. In the second story, titled 'Sylvia's Voice,' Penny-Kitty

helps Sylvia to embrace her own unique thoughts and ideas. Sylvia overcomes self-consciousness and fear of self-expression. My twin sister, Sue, illustrated *Connection to the Heart.* I wrote the story and she illustrated it. My mother died when I was six years old. I found that writing this book was a very therapeutic experience for me. I believe that many of Penny-Kitty's messages to Sylvia are in fact messages that I have received from my mother in heaven." *[For information on Abdelsayed's work, see entry on Susan E. Sullivan in this volume.]*

*   *   *

ALLAN, Nicholas 1956-

Personal

Born on December 11, 1956, in Brighton, England; son of Frederick (an orthodontist) and Joan (Reed) Allan. *Education:* Slade School of Fine Art, B.A., 1980; University of East Anglia, M.A., 1981.

Addresses

Home—9 Arundel Terrace, Brighton, Sussex, England. *Agent*—A. M. Heath & Co. Ltd., 79 St. Martins Ln., London WC2N 4AA, England.

Career

Author and illustrator of books for children and young adults. Worked variously as a waiter, typist, and as a reader in a publisher's office.

Writings

FOR CHILDREN; SELF-ILLUSTRATED

The Hefty Fairy, Hutchinson (London, England), 1989.

The Magic Lavatory, Hutchinson (London, England), 1990, published as *The Thing that Ate Aunt Julia,* Dial (New York, NY), 1991.

Jesus's Christmas Party, Hutchinson (London, England), 1991, Random House, 1992.

Hilltop Hospital, Hutchinson (London, England), 1992.

The Queen's Knickers, Hutchinson (London, England), 1993.

The Pig's Book of Manners, Hutchinson (London, England), 1995.

Heaven, Hutchinson (London, England), 1996.

The Happy Princess: The Story of the Princess of Wales, Red Fox (London, England), 1997.

The Bird, Delacorte, 1997.

Stories from Hilltop Hospital, Hutchinson (London, England), 1997.

Jesus's Day Off, Doubleday, 1998.

Demon Teddy, Hutchinson (London, England), 1999.

Adios, Pajarito Adio!, Ediciones Ekare, 2000.

Fire Alert, Hutchinson (London, England), 2000.

Happy Birthday, Dr. Matthews, Red Fox (London, England), 2000.

Heart Trouble at Hilltop, Red Fox (London, England), 2000.

The Runaway Bed, Red Fox (London, England), 2000.

You're All Animals, Hutchinson (London, England), 2000.

FOR YOUNG ADULTS

The First Time (novel), Hutchinson, 1993.

Sidelights

Nicholas Allan once told *SATA* that his primary motivation for writing was revenge. Explaining his writing philosophy, the author noted that "writing fiction is often a form of revenge. In my own case, it's getting back at all those people—teachers, parents, priests—who inundate us with misinformation at an early age, leading to so much unhappiness and disillusionment later. So I've found the best way to shock is to write down things which are true." Allan explained that he especially enjoys writing children's books because they allow him to always side with children against adults. For example, his 1990 work, *The Magic Lavatory* (published in the United States as *The Thing that Ate Aunt Julia*), tells the story of Jeffrey, on orphan child who lives with his obsessive aunt. She will not allow Jeffrey to play in her tidy house, until one day when Jeffrey finds a magic goo that brings objects to life. When the aunt finds Jeffrey using the goo on her crockery, she pours it down the toilet, which comes to life. The toilet grows legs, has sharp teeth, and, beginning with the aunt, it eats everything in the house except Jeffrey, whom it befriends. They go out and create havoc until a reconciliation eventually occurs between aunt and child.

Allan's irreverence towards religion led him to write *Jesus's Christmas Party,* a book that tells the story of Jesus through the eyes of an inn keeper who only wants to get some sleep. Throughout the book, he is continuously awakened by late-night callers, including kings, shepherds, and angels. The author noted in *SATA* that he originally "wrote the story to be blasphemous." To his surprise, it had the opposite effect, with several clergymen writing to Allan and asking his permission to read the book to their congregations.

Allan is deeply concerned with using his fiction to convey the truth to his young readers. He explained in *SATA* that for him "all fiction writing, however apparently fanciful, is about making things more real, more truthful." His 1996 work, *Heaven,* continues this tradition by telling the story of Lily, who wakes up one day to find her dog, Dill, preparing for a trip to heaven. Allan uses the dialogue between Dill and Lily to speculate on what heaven will be like—and although Lily is sad after Dill's death, she comforts herself by remembering his vision of the afterlife.

In 1998 Allan issued *Jesus's Day Off.* In this work we encounter Jesus on a day when things are not going well—following a failed attempt at walking on water, Jesus is taking a day off, feeling guilty about his failures. A conversation with his father (God) assures him that all is well and Jesus goes to sleep knowing that there is more good work to be done the next day and onwards. Reviewing this work in the *Bulletin of the Center for Children's Books,* Elizabeth Bush noted that *Jesus's Day Off* has an "upbeat message" that will be "welcome in homes and Sunday schools where children are encouraged to know Jesus as a friend."

Allan explored another biblical tale in *The Bird,* which presents an alternate interpretation of the story of Noah's Ark. Characterizing Allan's interpretation of this classic tale as "creative and clever," *School Library Journal* contributor Martha Topol praised Allan for the "masterful" interplay between the text and artwork in the book.

In addition to children's books, Allan has also published a young adult novel, *The First Time,* in which he charts Jake's struggles with adolescence. A lonely boy who has just moved to a new school, Jake is determined to master the rites of passage that he perceives will initiate his adolescence, including experimentation with sexual experiences, drugs, and alcohol. Although this book deals with Jake's sexual insecurities in explicit detail, drawing some criticism from reviewers, a critic for *Junior Bookshelf* noted that the work is a "skilful portrayal of how it feels to be growing up."

Biographical and Critical Sources

PERIODICALS

Books for Keeps, January, 1996, Jill Bennet, review of *The Queen's Knickers,* p. 7; September, 1997, Clive Barnes, review of *The Pig's Book of Manners;* March, 1999, Ralph Gower, "Biblical Books for Children," pp. 3-7.

Books for Your Children, spring, 1994, J. Ousbey, review of *The Queen's Knickers,* p. 11.

Bulletin of the Center for Children's Books, December, 1998, Elizabeth Bush, review of *Jesus's Day Off,* p. 125.

Horn Book Guide, fall, 1997, Anne Deifendeifer, review of *Heaven,* p. 257; spring, 1999, Anne St. John, review of *Jesus's Day Off,* p. 20.

Junior Bookshelf, February, 1994, review of *The First Time,* p. 38.

Kirkus Reviews, December 1, 1997, review of *The Bird,* p. 1772.

Publishers Weekly, December 2, 1996, review of *Heaven,* p. 59; October 6, 1997, review of *Jesus's Christmas Party,* p. 58; March 2, 1998, review of *The Bird,* p. 67.

School Librarian, May, 1994, Susan Elkin, review of *The First Time,* p. 71; November, 1997, Lynda Jones, review of *Stories from Hilltop Hospital,* p. 184; autumn, 1999, Hazel Townson, review of *Demon Teddy,* p. 134.

School Library Journal, May, 1994, Brian Moses, review of *The Queen's Knickers,* p. 53; July, 1998, Martha Topol, review of *The Bird,* p. 64.

*   *   *

ALLEN, Pamela 1934-

Personal

Born April 3, 1934, in Devonport, Auckland, New Zealand; daughter of William Ewart (a surveyor) and Esma (a homemaker; maiden name, Griffith) Griffiths; married William Robert Allen (head of an art school), December 12, 1964; children: Ben, Ruth. *Education:* Elam School of Art (now Auckland University), diploma of fine art, 1954; attended Auckland Teachers Training College, 1955-56.

Addresses

Agent—Curtis Brown Ltd., 27 Union St., Paddington, Sydney, New South Wales 2021, Australia.

Career

Pio Pio District High School, New Zealand, art teacher, 1956; Rangitoto College, Auckland, New Zealand, art teacher, 1957-58, 1960-64; writer and illustrator, 1979—. *Member:* Australian Society of Authors, Children's Book Council of Australia, New Zealand Society of Authors, Children's Literature Foundation of New Zealand.

Awards, Honors

Picture Book of the Year commendation, Children's Book Council of Australia, and New South Wales Premier's Literary Award in children's book category, both 1980, and Book Design Award commendation, Australian Book Publishers Association, 1980-81, all for *Mr. Archimedes' Bath;* Australian Picture Book of the Year Award, Children's Book Council of Australia, and New South Wales Premier's Literary Award in chil-dren's book category, both 1983, honor diploma for illustration, International Board on Books for Young People, 1984, and Gaelyn Gordon Award, Children's Literature of New Zealand, 2001, all for *Who Sank the Boat?;* Children's Picture Book of the Year Award, Children's Book Council of Australia, 1984, for *Bertie and the Bear;* Russell Clark Award for Illustration, New Zealand Library Association, 1986, for *A Lion in the Night;* Australian Children's Book of the Year Award commendation, 1986, for *Watch Me;* represented in the Bologna International Illustrator's Exhibition, 1987, for *A Lion in the Night;* Helen Paul Encouragement Award, 1989, for *Fancy That;* Australian Picture Book of the Year Award commendation, Children's Book Council of Australia, 1990, for *I Wish I Had a Pirate Suit;* AIM Children's Book Award, New Zealand Picture Book of the Year, and shortlisted for Picture Book of the Year Award, Children's Book Council of Australia, all 1991, all for *My Cat Maisie;* shortlisted for Picture Book of the Year Award from Children's Book Council of Australia, 1993, and shortlisted for the Koala Award, 1999, both for *Belinda;* shortlisted for Russell Clark Award for Illustration, New Zealand Library Association, 1993, for *Mr. McGee Goes to Sea;* shortlisted for Picture Book of the Year, Children's Book Council of Australia, 1999, and winner of the inaugural Tasmania Children's Choice Award, both for *Mr. McGee and the Biting Flea.*

Writings

FOR CHILDREN; SELF-ILLUSTRATED

Mr. Archimedes' Bath, Collins (Australia and New Zealand), 1980.

Who Sank the Boat?, Thomas Nelson (Australia), 1982, Coward, 1983.

Bertie and the Bear, Thomas Nelson (Australia), 1983, Coward, 1984.

A Lion in the Night, Thomas Nelson (Australia), 1985, Orchard Books, 1986.

Simon Said, Thomas Nelson (Australia), 1985.

Watch Me, Thomas Nelson (Australia), 1985.

Herbert and Harry, Thomas Nelson (Australia), 1986.

Mr. McGee, Thomas Nelson (Australia), 1987.

Hidden Treasure, Putnam (New York, NY), 1987.

Fancy That!, Orchard Books, 1988.

I Wish I Had a Pirate Suit, Viking (Ringwood, Australia), 1989.

Simon Did, Orchard Books, 1988.

Watch Me Now, Orchard Books, 1989.

Herbert and Harry, Viking (Ringwood, Australia), 1990.

My Cat Maisie, Viking (Ringwood, Australia), 1990.

Black Dog, Viking (Ringwood, Australia), 1991.

Belinda, Viking (Ringwood, Australia), 1992.

Mr. McGee Goes to Sea, Viking (Ringwood, Australia), 1992.

Alexander's Outing, Viking (Ringwood, Australia), 1993.

Mr. McGee and the Blackberry Jam, Viking (Ringwood, Australia), 1993.

Clippity-Clop, Viking (Ringwood, Australia), 1994.

Waddle Giggle Gargle, Puffin (Ringwood, Australia), 1996.

The Bear's Lunch, Puffin (Ringwood, Australia), 1997.

Mr. McGee and the Biting Flea, Viking (Ringwood, Australia), 1998.

Mr. McGee and the Perfect Nest, Viking (Ringwood, Australia), 1999.

The Pear in the Pear Tree, Viking (Ringwood, Australia), 1999.

Can You Keep a Secret?, Viking (Ringwood, Australia), 2000.

Inside Mary Elizabeth's House, Viking (Ringwood, Australia), 2000.

Brown Bread and Honey, Viking (Ringwood, Australia), 2001.

Also contributor to *School* magazine (New South Wales, Australia).

ILLUSTRATOR

Jan Farr, *Mummy, Do Monsters Clean Their Teeth?,* Heinemann (New Zealand), 1975.

Jan Farr, *Mummy, How Cold Is a Witch's Nose?,* Heinemann (New Zealand), 1976.

T. E. Wilson, *Three Cheers for McGinty,* Heinemann (New Zealand), 1976.

Jan Wilson, *McGinty Goes to School,* Heinemann (New Zealand), 1976.

Jan Wilson, *McGinty the Ghost,* Heinemann (New Zealand), 1976.

Jan Wilson, *McGinty in Space,* Heinemann (New Zealand), 1976.

T. E. Farr, *Big Sloppy Dinosaur Socks,* Heinemann (New Zealand), 1977.

T. E. Farr, *Mummy, Are Monsters Too Big for Their Boots?,* Heinemann (New Zealand), 1977.

N. L. Ray, *The Pow Toe,* Collins (Australia), 1979.

Sally Fitzpatrick, *A Tall Story,* Angus & Robertson (Australia), 1981.

Nancy Antle, *Ordinary Albert,* HarperCollins (Pymble, Australia), 1997.

Allen's simple, humorous illustrations and repetitive text introduce children to Archimedes' principle in her **Mr. Archimedes' Bath.**

Sidelights

Pamela Allen is a well-respected picture book creator in Australia. Known best for her books geared toward small children, Allen works carefully to make the words and pictures in her books convey her message to her young audience. Although Allen knew from a young age that she wanted to be an illustrator, it was not until she had her own children that she finally began to write. Since then she has developed an exemplary reputation as an author and illustrator. Writing about Allen in *Twentieth-Century Children's Writers,* Kerry White called her award-winning book *Who Sank the Boat?* a "modern classic." White noted that Allen's books are extremely popular with preschoolers due to her masterful combination of text and illustrations. Allen herself once told *SATA,* "I see myself as an author/illustrator. I feel that you can't really separate a book into parts if it's a picture book." Most of her books, including *Mr. Archimedes' Bath, Who Sank the Boat?, Bertie and the Bear, A Lion in the Night,* and *Belinda,* are evidence of this philosophy.

Born in New Zealand in 1934, Allen knew from an early age that she wanted to be an artist, and she eventually convinced her parents to let her attend art school. Although she graduated at the age of twenty with an art diploma from the Elan School of Art, Allen did not begin writing and illustrating until after she and her family, including two children, moved to Sydney, Australia. It was then that she issued her first book, *Mr. Archimedes' Bath,* to critical and popular acclaim. The book shows Archimedes' discovery of water displacement. His realization of this theory comes after he is joined in his bath by a kangaroo, a goat, and a wombat. Praising her for the simple language and uncluttered illustrations, *Books for Your Children* critic P. Thompson lauded Allen for introducing "science in a wonderful and memorable way." Similarly, *Who Sank the Boat?* explores a scientific principle. In this tale of five animals who learn a wet lesson as they try to climb into a rowboat, Allen teaches children about balance. *Who Sank the Boat?* received numerous awards for illustration and children's writing in Australia.

Written for a young audience, Allen's books are suited to being read aloud. In fact, Allen once told *SATA* that it is only when they are read aloud that her books "come into existence." This principle is illustrated in *Bertie and the Bear,* a tale of a small child trying to scare away a bear. As he is joined in his attempts by a queen, king, admiral, and other courtly figures, the chase transforms into a merry parade, inviting reader participation in the cacophony of sounds produced by the characters in the book. Another chase, this time after a royal baby, is the subject of *A Lion in the Night,* which combines text and illustrations to lead the reader into replicating the actions of the characters in the book. White noted that water, chases, sounds, and cows are recurring motifs in Allen's works and that in each work the author invites her young readers to problem solve in "delightful cumulative scenarios that reward participation."

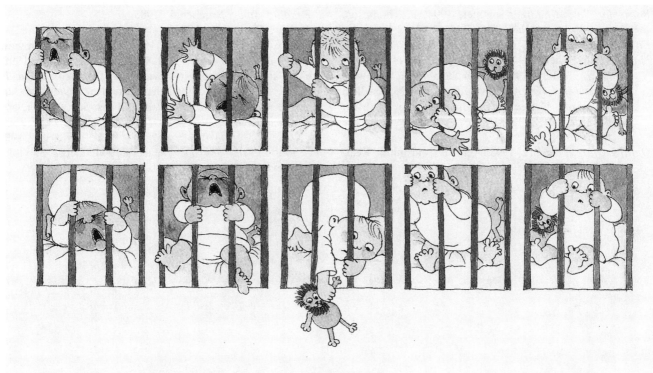

One night, when she had been
put to bed while it was still light,
she made a wish.

Illustration from **A Lion in the Night,** *written and illustrated by Allen.*

In a series of books that relate the adventures of the eccentric Mr. McGee, Allen delights her readers with such titles as *Mr. McGee and the Blackberry Jam, Mr. McGee and the Biting Flea,* and *Mr. McGee and the Perfect Nest.* These stories about the bowler-hatted Mr. McGee are written in rollicking rhyme, inviting pre-schoolers to both listen to the words and look at the pictures. Reviewing the series for *Magpies,* Nola Allen noted that the text of these books is designed for a "read-aloud audience" while the design and type placement encourages beginning readers to learn the words. The books have an almost "cinematic quality," asserted Allen, praising *Mr. McGee and the Biting Flea* and saying that parents and children "will bring it to life and proceed to replay it over and over again."

In *The Pear in the Pear Tree* Allen once again returns to the principles of science. As John and Jane attempt to pick a solitary pear from a point high up in a tree, the rhythmic text of the book introduces its young readers to the concept of physical forces, including gravity. Reviewing this work in *School Librarian,* Diane South-combe labeled this work "brilliant," noting that it is a "must" for any group of beginning readers. Margaret Phillips characterized the work in *Magpies* as "vintage unmistakable Pamela Allen," noting that the repetitious, rhyming text of the book will delight its young readers.

Allen once commented, "One does not go to school to learn to make a picture book. When I made the conscious decision to write and illustrate a picture book, I spent some time thinking about the order of my priorities. I put as my first priority the child. The child I had in mind was young and not yet able to read—a preschool child. Through my picture books I wanted to communicate with this young child. Young children gather meaning from many clues, language being only one possibility. I use pictures, sound, drama, and language. All of this only comes alive when it is shared. There is the adult, the child, and the book: the fun they have together is what it is all about."

Biographical and Critical Sources

BOOKS

Children's Literature Review, Volume 44, Gale (Detroit, MI), 1997.
Twentieth-Century Children's Writers, fourth edition, St. James Press (Detroit, MI), 1995.

PERIODICALS

Books for Keeps, May, 1994, Judith Sharman, review of *Mr. Archimedes' Bath,* p. 10; July, 1995, Judith Sharman, review of *Mr. McGee and the Blackberry Jam,* p. 6.

Books for Your Children, summer, 1994, P. Thompson, review of *Mr. Archimedes' Bath,* p. 7.

Five Owls, May, 1996, review of *Belinda,* p. 100.

Magpies, November, 1994, Nola Allen, review of *Clippity-Clop,* p. 23; July, 1996, Kevin Steinberger, review of *Who Sank the Boat?,* p. 10; July, 1998, Nola Allen, review of *Mr. McGee and the Biting Flea,* p. 24; May, 1999, Margaret Phillips, review of *The Pear in the Pear Tree,* p. 27.

Quill & Quire, February, 1995, Annette Goldsmith, "Real-Life Picture Shows," pp. 34-35.

Reading Time, Number 5, 1983.

Review, December, 1984.

School Librarian, February, 1994, Carol Woolley, review of *Mr. McGee and the Blackberry Jam;* autumn, 1998, Catriona Nicholson, review of *The Bear's Lunch,* p. 129; spring, 1999, Jane Doonan, review of *Mr. McGee and the Biting Flea,* p. 17; spring, 2000, Diane Southcombe, review of *The Pear in the Pear Tree,* p. 17.

School Library Journal, January, 1994, Debra S. Gold, review of *Belinda,* p. 80.

B

BAILEY, Debbie 1954-

Personal

Born September, 29, 1954, in Toronto, Ontario, Canada; daughter of Douglas and Gladys Serjeantson Lawson; married Stanley W. Bailey, July 9, 1983; children: Emily Sarah; stepchildren: Wally David, Owen Robert. *Education:* Ryerson University, B.A.A. (early childhood education), 1977; Ontario Teacher Education College, B.Ed., 1979; University of Toronto, M.Ed., 1981.

Addresses

Agent—Annick Press Ltd., 15 Patricia Ave., Willowdale, Ontario, Canada M2M 1H9.

Career

Kindergarten teacher in Calgary, Alberta, 1981-87; sessional instructor, Early Childhood Education Program, University of Calgary, 1987-91; teacher in Calgary, 1994-2001; Kindergarten Specialist, Calgary Board of Education, 2001—. *Member:* Canadian Society of Children's Authors, Illustrators, and Performers (CANSCAIP).

Awards, Honors

Grandma was selected as American Booksellers' "Pick of the List," 1994; Early Childhood News Directors' Choice Award, 1998, for *Grandma* and *Grandpa.*

Writings

FOR CHILDREN; "TALK-ABOUT-BOOK" SERIES

Toys, photographs by Susan Huszar, Annick Press (Willowdale, Canada), 1991.

Hats, photographs by Susan Huszar, Annick Press (Willowdale, Canada), 1991.

Shoes, photographs by Susan Huszar, Annick Press (Willowdale, Canada), 1991.

Clothes, photographs by Susan Huszar, Annick Press (Willowdale, Canada), 1991.

My Mom, photographs by Susan Huszar, Annick Press (Willowdale, Canada), 1991.

My Dad, photographs by Susan Huszar, Annick Press (Willowdale, Canada), 1991

Sisters, photographs by Susan Huszar, Annick Press (Willowdale, Canada), 1993.

Brothers, photographs by Susan Huszar, Annick Press (Willowdale, Canada), 1993.

Grandma, photographs by Susan Huszar, Annick Press (Willowdale, Canada), 1994.

Grandpa, photographs by Susan Huszar, Annick Press (Willowdale, Canada), 1994.

My Family, photographs by Susan Huszar, Annick Press (Willowdale, Canada), 1998.

The Playground, photographs by Susan Huszar, Annick Press (Willowdale, Canada), 1998.

Let's Pretend, photographs by Susan Huszar, Annick Press (Willowdale, Canada), 1999.

Families (compilation of six "Talk-About-Books"), photographs by Susan Huszar, Annick Press (Willowdale, Canada), 1999.

Happy Birthday, photographs by Susan Huszar, Annick Press (Willowdale, Canada), 2000.

The Hospital, photographs by Susan Huszar, Annick Press (Willowdale, Canada), 2000.

Good Night, photographs by Susan Huszar, Annick Press (Willowdale, Canada), 2001.

Some of Bailey's works have also been translated into French and Spanish editions.

Sidelights

Debbie Bailey told *SATA:* "Books have always been an important part of my life. As a child, I loved to read, and I am still an enthusiastic reader of just about anything. In university, my studies focused on teaching young children and I became much more aware of children's books and the importance of early literacy. I have taught kindergarten for a number of years, and this has given me an opportunity to become even more knowledgeable about books that children enjoy and the value of good literature in their lives.

"My days as a writer began not long after my daughter, Emily, was born in 1987. Knowing how important it was to begin reading to Emily at an early age, I went to the public library and began borrowing board books to share with her. The 'teacher' part of me carefully watched how she interacted with the books, watched which books she liked best and critiqued each one for content and appropriateness. It didn't take long for us to exhaust the available supply of board books at libraries and bookstores. At this point, I decided to try writing my own board books.

"What would I write about? I watched Emily to see what she seemed most interested in. Most of the books that I have developed deal with everyday aspects of a young child's world, such as *My Mom, Toys,* and *The Playground.* The text is brief in these books, which is appropriate for very young children. On some pages, the text is posed as a question. The books are called 'Talk-About-Books' because the text and the photographs are designed to encourage the adult and child sharing each book to talk about what they see on the pages." Reviewers of Bailey's works have appreciated the appropriateness of her books for very young children. All the books in her series include a combination of photographs and text intended to encourage discussion about things and situations that are relevant to a young child, focusing on such topics as clothes, playtime, siblings, and families. The books are washable and durable, making them extremely suitable for Bailey's intended audience. Commenting on *Shoes,* a book that includes pictures of children in a variety of types of shoes, *Canadian Materials* critic Joan Skogan noted Bailey's ability to create a "child's close-up world" and "highly" recommended the books for babies and children under the age of three.

Bailey continued for *SATA,* "When I was reading to Emily, I noticed that she was particularly fascinated by books that included photographs of other children. My good friend Susan Huszar is an accomplished photographer and was interested in working with me. Susan's photographs show a diverse and multi-cultural array of children and their families doing everyday things. We wanted to include a wide variety of people to better reflect our society, enabling more children to identify with the people in the books. Sue and I approached family members, neighbors, friends, day cares, and people on the street to find the families for our books. The photos were not taken in a studio but were taken in people's homes, backyards, and neighborhood parks. They show families being themselves and doing things that the readers can relate to and, again, talk about. I have been very fortunate to have such a talented partner whose photographs capture the warmth and joy that is unique to children and their families." Several critics have commented on Huszar and Bailey's inclusion of ethnically diverse photographs in their books, as well as Bailey's focus on clear and simple sentences that are designed to provoke discussion between adults and children. Steve Hardman, reviewing *Hats* and *My Dad* for *School Librarian,* noted the "engaging ethnically mixed" photographs in *Hats* and advocated the appropriateness of the series for children up to the age of six. Reviewing *Brothers* and *Sisters* for *Quill & Quire,* Ann Douglas lauded Bailey for including realistic details in her works, as well as her matter-of-fact handling of the business of being twins. Douglas also commented on Bailey's continued use of photographs from a "variety of ethnic backgrounds."

"My biggest thrill as an author," Bailey told *SATA,* "is to be at the public library and see children borrowing my books or to find out that my kindergarten students read them at home when they were little. My dream as an author is to provide the youngest children with a series of books that will give them an enjoyable and meaningful first step into the world of books. I hope that when an adult and child sit down to read a 'Talk-About-Book,' they share a close and rewarding time together which will leave a lasting impression that reading books is something wonderful."

Biographical and Critical Sources

PERIODICALS

Canadian Children's Literature, autumn, 1994, Hilary Turner, review of *Clothes, Toys, Brothers,* and *Sisters,* pp. 53-54; fall, 1997, Patricia Feltham, review of *Grandma,* p. 92, review of *Grandpa,* p. 92.

Canadian Materials, November, 1991, Ila D. Scott, reviews of *Clothes, My Dad,* and *Toys,* p. 352, Joan Skogan, reviews of *Hats, My Mom,* and *Shoes,* p. 352; September, 1993, Patricia L. M. Butler, review of *Brothers* and *Sisters,* p. 144.

Horn Book Guide, spring, 2000, Kitty Flynn, review of *Families,* p. 103.

Publishers Weekly, May 4, 1998, review of *My Family* and *The Playground,* p. 215.

Quill & Quire, May, 1993, Ann Douglas, review of *Brothers* and *Sisters,* p. 34; August, 1994, Fred Boer, review of *Grandma,* p. 35.

School Librarian, August, 1992, Steve Hardman, review of *Hats* and *My Dad,* p. 93; February, 1994, Carol Woolley, review of *Brothers* and *Sisters,* p. 15.

School Library Journal, January, 1995, Emily Kutler, review of *Grandma* and *Grandpa,* p. 81; August, 1998, Kathy Piehl, review of *My Family* and *The Playground,* p. 132; September, 1999, Susan Knell, review of *Happy Birthday* and *Let's Pretend,* p. 211; November, 2000, Maria Otero-Boisvert, review of *The Hospital,* p. 178.

*   *   *

BANAT, D. R.
See BRADBURY, Ray

BECKER, Neesa 1951-

Personal

Born January 14, 1951, in Philadelphia, PA; daughter of Jack (a builder) and Estelle (a homemaker) Becker; married Virgil A. Procaccino (a designer), September 10, 1978; children: Dana, Gabe. *Education:* Pratt Institute, B.F.A., 1972; Temple University, M.Ed., 1974; also attended Pennsylvania Academy of Fine Arts, 1993. *Politics:* Democrat. *Religion:* Jewish.

Addresses

Home—241 Monroe St., Philadelphia, PA 19147. *E-mail*—procac@aol.com.

Career

Worked as menswear designer in New York City, 1974-78; freelance illustrator in Philadelphia, PA, 1978—. Part-time art teacher at an elementary school in Philadelphia, 1991—; Settlement Music Schools, member of board of directors. Philadelphia Museum of Art, member. *Member:* Society of Illustrators.

Illustrator

Geoffrey T. Williams, *Antarctica: The Last Frontier,* Price, Stern (Los Angeles, CA), 1992.
When Robins Sing, Wright Group (San Diego, CA), 1993.
Fish Watching, Cornell University (Ithaca, NY), 1994.
Lola M. Schaefer, *Turtle Nest,* Richard C. Owen (Katonah, NY), 1996.
Coat Full of Bubbles, Richard C. Owen (Katonah, NY), 1998.
Flip Flop, Richard C. Owen (Katonah, NY), 1998.

Sidelights

Neesa Becker told *SATA:* "I began my career in art designing patterns and motifs for the fashion industry, but my first love, drawing, led me to a career as a freelance illustrator in the advertising and educational publishing markets. When my children attended a progressive independent school I joined the faculty, teaching art on a part-time basis in grades kindergarten through eight. Working with children has helped me understand how they relate to and understand my own illustrations and how to help children learn to read through the aid of clear and realistic illustrations."*

*   *   *

BLOBAUM, Cindy 1966-

Personal

Born June 8, 1966, in Galesburg, IL; daughter of Gary (an engineer) and Janet (a medical technologist; maiden name, Torline) Sickbert; married Philip L. Blobaum (a videographer), April 1, 1995; children: Emily, Jacob. *Education:* Eastern Illinois University, B.S., 1987; University of Oklahoma, M.L.S. (master's degree in liberal studies), 1998. *Hobbies and other interests:* Folk dancing, folk music, camping.

Addresses

Home—1210 37th St., Des Moines, IA 50311. *E-mail*—cindybb@juno.com.

Career

Pottawattamie County Conservation Board, Council Bluffs, IA, naturalist, 1992-94; Riverview Nature Island, Des Moines, IA, naturalist and project coordinator, 1995-99; Grand View College, Des Moines, instructor in science methods, 2000—. Fontenelle Forest, manager of nature center and project coordinator, 1993-96; consultant to Iowa Public Television. *Member:* National Association for Interpretation, National Science Teachers Association, Society of Children's Book Writers and Illustrators, Iowa Association of Naturalists.

Writings

Geology Rocks! 50 Hands-on Activities to Explore the Earth, illustrated by Michael Kline, Williamson Publishing (Charlotte, VT), 1999.

Work in Progress

A picture book, *Thundermuffs;* a young adult biography of Lillian Gilbreth; an insect activity book, *Insectigations.*

Sidelights

Cindy Blobaum told *SATA:* "My primary goal in writing is to help young people explore, explain, understand, and enjoy science, especially the natural world. Having spent seventeen years actively designing and delivering informal education programs across the country, I am distilling what I learned and developed to share with a larger audience."

Biographical and Critical Sources

PERIODICALS

School Library Journal, March, 2000, Kathryn Kosiorek, review of *Geology Rocks!,* p. 235.

*   *   *

BLUMBERG, Rhoda 1917-

Personal

Born December 14, 1917, in New York, NY; daughter of Abraham and Irena (Fromberg) Shapiro; married Gerald Blumberg (a lawyer), January 7, 1945; children: Lawrence, Rena, Alice, Leda. *Education:* Adelphi College, B.A. (magna cum laude), 1938; graduate study at Columbia University.

Rhoda Blumberg

Addresses

Home—Yorktown Heights, NY.

Career

Freelance writer. CBS Radio, New York City, researcher, 1940-44; NBC Radio, New York City, talent scout, 1945-46; Simon & Schuster, New York City, executive editor, "Travel Guides" series, 1973-74. Magazine writer, 1940—. *Member:* Authors Guild, Authors League of America, PEN America, Society of Children's Book Writers and Illustrators.

Awards, Honors

Outstanding Science Trade Book for Children Award, Children's Book Council/National Science Teachers Association, 1980, for *The First Travel Guide to the Moon; Boston Globe-Horn Book* Award, Golden Kite Award, Society of Children's Book Writers and Illustrators (SCBWI), American Library Association (ALA) Notable Book citation, all 1985, and Newbery Honor Book Award, ALA, 1986, all for *Commodore Perry in the Land of the Shogun;* Golden Kite Award, SCBWI, ALA Notable Book citation, both 1987, both for *The Incredible Journey of Lewis and Clark;* John and

Patricia Beatty Award, California Library Association, FOCAL Award, Los Angeles Library, Orbis Pictus Honor, National Council of Teachers of English, and ALA Notable Book citation, all 1989, all for *The Great American Gold Rush;* ALA Notable Book citation, 1991, for *The Remarkable Voyages of Captain Cook; Washington Post*/Children's Book Guild Award, 1977, for overall contribution to nonfiction.

Writings

Simon & Schuster Travel Guides, Cornerstone, 1974.
Firefighters, F. Watts, 1975.
Sharks, F. Watts, 1975.
First Ladies, F. Watts, 1977.
Famine, F. Watts, 1978.
Witches, F. Watts, 1979.
Backyard Bestiary, Coward, 1979.
UFO, F. Watts, 1979.
The Truth about Dragons, Four Winds, 1980.
First Travel Guide to the Moon: What to Pack, How to Go, and What to See When You Get There, Four Winds, 1980.
Freaky Facts, Wanderer, 1981.
Southern Africa: South Africa, Nambia, Swaziland, Lesotho, and Botswana, F. Watts, 1982.
Devils and Demons, F. Watts, 1982.
(With daughter, Leda Blumberg) *Dictionary of Misinformation,* Wanderer, 1982.
First Travel Guide to the Bottom of the Sea, Lothrop, 1983.
(With Leda Blumberg) *Simon & Schuster's Book of Facts and Fallacies,* Simon & Schuster, 1983.
Monsters, F. Watts, 1983.
Commodore Perry in the Land of the Shogun, Lothrop, 1985.
(With Leda Blumberg) *Lovebirds, Lizards, and Llamas,* Messner, 1986.
The Incredible Journey of Lewis & Clark, Lothrop, 1987.
The Great American Gold Rush, Bradbury (New York, NY), 1989.
The Remarkable Voyages of Captain Cook, Bradbury (New York, NY), 1991.
Jumbo, illustrated by Jonathan Hunt, Bradbury (New York, NY), 1992.
Bloomers!, illustrated by Mary Morgan, Bradbury (New York, NY), 1993.
Full Steam Ahead: The Race to Build a Transcontinental Railroad, National Geographic Society (Washington, DC), 1996.
What's the Deal? Jefferson, Napoleon, and the Louisiana Purchase, National Geographic Society (Washington, DC), 1998.
Shipwrecked! The True Adventures of a Japanese Boy, HarperCollins (New York, NY), 2000.

Sidelights

Rhoda Blumberg is the author of numerous nonfiction works for young readers. She has written on topics that range from sharks to railroads, and her books have won praise from reviewers for the author's ability to make her topics come alive. As the author once said in an autobiographical essay for *Sixth Book of Junior Authors* and Illustrators, "I love writing for children. What a joy it is to find information about a captivating subject that will eventually intrigue young readers." She describes herself as "a compulsive researcher, obsessed with and addicted to ferreting out information," and added that she is "especially interested in social history, and willingly endure[s] monotonous diaries and poorly written manuscripts when they reward [her] with surprising information about people and events."

Blumberg was born in 1917 in New York City and earned a degree from Adelphi College. She worked as a researcher for CBS Radio in New York City in the 1940s, and continued in that line of work as a freelancer for magazines until 1951. It was not until 1973 that Blumberg—a wife and mother of four—returned to work as executive editor of the Simon & Schuster "Travel Guides" series. From there, she began writing for the children's market. Her first published work for children, *Firefighters,* appeared in 1975. Among her other early books were *Sharks, First Ladies, Famine,* and *Witches,* but it was her first foray into historical writing that earned Blumberg tremendous critical accolades as well as several children's writing awards. Her 1985 book *Commodore Perry in the Land of the Shogun* presented the story of Matthew Perry, an American naval officer and diplomat, and his historic 1853 mission to Japan. Perry, with the backing of the United States, was determined to open up the country's ports to foreign ships. Japan's ruling shogun dynasty had all but closed the country to foreigners since 1600. Blumberg's book presents both views of the history-making visit, giving a bipartisan account of how each considered one another's dress and habits strange. Blumberg's *Commodore Perry in the Land of the Shogun* also makes use of illustrations by the artists who came along with Perry as well as reproductions of prints made by Japanese artists who also commemorated the visit. Writing in the *Washington Post Book World,* Michael Dirda commended Blumberg's grasp of her material. "Her writing is clear, crisp and alive with fascinating scraps of information," Dirda noted. John Buschman, reviewing the title for *School Library Journal,* also praised Blumberg's effort. "Especially good are the chapters and paragraphs explaining Japanese feudal society and culture," Buschman remarked.

Blumberg's next book tackled a similarly significant event. *The Incredible Journey of Lewis & Clark,* published in 1987, recounts the arduous two-year journey of Meriwether Lewis and William Clark to map out an overland route to the Pacific Ocean between 1803 and 1806. Along the way, they staked United States land claims and learned much about Native American culture. Blumberg's book details the hardships and triumphs of this seven-thousand-mile journey. Again, critics lauded her ability to make the past exciting for young readers. "Where she shines is in the imaginative use of extensive research to tell, compellingly and entertainingly, stories from history," noted *School Library Journal* writer Christine Behrmann.

In her 1989 book *The Great American Gold Rush,* Blumberg keeps with the territory of epochal nineteenth-century events. Here the topic is the "gold fever" that brought thousands to California after a nugget was discovered in 1849 at Sutter's Mill. Blumberg uses journals, letters, and other firsthand accounts of the hardships and treachery that befell the miners, few of whom actually struck it rich. *Washington Post Book World* reviewer Elizabeth Ward called it "a straightforward, beautifully written account." In 1991, Blumberg won praise for *The Remarkable Voyages of Captain Cook,* her account of the English sea captain who sailed around the world to chart the course of Venus, exploring the coasts of Australia and western North America along the way. The book reveals the legendary difficulties and danger that Cook and his crew faced on such a trip, both at sea and in the unfamiliar lands; Cook himself was slain in Hawaii in 1779. *School Library Journal* reviewer Trev Jones termed it "A fascinating, meticulously documented account that reads like an adventure novel," while Elizabeth S. Watson, writing in *Horn Book,* echoed the sentiments of other reviews in lauding Blumberg's forthright style: "Brutality is not overlooked," Watson noted, "nor is it stressed."

Blumberg's 1993 book *Bloomers!* acquaints readers with the first American women to defy custom and wear trousers. As her story reveals, it was a woman named Amelia Bloomer, who edited a women's political

Blumberg shares the history of bloomers from their shocking introduction in the 1850s to their adoption by suffragettes Elizabeth Cady Stanton, Amelia Bloomer, and Susan B. Anthony. (Cover illustration by Mary Morgan.)

Blumberg vividly presents the people, politics, and events leading to one of the most important land deals in history. (Cover illustration by John Buxton.)

magazine, who published the first illustrations of women in trousers, and the fashion statement caught on quickly. Bloomer was a friend of suffragette Elizabeth Cady Stanton, and to them and other like-minded women, the trousers were a symbol of freedom, as middle-class women of their day were ordinarily garbed in cumbersome skirts and tight corsets. "Young audiences will get a full sense of what life and attitudes were like in the mid-nineteenth century," noted Linda Greengrass in a *School Library Journal* review of *Bloomers!* Margaret A. Bush of *Horn Book* praised "Blumberg's straightforward narrative" and called the book "an effective history lesson that is both amusing and thought-provoking."

In 1996, Blumberg penned the story of another historic moment in American expansion with *Full Steam Ahead: The Race to Build a Transcontinental Railroad.* Her story takes into account the profit-minded railroad companies who drove their workers to complete the backbreaking job under a tight deadline. The author also chronicles the lives of the workers themselves—many of whom stayed in the area and helped give the early American West its reputation for lawlessness—as well as the Native Americans who were displaced from their ancestral lands and the Chinese immigrants brought in to work for what amounted to slave wages. "Both celebratory and grim, this illustrated history conveys the excitement of technology and also the terrible price

paid," remarked Hazel Rochman in *Booklist. Washington Post Book World* writer Dirda called *Full Steam Ahead* "enthralling" and said it "should appeal to any kid with a taste for trains, history, the old West, and good writing."

Nineteenth-century America continued to be Blumberg's preferred research topic, as evidenced by her 1998 work, *What's the Deal? Jefferson, Napoleon, and the Louisiana Purchase.* She sketches the key players in the 1803 deal that gave the United States an immense chunk of territory, from New Orleans north and west to Montana. As the book recounts, American president Thomas Jefferson, worried about Spain's territorial claims, sent emissaries to purchase New Orleans and west Florida from France; the emperor Napoleon, his treasury depleted, offered to sell the entirety of France's territory in this part of North America for fifteen million dollars. Blumberg's story recounts the tricky diplomatic maneuvers that involved appeasing Spain and several other European players before the deal was signed, which prompted *School Library Journal* reviewer Shirley Wilton to commend the author for her ability to create "an exciting and suspenseful tale out of the negotiations." *What's the Deal?* also includes a what-if? chapter, positing what might have ensued had France or Spain kept the territory, or had Britain gone to war for it, as was feared might occur. "The intersecting forces at play on the world stage are clearly delineated," declared *Horn Book*'s Mary M. Burns in her review. Randy Meyer, writing in *Booklist,* also delivered strong words of praise. "In Blumberg's talented hands, an event often depicted as just one more musty land deal from the olden days becomes a vibrant tale of greed, double-dealing, and political finesse," he declared.

While researching Captain Cook's travels for *The Remarkable Voyages of Captain Cook,* Blumberg discovered the true but relatively unknown story of Manjiro Nakahama, a Japanese boy rescued from a shipwreck by an American whaling ship. She relates the events of Manjiro's life in her 2000 offering, *Shipwrecked! The True Adventures of a Japanese Boy.* According to Blumberg's narrative, Manjiro journeyed to the United States on the American whaler, and completed his education in Massachusetts. He became proficient in English, and wrote several analytical papers comparing Japanese and American cultures. Eventually, Manjiro earned enough money to return to his family in Japan. Once he set foot on his native soil, however, he was imprisoned, according to the nineteenth-century Japanese law for dealing with citizens returning from foreign countries. Although he remained in jail for several months, Manjiro eventually became a samurai, and helped to negotiate the opening of Japanese ports to the world—a process which ultimately led to his contact with Commodore Perry. Reviewing *Shipwrecked!* for *Booklist,* Gillian Engberg praised Blumberg as "exemplary in both her research and writing," going on to note that the writer "hooks readers with anecdotes that astonish ... and she uses language that's elegant and challenging, yet always clear." Similarly, *School Library Journal*'s Andrew Medlar stated that Blumberg "packs a lot of excitement and drama into a few pages." The book also includes a variety of illustrations, including several drawings done by Manjiro himself.

Biographical and Critical Sources

BOOKS

Major Authors and Illustrators for Children and Young Adults, 6 volumes, Gale, 1993.
Sixth Book of Junior Authors and Illustrators, edited by Sally Holmes Holtze, H. W. Wilson, 1989, pp. 33-35.

PERIODICALS

Appraisal: Children's Science Books, number 3, 1980, Pamela R. Giller and Wayne Hanley, review of *Backyard Bestiary,* p. 13.
Booklist, June 1, 1998, Hazel Rochman, review of *Full Steam Ahead,* p. 1721; November 1, 1998, Randy Meyer, review of *What's the Deal?,* p. 491; February 1, 2001, Gillian Engberg, review of *Shipwrecked! The True Adventures of a Japanese Boy,* p. 1050.
Bulletin of the Center for Children's Books, January, 1993, Deborah Stevenson, review of *Jumbo,* p. 141.
Five Owls, September, 1994, Lois Ringquist, "Reading Across America," p. 1.
Horn Book, January, 1992, Elizabeth S. Watson, review of *The Remarkable Voyages of Captain Cook,* p. 88; September, 1993, Margaret A. Bush, review of *Bloomers!,* p. 616; November, 1998, Mary M. Burns, review of *What's the Deal?,* p. 752; September, 1999, Burns, review of *Commodore Perry in the Land of the Shogun,* p. 585.
Horn Book, March, 2001, review of *Shipwrecked!,* p. 225.
Interracial Books for Children Bulletin, number 4, 1984, Gail E. Myers, review of *Famine,* p. 7.
Kirkus Reviews, November 1, 1992, review of *Jumbo,* p. 1372; September 1, 1993, review of *Bloomers!,* p. 1140; May 15, 1996, review of *Full Steam Ahead,* p. 742.
New York Times Book Review, July 15, 2001, review of *Shipwrecked!,* p. 24.
Publishers Weekly, August 7, 1995, review of *The Incredible Journey of Lewis & Clark,* p. 462; February 12, 2001, "Better than Fiction," p. 214.
School Library Journal, October, 1985, John Buschman, review of *Commodore Perry in the Land of the Shogun,* p. 168; December, 1987, Christine Behrmann, review of *The Incredible Journey of Lewis & Clark,* p. 90; December, 1991, Trev Jones, review of *The Remarkable Voyages of Captain Cook,* p. 139; September, 1993, Linda Greengrass, review of *Bloomers!,* p. 222; October, 1998, Shirley Wilton, review of *What's the Deal?,* p. 150; February, 2001, Andrew Medlar, review of *Shipwrecked!,* p. 126.
Washington Post Book World, July 14, 1985, Michael Dirda, review of *Commodore Perry in the Land of the Shogun,* p. 8; November 5, 1989, Elizabeth Ward, "From a Flash in the Pan to a Glitter in the Sky," p. 20; March 14, 1993, Michael Dirda, review of *Jumbo,* p. 11; October 6, 1996, Michael Dirda, review of *Full Steam Ahead,* p. 11.*

BRADBURY, Ray (Douglas) 1920- (D. R. Banat, Leonard Douglas, William Elliot, Douglas Spaulding, Leonard Spaulding, Brett Sterling)

Personal

Born August 22, 1920, in Waukegan, IL; son of Leonard Spaulding (an electrical linesman) and Esther (Moberg) Bradbury; married Marguerite Susan McClure, September 27, 1947; children: Susan Marguerite, Ramona, Bettina, Alexandra. *Education:* Attended schools in Waukegan, IL, and Los Angeles, CA. *Politics:* Independent. *Religion:* Unitarian Universalist. *Hobbies and other interests:* Painting in oil and watercolors, collecting Mexican artifacts.

Addresses

Home—10265 Cheviot Drive, Los Angeles, CA 90064. *Office*—Bantam Books, 1540 Broadway Blvd., New York, NY 10036-4039. *Agent*—Don Congdon, 156 Fifth Ave., #625, New York, NY 10010.

Career

Newsboy in Los Angeles, CA, 1940-43; full-time writer, primarily of fantasy and science fiction, 1943—. *Mem-*

Ray Bradbury

ber: Writers Guild of America, Screen Writers Guild, Science Fantasy Writers of America, Pacific Art Foundation.

Awards, Honors

O. Henry Prize, 1947, and 1948; Benjamin Franklin Award for best story of 1953-54 in an American magazine, for "Sun and Shadow" in *The Reporter;* Commonwealth Club of California gold medal, 1954, for *Fahrenheit 451;* award from National Institute of Arts and Letters, 1954, for contribution to American literature; Boys' Clubs of America Junior Book Award, 1956, for *Switch on the Night;* Golden Eagle Award, 1957, for screenwriting; Academy Award nomination for best short film, 1963, for *Icarus Montgolfier Wright;* Mrs. Ann Radcliffe Award, Count Dracula Society, 1965, 1971; Writers Guild Award, 1974; World Fantasy Award, 1977, for lifetime achievement; D.Litt., Whittier College, 1979; Balrog Award, 1979, for best poet; Aviation and Space Writers Award, 1979, for television documentary; Gandalf Award, 1980; Body of Work Award, PEN, 1985; the play version of *The Martian Chronicles* won five Los Angeles Drama Critics Circle Awards; National Book Awards Foundation Medal for Distinguished Contribution to American Letters, 2000.

Writings

FOR YOUNG ADULTS

Switch on the Night (illustrated by Madeleine Gekiere), Pantheon (New York, NY), 1955, new edition (illustrated by Leo and Diane Dillon), Knopf (New York, NY), 1993.

R Is for Rocket (story collection), Doubleday (Garden City, NY), 1962.

S Is for Space (story collection), Doubleday (Garden City, NY), 1966.

The Halloween Tree (illustrated by Joe Mugnaini), Knopf (New York, NY), 1972.

The April Witch (illustrated by Gary Kelley), Creative Education (Mankato, MN), 1987.

The Other Foot (illustrated by Kelley), Creative Education (Mankato, MN), 1987.

The Foghorn (illustrated by Kelley; also see below), Creative Education (Mankato, MN), 1987.

The Veldt (illustrated by Kelley; also see below), Creative Education (Mankato, MN), 1987.

Fever Dream (illustrated by Darrel Anderson), St. Martin's (New York, NY), 1987.

The Smile, Creative Education (Mankato, MN), 1991.

Ahmed and the Oblivion Machines (illustrated by Chris Lane), Avon Books (New York, NY), 1998.

NOVELS

The Martian Chronicles (also see below), Doubleday (Garden City, NY), 1950, revised edition published as *The Silver Locusts,* Hart-Davis (London, England), 1951.

Fahrenheit 451 (also see below), Ballantine (New York, NY), 1953, abridged edition, Hart-Davis (London, England), 1954.

Dandelion Wine (also see below), Doubleday (Garden City, NY), 1957.

Something Wicked This Way Comes (also see below), Simon & Schuster (New York, NY), 1962.

Death Is a Lonely Business, Knopf (New York, NY), 1985.

A Graveyard for Lunatics: Another Tale of Two Cities, Knopf (New York, NY), 1990.

Green Shadows, White Whale, Knopf (New York, NY), 1992.

From the Dust Returned: A Family Remembrance, Morrow (New York, NY), 2001.

STORY COLLECTIONS

Dark Carnival, Arkham (Sauk City, WI), 1947, revised edition, Hamish Hamilton (London, England), 1948.

The Illustrated Man, Doubleday (Garden City, NY), 1951, revised edition, Hart-Davis (London, England), 1952.

Fahrenheit 451 (contains "Fahrenheit 451," "The Playground," and "And the Rock Cried Out"), Ballantine (New York, NY), 1953.

The Golden Apples of the Sun (also see below), Doubleday (Garden City, NY), 1953, revised edition, Hart-Davis (London, England), 1953.

The October Country, Ballantine (New York, NY), 1955.

A Medicine for Melancholy (also see below), Doubleday (Garden City, NY), 1959, revised edition published as *The Day It Rained Forever* (also see below), Hart-Davis (London, England), 1959.

The Ghoul Keepers, Pyramid Books, 1961.

The Small Assassin, Ace Books, 1962.

The Machineries of Joy, Simon & Schuster (New York, NY), 1964, abridged edition, Hart-Davis (London, England), 1964.

The Vintage Bradbury, Vintage Books (New York, NY), 1965.

The Autumn People, Ballantine (New York, NY), 1965.

Tomorrow Midnight, Ballantine (New York, NY), 1966.

Twice Twenty-Two (contains *The Golden Apples of the Sun* and *A Medicine for Melancholy*), Doubleday (Garden City, NY), 1966.

I Sing the Body Electric!, Knopf (New York, NY), 1969.

(With Robert Bloch) *Bloch and Bradbury: Ten Masterpieces of Science Fiction,* Tower, 1969 (published in England as *Fever Dreams and Other Fantasies*), Sphere, 1970.

(With Robert Bloch) *Whispers from Beyond,* Peacock Press, 1972.

Selected Stories, Harrap (London, England), 1975.

Long after Midnight, Knopf (New York, NY), 1976.

The Best of Bradbury, Bantam (New York, NY), 1976.

To Sing Strange Songs, Wheaton (Exeter, England), 1979.

The Stories of Ray Bradbury, Knopf (New York, NY), 1980.

Dinosaur Tales, Bantam (New York, NY), 1983.

A Memory of Murder, Dell (New York, NY), 1984.

The Toynbee Convector, Knopf (New York, NY), 1988.

Quicker Than the Eye, Avon Books (New York, NY), 1996.

Driving Blind, Avon Books (New York, NY), 1997.

PLAYS

The Meadow, first produced in Hollywood at the Huntington Hartford Theatre, March, 1960.

Way in the Middle of the Air, first produced in Hollywood at the Desilu Gower Studios, August, 1962.

Yesterday, Today, and Tomorrow, first produced in Hollywood at the Desilu Gower Studios, June, 1963.

The Anthem Sprinters, and Other Antics (includes *The Anthem Sprinters,* first produced in Beverly Hills at the Beverly Hills Playhouse, October, 1967), Dial (New York, NY), 1963.

The World of Ray Bradbury (three one-acts), first produced in Los Angeles at the Coronet Theater, October, 1964, produced off-Broadway at the Orpheum Theatre, October 8, 1965.

Leviathan 99 (radio play), British Broadcasting Corp., 1966, first produced in Hollywood at the Stage 9 Theater, November, 1972.

The Day It Rained Forever (one-act), Samuel French (New York, NY), 1966, also adapted as a musical by the same title (text by Bradbury and William Whitefield, music by Whitefield, and additional music and lyrics by Tom Gire), Dramatic Publishing (Woodstock, IL), 1992.

The Pedestrian (one-act), Samuel French (New York, NY), 1966.

Dandelion Wine (based on his novel of the same title; music by Billy Goldenberg), first produced at Lincoln Center's Forum Theatre, April, 1967.

Any Friend of Nicholas Nickleby's Is a Friend of Mine, first produced in Hollywood at the Actor's Studio West, August, 1968.

Christus Apollo (cantata; text by Bradbury, music by Jerry Goldsmith; first produced in Los Angeles at Royce Hall, University of California, December, 1969), Gold Stein Press (Newport Beach, CA), 1998.

The Wonderful Ice-Cream Suit and Other Plays (contains *The Wonderful Ice-Cream Suit,* first produced in Los Angeles at the Coronet Theater, February, 1965; *The Veldt* [based on his story of the same title], first produced in London, 1980; and *To the Chicago Abyss*), Bantam (New York, NY), 1972, also published as *The Wonderful Ice-Cream Suit and Other Plays for Today, Tomorrow, and Beyond Tomorrow,* Hart-Davis (London, England), 1973.

Madrigals for the Space Age (for mixed chorus and narrator, with piano accompaniment; text by Bradbury, music by Lalo Schifrin; first performed in Los Angeles at the Dorothy Chandler Pavilion, February, 1973), Associated Music Publishers, 1972.

Pillar of Fire and Other Plays for Today, Tomorrow, and Beyond Tomorrow (contains *Pillar of Fire,* first produced in Fullerton at the Little Theatre, California State College, December, 1973; *Kaleidoscope;* and *The Foghorn* [based on his story of the same title], first produced in New York, 1977), Bantam (New York, NY), 1975.

That Ghost, That Bride of Time: Excerpts from a Play-in-Progress, Roy A. Squires Press (Glendale, CA), 1976.

The Martian Chronicles (based on his novel of same title), first produced at the Colony Theater in Los Angeles, 1977.

Fahrenheit 451 (musical; based on his story of the same title), first produced at the Colony Theater in Los Angeles, 1979.

A Device Out of Time, Dramatic Publishing (Woodstock, IL), 1986.

Falling Upward, first produced in Los Angeles at the Melrose Theatre, March, 1988.

On Stage: A Chrestomathy of His Plays, Primus (New York, NY), 1991.

SCREENPLAYS

It Came from Outer Space, Universal Pictures, 1953.

The Beast from 20,000 Fathoms (based on his story, "The Foghorn"), Warner Bros., 1953.

Moby Dick, Warner Bros., 1956.

(With George C. Johnson) *Icarus Montgolfier Wright,* Format Films, 1962.

(Author of narration and creative consultant) *An American Journey,* U.S. Government for United States Pavilion at New York World's Fair, 1964.

(Under pseudonym Douglas Spaulding with Ed Weinberger) *Picasso Summer,* Warner Bros./Seven Arts, 1972.

Something Wicked This Way Comes (based on his novel of the same title), Walt Disney, 1983.

Also author of television scripts for *Alfred Hitchcock Presents, Jane Wyman's Fireside Theatre, Steve Canyon, Trouble Shooters, Twilight Zone, Alcoa Premiere,* and *Curiosity Shop* series. Author of forty-two television scripts for *Ray Bradbury Television Theatre,* HBO Cable Network, 1985-90.

POEMS

Old Ahab's Friend, and Friend to Noah, Speaks His Piece: A Celebration, Roy A. Squires Press (Glendale, CA), 1971.

When Elephants Last in the Dooryard Bloomed: Celebrations for Almost Any Day in the Year (also see below), Knopf (New York, NY), 1973.

That Son of Richard III: A Birth Announcement, Roy A. Squires Press (Glendale, CA), 1974.

Where Robot Mice and Robot Men Run Round in Robot Towns (also see below), Knopf (New York, NY), 1977.

Twin Hieroglyphs That Swim the River Dust, Lord John (Northridge, CA), 1978.

The Bike Repairman, Lord John (Northridge, CA), 1978.

The Author Considers His Resources, Lord John (Northridge, CA), 1979.

The Aqueduct, Roy A. Squires Press (Glendale, CA), 1979.

This Attic Where the Meadow Greens, Lord John (Northridge, CA), 1979.

The Last Circus, Lord John (Northridge, CA), 1980.

The Ghosts of Forever (five poems, a story, and an essay), Rizzoli (New York, NY), 1980.

The Haunted Computer and the Android Pope (also see below), Knopf (New York, NY), 1981.

The Complete Poems of Ray Bradbury (contains *Where Robot Mice and Robot Men Run Round in Robot Towns, The Haunted Computer and the Android Pope,* and *When Elephants Last in the Dooryard Bloomed*), Ballantine (New York, NY), 1982.

The Love Affair (a short story and two poems), Lord John (Northridge, CA), 1983.

Forever and the Earth: Radio Dramatization, limited edition, Croissant (Athens, OH), 1984.

Death Has Lost Its Charm for Me, Lord John (Northridge, CA), 1987.

With Cat for Comforter (illustrated by Louise Reinoehl Max), Gibbs Smith (Salt Lake City, UT), 1997.

Dogs Think That Every Day Is Christmas (illustrated by Louise Reinoehl Max), Gibbs Smith (Salt Lake City, UT), 1997.

Witness and Celebrate, Lord John (Northridge, CA), 2000.

OTHER

(Editor and contributor) *Timeless Stories for Today and Tomorrow,* Bantam (New York, NY), 1952.

(Editor and contributor) *The Circus of Dr. Lao and Other Improbable Stories,* Bantam (New York, NY), 1956.

(With Lewy Olfson) *Teacher's Guide: Science Fiction,* Bantam (New York, NY), 1968.

Zen and the Art of Writing and The Joy of Writing: Two Essays, Capra Press (Santa Barbara, CA), 1973.

(With Bruce Murray, Arthur C. Clarke, Walter Sullivan, and Carl Sagan) *Mars and the Mind of Man,* Harper (New York, NY), 1973.

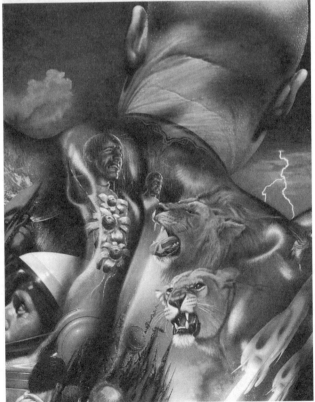

A man's eerie tattoos evoke tales of love, death, and humankind's past and future in Bradbury's imaginative work. (Cover illustration by Jim Burns.)

The Mummies of Guanajuato, Abrams (New York, NY), 1978.

Beyond 1984: Remembrance of Things Future, Targ (New York, NY), 1979.

(Author of text) *Los Angeles,* Skyline Press, 1984.

(Author of text) *Orange County,* Skyline Press, 1985.

(Author of text) *The Art of "Playboy,"* Alfred Van der Marck (New York, NY), 1985.

Yestermorrow: Obvious Answers to Impossible Futures, Joshua Odell/Capra Press (Santa Barbara, CA), 1991.

Journey to Far Metaphor: Further Essays on Creativity, Writing, Literature, & the Arts, Joshua Odell/Capra Press (Santa Barbara, CA), 1994.

Work is represented in over seven hundred anthologies. Contributor of short stories and articles, sometimes under pseudonyms, to *Playboy, Saturday Review, Weird Tales, Magazine of Fantasy and Science Fiction, Omni, Life,* and other publications.

Adaptations

Fahrenheit 451 was filmed by Universal in 1966. It was also adapted as an opera by Georgia Holof and David Mettere and first produced at the Indiana Civic Theater, Fort Wayne, IN, in November, 1988; *The Illustrated Man* was filmed by Warner Bros. in 1969; the story "The Screaming Woman" was filmed for television in 1972; the story "Murderer" was filmed for television by WGBH-TV in Boston in 1976; *The Martian Chronicles* was filmed as a television mini-series in 1980. Many of Bradbury's works have also been adapted as sound recordings or as CD-ROM productions.

Work in Progress

A novel, a book of essays, a poetry collection, and a screenplay.

Sidelights

With some sixty years of writing and over five hundred publications to his credit, Ray Bradbury is one of the grand old men of American letters. The recipient of the year 2000 Medal for Distinguished Contribution to American Letters from the National Book Award foundation, Bradbury has secured a place for himself on the classics bookshelf with novels such as *Fahrenheit 451* and *Something Wicked This Way Comes,* and thematic story collections such as *The Martian Chronicles* and *Dandelion Wine.* Widely known as a sci-fi and fantasy writer, Bradbury brought those genres into the mainstream with his popular books—several of which have been adapted for film—that emphasize humanism over technology and promote a healthy skepticism toward scientific "advances." Prolific in formats from novels to short stories to plays and screenplays and poetry, and equally comfortable writing for children as well as adults, Bradbury is, according to Jason Berner in the *Encyclopedia of American Literature,* "primarily a short-story writer ... noteworthy for his constant celebration of the human spirit." Berner further commented, "His works are, truly, not science fiction at all;

they are first and foremost philosophical/psychological stories dealing with human beings and human issues." Writing in the *Dictionary of Literary Biography,* George Edgar Slusser noted that "to Bradbury, science is the forbidden fruit, destroyer of Eden .... In like manner, Bradbury is a fantasist whose fantasies are oddly circumscribed: he writes less about strange things happening to people than about strange imaginings of the human mind."

Born in Waukegan, Illinois, in 1920, Bradbury grew up in a tradition of words and wordsmithing. His father, an electrical linesman, came from a family of newspaper editors and printers. The virtues of small-town life are celebrated in many Bradbury stories and form the backdrop entirely for the cycle of stories in *Dandelion Wine.* Growing up, Bradbury stored away visual memories that he much later pulled out of his memory bank for use in his fiction. Claiming to have total recall, a sort of photographic memory, Bradbury relies on this databank of images and memories. "Some of my first memories," he explained in Sam Moskowitz's *Seekers of Tomorrow,* "concern going upstairs at night and finding an unpleasant beast waiting at the next to the last step. Screaming, I'd run back down to mother. Then, together, we'd climb the stairs. Invariably, the monster would be gone. Mother never saw it. Sometimes I was irritated at her lack of imagination." All too real was his viewing, at age three, of the film *The Hunchback of Notre Dame,* an incident that sparked a lifelong interest in horror fiction. A few years later, a favorite aunt read him L. Frank Baum's *The Wizard of Oz* and this book would play a formative role in Bradbury's decision to write fantasy himself. Another favorite writer included Edgar Allan Poe.

However, for the young Bradbury it was not so much the classics as the pulps which dominated his reading. Science fiction came packaged in *Amazing Stories,* and the Buck Rogers comics became another staple. The Martian tales of Edgar Rice Burroughs, better known for the "Tarzan" books, also sparked an early interest in science fiction and space travel. An early writing effort came as a result of Burroughs: when Bradbury and a friend grew weary at the thought of waiting for the next installment of the series, they sat down with a roll of butcher paper and created their own illustrated book à la Burroughs. The world of circuses and traveling carnivals also captured his imagination while growing up in Waukegan.

In 1934, the Bradbury family moved West, first to Tucson, Arizona, where young Bradbury talked himself into a local radio job reading the comics to children, and then on to Los Angeles where he entered Los Angeles High School, determined to become a writer. A somewhat shy child with his peers, Bradbury had a large reserve of pluck when it came to meeting influential people. He knocked around the Hollywood studios as a youth, and also worked on his fiction, meeting such masters of sci-fi as Robert Heinlein and Henry Kuttner. Joining the Los Angeles chapter of the Science Fiction League the year before high-school graduation, Brad-

bury was already well on his way to his dream of becoming a writer. In 1938 he published his first short story in the club magazine.

High school was the extent of Bradbury's formal education; for several years after graduation he sold newspapers on the street during the day and labored on his stories after work. In 1941 he sold his first story, "Pendulum," to *Super Science Stories.* With the coming of the Second World War, Bradbury was exempted from military service because of eye problems, and for the next several years he made a regular living writing for the pulps, publishing in *Weird Tales* and *Detective Tales* each week. Married in 1947, Bradbury also published his first story collection, *Dark Carnival,* that year. More and more, his name was becoming known outside of the pulps: he had short stories published in *O. Henry Award Prize Stories* in 1947 and 1948, and in *Best American Short Stories,* and even sold a tale to the *New Yorker,* considered the standards-setter of literary taste at the time.

Despite all this, Bradbury was still barely eking out a living until he hit the mainstream with the publication of *The Martian Chronicles* in 1950. Encouraged by an editor at Doubleday to put together a novel for publication, Bradbury suddenly saw that he had several short stories that could be grouped together, framed with the thematic element of settling Mars. The Mars of Bradbury's *Chronicles* is oddly not too unlike that of Earth: the atmosphere allows for similar living conditions; the planet's inhabitants even live in towns similar to those on this planet. The twenty-six chapters of the book are linked by the settling of Mars by Terrans between the years 1999 and 2026. No one protagonist carries the reader through these years; rather it is the meeting of two cultures that the novel examines. The final section, exploring the effects of nuclear war on Earth upon the Terran settlers on Mars, announces a major theme of Bradbury's: the prevention of nuclear holocaust on Earth.

The Martian Chronicles, a lyrical and basically optimistic account of man's colonization of Mars, is widely regarded as Bradbury's preeminent work. It blends many of his major themes and metaphors, including the conflict between individual and social concerns (that is, freedom versus confinement and conformity) and the idea of space as a frontier wilderness, a place where man sets out on a quasi-religious quest of self-discovery and spiritual renewal. In addition, *The Martian Chronicles* provides the author with an opportunity to explore what he perceives to be the often deadly attraction of the past as opposed to the future and of balance and stability versus change. As in many other Bradbury stories, this idea is expressed in *The Martian Chronicles* via the metaphor of the small, old-fashioned Midwestern town "Green Town, IL," which represents peaceful childhood memories of a world that man hesitates to abandon to the passage of time. In his contribution to *Voices for the Future: Essays on Major Science Fiction Writers,* A. James Stupple wrote: "Bradbury's point [in *The Martian Chronicles*] is clear: [The Earthmen] met their deaths because of their inability to forget, or at least resist, the past. Thus, the story of this Third Expedition acts as a metaphor for the book as a whole. Again and again the Earthmen make the fatal mistake of trying to recreate an Earth-like past rather than accept the fact that this is Mars—a different, unique new land in which they must be ready to make personal adjustments."

Russell Kirk believes that the greatest strength of *The Martian Chronicles* is its ability to make us look closely at ourselves. In *Enemies of the Permanent Things: Observations of Abnormality in Literature and Politics,* Kirk stated: "What gives [*The Martian Chronicles*] their cunning is ... their portrayal of human nature, in all its baseness and all its promise, against an exquisite stageset. We are shown normality, the permanent things in human nature, by the light of another world; and what we forget about ourselves in the ordinariness of our routine of existence suddenly bursts upon us as a fresh revelation.... Bradbury's stories are not an escape from reality; they are windows looking upon enduring reality." William F. Touponce noted in his study of Bradbury in *American Writers* that "Bradbury's fantastic worlds are not marred by an anemic otherworldliness that is sometimes to be found in writers of modern fantasy." Touponce went on to comment, "On the contrary, even when his stories offer an escape to other worlds, these other worlds exist primarily as intensifications of the life of this world."

Writing in *Analog Science Fiction and Fact* on a reprinting of *The Martian Chronicles* nearly half a century after its first publication, Tom Easton observed that the novel "gave science fiction a lyrically enchanting voice such as it had never had before.... And all that without a shred of the plausibility we so fondly think essential to 'real' SF: a habitable Mars, humans coming as they once did to the American West, settling, building, dreaming." Since the time of its original publication, *The Martian Chronicles* has become one of the standard books in the American canon, assigned in high schools across the United States, and inspiring a host of adaptations from plays to a CD-ROM in 1995. Writing in *Dictionary of Literary Biography,* Gary K. Wolfe called *The Martian Chronicles* "a seminal event in the history of science fiction's growing respectability," a respectability which was due in no little respect to a very positive early review by the British novelist, Christopher Isherwood.

Bradbury followed up this achievement the following year with another framed series of short stories, *The Illustrated Man.* Here the stories enact scenes witnessed on the skin of a rather frightening tattooed individual encountered on a country road in Wisconsin. Then in 1954, Bradbury published the novel *Fahrenheit 451.* A dystopian look at the future, the book features the fireman Guy Montag who lives in the twenty-fourth century. In that age, firemen do not put out fires; instead they set them, burning books whenever and wherever they find them. Reading is forbidden in this future world and huge television screens broadcast nonstop pabulum to a passive citizenry. Slowly, Montag becomes radical-ized, however, secretly collecting books he is supposed to burn. Finally, pursued by those for whom he once worked, Montag runs away to the countryside where he takes up with a band of renegade book lovers and watches from afar the destruction of the city during a war.

Publication of *Fahrenheit 451,* whose title is taken from the temperature at which paper burns, confirmed Bradbury as one of the most important writers of mid-century. As with *The Martian Chronicles,* the novel *Fahrenheit 451* has proved to be long-lived. Its themes of the defense of the imagination against the menace of technology and of individual freedom winning out over the dumbing down of society prove as relevant today as they did in the 1950s. Donald Watt, writing in *Ray Bradbury,* called *Fahrenheit 451* "the only major symbolic dystopia of our time," and a book "that injects originality into a literary subgenre." Written at the height of McCarthyism and of the Cold War, *Fahrenheit 451* is a mirror of the United States at mid-century and is considered one of Bradbury's strongest works, an imaginative and powerful blend of sci-fi and literature. Wolfe noted that this novel is Bradbury's "only work to approach *The Martian Chronicles* in popularity and influence." Writing in *Extrapolation,* Kevin Hoskinson noted a historical connection between these two best-known Bradbury titles: "Through *The Martian Chronicles* and *Fahrenheit 451,* Ray Bradbury has created a microcosm of early cold war tensions. Though the reader will perceive a degree of Bradbury's sociopolitical concerns from a reading of either novel, it is only through the reading of both as companion pieces that his full cold war vision emerges. From the perspective that America has wrestled itself free of the extremism of the McCarthyists and, thus far, has escaped nuclear war as well, Bradbury's cold war novels may have indeed contributed to the 'prevention' of futures with cold war trappings."

Another popular collection from the 1950s which uses Bradbury's framing technique is *Dandelion Wine,* a series of sketches based on Bradbury's own childhood in Illinois. Through the course of these stories the young protagonist, Douglas Spaulding, comes to realize that he is truly alive. *The October Country* and *A Medicine for Melancholy* are other popular and critically acclaimed story collections from this time. In the early 1960s, Bradbury published *Something Wicked This Way Comes,* a long-awaited novel that grew out of a short story and which deals with a sinister traveling carnival and its satan-like ringmaster. In this novel, according to Wolfe, Bradbury develops his "first true hero," Charles Holloway. Holloway and his son must do battle with the evil transformations wrought by a traveling carnival. Highly symbolic in structure and content, the novel was an attempt by Bradbury to claim his rightful place as a serious novelist, though Wolfe, for one, felt the attempt was unsuccessful: "A highly self-conscious work, full of allusions to early Bradbury stories ... the novel suffers from an artificially inflated style and a barely controlled wealth of imagery and incident." Bradbury turned his attentions after this time primarily to plays, television

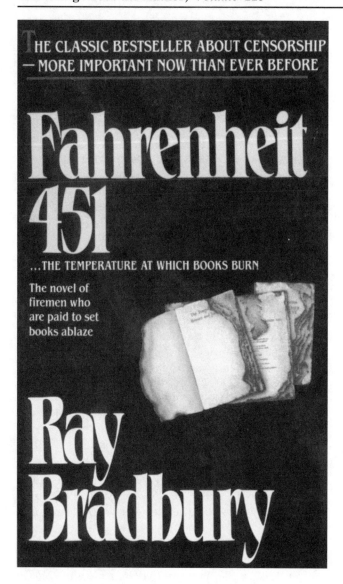

Guy Montag enjoys his job burning books until a seventeen-year-old girl and a professor convince him of a better future in Bradbury's classic novel. (Cover illustration by Donna Diamond.)

adaptations of his work, poetry, and short stories, including the popular *I Sing the Body Electric!*

Though known mainly for his work in the 1950s and 1960s, Bradbury has remained a popular writer; by the 1980s his works were garnering serious academic critical attention. His books for young readers, *Switch on the Night, The Halloween Tree,* and *Ahmed and the Oblivion Machines,* among others, continue many of the concerns of his books for adults. In the fable-like *Ahmed and the Oblivion Machines,* the twelve-year-old Ahmed is lost in the desert but saved by a gigantic statue which confers special powers on the boy. The picture book is, according to a writer for *Kirkus Reviews,* "occasionally breathtaking."

Bradbury has also continued to publish novels and short-story collections. *Death Is a Lonely Business,* a tip of the hat to hard-boiled detective novels of the 1940s, is a

murder mystery set in Venice, California, in the 1950s, and recalls Bradbury's early years. The same is true for *A Graveyard for Lunatics,* which is set in 1950s Hollywood and is narrated by the same anonymous writer of pulp fiction from *Death Is a Lonely Business.* Two short-story collections were also published in the 1990s: *Quicker Than the Eye* and *Driving Blind.* Both were mixtures of the spooky, the magical, and the sentimental. "Fans won't be disappointed," wrote a reviewer for *Publishers Weekly* of *Quicker Than the Eye.* "Ray Bradbury is The Master," declared *Kliatt's* Gail E. Roberts in a review of *Driving Blind.* Appraising the same title, a reviewer for *Publishers Weekly* commented, "The twenty-one stories in Bradbury's new anthology are full of sweetness and humanity."

In the end it is exactly this sense of humanity that has always set Bradbury apart. "It may be both reassuring to some," observed Wolfe, "and dismaying to others to discover that, on the basis of the evidence in his most recent fiction, Bradbury has hardly changed as a writer in decades; but it must also be said that no one writes quite like Bradbury, and that even if there are few masterpieces among his recent fiction, there is much fun, and a master's voice." According to Touponce writing in *American Writers,* "a close reading of [Bradbury's] major works ... reveals that his 'message' has always been the laughingly enthusiastic affirmation of life in this world." "I write for fun," Bradbury noted in an interview for *Future* magazine. "You can't get too serious. I don't pontificate in my work. I have fun with ideas. I play with them. I approach my craft with enthusiasm and respect. If my work sparks serious thought, fine. But I don't write with that in mind. I'm not a serious person, and I don't like serious people. I don't see myself as a philosopher. That's awfully boring. I want to shun that role. My goal is to entertain myself and others."

Biographical and Critical Sources

BOOKS

Berner, Jason, "Ray Bradbury," *Encyclopedia of American Literature,* edited by Steven R. Serafin, Continuum Publishing (New York, NY), 1999.

Concise Dictionary of American Literary Biography: Broadening Views, 1968-1988, Gale (Detroit, MI), 1989.

Contemporary Literary Criticism, Gale (Detroit, MI), Volume 1, 1973; Volume 3, 1975; Volume 10, 1979; Volume 15, 1980; Volume 42, 1987.

Dictionary of Literary Biography, Volume 2: *American Novelists Since World War II,* Gale (Detroit, MI), 1979, Volume 6: *Twentieth-Century American Science-Fiction Writers,* 1989.

Johnson, Wayne L., *Ray Bradbury,* Ungar (New York, NY), 1980.

Ketterer, David, *New Worlds for Old: The Apocalyptic Imagination, Science Fiction, and American Literature,* Indiana University Press (Bloomington, IN), 1974.

Kirk, Russell, *Enemies of the Permanent Things: Observations of Abnormality in Literature and Politics,* Arlington House (New Rochelle, NY), 1969.

Knight, Damon, *In Search of Wonder: Critical Essays on Science Fiction,* 2nd edition, Advent (Chicago, IL), 1967.

Moskowitz, Sam, *Seekers of Tomorrow: Masters of Modern Science Fiction,* Ballantine (New York, NY), 1967.

Nolan, William F., *The Ray Bradbury Companion,* Gale (Detroit, MI), 1975.

Platt, Charles, *Dream Makers: Science Fiction and Fantasy Writers at Work,* Ungar (New York, NY), 1987.

Slusser, George Edgar, *The Bradbury Chronicles,* Borgo (San Bernardino, CA), 1977.

Stupple, A. James, in *Voices for the Future: Essays on Major Science Fiction Writers,* Volume 1, edited by Thomas D. Clareson, Bowling Green State University Press (Bowling Green, OH), 1976.

Touponce, William F., "Ray Bradbury," *American Writers,* Supplement IV, Scribner's (New York, NY), 1996.

Touponce, William F., *Ray Bradbury and the Poetics of Reverie: Fantasy, Science Fiction, and the Reader,* UMI Research Press (Ann Arbor, MI), 1984.

Touponce, William F., *Naming the Unnamable: Ray Bradbury and the Fantastic after Freud,* Starmont House (San Bernardino, CA), 1997.

Watt, Donald, *Ray Bradbury: Writers of the Twenty-first Century Series,* edited by Martin H. Greenberg and Joseph D. Olander, Taplinger (New York, NY), 1980.

Wollheim, Donald, *The Universe Makers,* Harper (New York, NY), 1971.

World Literature Criticism, Gale (Detroit, MI), 1992.

PERIODICALS

Ad Astra, July-August, 1991.

Analog Science Fiction & Fact, March, 1989, p. 183; July, 1992, Tom Easton, review of *On Stage,* p. 311; July-August, 1997, Tom Easton, review of *The Martian Chronicles,* pp. 278-279.

Bloomsbury Review, March-April, 1997, Kathleen Cain, review of *A Medicine for Melancholy,* p. 17.

Booklist, March 1, 1992, Virginia Dwyer, review of *Yestermorrow,* p. 1191; April 15, 1993, Carolyn Phelan, review of *Switch on the Night,* p. 1522; February 1, 1994, Ray Olson, review of *The Bradbury Chronicles,* Volumes 4-5, p. 989; November 1, 1996, Ray Olson, review of *Quicker Than the Eye,* p. 458; November 15, 1997; October 1, 1998, Ray Olson, review of *Ahmed and the Oblivion Machines,* p. 312; November 1, 1998, p. 458.

Chicago Tribune, May 31, 1992, Thomas Flanagan, review of *Green Shadows, White Whale,* Section 14, pp. 6, 10.

Children's Literature Association Quarterly, spring, 1988, William F. Touponce, "Laughter and Freedom in Ray Bradbury's *Something Wicked This Way Comes,*" pp. 17-21.

Christianity Today, May 14, 1990.

Critique, spring, 1998, Rafeeq O. McGiveron, "'To Build a Mirror Factory': The Mirror and Self-Examination in Ray Bradbury's 'Fahrenheit 451,'" pp. 282-288.

English Journal, February, 1970, pp. 201-205.

Entertainment Weekly, October 15, 1993.

Extrapolation, December, 1971, pp. 64-74; fall, 1984; winter, 1995, Kevin Hoskinson, "'The Martian Chronicles' and 'Fahrenheit 451': Ray Bradbury's Cold War Novels," pp. 345-360.

Future, October, 1978, "Interview with Ray Bradbury."

Horn Book Guide, spring, 1997, Peter D. Sieruta, review of *The Halloween Tree,* p. 78.

Journal of Popular Culture, summer, 1973, pp. 227-248.

Kirkus Reviews, September 15, 1997, review of *Driving Blind,* p. 1422; November 1, 1998, review of *Ahmed and the Oblivion Machines,* p. 1597.

Kliatt, April, 1992, Naomi S. Myrvaagnes, review of *On Stage,* p. 24; January, 1999, Gail E. Roberts, review of *Driving Blind,* p. 15.

Locus, December, 1991, Gary K. Wolfe, review of *The Bradbury Chronicles* and *On Stage,* pp. 25, 58; February, 1994, Gary K. Wolfe, review of *Switch on the Night,* pp. 27, 29, 62; January, 1995, review of *Zen and the Art of Writing,* p. 47.

Los Angeles Times Book Review, October 20, 1996, Martin Zimmerman, review of *The Halloween Tree,* p. 8.

Magazine of Fantasy and Science Fiction, May, 1963, pp. 7-22.

National Review, April 4, 1967.

Newsweek, July 30, 1990, p. 54; November 13, 1995, "Sci-Fi for Your D: Drive," p. 89.

New York Times, April 24, 1983.

New York Times Book Review, August 8, 1951; December 28, 1969; October 29, 1972; October 26, 1980; December 11, 1988, p. 26; August 9, 1992, p. 3; January 25, 1998, review of *Quicker Than the Eye,* p. 24.

Omni, January, 1989; February, 1989.

Publishers Weekly, December 20, 1991, p. 71; September 30, 1996, p. 86; October 7, 1996, review of *Quicker Than the Eye,* p. 65; September 22, 1997, review of *Driving Blind,* p. 72; October 26, 1998, review of *Ahmed and the Oblivion Machines,* p. 49.

Reader's Digest, September, 1986.

School Library Journal, May, 1987; May, 1993, Gale W. Sherman and Bette D. Ammon, review of *The Ray Bradbury Chronicles: Volume 1,* pp. 35-36; December, 1994, Christine C. Menefee, "Imagining Mars: The New Chronicles," pp. 38-39.

Statesman (India), March 20, 2001.

Time, March 24, 1975; October 13, 1980; May 25, 1992, p. 68.

Voice of Youth Advocates, February, 1991, Tom Pearson, review of *A Graveyard for Lunatics,* pp. 349-350; April, 1993, Katharine L. Kan, review of *The Ray Bradbury Chronicles: Volume 3,* p. 32.

Washington Post, July 7, 1989.

Washington Post Book World, November 2, 1980, pp. 4-5; November 3, 1985, p. 7.

Writer's Digest, February, 1967, pp. 40-44, 47, 94-96; March, 1967, pp. 41-44, 87; December, 1974; February, 1976, pp. 18-25.*

BROOKS, Gwendolyn (Elizabeth) 1917-2000

OBITUARY NOTICE—See index for *SATA* sketch: Born June 7, 1917, in Topeka, KS; died of cancer, December 3, 2000, in Chicago, IL. Poet and novelist. Brooks was the first black writer to receive the Pulitzer Prize, which came in 1950 for her adult poetry collection *Annie Allen.* Much of what she wrote about related to black life— especially as it affected women—in the South as well as her adopted hometown of Chicago. As a writer for children, Brooks was best known as the creator of her first work of juvenile literature, *Bronzeville Boys and Girls,* which was published in 1959. Considered a classic for readers in the primary and middle grades, the book was often praised for reflecting the same sensitivity and literary skill that Brooks brought to her adult works. Brooks also developed *The Young Poet's Primer* (1980), a manual for high school and college students interested in learning the craft of poetry, and a collection of poems for young readers, 1983's *Very Young Poets.*

In 1971, she published the picture book *Aloneness,* a single long poem in free verse that focuses on the need for children to be alone. *The Tiger Who Wore White Gloves,* released in 1974, is another single poem, and was read by some critics as a pointed message to black readers. Brooks received numerous awards during her long career and was a Guggenheim fellow, poet laureate of Illinois for more than thirty years, and poetry consultant to the Library of Congress. She was also inducted into the National Women's Hall of Fame. In 1989 the National Endowment for the Arts presented her with a Lifetime Achievement Award for her work.

OBITUARIES AND OTHER SOURCES:

PERIODICALS

Chicago Tribune, December 10, 2000, sec. 4, p. 10.
Los Angeles Times, December 4, 2000, p. B4.
New York Times, December 5, 2000, p. C22.
Times (London), December 21, 2000.
Washington Post, December 5, 2000, p. B7.

C

CALDERONE-STEWART, Lisa
See CALDERONE-STEWART, Lisa-Marie

*   *   *

CALDERONE-STEWART, Lisa-Marie
1958-
(Lisa Calderone-Stewart)

Personal

Born January 14, 1958, in Montgomery, AL; daughter of Joseph Philip (a physician) and Constance (maiden name, Croce) Calderone; married Ralph P. Stewart III; children: Ralph P. IV, Michael J. *Education:* College of the Holy Cross (Worcester, MA), A.B., 1979; Lesley College (Cambridge, MA), M.Ed., 1980; Loyola University, M.P.S., 1996; Cardinal Stritch University (Milwaukee, WI), Ed.D., expected 2002; attended Aquinas College (Grand Rapids, MI). *Religion:* Roman Catholic.

Addresses

Office—c/o Archdiocese of Milwaukee, 3501 S. Lake Dr., P.O. Box 070912, Milwaukee, WI 53207-0912.

Career

Worked variously as an elementary school teacher, director of religious education, and swimming instructor in Massachusetts and Alabama, 1980-86; St. Stephen Parish, Saginaw, MI, parish youth ministry director, 1986-91; Diocese of Grand Island, NE, director of youth ministry, 1991-97; Archdiocese of Milwaukee, Milwaukee, WI, Office for Schools, Child and Youth Ministry, associate director, 1997—.

Writings

Faith Works for Junior High, St. Mary's (Winona, MN), 1994.

Faith Works for Senior High, St. Mary's (Winona, MN), 1995.

Lights for the World, St. Mary's (Winona, MN), 1995.

Prayer Works for Teens, St. Mary's (Winona, MN), Volume 1: *Rock, Aloe Plant, Children of God,* Volume 2: *Leaves, Nuts, The Four Elements,* Volume 3: *Water, The Four Seasons, Ojo de Dios,* Volume 4: *Bread, Puzzle, Ice and Snow,* 1997.

Life Works and Faith Fits: True Stories for Teens, St. Mary's (Winona, MN), 1999.

Know It! Pray It! Live It!: A Family Guide to the Catholic Youth Bible, St. Mary's (Winona, MN), 2000.

Contributor of "Teaching *Lectio Divina* to Young People" to *Bringing Catholic Youth and the Bible Together,* edited by Brian Singer-Towns, St. Mary's, 2000, and "Liturgical Catechesis" to *Vibrant Worship with Youth,* St. Mary's, 2000.

"IN TOUCH WITH THE WORD; LECTIONARY-BASED PRAYER REFLECTIONS" SERIES

Cycle C for Ordinary Time, St. Mary's (Winona, MN), 1997.

Cycle A for Ordinary Time, St. Mary's (Winona, MN), 1998.

Also author of other books in the series, including *Cycle B for Ordinary Time, Advent, Christmas, Lent,* and *Easter.*

AS LISA CALDERONE-STEWART; WITH ED KUNZMAN

Better Than Natural and Other Stories, St. Mary's (Winona, MN), 1999.

Meeting Frankenstein and Other Stories, St. Mary's (Winona, MN), 1999.

My Wish List and Other Stories, St. Mary's (Winona, MN), 1999.

Straight from the Heart and Other Stories, St. Mary's (Winona, MN), 1999.

That First Kiss and Other Stories, St. Mary's (Winona, MN), 1999.

Work in Progress

Faith Matters: All Year Long, a book of poems, stories, and short prayers in twelve chapters, one for each month.

Sidelights

In addition to working with the youth of several Catholic parishes, Lisa-Marie Calderone-Stewart has written some dozen books for St. Mary's Press, a Catholic publishing house. While *Faith Works for Junior High* and *Faith Works for Teens* each contain twelve faith formation sessions that are scripture-based and in the Catholic tradition, *Lights for the World* is a leader's manual for training high school students in leadership skills. *Prayer Works for Teens,* a four-volume collection of prayer experiences for young people, includes poems of various lengths to be used in different situations. Similarly, "In Touch with the Word" is a four-volume series of reflections on the weekly readings used at Catholic Sunday worship services. Each book includes separate reflection questions geared to adults, teenagers, and children, as well as a closing prayer, poem, or quotation. According to Jovian P. Lang of *Catholic Literary World,* "Not only will groups enjoy this work, but also individuals."

Life Works and Faith Fits is a collection of stories—some funny, according to the author, others inspiring—to show teenagers how faith and life are compatible. Calderone-Stewart also penned a five-book series with Ed Kunzman under the name Lisa Calderone-Stewart. Each book contains fictional stories that demonstrate the major teachings of the catechism of the Catholic Church through the examples of the characters' decisions and reactions. For example, *Better Than Natural and Other Stories* is based on the virtues and the beatitudes, *Meeting Frankenstein and Other Stories* is based on the Lord's Prayer, *My Wish List and Other Stories* deals with the seven sacraments, *Straight from the Heart and Other Stories* treats the ten commandments, and *That First Kiss and Other Stories* deals with the Apostle's Creed. Calderone-Stewart and her husband, Ralph Stewart, conduct workshops and retreats for Catholic youth and adults on such themes as images of Jesus, comic strip spirituality, global awareness, peacemaking, general prayer, general scripture exploration, and communication and self-discovery.

Biographical and Critical Sources

PERIODICALS

Catholic Literary World, March, 1999, Jovian P. Lang, review of *In Touch with the Word,* pp. 32-33.

CATTELL, James 1954-

Personal

Born November 19, 1954, in Wellington, New Zealand; son of Richard (a vicar) and Priscilla (a nurse; maiden name, Warrington) Cattell; married Dorelle Davidson (an artist); children: Ruby, Edith. *Education:* Attended Victoria University of Wellington, 1973-74, and University of Auckland, 1976-78.

Addresses

Home and office—113 Barkly St., St. Kilda, Victoria 3182, Australia. *E-mail*—james@honeyweatherand-speight.com.au.

Career

Honeyweather & Speight, Melbourne, Australia, partner, 1988—. Partner of a flower farm and a toy shop; sculptor and painter; puppeteer and performer as "The Wandering Washbasin."

Writings

(With Gary Crew; self-illustrated) *Gino the Genius,* Lothian (Port Melbourne, Australia), 2000.
(With Dorelle Davidson; self-illustrated) *Albuman's Quest,* Lothian (Port Melbourne, Australia), 2001.

Work in Progress

Author (with Dorelle Davidson) and illustrator of *Confessions of a Bad Dog.*

James Cattell

Sidelights

James Cattell told *SATA:* "As a child, I wrote a number of books as far as chapter 2, and illustrated them to chapter 3, then left blank pages with chapter headings up to chapter 10. I was very fond of short chapters and full stops. After the age of fourteen, I totally forgot about writing until I was about forty-two.

"I studied law, history, philosophy, literature, and art, but left university without a degree of any kind, determined to be a sculptor. In 1979 I left New Zealand and arrived in Melbourne, Australia.

"I worked for ten years as a puppeteer and street performer, and I lived surrounded by dusty sculptures and paintings. During this time I met my partner, Dorelle Davidson. After our daughter, Ruby, was born in 1987, we started an art business, where we produced murals, sculptural signs, and sometimes children's playgrounds. Life became very busy after our second daughter, Edith, was born in 1990.

"In 1999 we decided to try a new business and opened a toy shop in front of our home. The year before I had shown some drawings and sculptures to Helen Chamberlin (the children's publisher at Lothian) and Gary Crew. Gary Crew sent me the text for *Gino the Genius* soon after. Knowing nothing about the publishing industry, I had quite a difficult time illustrating the story, but everyone was most patient and eventually the book saw the light of day. It was an exhilarating experience.

"While working on the book, Dorelle and I tried our hands at writing some of our own stories. The first of these, *Albuman's Quest,* has been published, and *Confessions of a Bad Dog* will come out in 2002. Dorelle prefers writing in the peace and quiet of a small flower farm we have on the southern coast. I prefer to sit in our shop in St. Kilda and write to the sounds of arguments and screeching brakes, to which I add music."

Biographical and Critical Sources

ON-LINE

Honeyweather & Speight Web Site, http://www. honeyweatherandspeight.com.au/ (June 22, 2001).

*   *   *

CAVE, Kathryn 1948-

Personal

Born June 22, 1948, in Aldershot, Hampshire, England; daughter of Henry (a research scientist) and Eve (a teacher) Wilson; married Martin Cave (a professor), July, 1972; children: Eleanor, Joseph, Alice. *Education:* Oxford University, B.A., 1969; graduate studies at Massachusetts Institute of Technology, 1969-70, and Birmingham University, 1972-73. *Hobbies and other*

interests: Teaching tennis, coaching athletes, walking, poetry, theater, travel.

Addresses

Home—11 West Common Rd., Uxbridge, Middlesex UB8 IN2, England. *Office*—Frances Lincoln Ltd., 4 Torriano Mews, Torriano Avenue, London NW5 2RZ, England. *Agent*—Gina Pollinger, 222 Old Brompton Rd., London SW5 OBZ, England.

Career

Penguin Publishing, London, England, editor, 1970-71; Blackwell (publishers), Oxford, England, editor, 1971-72; Metier (publishers), Hayes, England, technical editor, 1987-88; Frances Lincoln Ltd., London, editorial director for children's nonfiction, 1990-92; writer.

Awards, Honors

Many Happy Returns and Other Stories was named one of the best ten books of the year by the Federation of Children's Book Group, 1986.

Writings

Dragonrise, illustrated by Liz Graham-Yooll, Blackie (London, England), 1984.

Many Happy Returns and Other Stories, illustrated by David Mostyn, Corgi (Ealing, England), 1987.

Just My Luck! And Other Stories, illustrated by David Mostyn, Corgi (London, England), 1987.

Just in Time, illustrated by Terry McKenna, Potter, 1988.

Poor Little Mary, Penguin, 1988.

Henry Hobbs, Alien, illustrated by Chris Riddell, Penguin, 1990.

Jumble, illustrated by Chris Riddell, Blackie (London, England), 1990.

William and the Wolves, Penguin, 1991.

Out for the Count, illustrated by Chris Riddell, Simon & Schuster, 1991.

Running Battles, illustrated by Derek Brazell, Penguin, 1992.

Andrew Takes the Plunge, illustrated by David Mostyn, Blackie Children's (London, England), 1994.

Something Else, illustrated by Chris Riddell, Viking (London, England), 1994.

Best Friends Forever, illustrated by Derek Brazell, Viking (London, England), 1994.

Create Your Own Masterpiece on a Journey through Art, illustrated by Melvin Bramich, Frances Lincoln (London, England)/National Gallery of Art (Washington, DC), 1994, published as *My Journey through Art: Create Your Own Masterpiece,* Barrons (Hauppauge, NY)/ National Gallery of Art (Washington, DC), 1994.

The Emperor's Gruckle Hound, illustrated by Chris Riddell, Hodder & Stoughton (London, England), 1996.

Horatio Happened, illustrated by Chris Riddell, Hodder Children's (London, England), 1998.

W Is for World: The Round-the-World ABC, Frances
Lincoln (London, England), 1998, Silver Press (Parsip-
pany, NJ), 1999.
Henry's Song, illustrated by Sue Hendra, Lion (Oxford,
England), 1999, Eerdmans (Grand Rapids, MI), 2000.
The Boy Who Became an Eagle, illustrated by Nick
Maland, Dorling Kindersley (New York, NY), 2000.

Sidelights

Kathryn Cave is the author of several books for children
that usually impart a moral lesson alongside a good dose
of humor. A former book editor in London, Cave has
teamed with illustrators to create picture books for
young readers, but she has also written for older
children. Cave was born in 1948 in Hampshire, England,
and grew up in a learned family headed by her research
scientist father and a mother who was a teacher by
profession. After finishing at Oxford University in 1969,
Cave took graduate courses at the Massachusetts Institute of Technology, but returned to London to work in
the publishing field. In the early 1970s she was an editor
at the Penguin and Blackwell houses; she left work
temporarily in 1972 to marry and begin a family. She
returned to work in 1987 as a technical editor and spent
the early 1990s as editorial director for children's
nonfiction at Frances Lincoln, another London firm.

Those afflicted with an overly vivid imagination fascinate Cave as a writer. "Most of my stories are concerned
with the gap between our own perceptions of reality and
those of other people," she once said. "I like the
borderline where logic turns into madness." Cave's first
book was *Dragonrise,* published in 1984. She wrote
several other picture books over the next few years,
including *Poor Little Mary* and *Henry Hobbs, Alien.* In
1991's *William and the Wolves,* Cave created a hero
whose plight was sure to resonate with many readers:
William is jealous of his sister, Mary, who seems to
receive much of the family's attention and praise for her
adorable imaginary lamb. The adults tell Mary that she
has a wonderful imagination, and even William's mother
mentions that he does not possess such a talent. So
William decides to imagine his own pack of imaginary
wolves—though the animals disappeared from England
around the sixteenth century—with the plan for them to
devour Mary's pet. But William's wolves become very
real to him, following him to school and causing havoc
at home. William concludes "that what imagination
caused was trouble. At the first opportunity, he would
abandon it for ever." Philippa Milnes-Smith, reviewing
William and the Wolves in *Books for Keeps,* called it "a
warm, witty, and appealing book which successfully
represents the complexity of family life."

Another work from Cave published that same year is
Out for the Count, one of many collaborative efforts
with illustrator Chris Riddell. Its focus is young Tom,
who cannot sleep, and so at his father's suggestion he
tries to count various animals. He begins with seven
sheep, which lead his imagination into the woods, where
he encounters twelve wolves; he then finds himself at

sea with forty-five pirates, in the South Pole with fifty-
four penguins, then facing ninety-seven Bengal tigers.
Finally, Tom decides to return to the safety of his bed.
"Cave's bouncy verse carries Tom through his caper at a
bracing clip," asserted a *Publishers Weekly* reviewer,
while *Books for Keeps* contributor Gwynneth Bailey
called it "a rhyming, rollicking adventure."

One of Cave's typical works for older readers is *Running
Battles,* published in 1992 and aimed at eleven- to
fourteen-year-olds. The story revolves around Karen,
who at fifteen is competitive and very assertive—but
focuses all of it on helping her younger sister, a talented
track star, succeed and eventually win Olympic gold. As
her sister's "manager," Karen bullies coaches, race
officials, and nearly everyone involved in her sister's
life, before realizing that her energies are generous
enough to spur her own achievements. *School Librarian*
reviewer Doris Telford called it a "lively, entertaining
story," with an "original and amusing" supporting cast
of characters. Cave has said that she was inspired to
write this particular book by her own daughter and her
athletic pursuits. As a parent at youth sporting events,
Cave said she "had plenty of chances to watch children,
parents and coaches cross that borderline, under the
influence of sheer obsession—it's always fascinating to
see single-minded pursuit of any objective (sometimes
it's horrifying too, of course)."

Cave returned to the picture-book format for younger
readers with the 1994 title *Something Else.* "Something"
is a gray blob with odd ears and blue fingers. Because he
is different, he is not allowed to join in and play with
others—a situation many five- to eight-year-olds might
recognize. His dilemma is resolved when a tangerine-
colored "something else" comes along—Something
initially rejects the newcomer, like the others, but has a
change of heart and the pair become fast friends.
Observer reviewer Kate Kellaway termed the book "a
pleasing variation on an old theme"

Friendship and its hardships is the theme of Cave's *Best
Friends Forever,* which appeared in 1994. Aimed at
readers from ages eight to eleven, the tale is once again a
familiar one: Sam and Alex declare themselves best
friends, and assert they will never fight. One day, a new
student arrives in class, and the teacher places Emma
between their desks. An intense rivalry ensues, which
leads to the inevitable physical confrontation. A *Junior
Bookshelf* reviewer termed it an "understated, quiet, yet
ultimately most satisfying tale." Cave again uses humor
to defuse a tense situation when a nervous junior
gardener at the Emperor's palace stammers on about a
very rare, very special breed of hound. "They're very
rare and exotic, and not in any of the books. They're
from Austria. They live in the mountains and hunt
gruckles." The gardener is talking about a litter of
puppies discovered on the royal grounds at the start of
The Emperor's Gruckle Hound, Cave's 1996 work.
Naturally, the Emperor insists on taking one, and Sam
the pup is raised in the lavish royal household as the
prized "Gruckle Hound." His identical brother Scruff,

meanwhile, has a far more adventurous puppyhood on the streets. One day, Sam escapes from the boredom of the palace, and the royal minions capture Scruff instead. Mary Hoffman, writing in *School Librarian,* termed it "a perfect little fable."

In 1999 Cave worked with the British relief agency Oxfam and publisher Frances Lincoln to create *W Is for World: The Round-the-World ABC,* an alphabet picture book whose proceeds were donated to Oxfam. Each letter depicts children in a different setting with photographs and a few lines of text about their culture. By showing youth from a wide variety of places around the globe and with Cave's text, the work delivers Oxfam's message that everybody needs the basics of shelter, food, heath care, and schooling. *Books for Keeps* reviewer Margaret Mallett called it "a warm and human journey" that helps youngsters "understand the joys and difficulties of people in different countries and circumstances."

Cave's 2000 title *Henry's Song* is one of a handful of her books to be published in the United States. Its title character is a yellow creature in a forest who wakes up one day so happy to be alive that he begins to sing. His neighbors, however, strongly object and tell him that he has a terrible voice and emits a tuneless noise. An unseen higher being, their creator, orders them to stop complaining about Henry and asks them what use their voices have, adding that he will demand the answer the next day. After much deliberation, the community decides to sing a song as their reply, but they ban Henry from participating. The creator corrects the situation when he does not hear Henry's voice. "This rhythmic, expressive little lesson reads aloud well," remarked *School Library Journal* reviewer Patricia Pearl Dole.

Biographical and Critical Sources

PERIODICALS

Books, autumn, 1998, review of *Horatio Happened,* p. 21.
Books for Keeps, January, 1994, Philippa Milnes-Smith, review of *William and the Wolves,* pp. 16-17; January, 1995, David Bennett, review of *Running Battles,* p. 8; January, 1996, Pam Harwood, review of *Best Friends Forever,* p. 9; Gil Roberts, review of *Jumble,* p. 10; July, 1996, Steve Rossen, review of *The Emperor's Gruckle Hound,* p. 12; January, 1999, Margaret Mallett, review of *W Is for World,* p. 21; September, 1999, Gwynneth Bailey, review of *Out for the Count,* p. 23.
Junior Bookshelf, April, 1992, review of *Out for the Count,* p. 53; October, 1994, review of *Best Friends Forever,* p. 169.
Observer (London), July 24, 1994, Kate Kellaway, "A Delicious Dose to Cure All Maladies," p. 19; August 22, 1999, James Shaw, "Mary Has a Little Lamb. William Has Six Wolves," p. 14.
Publishers Weekly, June 1, 1992, review of *Out for the Count,* p. 61; March 13, 2000, review of *Henry's Song,* p. 82.

School Librarian, May, 1993, Doris Telford, review of *Running Battles,* p. 72; November, 1994, Ingrid Broomfield, review of *Something Else,* p. 148; August, 1996, Mary Hoffman, review of *The Emperor's Gruckle Hound,* p. 105; summer, 1999, Rachel Ayers-Nelson, review of *W Is for World,* pp. 73-74.
School Library Journal, September 9, 2000, Patricia Pearl Dole, review of *Henry's Song,* p. 186.*

*   *   *

COONEY, Barbara 1917-2000

OBITUARY NOTICE—See index for *SATA* sketch: Born August 6, 1917, in Brooklyn, NY; died March 10, 2000, in Portland, ME. Illustrator, author. Cooney was the award-winning illustrator and author of numerous children's books. She won two Caldecott Medals for illustration, one for her drawings in a 1958 version of Chaucer's *Chanticleer and the Fox,* and the other in 1980 for her paintings in Donald Hall's *Ox-Cart Man. Miss Rumphius,* the 1982 book she wrote and illustrated, earned several awards, including Best Book of the Year from the *New York Times.* The work was also adapted as a filmstrip and cassette in 1984. Her final writing was the 1996 *Eleanor;* her final published illustrations came in Mary Lin Ray's *Basket Moon.* A generous but quiet benefactress, in 1997 Cooney donated nearly a million dollars for a new library to be built in her hometown of Damariscotta, Maine.

OBITUARIES AND OTHER SOURCES:

PERIODICALS

Chicago Tribune, March 14, 2000, section 2, p. 8.
Los Angeles Times, March 14, 2000, p. A20.
New York Times, March 15, 2000, p. A27.
Washington Post, March 15, 2000, p. B5.

*   *   *

CUMMINGS, Phil 1957-

Personal

Born December 22, 1957, in Port Broughton, South Australia, Australia; son of Cyril Gordon (a carpenter and builder) and Rachel Henrietta Arbon (a homemaker) Cummings; married Susan Chalmers (a teacher), February 1, 1987; children: Benjamin David, Alyssa Claire. *Education:* Received diploma in teaching from Salisbury College of Advanced Education, South Australia. *Hobbies and other interests:* Listening to music, playing guitar, sports, reading, "playing with my kids."

Addresses

Home—7 Robert Rd., Hillbank, South Australia 5112, Australia. *Office*—P.O. Box 84, Para Hills, South Australia 5096, Australia.

Career

Education Department of South Australia, teacher, 1979-2000; full-time writer, 2000—.

Writings

Goodness Gracious!, illustrated by Craig Smith, Omnibus (Norwood, Australia), Orchard, 1992.

Tully and Claws, illustrated by Rob Mancini, Random House (Milsons Point, Australia), 1994.

Marty and Mei-Ling, illustrated by Craig Smith, Random House (Milsons Point, Australia), 1995.

Monster, Monster, Big and Hairy, illustrated by Marina McAllan, Macmillan Education Australia (South Melbourne, Australia), 1995.

Surfing the Mudgiewallop Pool, illustrated by Mark Payne, Macmillan Education Australia (South Melbourne, Australia), 1996.

Sid and the Slimeballs, illustrated by Stephen Axelson, Heinemann (Port Melbourne, Australia), 1996.

African Animal Crackers, illustrated by Cameron Scott, Rigby Heinemann (Port Melbourne, Australia), 1996.

Angel (novel), Random House Australia (Milsons Point, Australia), 1997.

The Great Jimbo James, illustrated by David Cox, Omnibus (Norwood, Australia), 1997.

A Piece of Mind, Random House Australia (Milsons Point, Australia), 1999.

Lavinia Lavarr, illustrated by Terry Denton, Lothian (Port Melbourne, Australia), 2000.

Eggs for Breakfast, Pearson Education (South Melbourne, Australia), 2000.

Breakaway (novel), Random House Australia (Milsons Point, Australia), 2000.

The Rented House (novel for younger readers), Random House Australia (Milsons Point, Australia), 2000.

On the Run (novel for younger readers), Random House Australia (Milsons Point, Australia), 2001.

Spike, illustrated by David Cox, Omnibus/Ashton, 2001.

Also author of *Midge Mum and the Neighbors* and *Find My Friends,* both published in Australia.

Sidelights

Australian author Phil Cummings is known for his rhyming picture books and two juvenile novels featuring boy protagonists. The novel *Angel* deals with the topic of a dead brother who visits his sibling at night in the form of an angel, while *A Piece of Mind* explores peer group pressure. Used to following his pack of friends on their trouble-making pranks, Matt, the young protagonist of *A Piece of Mind,* worries when he begins hearing voices in his head urging him on to more dangerous stunts. Writing in *Magpies,* Cecile Grumelart praised *A Piece of Mind* for its verisimilitude, predicting that it would appeal to boys seven to nine years old, particularly those interested in in-line roller skating.

While most of his books were published in Australia, the picture book *Goodness Gracious!* appeared in the United

Phil Cummings

States and caught the attention of American reviewers. The story revolves around a red-headed, pigtailed girl who romps with such fanciful creatures as a witch, a pirate, and a wild baboon. "It's the words that will hold them," asserted Hazel Rochman in *Booklist.* "The word play is imaginative and appealing," claimed Lauralyn Persson in a *School Library Journal* review. Over the course of this rhyming tale, different body parts are highlighted, making it a "delightfully creative expansion of a truly childlike activity," according to a *Kirkus Reviews* critic.

Cummings once told *SATA:* "I love to write. It's great to come up with something that entertains others, particularly 'little' others. Writing books for young children presents numerous rewards for me. Giving them language to play with, use and expand upon, is fuel for my creativity. Creating characters, settings, and images and moulding them like clay is also exciting.

"I am the youngest of a family of eight children. I grew up in the dusty town of Peterborough in the mid-North of the state of South Australia. In my most recent works, it is the experiences from those wonderfully adventurous years that I am now calling upon as I write. And, you know, I don't think there are going to be enough years in my life to record them *all* in print, but I'm going to give a real good try."

Biographical and Critical Sources

PERIODICALS

Booklist, January 16, 1992, Hazel Rochman, review of *Goodness Gracious!*, p. 950.

Kirkus Reviews, January 15, 1992, review of *Goodness Gracious!*, p. 113.

Magpies, September, 1999, Cecile Grumelart, review of *A Piece of Mind*, p. 34.

School Library Journal, July, 1992, Lauralyn Persson, review of *Goodness Gracious!*, pp. 57-58.

D

DALE, Kim 1957-

Personal

Born March 16, 1957, in Melbourne, Australia; daughter of Faye (a film producer; maiden name, Nicholls) Waller; married Peter Dale, April, 1983; children: Simon, Harry, Georgia. *Education:* Attended high school. *Politics:* "Never!" *Religion:* "My own."

Addresses

Office—c/o Lothian, 11 Munro St., Port Melbourne, Victoria 3207, Australia.

Career

Professional stage actress, beginning in 1968; television actress, 1968-80; Billboard Night Club, Melbourne, Australia, director, 1980-81; Intuition (nursery, florist, and garden design company), Prahran, Australia, managing director, 1982-93; writer. Stage appearances include roles in *The Princess and the Sorcerer, Half a Sixpence, Carousel, The Boyfriend,* and *The King and I;* appeared on Australian television programs; musical performer throughout Australia and Asia, including record albums for Astor and Full Moon Records; also appeared as a model and in television commercials.

Awards, Honors

Acting awards include Sun Award, 1970, for *Half a Sixpence,* and Duhig Ford Prize, 1972, for *The Boyfriend.*

Writings

What Am I, Lothian (Port Melbourne, Australia), 2000.

Work in Progress

Eyes in the Dark, about the nocturnal wildlife of Australia; *Bush Baby Max,* "a true story about a duck."

Kim Dale

Sidelights

Kim Dale told *SATA:* "As a child my greatest loves were singing, drawing animals, and giving a home to every stray dog and horse I found. Somewhere along the way through adulthood I got lost, but now at forty-three, I've come back. They say 'Life begins at forty.' I'd have to agree. I have two horses, a dog, an abundance of wildlife to share our garden, and many ailing visitors who temporarily board here, especially birds.

"The first of my paintings was started six years ago. My mother, Faye, had written a story named 'Doon' and suggested that I try illustrating it. I hadn't drawn for thirty years. I painted animals first, just to get the feel of watercolor, which I had never used before. I completed 'Doon,' and it was taken to Lothian Books. Lothian was impressed by the wildlife illustrations, in particular the sea eagle.

"When I was first painting I believe Mother Nature herself said: if this is what you are to do, then do it from the heart. A hatchling magpie fell out of its nest. Saving it took 300 worms a day and an electric blanket for warmth. As the weeks went on there were a fledgling magpie, a kookaburra, two doves, and a rosella, all with different feeding needs every half-hour. (Thank goodness my husband, Peter, and our children were away for five weeks.) It was a wonderful time in my life. Those birds and many more since then have been my greatest teachers. I am now being licensed for a wildlife career. It is the caring that satisfies me the most, but the experience has also offered ideas for future stories. What the animals give us is precious, and hopefully I can pass my love for them on to many other people.

"One little blackbird that I reared and released lives in our garden. As a mother I know her voice among many others. She is totally wild now, but she surprised me recently when, having left the door open, I watched her come into the house with her mate and sit on the edge of our fruit basket. The two chatted away for an hour. I told her I thought her boyfriend was very handsome. Then off they flew. Many other times I walked in to find a magpie sitting on the chair or picking up crumbs off the kitchen floor. I thank them for their trust.

"I had very little formal education in the arts. When I finished my book and interest was being shown, I got nervous and felt I should have some lessons, not really knowing how I could recreate the backgrounds. I don't pre-sketch and throw paint on; it all happens then and there. Along the way I have literally been blessed with the right people at the right time. Jenny Phillips, a brilliant botanical artist, helped me refine my work and understand more technique, but the greatest learning has come through nature itself. I'm still a beginner with a long way to go, so now I tread gently with respect.

"The advice I would give to anyone aspiring to write and illustrate is to play like a child, be free, and don't worry or compare yourself with anyone else. Just believe: the moment self-doubt disappears, magic happens. I started painting at thirty-eight, when my business of fifteen years failed due to the economy. I lost everything financially and am beginning my life again. It's richer than it's ever been, and that's not in dollars. There's hope for us all, if we are willing to try.

"I have been blessed with a fantastic mother, who got me going and hasn't stopped supporting me in every way; a rare husband who has kept me on track when self-doubts creep in and self-discipline is needed; and many wonderful people who freely offered their knowledge. It's fun to feel like a kid again."

* * *

De GOLDI, Kate
See De GOLDI, Kathleen Domenica

* * *

De GOLDI, Kathleen Domenica 1959-
(Kate De Goldi)

Personal

Born August 18, 1959, in Christchurch, New Zealand; daughter of Ronald James (a lawyer) and Frances Kathleen (a cellist; maiden name, Anderson) De Goldi; married Bruce Robert Foster (a photographer), November 14, 1990; children: Luciana Domenica De Goldi, Jack Francis Allesandro Foster. *Education:* Attended University of Canterbury. *Politics:* "Social Democrat—Labour voter." *Religion:* Roman Catholic.

Addresses

Home—41 Waitohu Rd., York Bay, Wellington, New Zealand.

Kathleen Domenica De Goldi

Career

Waimairi County Library, library assistant, 1979-84; Christchurch Marriage Guidance Council, research assistant, 1985-86; full-time writer and teacher of creative writing, 1986—. New Zealand National Radio, radio reviewer of children's books; *Bookenz* (television program), presenter; Victoria University, children's writing workshop tutor. *Member:* New Zealand Book Council (member of board of directors), Wellington Children's Book Association (president).

Awards, Honors

Short story award from American Express, 1988, for "Parkhaven Hotel"; Katherine Mansfield short story award, 1992, for "A Girl's Best Friend"; Children's Book Awards Senior Fiction Winner, *New Zealand Post,* and Esther Glen Medal, Library and Information Association of New Zealand Aotearoa, both 1997, both for *Sanctuary;* Children's Book Awards Senior Fiction Honour Book, *New Zealand Post,* 2000, for *Closed, Stranger.*

Writings

UNDER NAME KATE De GOLDI

Like You, Really (stories; includes "Parkhaven Hotel" and "A Girl's Best Friend"), Penguin Books (Auckland, New Zealand), 1994.
Sanctuary (young adult novel), Penguin Australia (Auckland, New Zealand), 1996.
Love, Charlie Mike (young adult novel), Penguin Australia (Auckland, New Zealand), 1997.
Closed, Stranger (young adult novel), Penguin Australia (Auckland, New Zealand), 1999.

Work in Progress

A children's novel, *Monumental Mason.*

Sidelights

Kathleen Domenica De Goldi told *SATA:* "I began writing in 1987 shortly after the birth of my daughter, Luciana. My first lucky break was winning the American Express short story award in 1988, with my second completed story. This story, 'Parkhaven Hotel,' and another, 'A Girl's Best Friend,' formed the basis of my short story collection *Like You, Really,* published in 1994. My first published young adult novel was *Sanctuary,* which won the senior fiction prize in the *New Zealand Post* Children's Book Awards.

"I have concentrated on young adult fiction since 1996. It's a genre I read widely as a teenager and have continued to follow in my adult years. I find teenage protagonists—solipsistic, egocentric, passionate, and extreme as they often are—provide particularly interesting character arcs and, inevitably, white-hot story lines. I am also a radio reviewer of children's books and the front-person for a television books program, so I maintain a passionate interest in literature generally.

"My adult fiction has been particularly influenced by the inimitable Canadian writer Alice Munro and by American fiction writers Lorrie Moore, Louise Erdrich, and Ellen Gilchrist. The young adult writers I particularly admire are Jane Gardam, Jan Mark, Robert Cormier, and Philip Pullman; my most admired children's writer is, I think, E. L. Konigsburg, followed by David Almond.

"I divide my working life between my broadcast commitments and my writing. I also spend quite a bit of time each year teaching creative writing in schools, addressing teacher and librarian conferences, and speaking at writers' festivals.

"I write whenever I can, but work best in the mornings, after an hour's bush-walking. I hope most earnestly to inspire through my books the same love of story and reading that nurtured me throughout a book-filled childhood and young adulthood. My only two pieces of advice to aspiring writers is: read (reading was my sole creative writing tutor) and just do it (if you want to write, the only remedy is to sit down and begin).

"*Closed, Stranger,* my most recent book, evolved out of a long-time interest in the competitive nature (as I had observed it) of young male friendship and the business of adoption, particularly in the emotional lives of adopted children.

"In the last year I have been drawn increasingly 'back' to children's fiction, as distinct from young adult fiction. *Monumental Mason* is about the conversations between a twelve-year-old girl and a secret friend (Mason) she makes in the period immediately following her father's death."

*　　*　　*

de REGNIERS, Beatrice Schenk (Freedman) 1914-2000 (Tamara Kitt)

OBITUARY NOTICE—See index for *SATA* sketch: Born August 16, 1914, in Lafayette, IN; died March 1, 2000, in Washington, DC. Editor, author. De Regniers was the writer of dozens of children's books. Her first work, published in 1953, was entitled *The Giant Story;* following that book were nearly forty others, including her 1961 *Who Likes the Sun?,* her self-illustrated *Little Book,* and *The Way I Feel, Sometimes,* which was a collection of poetry published in 1988. During the 1960s, she published five books under the pseudonym Tamara Kitt, such as her 1967 *Sam and the Impossible Thing.* In 1965 she earned the Caldecott Award for *May I Bring a Friend?* In addition to her own stories, de Regniers' list of published works includes retellings of classics, such as *Red Riding Hood.*

OBITUARIES AND OTHER SOURCES:

PERIODICALS

New York Times, March 8, 2000, p. C24.

Washington Post, March 7, 2000, p. B7.

*   *   *

DeFORD, Deborah H.

Personal

Married; children: three.

Addresses

Home—Connecticut. *Agent*—c/o Reader's Digest Association, 260 Madison Ave., Fl. 16, New York, NY 10016.

Career

Author, editor, lecturer, and teacher.

Writings

(With Harry S. Stout) *An Enemy among Them* (novel), Houghton (Boston, MA), 1987.

FOR ADULTS

(Editor) *Are You Old Enough to Read This Book? Reflections on Midlife,* introduction by Linda Ellerbee, Reader's Digest Association (New York, NY), 1997.

The Simpler Life: An Inspirational Guide to Living Better with Less, Reader's Digest Association (New York, NY), 1998.

Seeking a Simpler Spirit: An 8-week Guide toward a Lifelong Relationship with God, Reader's Digest Association (New York, NY), 1999.

Sidelights

Deborah DeFord's debut novel *An Enemy among Them,* written with Harry S. Stout, tells the tale of the American Revolution through a crucial battle at Stony Point, Pennsylvania. The protagonist, Margaret, belongs to a family supportive of the colonists-turned-revolutionaries. She meets a young mercenary from Germany who has been captured and is under guard by her father, who has enlisted the young man to make boots for the colonial army. The mercenary, Christian, was responsible for injuring Margaret's brother in a previous battle, a fact which troubles Christian as he becomes more and more fond of Margaret. In the end, Christian takes the side of the American revolutionaries. He and Margaret deliver crucial information about Loyalist plans that enables the colonists to foil Loyalist battle strategies at Stony Point.

Reviewing the young adult novel in *School Library Journal,* Christian Behrmann commended the historical research that serves as a foundation for *An Enemy among Them,* but found both characters and plot routine and underdeveloped. A *Publishers Weekly* reviewer agreed, calling the story an "absorbing historical romance" that is "marred by inflated writing and too neat coincidences." While acknowledging that "at times

During the American Revolutionary War, a young Hessian soldier becomes a prisoner in a German home. (Cover illustration by Paul Mock.)

coincidence intrudes and motivation is stretched" in the narrative, a *Kirkus Reviews* contributor commended DeFord and Stout for their "action-filled account of a difficult time in the quest for freedom." *Kliatt*'s Donna L. Scanlon concurred with this assessment, commenting that the writers "ably combine their talents to produce a vivid and historically accurate portrait of the war's impact on a single family."

In addition to authoring fiction, DeFord edited the essay collection *Are You Old Enough to Read This Book? Reflections on Midlife,* which addresses various aspects of men and women's middle years. Contributors include over-fifty notables John Updike, Arthur Miller, and Dr. Ruth Westheimer, among others. The book contains essays, interviews, and quizzes spanning a range of topics, including marriage, single life, work and retirement, parenting, the role of the grandparent, the ability to change one's outlook, and end-of-life issues.

Pursuing a religious vein, DeFord wrote *Seeking a Simpler Spirit: An 8-week Guide toward a Lifelong Relationship with God* (1999), for those interested, to provide a structure for maintaining a relationship with God.

Biographical and Critical Sources

PERIODICALS

Booklist, October 1, 1997, Mary Carroll, review of *Are You Old Enough to Read This Book?,* p. 279.
Book Page, March, 1998, p. 23.
Bulletin of the Center for Children's Books, September, 1987, p. 6.
Kirkus Reviews, October 1, 1987, review of *An Enemy among Them,* pp. 1459-1460.
Kliatt, January, 1995, Donna L. Scanlon, review of *An Enemy among Them,* p. 7.

Library Journal, December, 1997, Susan E. Burdick, review of *Are You Old Enough to Read This Book?,* p. 127.
Publishers Weekly, October 9, 1987, review of *An Enemy among Them,* p. 88; November 3, 1997, review of *Are You Old Enough to Read This Book?,* p. 72.
School Library Journal, September, 1987, Christian Behrmann, review of *An Enemy among Them,* p. 194.
Voice of Youth Advocates, October, 1987, p. 199.

ON-LINE

Senior Times Books, http://seniortimes.com/feb98/books (November 10, 1998).*

*   *   *

DOUGLAS, Leonard
See BRADBURY, Ray

E–F

ELLIOT, William
See BRADBURY, Ray

*　　*　　*

FEINBERG, Barbara Silberdick 1938-

Personal

Born June 1, 1938, in New York, NY; married Gerald Feinberg (a physicist), August 9, 1968 (died April 21, 1992); children: Jeremy R., Douglas L. *Education:* Wellesley College, B.A., 1959; Yale University, M.A., 1960, Ph.D., 1963. *Politics:* Independent. *Hobbies and other interests:* Collecting antique autographs of historical personalities, knitting and crocheting, raising/cultivating African violets and other plants, working out daily at the gym, enjoying music of the 1920s and 1930s, enjoying her Yorkshire terrier, Holly, "who keeps me on her schedule—waking me in the morning to feed her and nudging me to bed at night."

Addresses

Office—c/o Millbrook Press, 2 Old New Milford Rd., Brookfield, CT 06804.

Career

City College of the City University of New York, New York, NY, lecturer, 1963-66, instructor in political science, 1966-67; Brooklyn College of the City University of New York, Brooklyn, NY, visiting lecturer in political science, 1967-68; Seton Hall University, South Orange, NJ, assistant professor of political science, 1968-70; Hunter College of the City University of New York, New York, NY, adjunct assistant professor of political science, 1970-73; freelance writer and editor, 1973—. *Member:* Phi Beta Kappa.

Awards, Honors

Woodrow Wilson Prize, Wellesley College, 1959, for essay on modern politics; Durant Scholar, Wellesley College; Yale University summer stipend. *American Political Scandals: Past and Present, Harry S. Truman,* and *Next in Line: The American Vice President* were all selected by the New York Public Library as "Books for the Teen Age."

Writings

JUVENILE NONFICTION

Franklin Roosevelt: Gallant President, Lothrop, 1981.

Barbara Silberdick Feinberg

34

Marx and Marxism, F. Watts, 1985.

The Constitution: Yesterday, Today, and Tomorrow, Scholastic, 1986.

Watergate: Scandal in the White House, F. Watts, 1990.

American Political Scandals: Past and Present, F. Watts, 1992.

The National Government, F. Watts, 1993.

State Governments, F. Watts, 1993.

Local Governments, F. Watts, 1993.

Words in the News: A Student's Dictionary of American Government and Politics, F. Watts, 1993.

Harry S. Truman, F. Watts, 1994.

John Marshall: The Great Chief Justice, Enslow, 1995.

The Cabinet, Twenty-First Century Books, 1995.

Electing the President, Twenty-First Century Books, 1995.

Black Tuesday: The Stock Market Crash of 1929, Millbrook, 1995.

Hiroshima and Nagasaki, Children's Press, 1995.

Next in Line: The American Vice Presidency, F. Watts, 1996.

Term Limits for Congress?, Twenty-First Century Books, 1996.

The Constitutional Amendments, Twenty-First Century Books, 1996.

Patricia Ryan Nixon, Children's Press, 1998.

American's First Ladies: Changing Expectations, F. Watts, 1998.

Bess Wallace Truman, Children's Press, 1998.

Edith Kermit Carow Roosevelt, Children's Press, 1999.

General Douglas MacArthur: An American Hero, F. Watts, 1999.

The Dictionary of the U.S. Constitution, F. Watts, 1999.

The Changing White House, Children's Press, 2000.

Abraham Lincoln's Gettysburg Address: Four Score and More, Twenty-First Century Books, 2000.

John McCain, Serving His Country, Millbrook Press, 2000.

Joseph Lieberman, Keeping the Faith, Millbrook Press, 2001.

The Articles of Confederation, Millbrook Press, 2001.

Contributor to *The Young Reader's Guide to American History,* Houghton, 1994.

Sidelights

Barbara Silberdick Feinberg is a former political science professor who has written numerous books on this subject for children and young adults. "I write because I enjoy learning about people and about important events and then sharing what I have discovered with my readers," she told *SATA.* "Sometimes my books have a personal significance. For example, *General Douglas MacArthur* is dedicated to my uncle Charlie who was a medic serving in the Pacific on an atoll near New Guinea during World War II. Uncle Charlie would never speak about his military experiences. However, he was willing to read and critique my manuscript. He approved of how I treated his very controversial commander. Like many veterans of his generation, he still refused to talk about the war! How I wish he had. He died in 1999."

Feinberg's books on politics for young readers are much admired by audiences and critics for their extensive

research, organization, and clear and interesting prose style. In *Words in the News: A Student's Dictionary of American Government and Politics,* for example, Feinberg covers five hundred terms useful to students in civics courses, including such occasionally controversial terms as communism, gerrymander, and conservative. *Booklist* reviewer Julie Corsaro praised *Words in the News* as "up-to-date" and well-researched, concluding, "This dictionary ... should be useful and entertaining for students in government studies classes." Other useful resources for middle-school students in civics classes include Feinberg's *Electing the President* and *The Cabinet.* In a *Booklist* review of *Electing the President,* Mary Harris Veeder remarked that Feinberg manages to "convey the sense that our government and our political processes are still evolving."

Turning to the personalities behind the institutions, Feinberg has published several biographies of presidents, first ladies, and other significant figures in the history of the United States government. Her *Harry S. Truman* treats a figure in twentieth-century politics whose reputation has undergone a revolution since his term in office. Feinberg cites telling incidents from Truman's youth that helped shape his values and ambition, recounts his rise in the political ranks, and examines the challenges of his two terms as president, "perceptively analyzing Truman's subsequent impact on U.S. foreign and domestic policy," according to Mary Romano Marks in *Booklist.* Later biographies *Bess Wallace Truman, Patricia Ryan Nixon,* and *Edith Kermit Carow Roosevelt* were preceded by a collective history of the role of the wife of the American president, *America's First Ladies: Changing Expectations.* Here Feinberg addresses the women's differing responses to national expectations regarding their involvement in campaigning and making policy, social activities and fulfillment of family responsibilities, leadership in fashion-setting, and speaking out on favorite causes. The author draws on this material to "provide many lively anecdotes drawn from a wide range of sources," observed Anne O'Malley in *Booklist.*

Beyond institutions and personalities, Feinberg has also turned her attention to pivotal documents in American political history. Beginning with *The Constitution: Yesterday, Today, and Tomorrow* and *The Constitutional Amendments,* Feinberg then wrote *The Dictionary of the U.S. Constitution,* which is similar in orientation and audience focus to her *Words in the News.* In addition to entries on the Constitution itself, its amendments, and articles, the author includes information on many related terms such as the *Federalist Papers,* Habeas corpus, and freedom of speech. In *Abraham Lincoln's Gettysburg Address: Four Score and More,* Feinberg gives background on one of the most famous speeches in American history and "reveals surprising facts about the speech and its context," Catherine Andronik reported in *Booklist.* Feinberg's research extends to contemporary responses to the speech, which have been mixed, and communicates a variety of perspectives on the now-revered historical figure. Feinberg's accomplishment, according to Patricia Ann Owens in *School Library*

Journal, is that she answers a myriad of questions a middle school student might have about the Gettysburg Address "while she fosters a deeper appreciation for the memorable, inspirational words."

Biographical and Critical Sources

PERIODICALS

Booklist, November 1, 1992, Gary Young, review of *American Political Scandals,* p. 499; March 1, 1994, Julie Corsaro, review of *Words in the News,* p. 1257; September 1, 1994, Mary Romano Marks, review of *Harry S. Truman,* p. 32; September 1, 1995, Mary Harris Veeder, review of *Electing the President,* p. 68; March 1, 1999, Anne O'Malley, review of *America's First Ladies,* p. 1163; December 15, 1999, review of *The Dictionary of the U.S. Constitution,* p. 799; November 15, 2000, Catherine Andronik, review of *Abraham Lincoln's Gettysburg Address,* p. 637.

Book Report, September-October, 1994, Ron Marinucci, review of *Words in the News,* p. 60; November-December, 1994, review of *Harry S. Truman,* p. 51.

Publishers Weekly, May 8, 1981, Jean F. Mercier, review of *Franklin F. Roosevelt,* p. 255.

School Library Journal, December, 1981, review of *Franklin D. Roosevelt,* p. 62; August, 1986, James Steed, review of *Marx and Marxism,* p. 100; January, 1993, Jonathan Betz-Zall, review of *American Political Scandals,* p. 137; January, 1994, Eunice Weech, review of *The National Government* and *State Governments,* p. 121; May, 1994, Daryl Grabarek, review of *Words in the News,* p. 140; September, 1994, Pat Katka, review of *Harry S. Truman,* p. 248; August, 1995, Pat Katka, review of *John Marshall,* p. 160; October, 1995, Ann M. Burlingame, review of *The Cabinet,* p. 146; August, 1996, Jeffrey A. French, review of *Term Limits for Congress?,* p. 153; February, 1997, Mary Mueller, review of *Next in Line,* p. 114; January, 1999, Debbie Feulner, review of *America's First Ladies,* p. 139; July, 1999, review of *The Dictionary of the U.S. Constitution,* p. 148; July, 1999, Herman Sutter, review of *Douglas MacArthur,* p. 106; December, 1999, Mary Mueller, review of *The Dictionary of the U.S. Constitution,* p. 148; January, 2001, Patricia Ann Owens, review of *Abraham Lincoln's Gettysburg Address,* p. 144.

*   *   *

FERRARI, Maria

Personal

Born in Brooklyn, NY; daughter of Frank and Giuseppina Ferrari. *Education:* Syracuse University, B.S. (communications).

Addresses

Home—311 West 19th St., #62, New York, NY 10011. *E-mail*—m14ferrari@aol.com.

Career

Self-employed still-life photographer, 1985—.

Illustrator

Carol Wallace, *Victorian Treasures: An Album and Historical Guide for Collectors,* Harry Abrams (New York, NY), 1993.

Rebecca Kai Dotlich, *What Is Round?,* HarperCollins (New York, NY), 1999.

Rebecca Kai Dotlich, *What Is Square?,* HarperCollins (New York, NY), 1999.

Rebecca Kai Dotlich, *What Is a Triangle?,* HarperCollins (New York, NY), 2000.

Sidelights

Maria Ferrari is a professional photographer who has illustrated a series of books written for preschoolers by Rebecca Kai Dotlich. These books, including *What Is Round?, What Is Square?,* and *What Is a Triangle?,* introduce the youngest audiences to basic concepts of shape through a rhyming text heavy on alliterative effects and photographed objects that critics praised as perfectly designed for the preschool audience. At the close of each book, a double-page photo of a myriad of objects is displayed so that children can test what they have learned about the concepts of round, square, and triangular by sifting through some objects that do not belong. "The book works on multiple levels," avowed Kathy Broderick in a review of *What Is Round?* in *Booklist,* citing Dotlich's text for building vocabulary and sound recognition and Ferrari's photos for "challenging" her audience to find the circles in the world all around them. *School Library Journal* contributor Susan Marie Pitard faulted *What Is Round?* for including objects that are not perfect circles, such as garbanzo beans, or do not always come in circular shapes, such as bells. However, Pitard added praise for Ferrari's photographs, dubbing them "bright and uncluttered, perfect for attracting the attention of preschoolers."

The critical response to *What Is Square?* and *What Is a Triangle?* mirrored the response to the first book. Jackie Hechtkopf offered unqualified praise for *What Is Square?* in *School Library Journal,* citing the photography, the design and layout of the pages, and Dotlich's catchy rhyming text equally. "This superbly crafted concept book will quickly become a favorite," Hechtkopf predicted. Like Pitard, however, *School Library Journal* reviewer Ellen Heath took issue with the author and illustrator of *What Is a Triangle?* for using birthday hats and ice-cream cones as examples of triangles when these objects are actually cones. Heath did add, however, that the book's text is accompanied by Ferrari's "colorful photos of common objects set against bright backgrounds."

Biographical and Critical Sources

PERIODICALS

Booklist, July, 1999, Kathy Broderick, review of *What Is Round?,* p. 1950.

School Library Journal, April, 1999, Susan Marie Pitard, review of *What Is Round?,* p. 113; August, 1999, Jackie Hechtkopf, review of *What Is Square?,* p. 145; November, 2000, Ellen Heath, review of *What Is a Triangle?,* p. 140.

*   *   *

FIGLER, Jeanie 1949-

Personal

Born December 30, 1949, in Rahway, NJ; daughter of Louis and Dorinda (Spadaro) Ciraolo; married Ray Figler (a body shop instructor at a vocational school), August 10, 1975; children: Michael, Daniel. *Education:* Attended Raritan Valley College; earned diploma from Children's Institute of Literature. *Politics:* Republican. *Religion:* Christian. *Hobbies and other interests:* Music (including piano), travel, reading.

Addresses

Home—Flemington, NJ. *Agent*—Arthur Fleming Associates, San Diego, CA.

Jeanie Figler

Career

Writer. MAACO Auto Painting and Body Works, North Brunswick, NJ, past vice president, co-owner, and secretary, ending 1994; also worked as administrative assistant.

Writings

Majestic Blue Horses, Laredo Publishing (Beverly Hills, CA), 1999.

Contributor to *Poetic Voices of America,* 1992.

Work in Progress

Bloody Bones, a suspense novel; *Volcano Dancer,* a sequel to *Majestic Blue Horses.*

Sidelights

Jeanie Figler told *SATA:* "I first became interested in writing short stories when I was in the sixth grade. At the time, *Life* magazine always had an unusual picture on the last page. The class had to write a story about it. Being a thrill-seeker even at a young age, I loved to write adventurous and perhaps far-fetched stories. I also wrote little blurbs with cartoon characters and humorous 'mad-libs.'

"I have two teenage sons who also inspired some of my writing. With my vivid memory of my own childhood, I can easily relate to the young characters I write about. The free-spirited little kid in me is very active, and writing for this age group keeps me in tune to the ever-changing world.

"I love to travel and, whenever I take a trip, I try to do something unusual—trying to test my limits. Then I incorporate my escapades into my stories. My husband never knows where I'll drag him. Although he will protest, he will enjoy the experience."

*   *   *

FREEDMAN, Russell (Bruce) 1929-

Personal

Born October 11, 1929, in San Francisco, CA; son of Louis N. (a publisher's representative) and Irene (an actress; maiden name, Gordon) Freedman. *Education:* Attended San Jose State College (now University), 1947-49; University of California, Berkeley, B.A., 1951. *Hobbies and other interests:* Travel, photography, film-making.

Career

Associated Press, San Francisco, CA, reporter and editor, 1953-56; J. Walter Thompson Co. (advertising agency), New York City, publicity writer for television, 1956-60; Columbia University Press, New York City, associate staff member of Columbia Encyclopedia, 1961-63; editor, Crowell-Collier Educational Corp., 1964-65; freelance writer, 1961—. Writing workshop instructor, New School for Social Research, 1969-86. *Military service:* U.S. Army, Counter Intelligence Corps, 1951-53; served in Korea. *Member:* Authors Guild, PEN, Society of Children's Book Writers and Illustrators.

Awards, Honors

Western Heritage Award, National Cowboy Hall of Fame, 1984, for *Children of the Wild West;* Spur Award Honor Book citation, Western Writers of America, 1985, and Jefferson Cup Award, 1986, both for *Cowboys of the Wild West;* Golden Kite Award Honor Book citation, Society of Children's Book Writers, 1987, Newbery Medal, American Library Association, and Jefferson Cup Award, both 1988, all for *Lincoln: A Photobiography;* Jefferson Cup Award Honor Book citation, 1988, for *Indian Chiefs;* Golden Kite Award Honor Book citation, 1988, for *Buffalo Hunt;* Golden Kite Award Honor Book citation, 1990, Orbis Pictus Award, National Council of Teachers of English, and Jefferson Cup Award, both 1991, all for *Franklin Delano Roosevelt;* Golden Kite Award, 1991, Jefferson Cup Award, and Newbery Honor Book citation, both 1992, all for *The Wright Brothers: How They Invented the Airplane; Washington Post*/Children's Book Guild Nonfiction Award, 1992, for distinguished work in the field of nonfiction for children; Golden Kite Award Honor Book citation, 1992, for *An Indian Winter;* Golden Kite Award, 1993, *Boston Globe-Horn Book* Award, 1994, and Newbery Honor Book citation, 1994, all for *Eleanor Roosevelt: A Life of Discovery;* Golden Kite Award, 1994, for *Kids at Work: Lewis Hine and the Crusade against Child Labor;* Spur Award, Western Writers of America, 1996, for *The Life and Death of Crazy Horse;* Laura Ingalls Wilder Medal, American Library Association, 1998, for body of work; Golden Kite Award, 1998, for *Martha Graham: A Dancer's Life.* Freedman's books have appeared on numerous "best" or "outstanding" book lists, including lists compiled by such organizations as the American Library Association, the Junior Literary Guild, the Child Study Association of America, and the Children's Book Council, and such periodicals as *School Library Journal, Horn Book,* and *Booklist.*

Writings

NONFICTION; FOR YOUNG ADULTS

Teenagers Who Made History, portraits by Arthur Shilstone, Holiday House (New York, NY), 1961.

Two Thousand Years of Space Travel, Holiday House (New York, NY), 1963.

Jules Verne: Portrait of a Prophet, Holiday House (New York, NY), 1965.

Thomas Alva Edison, American R.D.M. (New York, NY), 1966.

Scouting with Baden-Powell, Holiday House (New York, NY), 1967.

(With James E. Morriss) *How Animals Learn,* Holiday House (New York, NY), 1969.

Russell Freedman

(With James E. Morriss) *Animal Instincts,* illustrated by John Morris, Holiday House (New York, NY), 1970.

Animal Architects, Holiday House (New York, NY), 1971.

(With James E. Morriss) *The Brains of Animals and Man,* Holiday House (New York, NY), 1972.

The First Days of Life, illustrated by Joseph Cellini, Holiday House (New York, NY), 1974.

Growing Up Wild: How Young Animals Survive, illustrated by Leslie Morrill, Holiday House (New York, NY), 1975.

Animal Fathers, illustrated by Joseph Cellini, Holiday House (New York, NY), 1976.

Animal Games, illustrated by St. Tamara, Holiday House (New York, NY), 1976.

Hanging On: How Animals Carry Their Young, Holiday House (New York, NY), 1977.

How Birds Fly, illustrated by Lorence F. Bjorklund, Holiday House (New York, NY), 1977.

Getting Born, illustrated with photographs and with drawings by Corbett Jones, Holiday House (New York, NY), 1978.

How Animals Defend Their Young, Dutton (New York, NY), 1978.

Immigrant Kids, Dutton (New York, NY), 1980.

Tooth and Claw: A Look at Animal Weapons, Holiday House (New York, NY), 1980.

They Lived with the Dinosaurs, Holiday House (New York, NY), 1980.

Animal Superstars: Biggest, Strongest, Fastest, Smartest, Prentice-Hall (Englewood Cliffs, NJ), 1981.

Farm Babies, Holiday House (New York, NY), 1981.

When Winter Comes, illustrated by Pamela Johnson, Dutton (New York, NY), 1981.

Can Bears Predict Earthquakes? Unsolved Mysteries of Animal Behavior, Prentice-Hall (Englewood Cliffs, NJ), 1982.

Killer Fish, Holiday House (New York, NY), 1982.

Killer Snakes, Holiday House (New York, NY), 1982.

Children of the Wild West, Clarion Books (New York, NY), 1983.

Dinosaurs and Their Young, illustrated by Leslie Morrill, Holiday House (New York, NY), 1983.

Rattlesnakes, Holiday House (New York, NY), 1984.

Cowboys of the Wild West, Clarion Books (New York, NY), 1985.

Sharks, Holiday House (New York, NY), 1985.

Indian Chiefs, Holiday House (New York, NY), 1987.

Lincoln: A Photobiography, Clarion Books (New York, NY), 1987.

Buffalo Hunt, Holiday House (New York, NY), 1988.

Franklin Delano Roosevelt, Clarion Books (New York, NY), 1990.

The Wright Brothers: How They Invented the Airplane, photographs by Orville and Wilbur Wright, Holiday House (New York, NY), 1991.

An Indian Winter, paintings and drawings by Karl Bodmer, Holiday House (New York, NY), 1992.

Eleanor Roosevelt: A Life of Discovery, Clarion Books (New York, NY), 1993.

Kids at Work: Lewis Hine and the Crusade against Child Labor, with photographs by Lewis Hine, Clarion Books (New York, NY), 1994.

The Life and Death of Crazy Horse, drawings by Amos Bad Heart Bull, Holiday House (New York, NY), 1996.

Out of Darkness: The Story of Louis Braille, illustrated by Kate Kiesler, Clarion Books (New York, NY), 1997.

Martha Graham: A Dancer's Life, Clarion Books (New York, NY), 1998.

Babe Didrikson Zaharias: The Making of a Champion, Clarion Books (New York, NY), 1999.

Give Me Liberty!: The Story of the Declaration of Independence, Holiday House, (New York, NY) 2000.

In the Days of the Vaqueros: America's First True Cowboys, Clarion Books (New York, NY), 2001.

Confucius: The Golden Rule, illustrated by Frederic Clement, Arthur A. Levine, in press.

OTHER

Holiday House: The First Fifty Years (adult), Holiday House (New York, NY), 1985.

Contributor to *Columbia Encyclopedia,* 3rd edition, and *New Book of Knowledge Annual, 1981-89.* Also contributor to periodicals, including *Cricket, Ranger Rick, Horn Book,* and *School Library Journal.*

Adaptations

Lincoln: A Photobiography was adapted as a filmstrip and video, McGraw-Hill Media, 1989.

Sidelights

The author of more than forty nonfiction books for children, Russell Freedman has been honored with many major awards: the Newbery Medal for *Lincoln: A Photobiography* (Freedman was the first nonfiction author in thirty-two years to win the Newbery and one of only a handful of nonfiction authors to be honored with the medal since it was first presented in 1922); two Newbery Honors, for *The Wright Brothers: How They Invented the Airplane,* and *Eleanor Roosevelt: A Life of Discovery;* several Golden Kite awards for other biographies, as well as the *Washington Post*/Children's Book Guild Nonfiction Award; and in 1998 he was awarded the prestigious Laura Ingalls Wilder Award for the entire body of his work. This respected author has written on subjects such as famous teenagers, animal behavior, and American presidents, and his books are noted for their understandable and entertaining presentation of often-complex information. Freedman pioneered the form he calls a "photobiography," first used in his Lincoln biography, and has continued to employ this creative mix of text and image with a dozen more popular biographies and history books. Dubbed the "John McPhee of juvenile writers" by Michael Dirda in the *Washington Post Book World,* Freedman writes books that often "build on a suite of historical photographs or paintings, enhanced by a sleekly written, factual text," according to Dirda.

If writing comes naturally to Freedman, he may credit both nature and nurture. Born in 1929 in San Francisco, Freedman grew up in an atmosphere where literary

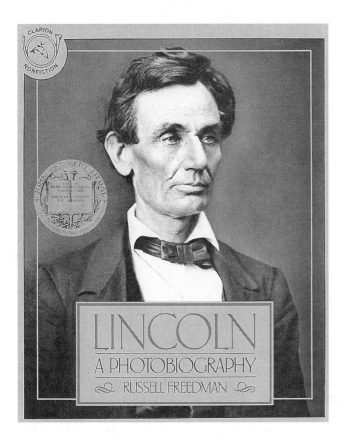

Freedman received the Newbery Award for this comprehensive photobiography.

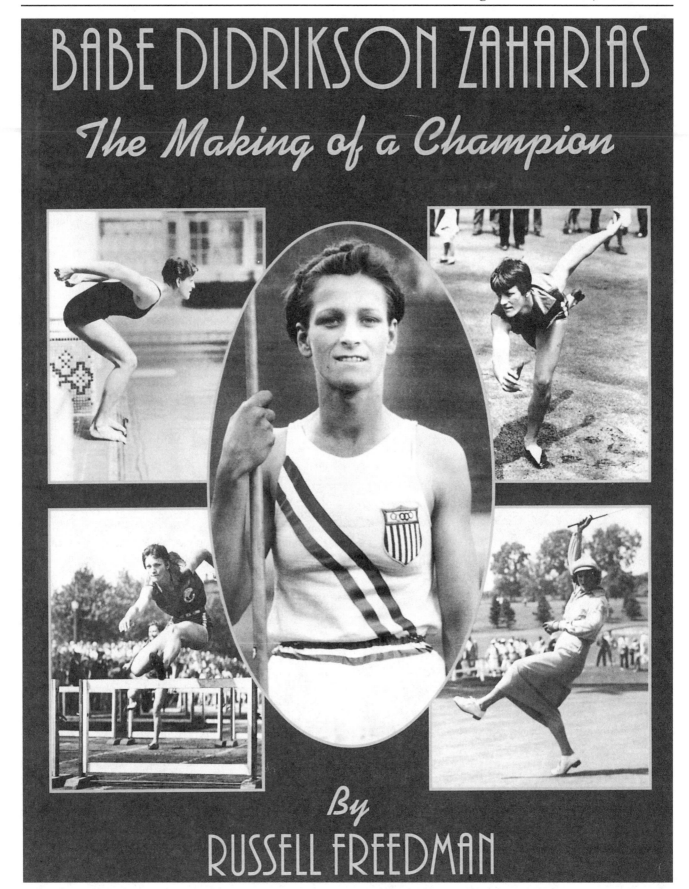

BABE DIDRIKSON ZAHARIAS
The Making of a Champion

By
RUSSELL FREEDMAN

Freedman includes reminiscences and rare photographs in this photobiography of the most accomplished woman athlete who ever lived.

accomplishments were encouraged. "My father was a great storyteller," Freedman related in his Newbery Medal acceptance speech, reprinted in *Horn Book.* "The problem was, we never knew for sure whether the stories he told were fiction or nonfiction." Freedman's father, a book salesman, met Russell's mother, a clerk, in the bookstore where she worked. "I had the good fortune to grow up in a house filled with books and book talk," the author stated, and often filled with visiting authors as well: writers such as John Steinbeck, William Saroyan, and John Masefield all came to dinner at one time or another.

From 1947 to 1949, he attended San Jose State College and graduated in 1951 with a B.A. from the University of California at Berkeley. For the next two years he served with the U.S. Counter Intelligence Corps, part of that time in combat duty in Korea with the 2nd Infantry Division. After his stint in the Army, Freedman went to work for the Associated Press in San Francisco as a reporter and editor. "That was where I really learned to write," he told Frank J. Dempsey in a *Horn Book* interview. He also wrote publicity pieces for television until he came upon something that would change the direction of his life. Freedman found an article about a blind sixteen-year-old boy who had invented a Braille typewriter. Freedman also learned that another blind sixteen-year-old, Louis Braille, had originally developed the Braille system. The article served as the inspiration for *Teenagers Who Made History,* Freedman's first book.

Since the late sixties Freedman has written more than twenty books on animal behavior, a subject that has interested him since his youth. He collaborated with James E. Morriss on a series of books that seeks to explain, in simple language, some of the scientific concepts of the animal kingdom. As the titles indicate, the books cover subjects such as *How Animals Learn, Animal Instincts,* and *The Brains of Animals and Man.* The books were well received by the educational community, as reflected in their appraisal by a reviewer in *Science Books: A Quarterly Review,* which stated that Freedman and Morriss's *How Animals Learn* and *Animal Instincts* "are among the best for beginning naturalists."

In 1980 Freedman took a break from chronicling wildlife to write a book on a different kind of animal— the human. While attending a photographic exhibit at the New York Historical Society, Freedman was struck by the photographs of children in nineteenth- and early twentieth-century America. "What impressed me most of all was the way that those old photographs seemed to defy the passage of time," he wrote in *Horn Book.* Freedman decided to tell the story behind the photographs, attempting to convey through his words—and some of those very same pictures—a sense of what life was like in those suspended moments of history. The resulting book was titled *Immigrant Kids.* The book proved to be a turning point; Freedman continued to produce books on animals, but he was increasingly

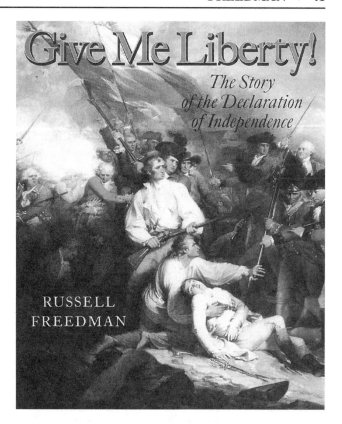

Freedman describes the events, personalities, and politics leading to the creation of the Declaration of Independence.

turning his writing attention to people. The books *Children of the Wild West* and *Cowboys of the Wild West* followed, earning praise for their accurate portrayal of life in the old West. Richard Snow, for example, wrote in the *New York Times Book Review* that *Children of the Wild West* "is a good introduction for young readers to the patterns of life in a Wild West that had nothing at all to do with gambling halls and shootouts."

Cowboys of the Wild West uncovered many myths about this often-romanticized group. A *Publishers Weekly* reviewer wrote: "Cowboys, readers discover, were really boys. Many were teenagers, a few 'old hands' were in their early twenties; and they were responsible for driving great herds across the plains in the 1800s." Freedman stays away from romanticizing the cowboys, instead describing the many difficulties of life on the range. George Gleason, writing in the *School Library Journal,* praised the work, declaring that it is "certainly a book to linger over and turn to again and again."

Freedman followed up these two books with a study of Native Americans entitled *Indian Chiefs* (1987). The work features six tribal leaders, including Sitting Bull and Red Cloud. Complete with archival photographs, Freedman gives a balanced picture of the lives and decisions of the great chiefs. Karen P. Zimmerman, writing in *School Library Journal,* stated that the account is factual and concluded that Freedman "does not romanticize the Indian viewpoint, nor is he judgmental against the whites." In *Buffalo Hunt* (1988) Freedman chronicles the importance of the great buffaloes to Native Americans and how their disappearance impacted the Indians' lives.

After discovering the truths behind the myths associated with life in the old West, Freedman decided to separate fact from fiction with respect to one of American history's most intriguing characters, Abraham Lincoln. In his quest to accurately research the book that would become *Lincoln: A Photobiography,* Freedman traveled to Lincoln's birthplace in Kentucky, then to the numerous Lincoln historical sites in Springfield, Illinois, and finally to Ford's Theater in Washington, D.C., where Lincoln was assassinated. Freedman was also allowed to examine some of the former president's original handwritten documents, including a letter to Lincoln's wife, Mary, and first-draft notes on his famed Emancipation Proclamation. Freedman's commitment to presenting the facts paid off; critical and popular response toward the book was very favorable. Elaine Fort Weischedel proclaimed in *School Library Journal:* "Few, if any, of the many books written for children about Lincoln can compare with Freedman's contribution."

Following the success of *Lincoln,* Freedman continued to write on historical figures in photobiographies, including *Franklin Delano Roosevelt, Eleanor Roosevelt: A Life of Discovery,* and *The Wright Brothers: How They Invented the Airplane.* For the first volume, Freedman once again did painstaking research to write a volume about a man whose life had already been chronicled extensively. In *Franklin Delano Roosevelt,* Freedman tries to bring to life the complicated personal world of the famous president, and the result, according to Alan Brinkley in the *New York Times Book Review,* is "sensitive [and] evocative.... It presents Roosevelt as an attractive and admirable public figure." Roosevelt's wife is also spotlighted in *Eleanor Roosevelt: A Life of Discovery,* a "sensitive portrayal" which "captures the spirit" of this remarkable woman, according to *Horn Book*'s Elizabeth S. Watson.

Freedman's interest in inventors led him to write the book *The Wright Brothers: How They Invented the Airplane* (1991). The "author's careful research yielded a completely engrossing volume," according to Margaret A. Bush in the *Horn Book,* which "draws deeply on letters, diaries, and other well-documented sources." Freedman dips into the characters of the Wright brothers, showing that their complementary personalities and life experiences helped them become the inventors of modern flight. Critics praised Freedman's selection of photographs and his storytelling ability. Bush claimed that the resulting book is a "fresh, illuminating look at an old story."

Freedman's next book topic was controversial as he profiled Lewis Hine, an early photographer of poor children involved in child labor. *Kids at Work: Lewis Hine and the Crusade against Child Labor* was published in 1994. Lewis Hine took photographs of children

of immigrants in the early 1900s. During those days, it was not uncommon for young children to work in dangerous conditions in the factory. These jobs often left the children seriously injured, or dead. Hine took the photographs to publicize these atrocities to the general public. Freedman told Shannon Maughan in *Publishers Weekly* that Hine was able to use "a camera as a tool for social change." Iris Tillman Hill wrote in the *New York Times Book Review* that "Those who want to share a lived sense of history with young children could not do much better than to look at these photographs and read this book with them."

In 1996, Freedman returned to Native American history to write *The Life and Death of Crazy Horse,* a biography of the great Lakota Sioux chief. Unlike other leaders of the era, Crazy Horse was a quiet, modest man who was also an excellent leader and tactician. He led groups in fights along the Oregon and Bozeman trails, including the Battle of the Little Bighorn, in an attempt to stem the tide of infiltration by pioneers. However, his life ended in a U.S. Army prison, with the fate of Native Americans looking very dim. A *Publishers Weekly* reviewer remarked, "No dry history this, but a story certain to sweep readers along its tragic path."

Freedman returned to the subject of his first children's book in *Out of Darkness: The Story of Louis Braille* (1997). Braille was blinded at the age of three after a knife accident. He learned not to turn his injury into a tragedy and worked hard to be accepted into a special school for the blind in Paris at the age of twelve and slowly developed the alphabet which today bears his name. Martha V. Parravano, reviewing Freedman's biography in *Horn Book,* said that *Out of Darkness* "brings the central figure to life as vividly as only Freedman can." In *Booklist,* Hazel Rochman claimed that Freedman "tells the momentous story in quiet chapters in his best plain style."

In 1998, Freedman published his first biography on an artist. His *Martha Graham: A Dancer's Life* was yet another photobiography, this time of the American dancer, teacher, and choreographer who, born in Pittsburgh in 1895, went on to become one of the seminal figures in the world in modern dance. "Freedman's focus," noted *Booklist*'s Rochman, "is on how [Graham] created a thrilling new modern dance language that connected movement with emotion...." Rochman concluded that this was another "great Y[oung] A[dult] title that will appeal to adults as much as to teens." A reviewer for *Publishers Weekly* commented that the "venerable author hooks readers in immediately" in this "outstanding biography [which] speaks not only to dancers but to anyone interested in the arts, history, or the American entrepreneurial spirit." Reviewing the same title in *New York Times Book Review,* Theodore W. Striggles felt that "Freedman has written a fine introduction to Martha Graham, and not just for the young readers...." Striggles concluded, "*Martha Graham* is so smoothly written that there are only a few moments during which the adult reader is reminded of the primary audience for whom the book is intended...." "Once again, preeminent biographer Russell Freedman proves the art of nonfiction," announced *Horn Book*'s Susan P. Bloom in a highly favorable review of *Martha Graham*. Bloom further commented, "No reader, whether interested in dance or not, will want to miss Graham's extraordinary story, Freedman's remarkable achievement."

From dance, Freedman turned his hand to sports, chronicling the remarkable career of Babe Didrikson, who broke records in golf, track and field, and other sports, and all at a time when opportunities for females in athletics were very limited. "Freedman is on top of his game with this engaging profile of one of this century's most remarkable athletes and larger-than-life personalities," wrote Luann Toth in a *School Library Journal* review of *Babe Didrikson Zaharias: The Making of a Champion*. Once again Freedman blended thorough research, clear prose, and a wealth of visual images to come up with a superlative biography. Toth concluded, "Befitting a champion, this superbly crafted, impeccably documented biography ranks head and shoulders above its peers." A reviewer in *Horn Book* felt that "Freedman's measured yet lively style captures the spirit of the great athlete," and that the plentiful black-and-white photographs "capture Babe's spirit and dashing good looks." A contributor for *Publishers Weekly* called Freedman's biography "exemplary," and concluded that this "celebratory work gives readers a chance to cheer Zaharias's legendary life."

Freedman welcomed in the new millennium with a piece of more orthodox history, *Give Me Liberty!: The Story of the Declaration of Independence*. *Horn Book*'s Mary M. Burns noted that Freedman, a "dependable historian and biographer ... is also an exciting writer who can make readers feel that they are witnesses to significant happenings." With *Give Me Liberty!*, he takes the reader into the story leading to the drafting and acceptance of the Declaration of Independence, from the Boston Tea Party to the signing of the document that announced American sovereignty. "Freedman weaves a tapestry that combines political observations, character interpretations, and popular sentiments in a style accessible to middle-school readers yet equally appealing to adults," commented Burns. "How does [Freedman] do it?" wondered GraceAnne A. DeCandido in a *Booklist* review of the same book. DeCandido went on to note, "Once again Freedman takes a crucial moment in American history and imbues it with living grace and powerful tension." Leah J. Sparks also had high praise for Freedman in a *School Library Journal* review: "Known for his stellar biographies and superb nonfiction, Freedman now offers a fine book about the creation of the nation's most important historical documents."

Biography is the format in which Freedman most likes to write. In an interview with James Cross Giblin in *Horn Book*, Freedman expanded on his reasons for writing nonfiction for children: "A writer of books for children has an impact on readers' minds and imaginations that very few writers for adults can match. But beyond that, writing nonfiction for children gives me, or any writer, tremendous artistic freedom. I can write about almost any subject that interests me and that I believe will interest a child. I can be a generalist rather than a specialist.... It's a much greater challenge to convey the spirit and essence of a life in a hundred pages than to write a 600- or 800-page 'definitive' tome that includes every known detail about that life. A nonfiction children's book requires concision, selection, judgment, lucidity, unwavering focus, and the most artful use of language and storytelling techniques. I regard such books as a specialized and demanding art form."

Biographical and Critical Sources

BOOKS

Children's Literature Review, Volume 20, Gale (Detroit, MI), 1990.
Meet the Authors and Illustrators, Volume II, Scholastic (New York, NY), 1993.
Twentieth-Century Young Adult Writers, 1st edition, St. James Press, 1994.
Ward, Martha E., *Authors of Books for Young People,* Scarecrow Press (Metuchen, NJ), 1990.

PERIODICALS

Booklist, July, 1993, p. 1962; June 1, 1996, p. 1721; March 1, 1997, Hazel Rochman, review of *Out of Darkness: The Story of Louis Braille,* pp. 1157-1158; April, 1998, Hazel Rochman, review of *Martha Graham: A Dancer's Life,* p. 1324; January 1, 1999, p. 782; July, 1999, p. 1932; March 1, 2000, p. 1248; March 15, 2000, p. 1359; October 1, 2000, GraceAnne A. DeCandido, review of *Give Me Liberty!: The Story of the Declaration of Independence,* p. 336.
Bulletin of the Center for Children's Books, May, 1987, p. 167; January, 1988; June, 1992, p. 260; May, 1997, p. 321.
Horn Book, January-February, 1986, Russell Freedman, "Perusing the Pleasure Principle"; March-April, 1986, pp. 220-221; January-February, 1987, pp. 104-107; July-August, 1987, p. 483; March-April, 1988, p. 222; July-August, 1988, Russell Freedman, "Newbery Medal Acceptance," pp. 444-451; July-August, 1988, Frank J. Dempsey, "Russell Freedman," pp. 452-456; March-April, 1991, pp. 213-214; July-August, 1991, Margaret A. Bush, review of *The Wright Brothers: How They Invented the Airplane,* pp. 475-476; January-February, 1994, Elizabeth S. Watson, review of *Eleanor Roosevelt: A Life of Discovery,* p. 87; November-December, 1994, p. 744; May-June, 1997, Martha V. Parravano, review of *Out of Darkness: The Story of Louis Braille,* pp. 339-340; July-August, 1998, James Cross Giblin, "Russell Freedman," pp. 455-459; July-August, 1998, Susan P. Bloom, review of *Martha Graham: A Dancer's Life,* pp. 511-512; September-October, 1999, review of *Babe Didrikson Zaharias: The Making of a Champion,* p. 623; July-August, 2000, p. 426; January-February, 2001, Mary M. Burns, review of *Give Me Liberty!: The Story of the Declaration of Independence,* p. 109.

Junior Literary Guild, October, 1987; March, 1988.

Kliatt, November, 1992, p. 26; September, 1996, p. 4; July, 1998, p. 32.

New York Times Book Review, November 13, 1983, Richard Snow, review of *Children of the Wild West,* p. 52; January 24, 1988, p. 37; March 17, 1991, Alan Brinkley, review of *Franklin Delano Roosevelt,* p. 26; November 14, 1993, p. 40; November 13, 1994, Iris Tillman Hill, review of *Kids at Work: Lewis Hine and the Crusade against Child Labor,* p. 23; May 17, 1998, Theodore W. Striggles, review of *Martha Graham: A Dancer's Life,* p. 29.

Publishers Weekly, November 15, 1985, review of *Cowboys of the Wild West;* November 27, 1987, review of *Lincoln: A Photobiography,* p. 86; May 3, 1991, p. 73; May 4, 1992, p. 58; June 21, 1993, p. 105; July 19, 1993, Shannon Maughan, interview with Russell Freedman, pp. 228, 234; June 17, 1996, review of *The Life and Death of Crazy Horse,* p. 67; April 6, 1998, review of *Martha Graham: A Dancer's Life,* p. 80; July 19, 1999, review of *Babe Didrikson Zaharias:*

The Making of a Champion, p. 196; February 14, 2000, p. 99; November 6, 2000, p. 93.

School Library Journal, December, 1985, George Gleason, review of *Cowboys of the Wild West,* p. 99; May, 1987, Karen P. Zimmerman, review of *Indian Chiefs,* pp. 110-111; December, 1987, Elaine Fort Weischedel, review of *Lincoln: A Photobiography,* pp. 93-94; July, 1999, Luann Toth, review of *Babe Didrikson Zaharias: The Making of a Champion,* p. 106; October, 2000, Leah J. Sparks, review of *Give Me Liberty!: The Story of the Declaration of Independence,* p. 183; December, 2000, p. 53.

Science Books and Films, December, 1977, p. 166.

Science Books: A Quarterly Review, May, 1970, review of *How Animals Learn* and *Animal Instincts,* pp. 2-3.

U.S. News and World Report, December 5, 1994, p. 96.

Voice of Youth Advocates, June, 1996, p. 48.

Washington Post Book World, July 12, 1992, Michael Dirda, review of *An Indian Winter,* p. 8.

Wilson Library Bulletin, September, 1994, p. 121; June, 1995, p. 48.

G

GARANT, Andre J. 1968-

Personal

Born October 9, 1968, in Boston, MA; son of Phil (a professor) and Jeanne (a mayor; maiden name, Maltais) Garant. *Education:* St. Michael's College, B.S., 1991. *Politics:* Republican. *Religion:* Roman Catholic. *Hobbies and other interests:* Reading, writing, music, travel.

Addresses

Home—4001 North Main St., No. 718, Fall River, MA 02720. *Office*—Lightolier, 631 Airport Rd., Fall River, MA 02720. *E-mail*—ajgolden@ici.net.

Career

IGHL, East Moriches, NY, accountant, 1993-95; Charlton Hospital, Fall River, MA, auditor, 1995-98; Neptco, Pawtucket, RI, accountant, 1998-2000; Lightolier, Fall River, MA, accountant, 2000—. Religious education instructor.

Writings

I'm Gonna Win, Morris Publishing (Kearney, NE), 1999.
Slap Shot, 1st Books Library (Bloomington, IN), 2000.
Slam Dunk, 1st Books Library (Bloomington, IN), 2000.
The Kid from North Park, Morris Publishing (Kearney, NE), 2000.

Sidelights

Andre J. Garant told *SATA:* "I first became interested in writing for children between the ages of nine and thirteen while taking a home-study course from the Institute of Children's Literature. After receiving my certificate in 1997, I actively began writing novels for boys and girls at the middle-school level. One of my very first manuscripts, *I'm Gonna Win,* is the story of an eleven-year-old boy named Matthew Casey. Matthew is a very conceited boy who must learn to overcome his bad attitude by learning an important lesson in life. The sequel to this story is *Slam Dunk.*

"My purpose in writing for middle-school children is to help revive their interest in reading. Many kids at this age become disinterested in reading and often turn to other activities that are not mind-stimulating. I visit schools and speak to kids firsthand about my writing, and usually when I leave the group at the end of my presentation, they are very excited about reading my books. Many boys and girls who are happy about reading can't wait to get home and log onto the Internet to view some of my books. Even if I only reach out to one child at each school, then I have met my goal. For me, writing books is not about making money. It's about helping children realize the importance of reading at a young age, in order to develop their oral and written

Andre J. Garant

Goalie Trevor is outraged when the coach asks a girl to join the team in Garant's novel for middle-graders.

communication skills fully. This is a necessity to success later on in life.

"My books are written in realistic and modern-day tones, with dialogue reflected to portray what kids are actually saying. I do, however, stay away from bad language, as I feel this only demonstrates to children that such language is acceptable to use. Realistic dialogue weaves kids into the story and makes them want to finish the book. It is like using good bait on a fishing rod. If kids are bored by what they are reading, then chances are they will not finish the book. Although most of my books deal with sports (the favored topic among kids), I have many manuscripts written about other subjects, such as school life, family life, friends, humorous situations, and death and dying. I have written about everything from food fights in the school cafeteria to a young boy who witnesses the death of his best friend. I want my readers to enjoy what they are reading, but also to learn something at the same time.

"I am just starting to do something fun in my books. All of the books that I have published to date (except one) do not have any inside illustrations. For my latest book, *The Kid from North Park,* I have asked many children to draw illustrations for the text. For each illustration I decided to include, I list a caption underneath it along with the child's name, age, and town of residence. This allows children to be their own illustrators, and it gives other kids who read the book some insight about what other children's artistic abilities might be. It also provides a quick geography lesson. Children love the idea and provide numerous drawings. The basic idea for me is to make a book as much about children as possible—not only written for children, but illustrated by them. The next step for me might be to have a child co-author a book with me. Now that would be fun! Happy reading!"

* * *

GHERMAN, Beverly 1934-

Personal

Born December 12, 1934, in Salt Lake City, UT; daughter of Leon (a dress shop owner) and Pearl (a dress shop owner; maiden name, Olish) Isenberg; married Charles R. Gherman (a physician), August 5, 1956; children: Gregory, Cindy. *Education:* University of California at Berkeley, B.A., 1956; graduate studies at San Francisco State University, 1968-70.

Addresses

Home—San Francisco, CA.

Career

University of California, San Francisco, medical researcher, 1956-58; San Francisco school system, teacher's aide, 1967-74; Kaiser Permanente, San Francisco, medical researcher, 1975; Jewish Community Library, San Francisco, library assistant, 1976-80; freelance writer.

Writings

Georgia O'Keeffe: The "Wideness and Wonder" of Her World, Atheneum (New York, NY), 1986.
Agnes de Mille: Dancing Off the Earth, Atheneum (New York, NY), 1990.
Sandra Day O'Connor: Justice for All ("Women of Our Time" series), illustrated by Robert Masheris, Viking (New York, NY), 1991.
E. B. White: Some Writer!, Atheneum (New York, NY), 1992.
The Mysterious Rays of Dr. Röntgen, illustrated by Stephen Marchesi, Atheneum (New York, NY), 1994.
Robert Louis Stevenson: Teller of Tales, Atheneum (New York, NY), 1996.
Norman Rockwell: Storyteller with a Brush, Atheneum (New York, NY), 2000.

Norman Rockwell
STORYTELLER WITH A BRUSH

Beverly Gherman

Full-color reproductions of Norman Rockwell's paintings illustrate Beverly Gherman's biography of the popular American artist. (Cover painting, The Soda Jerk, *detail, by Norman Rockwell.)*

Sidelights

Beverly Gherman is the author of a number of nonfiction works for young readers that profile the lives of people who have made a difference. Focusing on artists Georgia O'Keeffe and Norman Rockwell, writers E. B. White and Robert Louis Stevenson, and U.S. Supreme Court Justice Sandra Day O'Connor, among others, Gherman's books are sparked by her curiosity about factors in life that motivate certain people to greatness. Important in their role as resources for young people, her biographies have been praised as easy to read and useful in sparking further interest among readers. Commenting on her 1994 biography of the German scientist who discovered the X-ray in 1895, Elizabeth Bush noted in the *Bulletin of the Center for Children's Books* that in *The Mysterious Rays of Dr. Röntgen* Gherman "deftly select[s] details" for inclusion in her portrait of the Nobel Prize winner, and retains a "tenacious ... grip [on] the reader's attention" by showing how Röntgen's discovery affected the work of those scientists who came after him. "As I search for a new subject to study, I find myself back at the library," Gherman once explained to *SATA*, "reading about interesting people, snooping into what makes them tick, just as I've always done."

Born in Salt Lake City, Utah, in 1934, Gherman developed an early love of writing. As she told *SATA*, "I ... composed my first biography in the fourth grade when I decided to tell the story of Native American Sacajawea. I compiled it in the form of a daily journal, written as she led the early nineteenth-century expedition of Meriwether Lewis and William Clark across the country." Finding few resources in her local library, Gherman was forced to rely on her creative abilities and made things up. "Then I spent as much time trying to make the journal look old as I had spent on writing it." It would take the budding author a few more years to learn that writing biographies required faithfulness to the facts.

Throughout elementary school, Gherman would often be found with her nose in a book. Favorites included Margaret Mitchell's *Gone with the Wind,* Erskine Caldwell's *Tobacco Road,* Louisa May Alcott's *Little Women* and *Little Men,* and absolutely anything by Pearl S. Buck. "In seventh grade," she recalled, "I read Nathaniel Hawthorne's book *The Scarlet Letter* but was not allowed to give an oral report to my class. My teacher felt that I might shock the other students because the book was written for adult readers, not children. I read biographies all the time, even though most of my friends thought I was strange. I was preparing for the future."

A frequenter of libraries, Gherman began working as a librarian's assistant in 1976, after raising her family. "I loved being surrounded by books—their smell, crisp new pages, words, and ideas. But it never occurred to me that I might someday want to write books." However, witnessing the positive impact children's books had on young people made Gherman realize that writing such books could provide her with a channel for her own curiosity. She enrolled in a writing class held by children's author Susan Terris and soon realized "that although I had read incessantly, I had no idea how to write a children's book." The education she received from Terris, as well as the encouragement and constructive criticism she gained from her fellow students, helped her hone her prose for young readers. In the mid-1980s her proposal for a biography of American artist Georgia O'Keeffe was accepted by New York City publisher Atheneum, and Gherman went to work polishing her prose and tracking down illustrations for the book. "I found some of her early drawings from boarding school and several pictures of O'Keeffe as a young woman," she recalled, adding, "At times I felt like a detective searching for clues." *Georgia O'Keeffe: The "Wideness and Wonder" of Her World* was published in 1986.

Researching the life of illustrator Norman Rockwell also allowed Gherman to indulge in her interest in art. Calling *Norman Rockwell: Storyteller with a Brush* a "most appealing introduction to a most accessible American artist," *Booklist* contributor Carolyn Phelan praised the author for her coverage of Rockwell's early years and the way in which childhood influences could be traced to his mature art works. Rockwell's legacy—his slice-of-Americana cover illustrations for the *Saturday Evening Post* as well as his controversial painting "The Problem We All Live With" and its depiction of a young African-American girl's confrontation with racism—is also reflected in Gherman's book. Mary M. Burns declared it "[r]emarkable for capturing its subject in so limited a space" in her *Horn Book* review. *Norman Rockwell* also earned praise from *School Library Journal* contributor Patricia Mahoney Brown, who wrote that Gherman's "writing style is free-flowing and [her] words capture the naturalness of Rockwell's paintings."

Gherman's third book project was a biography about Supreme Court Justice Sandra Day O'Connor, which publisher Viking requested as part of their "Women of Our Time" series. While meeting with a supreme court justice was intimidating to Gherman, her natural curiosity finally won out over fear. "I decided I wanted to know about this woman who was not much older than myself and had grown up about the same time," the author explained to *SATA*. "I wondered what had given her the drive to achieve such a goal. Where had she gained the confidence?" In addition to her interview with O'Connor, Gherman spoke to several of the justice's friends from grammar school and college. "Soon, I felt that I was able to see her as a person behind the black robe and the facade of the Supreme Court. I learned that she had been given a sense of responsibility when growing up on her family's Arizona ranch. Because she was bright and able to handle every task given to her at an early age, she never doubted her own abilities." When the biography was published in 1991, *School Library Journal* contributor April L. Judge dubbed *Sandra Day O'Connor: Justice for All* "concise and very readable," and noted that the book effectively reflects O'Connor's belief that the "individual can make things happen."

Several of Gherman's biographies have focused on other writers. The twentieth-century journalist and author E. B. White fascinated Gherman because of the fact that writing never came easily to him. "White was concerned about writing well," she explained to *SATA*. "He labored over every column he wrote for the *New Yorker* magazine. He cared about the creatures of the world, beginning with the chickens, geese, and pig on his Maine farm." White's affection for his pig would be shared by many readers after publication of his best-known book, *Charlotte's Web,* and Gherman discusses this phase of his career in detail in her 1992 book, *E. B. White: Some Writer!* Praised by *Five Owls* reviewer Gary D. Schmidt for "mak[ing] the man accessible as a real human being to young readers," Gherman's biography was also cited by James Cross Giblin in the *Washington Post Book World* as a "serviceable outline of the author's life and career that may prove useful for ... book reports."

Another author who comes under scrutiny by Gherman is British writer Robert Louis Stevenson, a Victorian world traveler whose *Jungle Book* and *Just So Stories* belied the ill health he suffered through much of his life. In *Robert Louis Stevenson: Teller of Tales,* Gherman "tells a fine tale herself, making Stevenson and his world vivid to readers," commented a *Kirkus Reviews* contributor, while in *School Library Journal* critic Susan M. Moore added that this "clearly written" biography uses many primary sources—including letters and diaries from Stevenson and his friends and family—to present the events of the author's life.

Biographical and Critical Sources

PERIODICALS

Booklist, May 15, 1990; March 1, 1991; December 1, 1994, Hazel Rochman, review of *The Mysterious Rays of Dr. Röntgen,* p. 671; October 1, 1996, Hazel Rochman, review of *Robert Louis Stevenson: Teller of Tales,* p. 328; February 15, 2000, Carolyn Phelan, review of *Norman Rockwell: Storyteller with a Brush,* p. 1108.

Bulletin of the Center for Children's Books, February, 1991, Zena Sutherland, review of *Sandra Day O'Connor: Justice for All,* pp. 140-141; October, 1994, Elizabeth Bush, review of *The Mysterious Rays of Dr. Röntgen,* p. 46.

Five Owls, September-October, 1992, Gary D. Schmidt, review of *E. B. White: Some Writer!,* p. 19.

Horn Book, March, 2000, Mary M. Burns, review of *Norman Rockwell,* p. 210.

Kirkus Reviews, March 1, 1986; September 1, 1996, review of *Robert Louis Stevenson,* p. 1321.

Publishers Weekly, March 21, 1986; April 13, 1990.

School Library Journal, July, 1991, April L. Judge, review of *Sandra Day O'Connor,* p. 80; September, 1994, Christine A. Moesch, review of *The Mysterious Rays of Dr. Röntgen,* p. 228; February, 1997, Susan M. Moore, review of *Robert Louis Stevenson,* p. 115; February, 2000, Patricia Mahoney Brown, review of *Norman Rockwell,* p. 132.

Washington Post Book World, May 10, 1992, James Cross Giblin, review of *E. B. White,* p. 19.*

* * *

GOLDBERG, Jan

Personal

Born in Chicago, IL; daughter of Sam and Sylvia (Tulsky) Lefkovitz; married Lawrence Goldberg (a teacher), August 19, 1977; children: Sherri Cohn, Deborah Sattley, Marci Barth (stepdaughter). *Education:* Roosevelt University, B.A. (elementary education). *Hobbies and other interests:* Reading, puzzles, time with family.

Jan Goldberg

Addresses

Home—924 Long Rd., Glenview, IL 60025. *E-mail*—JanGold1@aol.com.

Career

Nonfiction writer and educator. Freelance writer, 1990—. Presenter of writing workshops for adults and children. *Member:* National Writer's Union, Society of Children's Book Writers and Illustrators, American Society of Journalists and Authors.

Awards, Honors

Perfectionism: What's Bad about Being Good? was named among New York Public Library's Books for the Teen Age, 2000.

Writings

NONFICTION

Great Jobs for Music Majors, VGM Career Horizons (Lincolnwood, IL), 1997.

Great Jobs for Computer Science Majors, VGM Career Horizons (Lincolnwood, IL), 1997.

Great Jobs for Theater Majors, VGM Career Horizons (Lincolnwood, IL), 1998.

Great Jobs for Accounting Majors, VGM Career Horizons (Lincolnwood, IL), 1998.

(With Miriam Adderholdt) *Perfectionism: What's Bad about Being Too Good?,* revised edition, Free Spirit (Minneapolis, MN), 1999.

Careers in Journalism, VGM Career Horizons (Lincolnwood, IL), 1995, second edition, 1999.

"CAREERS WITHOUT COLLEGE" SERIES

Security Guard, Capstone Press (Mankato, MN), 1998.
Medical Record Technician, Capstone Press (Mankato, MN), 1999.
Fire Fighter, Capstone Press (Mankato, MN), 1999.
Private Investigator, Capstone Press (Mankato, MN), 1999.

"OPPORTUNITIES" SERIES

Opportunities in Horticulture Careers, VGM Career Horizons (Lincolnwood, IL), 1995.
Opportunities in Research and Development Careers, VGM Career Horizons (Lincolnwood, IL), 1997.
Opportunities in Entertainment Careers, VGM Career Horizons (Lincolnwood, IL), 2000.

"CAREERS FOR YOU" SERIES

Careers for Class Clowns and Other Engaging Types, VGM Career Horizons (Lincolnwood, IL), 1998.
Careers for Courageous People and Other Adventurous Types, VGM Career Horizons (Lincolnwood, IL), 1998.
Careers for Competitive Spirits and Other Peak Performers, VGM Career Horizons (Lincolnwood, IL), 1999.
Careers for Color Connoisseurs and Other Visual Types, VGM Career Horizons (Lincolnwood, IL), 1999.
Careers for Patriotic Types and Others Who Want to Serve Their Country, VGM Career Horizons (Lincolnwood, IL), 1999.
Careers for Extroverts and Other Gregarious Types, VGM Career Horizons (Lincolnwood, IL), 1999.
Careers for Persuasive Types and Others Who Won't Take No for an Answer, VGM Career Horizons (Lincolnwood, IL), 2000.
Careers for Scientific Types and Others with Inquiring Minds, VGM Career Horizons (Lincolnwood, IL), 2000.
Careers for Geniuses and Other Gifted Types, VGM Career Horizons (Lincolnwood, IL), 2000.
Careers for Homebodies and Other Independent Souls, VGM Career Horizons (Lincolnwood, IL), 2000.
Careers for Puzzle Solvers and Other Methodical Thinkers, VGM Career Horizons (Lincolnwood, IL), 2002.

"ON THE JOB" SERIES

Real People Working in Communications, VGM Career Horizons (Lincolnwood, IL), 1997.
(With Blythe Camenson) *Real People Working in Engineering,* VGM Career Horizons (Lincolnwood, IL), 1997.
(With Blythe Camenson) *Real People Working in Law,* VGM Career Horizons (Lincolnwood, IL), 1997.
(With Blythe Camenson) *Real People Working in Education,* VGM Career Horizons (Lincolnwood, IL), 1997.
(With Blythe Camenson) *Real People Working in Helping Professions,* VGM Career Horizons (Lincolnwood, IL), 1997.
Real People Working in Science, VGM Career Horizons (Lincolnwood, IL), 1998.
Real People Working in Government, VGM Career Horizons (Lincolnwood, IL), 1998.
Real People Working in Entertainment, VGM Career Horizons (Lincolnwood, IL), 1999.

OTHER

Contributor to books published by Publications International (Lincolnwood, IL), including *Sister,* 1999, *Grandmother,* 1999, and *Friend,* 1999; reviser for *Horizon in My Pocket,* Camp Fire Boys and Girls (Kansas City, MO).

Also contributor to textbooks, teacher's manuals, and other educational publications for Scott Foresman, Addison-Wesley, and General Learning Corporation. Contributor to periodicals, including *Career World, American Careers, Parenting, Bloomsbury Review, Correspondent, Friendly Exchange,* and *Successful Student.* Several of Goldberg's books have been translated into Chinese.

Sidelights

Jan Goldberg is a nonfiction writer who specializes in helping young job-seekers combine their unique skills and personality types into a rewarding job or career. Although trained as an educator, Goldberg decided instead to embark upon a career as a freelance journalist, and through her efforts to successfully establish her own career she realized the need for interesting, engaging books on the subject of career development. Her prolific output, which includes such books as *Careers for Competitive Spirits and Other Peak Performers, Great Jobs for Computer Science Majors, Opportunities in Horticulture Careers,* and *Careers for Homebodies and Other Independent Souls,* attests to Goldberg's creative approach to one of a young adult's most important concerns: What do I want to be when I grow up? In a review of *Great Jobs for Computer Science Majors* in the *St. Louis Post-Dispatch,* writer Jim Clarkson praised the book as "an excellent resource . . . . More than just a book about career paths, Goldberg provides a wealth of information about self-assessment and job search."

Born in Chicago, Illinois, Goldberg came to a love of reading early. Visits to the book bindery where her grandfather worked "produced a magic combination of sights and smells" that Goldberg commented to *SATA* have remained vivid in her memory even as an adult. "Childhood was filled with composing poems and stories, reading books, and playing library," the author also remembered. School newspapers in both elementary and high school provided her with an outlet for her writing, and after she enrolled at Roosevelt University, her part-time job at the school's College of Business Administration further honed her talent for clear, concise prose.

Graduating from college with a degree in elementary education, Goldberg eventually embarked on a career as a freelance writer and contributed a number of articles about career development to magazines. Soon she was working with educational publishers such as Scott Foresman and Addison-Wesley, while her magazine submissions had expanded to feature articles in such periodicals as *Parenting Magazine* and *Complete Woman.* By 2000 Goldberg could list over four hundred published articles to her credit.

In addition to her work for magazines, Goldberg joined with vocational publisher VGM Career Horizons to produce nonfiction books focusing on her area of expertise: the job search. In her 1995 work *Careers in Journalism,* she speaks with authority on the different directions available to writers—technical writers, business writers, electronic media writers, editors, freelance journalists, etc.—and discusses each of these fields in detail. In addition to noting salary ranges, job descriptions, and industry overviews, Goldberg also includes interviews with journalism professionals, all of which combine to provide "some good practical advice about getting started" in a journalism career, according to *Voice of Youth Advocates* contributor Christine Miller. Comparing *Careers in Journalism* with other, more narrowly focused vocational guidebooks on the same subject, Miller dubbed Goldberg's work "no ordinary so-you-want-to-be-a-reporter book." Related books by Goldberg include 1997's *Real People Working in Communications,* a volume in VGM's "On the Job" series that *Kliatt* reviewer Paula Rohrlick called "Useful for all [library] career collections."

While some of Goldberg's career guides take a traditional approach, her contributions to the "Careers for You" series published by VGM Career Horizons are by contrast unique. With titles like *Careers for Color Connoisseurs and Other Visual Types, Careers for Class Clowns and Other Engaging Types,* and *Careers for Courageous People and Other Adventurous Types,* Goldberg provides a "good starting place for students and others who are just starting to think about what kind of work they'd like to do," according to Rohrlick in another *Kliatt* review. In *Careers for Class Clowns* readers are encouraged to examine their interests before making a career choice, and the comedic-inclined are presented with such vocational options as comedian, juggler, magic and other performance jobs, while *Careers for Courageous People* tempts risk-takers with everything from astronaut to beekeeper to law enforcement officer. Goldberg's approach to career choices in her "Careers for You" titles still offers the same factual detail with regard to job outlook, job description, and

working conditions as her more traditional books, but she also "convey[s] enthusiastically the possibilities that exist" in the modern workplace, in the Rohrlick's opinion.

In addition to building her own career in the field of vocational self-help publishing, Goldberg has combined her talent for writing with her love of teaching by designing presentations that provide her audience with the nuts and bolts of making a go of a career in freelance writing in both magazines and book-length nonfiction. Besides working with adult groups, she also organizes and presents workshops for young adults and children who want help developing their personal reading and writing skills. Furthermore, her work with co-author Miriam Adderholdt of the highly praised *Perfectionism: What's Bad about Being Too Good?* helps today's over-achieving teens break the cycle of perfectionism that often blocks efforts to pursue long-term goals such as developing new skills.

Biographical and Critical Sources

PERIODICALS

Kliatt, January, 1995, Paula Rohrlick, review of *Careers in Journalism,* p. 28; March, 1997, Paula Rohrlick, review of *Real People Working in Communications,* pp. 27-28; January, 1998, Paula Rohrlick, review of *Careers for Courageous People and Other Adventurous Types,* p. 26; January, 1999, Paula Rohrlick, review of *Careers for Class Clowns and Other Engaging Types,* pp. 26-27; July, 1999, Paula Rohrlick, review of *Careers for Color Connoisseurs and Other Visual Types,* p. 30; November, 1999, review of *Perfectionism.*

St. Louis Post-Dispatch, August 16, 1998, Jim Clarkson, "Information Technology Professionals Are Seeing Salary Increases."

Voice of Youth Advocates, April, 1995, Christine Miller, review of *Careers in Journalism,* p. 45.

Youth Today, December-January, 2000, review of *Perfectionism.**

H

HALE, Bruce 1957-

Personal

Born October 30, 1957, in Los Angeles, CA; son of Clark (in industrial relations) and Ann (a homemaker) Hale; married Janette Cross (a dancer), 1993. *Education:* Attended University of California—Davis, 1975-77; University of California—Los Angeles, B.A. (economics), 1980. *Hobbies and other interests:* Hiking, swimming, yoga.

Addresses

Office—P.O. Box 91835, Santa Barbara, CA 93190-1835. *Agent*—Steven Malk, Writer's House, 3368 Governor Dr., #224F, San Diego, CA 92122.

Career

Asuka Communications (advertising firm), Tokyo, Japan, 1982-83; Trade Publishing (magazines), Honolulu, HI, 1983-86; GTE Hawaiian Tel (phone company), Honolulu, 1986-89; self-employed writer, actor, and illustrator, 1989—. *Member:* Dramatists Guild, Society of Children's Book Writers and Illustrators (former regional advisor for Hawaii chapter).

Writings

SELF-ILLUSTRATED

Legend of the Laughing Gecko: A Hawaiian Fantasy, Words and Pictures (Honolulu, HI), 1989.
Surf Gecko to the Rescue!, Geckostufs (Honolulu, HI), 1991.
Moki and the Magic Surfboard: A Hawaiian Fantasy, Words and Pictures (Honolulu, HI), 1996.
Moki the Gecko's Best Christmas Ever, Words and Pictures (Honolulu, HI), 1998.
How the Gecko Lost His Tail, Words and Pictures (Honolulu, HI), 1999.

Bruce Hale

The Chameleon Wore Chartreuse: From the Tattered Casebook of Chet Gecko, Private Eye, Harcourt (San Diego, CA), 2000.
The Mystery of Mr. Nice: A Chet Gecko Mystery, Harcourt (San Diego, CA), 2000.
Farewell, My Lunch Bag: A Chet Gecko Mystery, Harcourt (San Diego, CA), 2001.

The Big Nap: A Chet Gecko Mystery, Harcourt (San Diego, CA), 2001.

The Legend of Ghost Gecko, Words and Pictures (Honolulu, HI), 2002.

Sidelights

Bruce Hale told *SATA:* "I love disappearing into a story, whether I'm writing or reading it. And I love humor. While I'm writing, if I can crack myself up or if I surprise myself, I know I'm doing a good job. I feel fortunate to be an illustrator, too—so that I can create the reader's entire experience in my books."

Hale is the creator of a series of humorous chapter books featuring fourth-grade amateur sleuth Chet Gecko and his sidekick, Natalie Attired. Using the riffs first made popular in hard-boiled detective stories of decades past, Hale's protagonist spouts outlandish similes and slang as he narrates tales such as *The Mystery of Mr. Nice,* in which Chet suspects his school principal has been replaced by an imposter, and *The Chameleon Wore Chartreuse,* in which a chameleon suspects her brother has been abducted by an angry Gila monster named Herman. Chuckling at Hale's "corny jokes, clever wordplay, and amusing asides," Sharon McNeil, reviewing *The Mystery of Mr. Nice* in *School Library Journal,* praised the author's ability to keep the pacing of his faux-gumshoe mysteries swift. Hale's black-and-white cartoons add to the humor of his tales in their depiction of a range of animal characters who take the role of the other schoolchildren at Emerson Hicky Elementary School, where the main action of the stories takes place. In a *Publishers Weekly* review of *The Chameleon Wore Chartreuse,* a critic noted that since Hale's emphasis is on humor rather than on the element of mystery in his plots, mystery fans may not be entirely satisfied with the tales of Chet Gecko, "but beginning readers especially will appreciate the offbeat, likable cast and quirky comedy." However, for Connie Fletcher, who reviewed *The Mystery of Mr. Nice* in *Booklist,* "the swift plot, clever wisecracking, and hard-boiled style make this chapter book a terrific read."

Biographical and Critical Sources

PERIODICALS

Booklist, November 1, 2000, Connie Fletcher, review of *The Mystery of Mr. Nice,* p. 539.

Publishers Weekly, May 1, 2000, review of *The Chameleon Wore Chartreuse,* p. 71.

School Library Journal, December, 2000, Sharon McNeil, review of *The Mystery of Mr. Nice,* p. 145.

*   *   *

HALVORSON, Marilyn 1948-

Personal

Surname is pronounced "*Hall*-vor-son"; born January 17, 1948, in Olds, Alberta, Canada; daughter of Trygve (a rancher) and Irene (a teacher; maiden name, McCon- nell) Halvorson. *Ethnicity:* "Norwegian-Irish." *Education:* University of Calgary, B.Ed. *Politics:* Conservative. *Religion:* Protestant. *Avocational interests:* Riding, photography, art, wilderness conservation, reading, hiking, gardening.

Addresses

Home—Box 9, Site 14, R.R. 2, Sundre, Alberta, Canada T0M 1X0.

Career

County of Mountain View, Alberta, teacher at Didsbury School, 1968-71, and Sundre School, 1974-90. Rancher. *Member:* Writers Guild of Alberta.

Awards, Honors

Winner of Alberta Culture Writing for Youth Competition, 1982, for *Cowboys Don't Cry;* Children's Literature Award, Writers Guild of Alberta, 1987, for *Nobody Said It Would Be Easy.*

Writings

Cowboys Don't Cry, Irwin (Homewood, IL), 1984.

Let It Go, Delacorte (New York, NY), 1986.

Nobody Said It Would Be Easy, Delacorte (New York, NY), 1987, reprinted as *Hold On, Geronimo,* Delacorte (New York, NY), 1988.

Dare, General Publishing (Toronto, Ontario), 1988.

Marilyn Halvorson

Bull Rider, Macmillan (Don Mills, Ontario), 1989.
To Everything a Season: A Year in Alberta Ranch Country,
    Stoddart (Buffalo, NY), 1991.
Brothers and Strangers, Stoddart (Buffalo, NY), 1992.
Stranger on the Run, Stoddart (Buffalo, NY), 1992.
But Cows Can't Fly and Other Stories, Stoddart (Buffalo,
    NY), 1993.
Blue Moon, Macmillan, 1994 (Buffalo, NY).
Cowboys Don't Quit, Stoddart (Buffalo, NY), 1994.
Stranger on the Line, Stoddart (Buffalo, NY), 1997.

Contributor of stories to magazines for children.

Adaptations

The novel *Cowboys Don't Cry* was adapted as a
screenplay, directed by Anne Wheeler, and released in
1987.

Sidelights

Marilyn Halvorson brings her love of ranching, horses,
and country life to her young adult novels. *School
Library Journal*'s Jane Anne Hannigan observed that
Halvorson's writing often features characters who are
"tough on the outside but more vulnerable inside"; this
aspect of her work reflects the influence of both
television westerns and the classic western novels of
Zane Grey, both of which Halvorson loved as a child.
Her first book, *Cowboys Don't Cry,* is set in this rough
and ready milieu and draws from a number of Halvorson's personal interests, including Canada, ranching, and
horses. Her narrator, Shane Morgan, moves to a ranch in
Alberta with his father Josh, a former rodeo champion
who succumbed to alcoholism after the accidental death
of Shane's mother. Shane views the move as an
opportunity to start to repair his damaged relationship
with his dad, but neither father nor son are able to
openly discuss their grief and anger over Mrs. Morgan's
death. Still, Josh struggles valiantly to overcome his
cravings for alcohol, and Shane works to help support
his father's efforts, despite his resentment at the elder
Morgan's occasional lapses into drinking. A difficult
confrontation provides a chance for the pair to give vent
to their frustrations with each other and explore their
feelings. Reviewing the book for *School Library Journal,* Jack Forman found Shane to be a "rounded and
believable" character and concluded that Halvorson had
produced "a simply told, affecting narrative." While
Forman felt the text suffers from a "somewhat forced
epilogue," *Horn Book* reviewer Nancy C. Hammond
commented that despite the occasional "melodrama," the
text "is balanced by fresh observations."

Halvorson returned to a Canadian setting for *Let It Go,*
and its sequel *Hold On, Geronimo.* In the first book, best
friends Lance "Geronimo" Ducharme and Red Cantrell
are both burdened by the weight of family problems.
Red's older brother is brain dead after a drug-related
auto accident, and Lance's mother abandoned her family
when Lance was a young boy. When Red engineers a
meeting between Lance and his long-lost mother, all
does not go as planned—instead of being elated by his

mother's reappearance, Lance is crushed. He becomes
depressed and withdrawn, and begins taking drugs as he
struggles to come to terms with his new situation.
Although *School Library Journal*'s Libby K. White
complained that the narrative is "not involving," she
noted that the author's "descriptions of her home area
are interesting," and the characters are rendered "with
warmth and understanding."

Lance resurfaces in *Hold On, Geronimo,* still trying to
negotiate his difficult family connections, and his
ambition to become an artist. Lance is challenged by a
trying relationship with his step-cousin Kat. At the same
time, he must face the fact that a hand injury may
prevent him from winning a scholarship to art school. At
the novel's end, Lance's physical strength and emotional
courage are put to the test, when a small plane carrying
himself, Kat, and Red is caught in a severe winter storm.
Gerry Larson, writing in *School Library Journal,* praised
Hold On, Geronimo as "an exciting sequel to *Let It Go,*"
adding that "Lance's adolescent candor, anxieties, adventure, and courage" will appeal to many young
readers.

Halvorson once remarked: "I was an only child, alone on
the ranch a lot, and writing gave me a chance to develop
my imagination. I write books for young adults because,
after teaching junior high school students, I wanted to
'tell it like it is' to be a kid these days. My own favorite
writers are Wilbur Smith, Sue Grafton, and John
Grisham.

"I travel very little, keeping busy with the ranch, cattle,
four horses which I raised and trained myself, seven
cats, and two dogs, all of whom I love dearly. I love
country life and wouldn't trade it."

Biographical and Critical Sources

PERIODICALS

Calgary Herald, March 21, 1998; August 16, 1998;
    November 15, 1998.
Emergency Librarian, January-February, 1986.
Globe and Mail (Toronto), June 16, 1984; June 1, 1985;
    March 8, 1986.
Horn Book, May-June, 1985, Nancy C. Hammond, review
    of *Cowboys Don't Cry,* p. 316; September-October,
    1988, Nancy Vasilikis, review of *Hold on, Geronimo,*
    p. 631.
Publishers Weekly, December 12, 1986, Diane Roback,
    review of *Let It Go,* p. 56; June 10, 1988, Kimberly
    Olson Fakih and Diane Roback, review of *Hold On,
    Geronimo,* p. 82.
Quill and Quire, June, 1985.
School Library Journal, September, 1985, Jack Forman,
    review of *Cowboys Don't Cry,* p. 144; November,
    1986, Libby K. White, review of *Let It Go,* p. 101;
    May, 1988, Gerry Larson, review of *Hold On,
    Geronimo,* p. 108; August, 1992, Jane Anne Hanni-
    gan, review of *Meet the Author: Marilyn Halvorson,*
    p. 117.

HAMILTON, Martha 1953-

Personal

Born January 5, 1953, in Selmer, TN; daughter of Milford Hugh (a laborer) and Martha Madelyn (a homemaker) Hamilton; married Mitch Weiss (a storyteller), June 18, 1983. *Education:* Douglass College, Rutgers University, B.A., 1975; University of Michigan School of Library Science, M.L.S., 1976. *Politics:* Democrat. *Hobbies and other interests:* Gardening, running, hiking, playing tennis, reading, traveling, biking.

Addresses

Home and office—954 Coddington Rd., Ithaca, NY 14850.

Career

Storyteller, author. Elmira College, Elmira, NY, reference librarian, 1976-79; Cornell University, Ithaca, NY, reference librarian, 1979-84; professional storyteller, 1980—. *Member:* National Storytelling Network.

Awards, Honors

Anne Izard Storytellers' Choice Award, 1992, for *Children Tell Stories;* Storytelling World Gold Award, 1997, for *Stories in My Pocket;* Parents' Choice Recommendation, and National Parenting Publications Gold Award, both 1998, both for *Stories in My Pocket* (audiocassette); Storytelling World Gold Award, and Parents' Choice Approved Award, both 2000, both for *How and Why Stories;* National Parenting Publications Gold Award, 2000, for *How and Why Stories* (audio recording); Notable Social Studies Trade Book for Young People, National Council for the Social Studies/ Children's Book Council, 2001, for *Noodlehead Stories.*

Writings

WITH HUSBAND, MITCH WEISS

Tell Me a Story: Beauty and the Beast (videocassette), Kartes Video Communications, 1986.
Children Tell Stories: A Teaching Guide, R. C. Owen (Katonah, NY), 1990.
Stories in My Pocket: Tales Kids Can Tell, illustrated by Annie Campbell, Fulcrum (Golden, CO), 1996.
How & Why Stories: World Tales Kids Can Read and Tell, illustrated by Carol Lyon, August House (Little Rock, AR), 1999.
Noodlehead Stories: World Tales Kids Can Read and Tell, illustrated by Ariane Elsammak, August House (Little Rock, AR), 2000.
Through the Grapevine: World Tales Kids Can Read and Tell, illustrated by Carol Lyon, August House (Little Rock, AR), 2001.

Adaptations

Stories in My Pocket: Tales Kids Can Tell was adapted by Hamilton and Weiss as an audio recording on cassette, Fulcrum, 1998; *How & Why Stories: World Tales Kids Can Read and Tell* was adapted by Hamilton and Weiss as an audio recording on cassette and compact disc, August House, 2000.

Sidelights

Martha Hamilton and Mitch Weiss told *SATA:* "We are a husband-and-wife storytelling team known as 'Beauty and the Beast Storytellers.' We never say which is the beauty and which the beast—that's up to our listeners to decide. (We had the name *long* before the Disney movie!) We have been telling stories together since 1980, and have been full-time professional tellers since 1984. In addition to storytelling performances, we also teach kids to tell stories. Our books have come directly from our teaching experiences in the classroom. We feel strongly that children should be given the opportunity to tell stories because of the many benefits storytelling provides: increased self-esteem, poise and confidence when speaking in front of others, improved listening, writing, reading, and inventive thinking skills, and exposure to other customs and cultures. Perhaps most important, storytelling is a fun activity that children enjoy.

"Our first book, *Children Tell Stories: A Teaching Guide,* is a guidebook for teachers. It walks them, step by step, through a storytelling project. All of our other books are collections of stories for children. The stories are meant to be shared orally, whether read aloud or told without the book. From our experience, success with and enthusiasm for storytelling have a lot to do with whether or not one has chosen a good story. Our goal in writing these books is to provide a plethora of good stories written in lively, simple language that feels comfortable on the lips of children.

"When we write, we mostly work at two separate computers and edit each other's work. But when we come upon a thorny problem, the two of us sit at one computer and work together until we've solved it. It's not easy being married and working together so closely, both in performances and in our office at home. We think we are able to do it because we have great respect for one another, and, probably more important, we both have a good sense of humor!"

Working as a team, Martha Hamilton and Mitch Weiss have put together several books, audio recordings, and video tapes which both feature their storytelling and help teach others how to become storytellers themselves. In *Stories in My Pocket: Tales Kids Can Tell,* for example, the authors arrange thirty tales in order of ease of telling, printing them with appropriate breaks to aid in memorization and adding suggestions for gestures and actions on the facing page. An introduction aimed at child storytellers is filled with helpful advice on how to memorize stories and develop characters. A guideline for adults, including information on helping student storytellers deal with stage fright, rounds out the offering. The audiocassette version of *Stories in My Pocket* features student storytellers in action on one side and Weiss and Hamilton telling tales on the other. Liner notes provide tips from the tellers, and the result is a work that "provides storytellers with you-can-do-it-too encouragement," proclaimed John Sigwald in *Booklist.* Nancy L. Chu, writing in *School Library Journal,* also remarked on the inspirational effect of the use of child storytellers for the audio version of *Stories in My Pocket,* going on to praise Weiss and Hamilton for choosing a wide variety of stories from a number of different cultures. "This excellent collection would be particularly useful to teachers and librarians seeking to introduce storytelling to potential tellers of all ages," Chu concluded.

The focus is shifted slightly in *How and Why Stories: World Tales Kids Can Read and Tell.* Here the authors present twenty-five *pourquoi* tales, traditional stories that explain natural occurrences such as why dogs chase cats or how the tiger got his stripes. As in *Stories in My Pocket,* the emphasis in *How and Why Stories* is on encouraging children to become storytellers and giving them the tools to do so successfully, including advice on preparing and performing the tales printed in the book as well as general tips on storytelling. Writing in *School Library Journal,* Elizabeth Maggio called this "a useful book for anyone eager to learn the storytelling process." And, as in the audiotape version of *Stories in My Pocket,* the audio version of *How and Why Stories* features child narrators, serving to show Weiss and Hamilton's audience that kids really can be effective storytellers, as Paul Shackman remarked in *Booklist.* "The performances are both adorable and professional," claimed a reviewer in *Today's Librarian,* and "each story is bracketed by delightful musical interludes."

Continuing their works featuring short stories children can master, Weiss and Hamilton collected twenty-three tales from around the world in *Noodlehead Stories: World Tales Kids Can Read and Tell.* In addition to familiar stories such as "The Wise Fools of Gotham" and "Seven Foolish Fishermen," the authors and storytellers also include unusual stories about simpletons as well as discuss how different versions of the same story may be found in separate cultures. Calling the book "a good story-telling tool for children," *School Library Journal* reviewer Marlyn K. Roberts observed that the brevity of the stories "makes them easy for the youngest, most inexperienced storytellers to perform." Writing in *Booklist,* John Peters predicted that "budding tellers will find these short, simplified versions easy to learn and perform, particularly because each is followed by practical tips for delivery."

Weiss and Hamilton have also put out a videocassette, *Tell Me a Story: Beauty and the Beast,* which is a performance of their interpretation of four stories. "The well-chosen selections are ideal for the pair's expressive storytelling style," according to Constance Dyckman in a *School Library Journal* review.

Biographical and Critical Sources

PERIODICALS

Booklist, January 1, 1997, Karen Morgan, review of *Stories in My Pocket,* p. 850; November 15, 1998, John Sigwald, review of *Stories in My Pocket* (audiocassette), p. 604; May 15, 2000, Hazel Rochman, review of *How and Why Stories,* pp. 1755-1756; October 15, 2000, Paul Shackman, review of *How and Why Stories* (audiocassette and compact disc), p. 470; February 15, 2001, John Peters, review of *Noodlehead Stories: World Tales Kids Can Read and Tell.*

Bulletin of the Center for Children's Books, March, 1997, Janice M. Del Negro, review of *Stories in My Pocket,* p. 263; February, 2000, Janice M. Del Negro, review of *How and Why Stories.*

Horn Book, July-December, 1999, review of *How and Why Stories.*

Library Talk, January-February, 2000, Dorothy B. Bickley, review of *How and Why Stories,* p. 52.

School Library Journal, May, 1987, Constance Dyckman, review of *Tell Me a Story,* p. 53; August, 1998, Nancy L. Chu, review of *Stories in My Pocket* (audiocassette), pp. 78-79; January, 2000, Elizabeth Maggio, review of *How and Why Stories,* p. 146; July, 2000, Kirsten Martindale, review of *How and Why Stories,* p. 54; January, 2001, Marlyn K. Roberts, review of *Noodlehead Stories,* p. 146.

Today's Librarian, July, 2000, review of *How and Why Stories* (audiocassette and compact disc), p. 36.

ON-LINE

Beauty and the Beast Storytellers, http://www.people. clarityconnect.com/webpages3/bnb (April 28, 2001).

*   *   *

HAMILTON, Virginia (Esther) 1936-

Personal

Born March 12, 1936, in Yellow Springs, OH; daughter of Kenneth James (a musician) and Etta Belle (Perry) Hamilton; married Arnold Adoff (an anthologist and poet), March 19, 1960; children: Leigh Hamilton, Jaime Levi. *Education:* Studied at Antioch College, 1952-55, Ohio State University, 1957-58, and New School for Social Research, 1958-60.

Addresses

Agent—Arnold Adoff Agency, Box 293, Yellow Springs, OH 45387.

Career

"Every source of occupation imaginable, from singer to bookkeeper."

Awards, Honors

Notable Children's Book citation, American Library Association (ALA), 1967, and Nancy Block Memorial

Award, Downtown Community School Awards Committee, New York, both for *Zeely;* Edgar Allan Poe Award for best juvenile mystery, Mystery Writers of America, 1969, for *The House of Dies Drear;* Ohioana Literary Award, 1969; Newbery Honor Book, ALA, 1971, for *The Planet of Junior Brown;* Lewis Carroll Shelf Award, *Boston Globe-Horn Book* Award, 1974, Newbery Medal, ALA, and National Book Award, Association of American Publishers (AAP), both 1975, and Gustav-Heinemann-Friedenspreis für kinder und Lugendbucher (Dusseldorf, Germany), 1991, all for *M. C. Higgins, the Great;* Newbery Honor Book, ALA, Coretta Scott King Award, ALA, *Boston Globe-Horn Book* Award, and National Book Award nomination, AAP, all 1983, all for *Sweet Whispers, Brother Rush;* *Horn Book* Fanfare Award in fiction, 1985, for *A Little Love;* Coretta Scott King Award, ALA, *New York Times* Best Illustrated Children's Book citation, Children's Book Bulletin Other Award, and *Horn Book* Honor List selection, all 1986, all for *The People Could Fly: American Black Folktales; Boston Globe-Horn Book* Award, 1988, and Coretta Scott King Award, ALA, 1989, both for *Anthony Burns: The Defeat and Triumph of a Fugitive Slave;* Newbery Honor Book, ALA, 1989, for *In the Beginning: Creation Stories from around the World;* D.H.L., Bank Street College, 1990; Regina Medal, Catholic Library Association, 1990, for lifetime achievement; Hans Christian Andersen Award, International Board on Books for Young People, 1992, for body of work; Laura Ingalls Wilder Award for lifetime achievement, ALA, 1995; Coretta Scott King Award, ALA, 1996, for *Her Stories;* L.L.D., Wright State University.

Writings

FICTION; FOR CHILDREN

Zeely, illustrated by Symeon Shimin, Macmillan, 1967.
The House of Dies Drear, illustrated by Eros Keith, Macmillan, 1968.
The Time-Ago Tales of Jahdu, Macmillan, 1969.
The Planet of Junior Brown, Macmillan, 1971.
Time-Ago Lost: More Tales of Jahdu, illustrated by Ray Prather, Macmillan, 1973.
M. C. Higgins, the Great, Macmillan, 1974, published with teacher's guide by Lou Stanek, Dell, 1986.
Arilla Sun Down, Greenwillow, 1976.
Justice and Her Brothers (first novel in the "Justice" trilogy), Greenwillow, 1978.
Jahdu, pictures by Jerry Pinkney, Greenwillow, 1980.
Dustland (second novel in the "Justice" trilogy), Greenwillow, 1980.
The Gathering (third novel in the "Justice" trilogy), Greenwillow, 1981.
Sweet Whispers, Brother Rush, Philomel, 1982.
The Magical Adventures of Pretty Pearl, Harper, 1983.
Willie Bea and the Time the Martians Landed, Greenwillow, 1983.
A Little Love, Philomel, 1984.
Junius over Far, Harper, 1985.

Virginia Hamilton

The People Could Fly: American Black Folktales, illustrated by Leo and Diane Dillon, Knopf, 1985, published with cassette, 1987.
The Mystery of Drear House: The Conclusion of the Dies Drear Chronicle, Greenwillow, 1987.
A White Romance, Philomel, 1987.
In the Beginning: Creation Stories from around the World, illustrated by Barry Moser, Harcourt, 1988.
Anthony Burns: The Defeat and Triumph of a Fugitive Slave (historical reconstruction based on fact), Knopf, 1988.
The Bells of Christmas, illustrated by Lambert Davis, Harcourt, 1989.
The Dark Way: Stories from the Spirit World, illustrated by Lambert Davis, Harcourt, 1990.
Cousins, Putnam, 1990.
The All Jahdu Storybook, illustrated by Barry Moser, Harcourt, 1991.
Drylongso, illustrated by Jerry Pinkney, Harcourt Brace Jovanovich, 1992.
Many Thousand Gone: African Americans from Slavery to Freedom, illustrated by L. Dillon and D. Dillon, Knopf, 1993.
Plain City, Scholastic, 1993.
Her Stories: African American Folktales, Fairy Tales and True Tales, illustrated by Leo and Diane Dillon, Scholastic, 1995.
Jaguarundi, Blue Sky Press, 1995.
When Birds Could Talk and Bats Could Sing: The Adventures of Bruh Sparrow, Sis Wren, and Their Friends, illustrated by Barry Moser, Blue Sky Press, 1996.
A Ring of Tricksters: Animal Tales from America, the West Indies, and Africa, illustrated by Barry Moser, Blue Sky Press, 1997.

Second Cousins, Scholastic, 1998.

Bluish, Scholastic, 1999.

The Girl Who Spun Gold, Scholastic, 2000.

Wee Winnie Witch's Skinny: An Original Scare Tale for Halloween, illustrated by Barry Moser, Scholastic, 2001.

BIOGRAPHIES; FOR CHILDREN

W. E. B. Du Bois: A Biography, Crowell, 1972.

Paul Robeson: The Life and Times of a Free Black Man, Harper, 1974.

OTHER

(Editor) *W. E. B. Du Bois, The Writings of W. E. B. Du Bois,* Crowell, 1975.

(Author of introduction) Martin Greenberg, editor, *The Newbery Award Reader,* Harcourt, 1984.

Also author of *Illusion and Reality* (lecture presented at the Library of Congress in observance of National Children's Book Week), Library of Congress, 1976.

Adaptations

The House of Dies Drear was adapted for the Public Broadcasting Service series "Wonderworks" in 1984; *The Planet of Junior Brown* was adapted for Canada Television and Cable in 1998.

Sidelights

"Virginia Hamilton is the most important author currently writing for children in the United States," proclaimed Roberta Seelinger Trites in *African American Review.* Such a claim is not made lightly, for Hamilton—author of several dozen inspiring books for young readers which present realism, history, myth, and folklore to explore family relations and the African American parallel culture in America—has won an impressive list of awards. Her 1974 novel *M. C. Higgins, the Great* was the first work ever to win both the National Book Award and the Newbery Medal. Other titles since then have won Newbery Honors, Coretta Scott King Awards, an Edgar Alan Poe Award, and a flotilla of other prestigious honors. In 1992, Hamilton won the Hans Christian Andersen Medal from the International Board on Books for Young People, similar to a Nobel Prize for children's literature, and in 1995 she was awarded the Laura Ingalls Wilder Award from the American Library Association for lifetime achievement. Today she is generally and universally recognized as both a gifted and demanding storyteller. Ethel L. Heins, for example, wrote in *Horn Book:* "Few writers of fiction for young people are as daring, inventive, and challenging to read—or to review—as Virginia Hamilton. Frankly making demands on her readers, she nevertheless expresses herself in a style essentially simple and concise."

Hamilton's vision has been deeply influenced by her background. Born in Ohio in 1936, Hamilton is descended—on her mother's side of the family—from a fugitive slave, Levi Perry, who settled in the southern Ohio Miami valley town of Yellow Springs. The Perry family grew and prospered by farming the rich Ohio soil. "I grew up within the warmth of loving aunts and uncles, all reluctant farmers but great storytellers," Hamilton recalled in a *Horn Book* article by Lee Bennett Hopkins. "I remember the tales best of all. My own father, who was an outlander from Illinois, Iowa, and points west, was the finest of the storytellers besides being an exceptional mandolinist. Mother, too, could take a slice of fiction floating around the family and polish it into a saga."

While attending Antioch College on a scholarship, Hamilton majored in writing and composed short stories. Later on at Ohio State University, one of her instructors liked her stories enough to encourage the young student to leave college and test her skills in New York City. Hamilton was eager to experience the excitement of city life, and so in 1955, she began spending her summers in New York working as a bookkeeper. Later, she moved to the city permanently. Hamilton labored at a host of different jobs as she strove to become a writer, working at first in adult fiction, and then in children's fiction.

In 1967 her first novel, *Zeely,* was published. The tale of a girl named Geeder who discovers an older young woman feeding pigs on a farm and imagines she is a Watusi queen, *Zeely* is about looking to Africa and back to America for an African American heritage. An important influence on the creation of *Zeely* came after Hamilton married poet and anthologist Arnold Adoff, whom she met not long after arriving in New York City. The two newlyweds traveled to Spain and then to northern Africa. Hamilton's first novel reflects that eye-opening visit abroad. According to John Rowe Townsend in his *A Sounding of Storytellers: New and Revised Essays on Contemporary Writers for Children, Zeely* exemplifies the type of writing that Hamilton would produce throughout her career: there "is no taint of racism in her books.... All through her work runs an awareness of black history, and particularly of black history in America."

Hamilton won the Edgar Award for her next book, *The House of Dies Drear.* It is a novel set in contemporary times, but centered around the history of the Underground Railroad, the route that fugitive blacks took to escape slavery in the South before the Civil War. It "is a taut mystery, one which youngsters gulp down quickly and find hard to forget," attested Hopkins in *Horn Book.* In a 1987 sequel, *The Mystery of Drear House,* the story was brought to a conclusion. Hamilton's first Newbery Honor Book Award came in 1971 for *The Planet of Junior Brown,* featuring Buddy Clark, a street-wise leader in New York's world of homeless children, who shoulders the responsibilities of looking out for another child, Junior Brown, an overweight and emotionally troubled fellow eighth grader. A sense of family grows between Buddy, Junior, and an eccentric janitor who helps Buddy in his growth.

Hamilton's *M. C. Higgins, the Great* also emphasizes the importance of family. The story portrays the

Higginses, a close-knit family that resides on Sarah's Mountain in southern Ohio. The mountain has special significance to the Higginses, for it has belonged to their family since M. C.'s great-grandmother Sarah, an escaped slave, settled there. The conflict in the story arises when a huge spoil heap, created by strip mining, threatens to engulf their home. M. C. is torn between his love for his home and his concern for his family's safety, and he searches diligently for a solution that will allow him to preserve both. *M. C. Higgins, the Great* was highly praised by critics, including poet Nikki Giovanni who wrote in the *New York Times Book Review:* "Once again Virginia Hamilton creates a world and invites us in. *M. C. Higgins, the Great* is not an adorable book, not a lived-happily-ever-after kind of story. It is warm, humane and hopeful and does what every book should do—creates characters with whom we can identify and for whom we care." The novel won both the National Book Award and a Newbery Medal.

In books like *The Time-Ago Tales of Jahdu, Time-Ago Lost: More Tales of Jahdu, Jahdu,* and *The All Jahdu Storybook,* Hamilton takes an approach that utilizes the style of the traditional folktale. These works tell of the fantastic adventures of Jahdu and his "encounters [with] the allegorical figures Sweetdream, Nightmare, Trouble, Chameleon, and others," wrote Marilyn F. Apseloff in *Dictionary of Literary Biography.* "These original tales have a timeless quality about them; in addition, they reveal racial pride, as Jahdu discovers in [*The Time-Ago Tales of Jahdu*] that he is happiest when he becomes a part of a black family in Harlem." Similarly, in the collections *The People Could Fly: American Black Folktales, In the Beginning: Creation Stories from around the World,* and *The Dark Way: Stories from the Spirit World,* Hamilton retells old myths and folktales from her own black ancestry—as well as many other cultures—in an attempt to restore pride in this diverse and rich literary heritage.

With *In the Beginning,* Hamilton teamed up with illustrator Barry Moser for one of many fruitful collaborations. Elizabeth Ward, reviewing *In the Beginning* in the *Washington Post Book World,* found it to be "a thought-provoking book to pair with Genesis." This collection of creation stories won a Newbery Honor Award. Further team efforts involving Hamilton and Moser include *When Birds Could Talk and Bats Could Sing* and *A Ring of Tricksters: Animal Tales from America, the West Indies, and Africa.* In *When Birds Could Talk and Bats Could Sing,* Hamilton gathers and retells Bird tales from Alabama. *Horn Book*'s Nancy Vasilakis felt that Hamilton's "inimitable storytelling style" serves these fables well and that Moser's watercolor illustrations are among "some of his best work yet." A contributor for the *New York Times Book Review* observed that these bird and bat stories, which all have a moral and were originally told in a heavy black dialect, "have been charmingly retold and illustrated." Trickster stories from around the world form the core of *A Ring of Tricksters,* a "handsome, well-annotated anthology, [which is] a pleasure to read aloud," noted a writer for *New York Times Book Review. Booklist*'s Julie Corsaro

called *A Ring of Tricksters* "a stunning collection of trickster tales," and "an undeniably handsome and well-written book that showcases two masters at the top of their form."

Hamilton has written other picture books, as well, *The Bells of Christmas, Jaguarundi,* and *The Girl Who Spun Gold* among them. In the first book, readers learn what Christmas was like a hundred years ago in Ohio when a young boy celebrates the holiday with his family. *Booklist*'s Ilene Cooper called this a "warm story." The rain forest is evoked in Hamilton's *Jaguarundi,* in which two animals decide to depart for better habitat when their forest is threatened. Karen K. Radtke, reviewing the book in *School Library Journal,* called it an "original fantasy" that presents "cogent reasons for preserving the rain forest and its dwellers." In *The Girl Who Spun Gold,* published in 2000, Hamilton creates a "stirring picture book [that] will make even older readers think about a story they thought they knew," commented *Booklist*'s Hazel Rochman. This West Indian version of the Rumpelstiltskin story features Lit'mahn, a tiny monster, who spins three rooms of gold for the lovely Quashiba, the king's new bride. Rochman praised both words and pictures in this tale which shows "that evil is in the humans who love the beautiful maiden as well as in the scary monster who threatens her." *Horn Book*'s Robert Strang commented that Hamilton's version of the tale "not only has plenty of mischief in its own right but also gives some spirit to its heroine." Carol Ann Wilson, writing in *School Library Journal,* described the story as "a charming and visually stunning tale of cunning, greed, and quixotic good fortune."

Hamilton chronicles slavery in *Anthony Burns: The Defeat and Triumph of a Fugitive Slave* and in *Many Thousand Gone: African Americans from Slavery to Freedom.* In *Anthony Burns,* Hamilton relates the true story of an escaped slave who was captured and tried under the Fugitive Slave Act. The trial triggered riots and ended with Burns's return to his former owner. Hamilton based her account on court records, newspaper reports, biographies, and other primary sources. "Told in an appropriately restrained, unadorned style, incorporating verbatim the speeches of counsel for both sides, *Anthony Burns* is a work of simple, but noble, eloquence," praised Elizabeth Ward in *Washington Post Book World.* A reviewer for *Children's Book Review Service* remarked, "Black history comes alive in this striking, gripping, personalized account." Based on information found in nineteenth-century archives and oral histories, *Many Thousand Gone* contains biographical profiles of celebrated and obscure individuals that reveal their personal experiences with slavery. The stories provide insight on slavery in America from the early 1600s to its abolishment in 1865 with the ratification of the Thirteenth Amendment to the Constitution. "All of these profiles drive home the sickening realities of slavery in a personal way," asserted David Haward Bain in the *New York Times Book Review,* who added that "many also show how the experiences of individuals in the legal system worked in the larger struggle for freedom." Michael Dirda concluded in

Washington Post Book World that "as a kind of portrait gallery of the brave and resourceful, *Many Thousand Gone* deserves many thousand readers."

Hamilton serves up more African folktales in *Her Stories: African American Folktales, Fairy Tales and True Tales,* "possibly the first collection of such folk literature to focus exclusively on African-American women and girls," according to Veronica Chambers in the *New York Times Book Review.* Teaming up once again with Leo and Diane Dillon, illustrators for both *The People Could Fly* and *Many Thousand Gone,* Hamilton recasts stories dealing with animals, fairy tales, the supernatural, folkways, and true experiences that were passed down through oral history in several African languages, Spanish, and English. "Hamilton's retellings of these stories strike a nice balance between dialect and accessibility, modernizing just enough to make the stories easily readable without sacrificing the flavor of the originals," credited Jennifer Howard in *Washington Post Book World.* "The storytelling is dramatic and direct in this collection," noted Rochman in a *Booklist* review of this collection of nineteen folktale retellings.

The breadth of Hamilton's writing style is shown in several of her novels from the 1990s. With *Cousins* and its 1998 sequel *Second Cousins,* Hamilton takes a realistic look at family life. Concerned that her grandmother, in a nursing home, may die, young Cammy is unprepared for real tragedy when it strikes. Jealous of her pretty, intelligent, and wealthy cousin Patty Ann, Cammy is shocked and guilt-ridden when the girl drowns on a school field trip. A reviewer for *Publishers Weekly* called the book an "elegant, stirring tapestry of family life." In its sequel, *Second Cousins,* the action is picked up a year later with second cousin Elodie living with Cammy and her mother. Their budding friendship is threatened when a family reunion includes two other cousins and Elodie is tempted to drop Cammy for new friends. Joyce Sparrow, writing in *Voice of Youth Advocates,* noted that in *Second Cousins* "Hamilton continues her multi-generational story showing the powerful force of love that binds an extended family together." Janice M. Del Negro, writing in *Bulletin of the Center for Children's Books,* concluded that Hamilton's "masterful handling of the physical settings and her ability to create empathetic characters will carry readers through...."

Family relations are also showcased in *Drylongso,* but here the emphasis is on the mythic rather than the purely realistic. As a family battles drought on their Midwestern farm, a young man, Drylongso, mysteriously appears and helps the family find water and plant new seeds. Based on folktales from the Georgia Sea Islands, *Drylongso* is a tale where "fantasy and myth linger around the edges," according to Mary Harris Veeder in a Chicago *Tribune Books* review. Themes of family and cultural identity are dealt with in *Plain City,* the story of a young girl torn between two cultures. Buhlaire, a racially-mixed child, must come to terms with her own past when her long-absent father returns. "*Plain City* is

the kind of rich, well-written story we have come to expect from Hamilton," announced Alice F. Stern in *Voice of Youth Advocates.* A reviewer for *Publishers Weekly* called the book "a vibrant portrait of a gifted 12-year-old of mixed race in search of her identity." And in *Bluish,* Hamilton maintains a realistic tone to tell the story of ten-year-old Dreenie and her relations with the classmate called Bluish, whose skin has turned that hue from chemotherapy treatments to battle leukemia. Writing in *School Library Journal,* Katie O'Dell called the book a "sensitive and quiet story," but one that is "not fully realized." Del Negro, reviewing the novel in *Bulletin of the Center for Children's Books,* felt it "transcends genre labels with its honest and masterful depiction of the rewards and difficulties of friendship." *Booklist*'s Rochman labeled *Bluish* a "jumpy, edgy story of sorrow and hope, of kids trying to be friends."

In all her work, Hamilton deals with characterization, theme, and setting first, and with racial matters second. Although many of her books feature African American characters, and black history and folktales often play a part in each, Hamilton writes beyond narrowly defined racial themes. Topics from inter-generational family relations to peer pressure to sibling rivalry all appear in her books, as do larger historical issues. As Hamilton herself once said, "Books can, and do help us to live; and some may even change our lives." However this award-winning author was quick to add, "It is not a good thing to put sociological/didactic considerations before literary ones."

Biographical and Critical Sources

BOOKS

Children's Literature Review, Gale (Detroit, MI), Volume 1, 1976; Volume 8, 1985; Volume 11, 1986.
Contemporary Literary Criticism, Volume 26, Gale (Detroit, MI), 1983.
Dictionary of Literary Biography, Gale (Detroit, MI), Volume 33: *Afro-American Fiction Writers after 1955,* 1984, Volume 52: *American Writers for Children since 1960: Fiction,* 1986.
Egoff, Sheila A., *Thursday's Child: Trends and Patterns in Contemporary Children's Literature,* American Library Association, 1981.
Mikkelsen, Nina, *Virginia Hamilton,* Twayne (New York, NY), 1994.
Rees, David, *Painted Desert, Green Shade: Essays on Contemporary Writers of Fiction for Children and Young Adults,* Horn Book, 1984.
Sims, Rudine, *Shadow and Substance: Afro-American Experience in Contemporary Children's Fiction,* National Council of Teachers of English, 1982.
Townsend, John Rowe, *A Sounding of Storytellers: New and Revised Essays on Contemporary Writers for Children,* Lippincott, 1979.
Wheeler, Jill C., *Virginia Hamilton,* ABDO & Daughters (Minneapolis, MN), 1997.

PERIODICALS

African American Review, spring, 1998, Roberta Seelinger Trites, "'I Double Never Ever Never Lie to My

Chil'ren': Inside People in Virginia Hamilton's Narratives," pp. 146-156.

Best Sellers, January, 1983.

Booklist, August, 1982, p. 1525; April 1, 1983, pp. 1034-1035; July, 1985, p. 1554; February 15, 1994, Ilene Cooper, review of *The Bells of Christmas,* p. 1095; April 1, 1994, p. 1464; December 15, 1994, p. 753; April 15, 1995, p. 1516; November 1, 1995, Hazel Rochman, review of *Her Stories,* p. 470; January 1, 1998, Julie Corsaro, review of *A Ring of Tricksters,* p. 802; September 15, 1999, Hazel Rochman, review of *Bluish,* p. 257; August, 2000, Hazel Rochman, review of *The Girl Who Spun Gold,* p. 2134.

Bulletin of the Center for Children's Books, September, 1978, p. 9; March, 1981, p. 134; July-August, 1982, p. 207; November, 1983, pp. 50-51; April, 1985, p. 148; June, 1988; November, 1998, Janice M. Del Negro, review of *Second Cousins,* pp. 97-98; October, 1999, Janice M. Del Negro, review of *Bluish,* p. 54.

Chicago Tribune Book World, November 10, 1985, pp. 33-34.

Children's Book Review Service, April, 1985, p. 97; July, 1988, review of *Anthony Burns,* p. 146; October, 1992, p. 22; March, 1995, p. 90; October, 1995, p. 22; March, 1996, p. 91.

Children's Literature Association Quarterly, fall, 1982, pp. 45-48; winter, 1983, pp. 10-14, 25-27; spring, 1983, pp. 17-20; fall, 1986, pp. 134-142; winter, 1995-96, pp. 168-174.

Children's Literature in Education, winter, 1983; summer, 1987, pp. 67-75.

Christian Science Monitor, May 4, 1972, p. B5; March 12, 1979, p. B4; May 12, 1980, p. B9; March 2, 1984, p. B7; August 3, 1984.

Horn Book, October, 1968, p. 563; February, 1970; February, 1972; October, 1972, p. 476; December, 1972, Lee Bennett Hopkins, "Virginia Hamilton," pp. 563-569; June, 1973; October, 1974, pp. 143-144; April, 1975; August, 1975, pp. 344-348; December, 1976, p. 611; December, 1978, pp. 609-619; June, 1980, p. 305; October, 1982, Ethel L. Heins, pp. 505-506; June, 1983; February, 1984, pp. 24-28; September-October, 1984, pp. 597-598; September-October, 1985, pp. 563-564; March-April, 1986, pp. 212-213; January-February, 1988, pp. 105-106; March-April, 1989, pp. 183-185; July-August, 1993, p. 437; September-October, 1993, p. 621; March-April, 1994, p. 204; July-August, 1995, pp. 436-445; September-October, 1996, Nancy Vasilakis, review of *When Birds Could Talk and Bats Could Sing,* p. 604; January-February, 1998, p. 83; January-February, 1999, p. 61; September-October, 2000, Robert Strang, review of *The Girl Who Spun Gold,* p. 586.

Interracial Books for Children Bulletin, Numbers 1 and 2, 1983, p. 32; Number 5, 1984; Volume 15, number 5, 1984, pp. 17-18; Volume 16, number 4, 1985, p. 19.

Kirkus Reviews, July 1, 1974; October 15, 1980, pp. 1354-1355; April 1, 1983; October 1, 1985, pp. 1088-1089; March 1, 1996, p. 375.

Lion and the Unicorn, Volume 9, 1985, pp. 50-57; Volume 10, 1986, pp. 15-17.

Los Angeles Times Book Review, March 23, 1986; May 22, 1988, p. 11; December 17, 1989, p. 8; November 18, 1990, p. 8.

New York Times Book Review, October 13, 1968, p. 26; October 24, 1971, p. 8; September 22, 1974, Nikki Giovanni, review of *M. C. Higgins, the Great,* p. 8; December 22, 1974, p. 8; October 31, 1976, p. 39; December 17, 1978, p. 27; May 4, 1980, pp. 26, 28; September 27, 1981, p. 36; November 14, 1982, pp. 41, 56; September 4, 1983, p. 14; March 18, 1984, p. 31; April 17, 1985, p. 20; November 10, 1985, p. 38; November 8, 1987, p. 36; October 16, 1988, p. 46; November 13, 1988, p. 52; December 17, 1989, p. 29; November 11, 1990, p. 6; November 22, 1992, p. 34; February 21, 1993, David Haward Bain, review of *Many Thousand Gone,* p. 23; November 12, 1995, Veronica Chambers, review of *Her Stories,* p. 23; September 22, 1996, review of *When the Birds Could Talk and Bats Could Sing,* p. 28; April 19, 1998, review of *A Ring of Tricksters,* p. 32.

Publishers Weekly, January 18, 1993, p. 470; January 4, 1993, review of *Cousins,* p. 74; February 6, 1995, review of *Plain City,* p. 86; February 19, 1996, p. 214; October 6, 1997, p. 59; April 20, 1998, p. 69.

School Library Journal, December, 1968, pp. 53-54; September, 1971, p. 126; December, 1978, p. 60; March, 1980, p. 140; April, 1981, p. 140; April, 1983, p. 123; August, 1985, p. 97; December, 1994, Karen K. Radtke, review of *Jaguarundi,* p. 75; January, 1995, p. 70; February, 1996, pp. 70-71; December, 1996, p. 29; November, 1999, Katie O'Dell, review of *Bluish,* p. 158; September, 2000, Carol Ann Wilson, review of *The Girl Who Spun Gold,* p. 217.

Times (London), November 20, 1986.

Times Literary Supplement, May 23, 1975; July 11, 1975, p. 766; March 25, 1977, p. 359; September 19, 1980, p. 1024; November 20, 1981, p. 1362; August 30, 1985, p. 958; February 28, 1986, p. 230; October 30, 1987, p. 1205; November 20, 1987, p. 1286; July 29, 1988, p. 841.

Tribune Books (Chicago), October 16, 1988, p. 9; November 13, 1988, p. 6; February 26, 1989, p. 8; November 11, 1990; February 14, 1993, Mary Harris Veeder, review of *Drylongso,* p. 5.

Voice of Youth Advocates, August, 1980, pp. 31-32; October, 1983, p. 215; June, 1985, p. 130; October, 1988, p. 201; February, 1994, Alice F. Stern, review of *Plain City,* p. 367; August, 1997, p. 173; February, 1999, Joyce Sparrow, review of *Second Cousins,* p. 434.

Washington Post Book World, June 25, 1967, p. 12; November 10, 1974; November 7, 1976, p. G7; November 11, 1979; September 14, 1980, p. 6; November 7, 1982, p. 14; November 10, 1985; July 10, 1988, Elizabeth Ward, review of *Anthony Burns,* p. 11; April 8, 1990, p. 8; November 4, 1990, p. 19; December 9, 1990, p. 14; February 14, 1993, Michael Dirda, review of *Many Thousand Gone,* p. 10; December 5, 1993, Elizabeth Ward, review of *In the Beginning,* pp. 21, 26; December 10, 1995, Jennifer Howard, review of *Her Stories,* p. 17.

—Sketch by J. Sydney Jones

HARVEY, Roland 1945-

Personal

Born December 11, 1945, in Melbourne, Victoria, Australia; son of Herbert Bruce (a graphic artist) and Eveline Anne (a graphic artist) Harvey; married Rona Judith Sharpe (a teacher and astrologer), 1977; children: Sally Christina, Timothy Piers, Roland James, Sara Jane. *Education:* Royal Melbourne Institute of Technology, B.S. (environmental science), 1974, studied architecture, 1973-77. *Politics:* Green.

Addresses

Home—11 Selbourne Rd., Kew, Victoria 3101, Australia. *Office*—125 Auburn Rd., Hawthorn, Victoria 3122, Australia.

Career

Worked as a cadet executive for a corporation in Victoria, Australia, 1964-68; affiliated with Colonial Sugar Refining Co., Victoria, 1968-72; Roland Harvey Studios/The Five Mile Press, Collingwood, Victoria, managing director, 1977-90; Roland Harvey Studios/The Periscope Press, Hawthorn, Victoria, managing director, 1991—; writer and illustrator. *Member:* Black and White Illustrators Club, Icicles Ski Club, Gippsland Lakes Yacht Club.

Awards, Honors

Commendation, Children's Book Council of Australia (CBC), 1984, and shortlisted for best picture story book, Young Australians Best Book Award Council, 1986, both for *The Friends of Emily Culpepper;* Clifton Pugh Award, CBC, and shortlisted for the Junior Book of the Year Award, CBC, both 1986, for *Burke and Wills;* children's picture book of the year finalist, CBC, 1989, for *My Place in Space,* which also was named a CBC honor book.

Writings

SELF-ILLUSTRATED

Roland Harvey's Book of Christmas, Five Mile Press (Canterbury, Victoria, Australia), 1982.
Roland Harvey's First Ever Book of Things to Make and Do, Roland Harvey Studios, 1982.
Roland Harvey's Second Ever Book of Things to Make and Do, Roland Harvey Studios, 1983.
Roland Harvey's Incredible Book of Almost Everything, Five Mile Press (Canterbury, Victoria, Australia), 1985.
Burke and Wills, Five Mile Press (Canterbury, Victoria, Australia), 1985.
Roland Harvey's New Book of Christmas, Five Mile Press (Canterbury, Victoria, Australia), 1986.
Roland Harvey's Only Joking Take-Away Fun Book!, Ashton Scholastic, 1987.
The Real Me Book, Five Mile Press (Canterbury, Victoria, Australia), 1989.

(With Scott Riddle) *Crisis on Christmas Eve,* Periscope Press, 1991.
Roland Harvey's Drawing Book, Scholastic Australia (Sidney, Australia), 1996.
The Secret Record of Me, Roland Harvey Books (Port Melbourne, Australia), 1997.

ILLUSTRATOR

Lorraine Milne, *The Fix-It Man: Songs for Schools,* Macmillan, 1979.
Michael Dugan, compiler, *More Stuff and Nonsense,* Collins, 1980.
Alan Boardman, *Eureka Stockade,* Five Mile Press (Canterbury, Victoria, Australia), 1981.
Boardman, *The First Fleet,* Five Mile Press (Canterbury, Victoria, Australia), 1982.
Jean Chapman, *The Great Candle Scandal,* Hodder & Stoughton, 1982.
Ann Coleridge, *The Friends of Emily Culpepper,* Five Mile Press (Canterbury, Victoria, Australia), 1983.
Boardman, *The Crossing of the Blue Mountains,* Five Mile Press (Canterbury, Victoria, Australia), 1985, Scholastic (Sidney, Australia), 1997.
Boardman, *Great Events in Australia's History,* Five Mile Press (Canterbury, Victoria, Australia), 1985.
Jim Converse, *The Book of Australian Trivia,* Five Mile Press (Canterbury, Victoria, Australia), 1985.
Nette Hilton, *Dirty Dave the Bushranger,* Five Mile Press (Canterbury, Victoria, Australia), 1987, published as *Dirty Dave,* Orchard Books (New York, NY), 1990.
(With Joe Levine) Robin Hirst and Sally Hirst, *My Place in Space,* Five Mile Press (Canterbury, Victoria, Australia), 1988, Orchard Books (New York, NY), 1990.
Marcia Vaughan, *Milly Fitzwilly's Mousecatcher,* Periscope Press, 1991.
Jim Howes, *Islands in My Garden,* Roland Harvey Books (Port Melbourne, Australia), 1998.
Cathy Dodson, *Bass and Flinders,* Scholastic (Sidney, Australia), 1999.
Hilton, *What's a Bunyip?,* Roland Harvey Books (Port Melbourne, Australia), 1999.
Gwenda Smyth, *The Six Wonders of Wobbly Bridge,* Roland Harvey Books (Port Melbourne, Australia), 1999.
Kate Ryan, *Belvedere Dreaming,* Roland Harvey Books (Port Melbourne, Australia), 2000.
Gael Jennings, *Sick As: Bloody Moments in the History of Medicine,* Roland Harvey Books (Port Melbourne, Australia), 2000.
Kate Ryan, *Belvedere in the City,* Roland Harvey Books (Port Melbourne, Australia), 2000.

Sidelights

Roland Harvey told *SATA:* "Some of my earliest memories are of our holiday house in the mountains. We were fifty meters from the edge of the forest, and the name of our house, 'Joalah' meant 'home of the lyrebird.' We spent most of our time there listening to and feeding those beautiful birds, climbing waterfalls, and generally getting very dirty. I wrote my first books there: exercise books with bits of leaf, fern, feathers, and sometimes whole logs stuck in them.

Roland Harvey's detailed drawings depict where Henry lives as the boy gives not only his address but his exact position in the universe to a bus driver. (From My Place in Space, *written by Robin and Sally Hirst.)*

"My parents were both graphic artists, which gave me a lot of confidence in my drawing. It also stalled my entry into the real world of illustrating: my mum and dad had suffered in the Great Depression. So I tried a number of other careers and finally architecture, which I loved. Ironically, another depression in the building trade pushed me from architecture into illustrating, then writing and illustrating, and then publishing, writing, and illustrating. I love that even more.

"My first real success came with an attempt to present history in an interesting way. It was on that project that I discovered I work best in a team. *Eureka Stockade,* the true story of the Gold Rush in Australia and the miners' struggle against repression, was developed with Alan Boardman and was really the birth of my 'style.' In the illustrations of that book, little challenges and questions lurk in every corner, tiny tragedies and comedies are enacted off center stage. I later worked on other history books as well as *My Place in Space,* an interesting collaboration between two astronomers (Robin and Sally Hirst), an airbrush wizard (Joe Levine) and me. I hope to extend the concept in order to tackle even more difficult subjects like 'time,' all the while trying to make such difficult subjects accessible and fun.

"I don't feel bound to book illustrating; a lot of my time goes toward developing my very Australian cards, kids' calendars, posters and 'other things.' I listen a lot to what my kids say about my books, such as 'Dad—you can't say that!' or 'The reindeer wouldn't be rude to

Santa!' I also notice kids laugh at anything to do with toilets."

Roland Harvey is much admired as an Australian illustrator for his intricately detailed drawings and humor, as well as historical veracity, in young adult books of fiction and nonfiction alike. Three early efforts, *The First Fleet* and *Eureka Stockade,* both written by Alan Boardman, and *Burke and Wills,* which Harvey wrote and illustrated, are historical treatments of important moments in Australia's past. *The First Fleet* tells the story of the first transport ship of convicts from England, for example, and *Burke and Wills* recounts the nineteenth-century Australian explorers' tragic bid to be the first to make the north-south trek across the Australian continent—Robert Burke and Williams Wills were successful in the attempt, but died on the return journey, along with all of their crew but one. The books were reissued fifteen years after they first appeared, and "Roland Harvey's whimsical wash and line drawings throughout the text remain—and will surely create as much pleasure today as when they first appeared," wrote Rayma Turton in *Magpies,* attesting to the fact that the illustrations bear hours of scrutiny by fascinated young people.

Harvey has produced several books that share his art techniques with young readers, including *Roland Harvey's First Ever Book of Things to Make and Do* and *Roland Harvey's Drawing Book.* As in his illustrations for middle-grade histories, the artwork in *Roland Harvey's Drawing Book* provides opportunities for laughter as well as learning, and in clearly written asides and captions conveys a tremendous amount of information about drawing techniques such as perspective, light and tone, and shape. Special attention is paid to techniques used in drawing people and animals. "In short," concluded Kevin Steinberger in *Magpies, Roland Harvey's Drawing Book* "is quite the most thorough and engaging drawing manual for children I've ever seen."

Harvey teamed up with Scott Riddle to compose the story of *Crisis on Christmas Eve,* a humorous story about the time Santa Claus was stranded in Australia on Christmas Eve. With his reindeer on strike and the heat getting him down, Santa luckily gets some help from the enthusiastic denizens of Green's station, who with a little magic make sure that Christmas will arrive after all. The result is a "highly original and hilarious offering which will give young readers hours of pleasure," averred Cathryn Crowe in *Magpies.*

Biographical and Critical Sources

PERIODICALS

Magpies, November, 1992, Cathryn Crowe, review of *Crisis on Christmas Eve,* p. 28; July, 1996, Kevin Steinberger, review of *Roland Harvey's Drawing Book,* pp. 40-41; March, 1997, Rayma Turton, review of *The First Fleet, Eureka Stockade* and *Burke and Wills,* p. 24.*

*   *   *

HERNANDEZ, Natalie Nelson 1929-

Personal

Born March 28, 1929, in Chicago, IL; daughter of Lester L. (a farmer) and Myra Maria (a homemaker; maiden name, Lightcap) Nelson; married Tony Y. Hernandez (a teacher), March 20, 1953; children: Shirley A. Hernandez Greene, Diana Hernandez Wilburn, Tony Y., Jr. *Education:* University of Illinois, B.A.; California Polytechnic State University, teaching credential. *Hobbies and other interests:* Reading, horseback riding, history.

Addresses

Home and office—Santa Ines Publications, 330 West Highway 246, No. 232, Buellton, CA 93427. *E-mail*—hernan@sbceo.org.

Career

Solvang School District, Solvang, CA, elementary school teacher, 1966-91. Cofounder, Hands On, Inc., 1987—. Volunteer literacy educator, tutoring in English and reading; La Purisima Mission, tour guide. *Member:* Retired Teachers Association.

Writings

Stowaway to California! Adventures with Father Junipero Serra, illustrated by Claudia Nolan, Santa Ines Publications (Buellton, CA), 1994.
Mapmakers of the Western Trails: Adventures with John Charles Fremont, illustrated by Claudia Nolan, Santa Ines Publications (Buellton, CA), 1997.
Captain Sutter's Fort: Adventures with John A. Sutter, Santa Ines Publications (Buellton, CA), 1999.

Contributor to equestrian magazines.

COAUTHOR OF MATH ACTIVITY BOOKS

Measurement, Hands On, 1988.
Statistics, Probability, and Graphing, Hands On, 1988.
Algebra, Hands On, 1989.
Geometry, Hands On, 1989.
Logic, Hands On, 1989.
Number and Operations, Hands On, 1991.
Patterns and Functions, Hands On, 1991.

Coauthors include Linda-Sue Brisby, Andy Heidemann, Jeanette Lenger, Ron Long, Petty Pfau, Scott Purdy, and Sharon Rodgers.

Work in Progress

Research on California history and on the preservation of equestrian trails.

Sidelights

Natalie Nelson Hernandez told *SATA:* "I was born in Chicago, Illinois, on March 28, 1929. I graduated from the University of Illinois with a B.A. in Spanish. I worked for the Department of the Army, traveling to Japan, where I met and married my husband Tony in

Natalie Nelson Hernandez

1953. After teaching school in California for twenty-five years, I retired and began writing historical novels for young people.

"I am especially interested in the history of California. I want to make history interesting to young people. Remembering how much my fourth-graders enjoyed

historical novels such as *By the Great Horn Spoon!* and *Island of the Blue Dolphins,* I believe there is a need for more of this type of fiction.

"In 1987, with seven other teachers in Solvang, California, I formed Hands On, Inc., to write and publish math books of manipulative activities."

Autobiography Feature

Nonny Hogrogian

1922-

I was born at 2854 Kingsbridge Terrace in The Bronx, New York, to Rachel and Mugerdich Hogrogian on the seventh day of May in 1932.

I was born into a family of six, including my Uncle Bobby who was just preparing to be married. I am told, though I remember none of it, that he would toss me in the air and catch me, singing "Hey, Nonny, Nonny and a Ha-Cha-Cha." I must have loved it for he did it often enough that Nonny was the only name I answered to.

When Uncle Bobby left I became the sixth member of the family—my grandparents, Roupen Hrahad and Ehleezah, being the heads, then my parents, and my sister Gloria Zabel.

My first memory was of being in a carriage on the stone porch of our house. I remember the stones and being very high up (we were living two stories up from the street). The sky was very blue with soft white, fluffy clouds that floated by. The air was cool and crisp and I wanted to be moved in to the warmth and comfort of my home and family. I cried and screamed. But my mother was determined that I would have my sleep alone in the fresh air. She came out, tucked me in, and purred some words to me ... and left me alone again.

My grandparents were born in Ersingah, Armenia (now and at that time a part of Turkey), long before the massacres; but there were always troubled times for them. Ehleezah was the daughter of a wealthy silk merchant and Roupen Hrahad was the youngest son of a long line of tillers of the soft black earth on which babies were laid in olden times. Their name was Hogh-grogh-ian (with a couple of more h's) which means earth-carriers. One day when they were digging the soil they came upon a buried treasure which belonged to a fifth-century Armenian king. They kept the treasure a secret for a long time because they were afraid of the Turkish officials, but as time went on, their affluence became more and more apparent. They bought a mansion with quarters for all the sons and their

families. But aside from the tapestries on their walls and the few gold circlets the women wore, they lived a simple life. My grandfather was a quiet man, a reader and a dreamer. He had a small shop in the Armenian sector of the city where he did very little business but had a lot of free time for reading.

Ehleezah was a fifteen-year-old with a strong passion for life and a very sharp tongue.

Their families arranged the union.

A horse-drawn carriage took the young bride and groom along the Euphrates River to her new home. They had a difficult marriage from the beginning.

By the time I knew them, they were sharing the same house and family but not much else. And the air held the tension of their non-compatibility. We jokingly called it "divorce, Armenian style."

My father came to America when he was thirteen, along with the two youngest children and my grandmother. The oldest son had come earlier to help his father earn enough money to bring the whole family to America. The wealth was all left behind to the plunder of the Turks, the only remnants being my grandmother's silk underwear.

On my mother's side the influences and circumstances were not so different. She was born on the island of Cyprus during her family's emigration from their troubled Armenia. She was a baby when she arrived in this country and was caught in the difficulties of growing up in two cultures. She wasn't allowed to attend the local high school because it was coeducational, but her mother secretly agreed to send her to a business school so that she could at least learn some secretarial skills. By the time my mother was seventeen her family and my father's had arranged a match, and when she was eighteen they were married.

For the most part our home was warm and our life was full. My father was the only one of his family to keep a job during the Depression, and that, coupled with the fact that we lived with my grandparents, made our home the hub of

Nonny Hogrogian

the whole family on my father's side. At least once a week there would be a big family gathering at our dining room table with places set even at the corners. We children would eat in the kitchen but after the meal we would run into the dining room and climb on someone's lap and listen to Nasreddin Hodja stories and finally to my Uncle Onnig as he sang the songs of the old country.

Talent, if that is what you call it, ran strong in my family. My father, a photoengraver by trade, was an artist in his heart. He was short and handsome, shy and serious, and what he cared about was God, family and work, painting and gardening. I am not sure of his order of importance except that he put his responsibility for being a good householder first before anything. That included family, work, home, and garden. As for his connection with God, I didn't clearly understand it as a child. He didn't go to church every Sunday as my grandfather did, but whenever there were some quiet moments in his day he would pick up the Bible and read it, always keeping it private. As for his painting and artwork, it took up a small corner of our living room and in the evening after work and on weekends he would stand before his easel and paint.

My mother, it seemed to me, could do almost anything with her hands and do it well. She sewed for all the women in the family and during the Depression, when money was so scarce, she helped the family income by crocheting silk evening purses at home. She called it piecework.

Once a week she and my dad would go to a sketch class together. I thought that her drawings were beautiful, but you couldn't convince her of that. She also was a great cook, although she didn't show it when I was little because she took her place in the kitchen as my grandmother's

helper. She washed the dishes and helped to form the dough and chopped the onions and never complained that she wanted a more creative job. But when her opportunities came she made the best apple pies I've ever eaten, along with many other incredible main dishes and desserts. Preparing food with simplicity and interest was always her way and the results of her labors—superb!

The pattern of my life was set very early. My fascination with artwork and fine handwork goes back as far as I can remember. Love of work itself was strong in the family and whenever there were spare moments someone would start a new project. And so, with these influences, when I was about three or four years old, I began to putter with my father's paints and brushes.

My grandfather, who had a large basement room that was his study and sleeping quarters, had many, many books. One wall of his room was filled with them. The books were mostly in Armenian but there was one shelf (or maybe two) which I could reach that had books in English—Evangeline, Joan of Arc, King Arthur. Andersen's *Fairy Tales* and Grimm's, some poetry—all beautifully illustrated. He never said they were our books. But he couldn't read them. They were simply there and we were welcome to go there anytime to read them. He never needed to tell us to treat them with respect. It was like a library in his room and all the books were so well cared for. Papa would sit at his desk reading his Armenian journals and I would sit in the big chair by the bookcase going through the illustrated books and dreaming about the possibility of making such beautiful pictures.

There was a time, between the discovery that I could use my hands to paint or draw and the point when artwork became a serious part of my life, that I remember very little about. But I do recall a few incidents connected with artwork. I was shy and retiring and embarrassed to be in any situation outside my immediate family life, which kept me comfortable and (I thought) secure. I knew that I had a gift that everyone didn't have, and I used it for the attention that I didn't know how to get in any other way. Once when I was ill and in bed, someone brought me a gift of some Walt Disney comic books. I read through them and was pretty quickly bored until I began to notice exaggerations of line that were used to create certain expressions on the animals' faces. I became fascinated. Eyebrows tilting down into the center of the face made the character look angry, and tilting up in the center, made him look innocent or wondering. I borrowed my mother's little purse-mirror and began to make faces in it. It was true! I knew then that I could also draw these expressions on paper. I began to imitate Walt Disney characters until I excelled at drawing them. The word quickly got around my classroom at school that I could draw a mean Donald Duck or Mickey Mouse. It became my entry ticket to life on this planet and I used it— to please the teachers, to attract "friends," to have adults exclaim over me, and for my own amusement when I was alone. And in its own way, it worked.

There were a few incidents in grammar school that left strong impressions on me. One incident brought into perspective something about my artistic ability. We were drawing Thanksgiving pictures. It was clear to me that I could draw a pumpkin. I knew pumpkins ... the stem end

... those beautiful rounded ribs that grew up and out and around from the center. I could even draw the pilgrims or facsimiles in pilgrim's clothing; but when it came to the turkey, I was stuck. I knew I couldn't draw one because I hadn't seen a live one and the pictures were unclear to me. I could draw a cartoon based on a picture of a turkey but I had no sense of what a real turkey was. Years later, my husband wrote this poem after we had shared our life on a piece of land with "Penelope and Franklyn Turkey."

Turkeys

Say it: the tom is all ego and male.
Puffs one second, unpuffs the next.
And what is the cause of his puffing,
and why did he cease?
A cat will leap from a butterfly
shadow sometimes, but he will do so
with humor, enjoying his own fright
in a game he plays for himself.
But for the tom it is not even
butterfly shadows.
It is simply, one moment all feathers
and fight, the next minute
nothing—Mr. Nonentity himself.

It's a hell of a life. Consider it!
The fluff and feathers serve no purpose,
and signal his own fear—though he
pretends to be scaring others off—
and his face (that turns blue from fear)
and that silly, flappy foreskin on his face.
Really!—is that what ego is all about?

But then there is the hen, all squawk
and whining sex. Everything, just everything,
is a complaint. Come here, go away (she says
to Tom), get me more, get me less. Why can't
you see what I want? You never can, you
never will. Oh, never mind ... it's too late,
and doesn't matter anyhow.

Oh God, the point is clear, why You
have put turkeys here.

Although I could not formulate it, the point was clear to me as a child ... that I must know something in order to depict it (as David knows turkeys). Knowing must come from "seeing," which brings an understanding between myself and the thing drawn.

Other than one or two more such incidents that clarified for me something important about artwork, I don't remember working at it with intention ... until that time between my twelfth and thirteenth year when I was forced to think about my future. And that meant which high school I would attend. It was natural that I would dream about going to Music and Art High School in New York. It was the school for future artists. And everyone assumed that I would be an artist, including me. So I applied. The times were difficult for my family. My grandfather and grandmother had both just died and within two months of each other. The rest of us were trying to pick up the pieces of our lives and find the inevitable new directions that would be true for each of us.

There were tests to pass before a student was accepted at Music and Art High School. We were to be judged by an examination on the basis of portfolios of our past work. I had no idea how to go about putting together a portfolio, but I thought a variety of my work would show what I could do. I picked out about six or eight of my best drawings and my father bought a manila envelope for me to carry them in.

The day came. I was the only child from my school who tried out for Music and Art High School. I took a trolley car, a bus, and a subway to get there. It was the first time away from my neighborhood that I was completely alone. It felt very strange but somehow right that I was alone in this endeavor. When I arrived at the school everyone looked as if they belonged except me. Every child I saw had a big black, shiny portfolio filled with drawings. They seemed to have prepared for this for a long time. I wished I could hide myself but my wish to go to the school was stronger, so I stayed in the line and opened my skimpy little envelope and showed my few doodles. The woman hardly looked at them and condescendingly moved me on.

I was confident that the test would make up for my lack of a proper portfolio. I knew I could draw.

Wedding portrait of parents, Rachel and Mugerdich Hogrogian.

The tester (as she was called) came to the front of the room. The atmosphere was tense. I was perspiring for the first time in my young life.

She talked about the true test of talent. She said there was one sure proof of a person's talent: whether or not a person could do a good contour drawing. "You will know for yourself," she said, "when you have completed this test whether or not you should pursue this work."

I didn't know what a contour drawing was and that scared me, but it infuriated me that she could say it would decide my future. She gave the rules. She said no previous training was necessary, or even relevant. Either we were able to do a contour drawing, or not. We were to draw the model with one fluid line, without taking our hand from the page or our eyes from the model. Anyone who did would be disqualified.

The tension in the room mounted and my wet hand clutched my pencil tighter. The paper was flimsy. My dad

Author's father, Mugerdich Hogrogian, in front of the house where Nonny was born in New York.

had always given me good paper to draw on. The model came up to pose. I had never drawn from a live model before. The tester said our drawing should fill the page. How could I be sure I was filling the page without looking at the paper? My rigid hand began to move on the page. I sneaked a peak. I had drawn the ugliest little squiggle. The shock of my ugly drawing cleared my head a little and I realized that it happened because her tight rules had filled me with fear. I would simply turn the paper over and begin from a freer place in myself. I knew I could do it. My mistake was in asking permission to start again. She smiled condescendingly and said the proof was on the page. There was no second chance. I began to cry from rage and frustration. She gave me some water to calm me and I went home, but my future was decided that day. The seeds of my talent were sown before I was born but the fertilizer they needed to push out of their shells was given to me in the judgment of the examiners that day. (I went on and trained myself to excel at contour drawing.)

During my high school years my parents sent me to study painting and charcoal drawing with my Aunt Angele who was our official family artist. Aunt Angele was born in Constantinople and studied at the Sorbonne; she wore colorful French berets with a contrasting scarf around her neck. Several times a week she would spend her whole day at the Metropolitan Museum copying the paintings of the "old masters." Her copies were exquisite. The walls of her apartment were covered with them and some originals as well. Mainly, she encouraged me and pointed out certain things I didn't see or avoided seeing, always making it seem more possible to stretch myself, and my skill. I worked with Aunt Angele every Saturday morning for about two years. Then one day I heard there were Saturday art classes for young people at Pratt Institute in Brooklyn. I took an illustrating class there with a young woman who was training to be a teacher.

I jumped at any chance to hone my skill. In high school I spent my study periods hand-lettering cards for one of my teachers and I worked on scratchboard illustrations for my high school magazine. One hot summer my family drove out to California and after seeing one cotton field too many, I slouched in the back seat of the car with my feet up on the back of the front seat, and I began to draw. I spent at least five days of the journey crossing America drawing my feet and I've always enjoyed drawing feet since then.

During my high school years I also hand-painted greeting cards. There was a woman (a friend of one of my art teachers) who hand-printed greeting cards for one of the more elegant stores on Fifth Avenue. I painted them for her in dry-brush technique for a nickel a card. It hardly paid since I took pains to make each one as beautiful as I possibly could, and the deadlines came up too quickly. Sometimes my family would even help paint in the little red bows while I concentrated on dry-brushing the fluffy little poodles. It was a short-lived experience but good training.

When it came time to go to college, my family assumed that I would attend Hunter College since all the girls in the family had gone there. But I applied to The Cooper Union. I don't know where I found the nerve but the day of the examination I woke up with a pounding headache. It didn't stop me. I took my place in the large auditorium where there were two or three empty seats between each applicant and each applicant's seat contained the examination booklet. We were told to turn the first page after the bell sounded. I turned it. The instructions told me to complete the incomplete drawing on the page. It seemed ugly to me. How could I possibly complete it? I realized that they not only wanted me to complete it but to tack on some personality—pizazz—call it what you will. My headache became worse. I realized that I neither would nor could do what they wanted. I closed the booklet and put down my pencil and walked out into the fresh air. I did attend Hunter like all the women in my family and it was no worse nor better than Walton High School. I was an art major with an art history minor and I filled my programs with as many art classes as I could fit in. And when I graduated I didn't fit into a slick art school mold but had had many, many hours of artwork behind me and a smattering of many different techniques. I was ready to go out and find my way in the world.

I had found a few jobs after I graduated from Hunter but they were all horrid. I was either fired after a few days or I quit before they had the chance to fire me. I didn't know what I wanted to do but I knew I needed to do artwork and I was beginning to notice that my college portfolio was not knocking the employers dead. I supposed I could stay home and spend six months working on a new one but I felt the time had come to earn some money.

Was I really as untalented as the interviews made me feel? Every time I had a bad one I would want to throw out my portfolio, crawl into bed, and stay there. But I knew I couldn't stay there forever. The only thing that egged me on was that my mom was always nudging me to study the secretarial skills because there was security in secretarial work. That simply made me want a job that required my own skills even more.

I finally began checking the employment agencies. There was one that was known for having jobs for people interested in publishing. They had one job available for a "girl Friday" in the advertising department of William Morrow. Could I type, the woman asked. Yes, I lied. I had taken one class in college (at my mother's insistence), which I failed. What was my speed, she wanted to know. "Oh, I'm not very fast, but I can type well enough for a girl Friday." "Well, I suppose it won't do any harm to send you down there," she replied. "I'll call Mr. Baker and see if you can have an interview this afternoon." He said "yes" if I came right away and so I grabbed the first cab I could hail.

I felt at home with Ross W. Baker III (better known as Jerry). He asked me a few questions, about my schooling and my typing skills. I told him I was slow but accurate. He looked through my portfolio and I could tell he liked my work. Maybe he has no taste, I thought, since he was almost the first person since college who responded in a positive way. He asked me questions about technique and I relaxed and chatted with him. Then he told me he wanted to give me a short typing test. Even that didn't throw me. I just laughed and told him I couldn't type fast enough to be tested. I had to face it anyway. I hunted and pecked a few letters on his old machine and my heart began to sink. "It's no use," I said. "I can't type well enough."

Nonny at about three with older sister, Gloria, at camp in the Catskills.

"I can see that," he answered. "Well, let me take another look at your portfolio."

The interview was soon over and although he said he would call me, I had lost all hope.

Two weeks went by and one day Jerry Baker did call me. I could hardly believe it. He asked if I had found a job yet and said he'd like to see my portfolio again, and he couldn't seem to remember—had I taken a typing test? I reminded him that I was too slow for a typing test.

"Well, why don't you just come in and let me take another look at your portfolio and maybe you can type a few short sentences."

I wasn't about to argue with that. I was beginning to think that Jerry Baker was a little weird, but I was also beginning to feel that there might be a place for me in this world and that it could be at William Morrow and Company.

At my second interview we went through the usual amenities; he checked out my portfolio again and had me struggle with the typewriter again. Then he excused himself and took my portfolio with him.

About fifteen minutes later he came back and told me he wanted me to meet the president of the company. He looked nervous and it was catchy. I wanted the job very much. He led me through the old office building and we descended the circular metal staircase to the floor below and Thayer Hobson's office. Jerry introduced us and then disappeared. Thayer Hobson was an elegant, blustery old codger, seated at the biggest, most beautiful desk I ever saw. When I commented on it, he grinned and told me his first wife (the Jewess, he called her) had it made for him. I knew he was testing me so I responded and asked if she was Laura Z. Hobson. I knew, of course, that it must be.

He told me he heard I couldn't type but he really didn't seem to care. He spoke about how one was spoon-fed in college—but that working was more like graduate studies. One had to figure out things for oneself. I wondered if he knew how much I would have to figure out, like all the things I lied about being able to do—like paste-ups and layouts. I would simply figure it out.

I loved Thayer Hobson and I loved those offices. I practically floated back to Jerry's office. He was standing at his window aiming a paper airplane at the street below. He jumped when he saw me. After asking how things went, he excused himself again. I waited in silence, but I was singing inside. I knew already that the job was mine.

I began work at Morrow the Monday after my interview. I arrived at a quarter to nine, a shade anxious. Richard, the assistant advertising manager, was there to let me in. It turned out that he had worked there for twenty-five years in the same job, placing ads in newspapers and guiding new people (including Jerry Baker, when he began to work there) through their early difficulties. Richard helped me through many disasters during my first months at Morrow.

Betty was the copy chief of the department. She was a mannish, short-tempered woman who shared Richard's office when she was around. She came in late, took long lunch hours, and left early. But when she worked, her typewriter flew and she expected those who worked for her to work with the same clarity and speed.

There were also two secretaries (also named Betty)—one old and crotchety and the other a young Belgian-Jew who had been hidden away by some nuns during the war. She was more Catholic than Jewish although she was always bringing in samples of her mother's wonderful gefilte fish.

The elder secretary Betty did a bit of typing for Jerry but she spent most of her time going through newspapers from all over the country, clipping reviews of Morrow books.

There was one additional job in the department: a copywriter. It was the only job in the department that turned over while I was there. But whichever copywriter happened to be there at the time, that person became my friend. They came from schools like Radcliffe, Smith, and Reed—and I learned from them about books and music and politics and even art. As Thayer Hobson had told me, my education was just beginning.

My own small corner of that department was wonderful. My job consisted of working with book-jacket artists, choosing type, getting the artwork approved—starting with Jerry and then each of six salesmen and finally Thayer Hobson. I always argued with the salesmen because they would want the lettering bigger and brighter on every jacket. But I even enjoyed my anger at them.

Hogrogian at Art Students' League, New York, about 1970.

I did jacket mechanicals and small ads; and whenever they wanted to save money on a book, I would offer to do the jacket art myself. I'd stay after hours and sneak into the jacket files and examine how other artists did their work. I studied the different methods until I understood how type and color separations worked best for me.

There weren't many great writers at Morrow then but there were some good ones. And they always had at least one book on the *New York Times* best-seller list.

Earle Stanley Gardner was Thayer Hobson's first author and "Uncle Earle," as we called him, came to visit a couple of times a year with big boxes of candied fruit from sunny California.

I loved that job until the day I left. I worked as hard as I could for myself and for the company. Almost everything I know about type and design I learned from struggling with them at Morrow. It was a time of awakening for me and I never missed an opportunity. Every person that I met there was unlike anyone I had met before. Everything in my life seemed alive and open and new. I worked at Morrow for three years, which is the longest I ever stayed at any job. I realized finally that my time there was over, and I left to try to do my own artwork. But I left a bit of my heart there, too.

I was twenty-four years old and entering a more difficult time in my life. I had been working at wood-cutting at about the time I left Morrow. I added all of my woodcuts to my portfolio, removed a few old pieces, and went to see Estelle Mandel, an artist's agent whom I had worked with at Morrow. I heard that she took a forty-percent commission from her clients but that she was one of the best agents. Estelle wasn't impressed. "Do line drawings," she said. "That's what art directors are buying now."

"But I don't do line drawings. I'm doing woodcuts now. Maybe there is an art director somewhere who will like them."

"I wish it were true, Nonny, but they are just not commercial enough. You go home and do about fifty line drawings and then come back and see me."

My life was entering a new phase and whatever I tried seemed not to work.

One evening while I was visiting my sister, she mentioned something about the Haystack Mountain School of Crafts in Maine. In fact, she said, there was a young Armenian-American designer that she knew who would be teaching there that summer. She thought I might be able to get a scholarship.

Well, to make a long story short, I got the only scholarship I have ever gotten, and not because my work was thought to be so great, but because Ruben Eshkhanian, the young Armenian-American designer, worked for Jack Larsen, the textile king, who was on the board of directors of the school and my sister bought a lot of fabrics from Larsen as part of her job. I didn't care how it happened. I needed the opportunity, and I took it.

Sixteen of us scholarship students arrived two days before the paying guests—in time to clean out the cabins, and to get acquainted with each other, our studios, the rules, and the summer chores.

Maine was different from New York, right down to the bugs. By my second day there, I was covered with welts. My first job was to clean out the bureaus and put bed linens in each room. The bureaus were filled with toilet paper

nests of mice! Ugh! Didn't these people know that I was a city girl? After cleaning out about five drawers I began to notice the baby mice in detail. They were actually cute. Walt Disney wasn't making it all up. They really looked like his drawings—big ears and all.

Our quarters were primitive and there was a shortage of water. We were not allowed to do our own laundry or even to bathe more than once a week. I couldn't believe it. There was a woman who worked for the school who washed our clothes in the brook for a small fee, but we were warned not to expect them to stay bright with the hard water of Haystack Mountain. It was a good, difficult summer for me but I began as a misfit and remained one all summer long.

There were sixty people in all, including the scholarship students, the paying guests, and the director, Fran Merritt, and his wife, Priscilla. The scholarship students were supposed to shine as guides and examples to the paying guests. One of my duties was to wait on the table where I ate plus the one next to mine. I was never the picture of grace, but if I looked anything like I felt as I juggled huge trays of food through the dining room, I must have been quite a sight.

I only worked at two woodcuts the whole summer long. I went to the first Friday night seminar and realized that I had no connection with what the rest of the people were saying about art, so I never attended another of their seminars. I realize in writing this that I never really understood what my relation to artwork was, but I knew somewhere inside that it was what it was, and that I had a responsibility to work with it as best I could. My work at Haystack was disliked. The acceptable form there was more experimental—more "creative"—more modern— more abstract. The unspoken consensus of opinion was that it was a mistake for me to be there but they would have to suffer it. I realized this after my first woodcut which I tried

With husband, David Kherdian, in Armenia, 1971.

to do in a modern Japanese technique (taught by my woodcutting instructor, Hodaka Yoshida). The method had no life in it for me. My work seemed dead even to me. I burned the woodblocks.

I spent the rest of the summer playing hooky from the print shop. I wove a small rug, I tried to throw some clay, I played at woodcarving but, most of all, I experienced what it was to be nearly alone with sixty other people.

It was in a way a wonderful summer. Even the wasps began to accept me. I went for a walk one day with a young man named Peter, also a misfit. Suddenly Peter flung me across the road, grabbed an old tree limb, and seemed to be fighting with the dead leaves on the ground. But the leaves were moving and I realized that Peter had saved me from stepping on an eight-foot golden adder. Of course, I fell in love with him but our relationship was like being in the army together. We knew that when we walked away from Haystack it would all be behind us.

The last week of the summer Peter spent the evenings sitting on a tall stool in the print shop as I cut my first real woodblock of the summer (of Peter, of course). Peter said it was good, I knew it was good, and no one else commented. But I knew that for that summer I had kept the skill protected inside me, just where it belonged.

You've heard a bit now about my first twenty-four years. The next thirty years included my good fortune in illustrating and my marriage to David Kherdian (a late and special marriage), and more. But my life as an illustrator is what I have tried to concentrate on here. I tried to retire from illustrating many times in my life, the first time—almost before I started—when I thought of changing my major so I could become an occupational therapist. The second time was a couple of months before I received the Caldecott Award in 1966. The award turned everything around and I forgot about going back to school for my Master's degree.

I have just gone through another bout of trying to retire and now I am beginning to get interested in what exactly is

At work in the print shop at Two Rivers Press.

going on here. I see, for one thing, that I only make a pretense of not caring enough about my work. In fact, I identify completely with my work and if anyone dares to "slight" it, I am very quick to shut down the doors, to bar my work from the offenders. Beyond that, I am always dissatisfied with my work, always left with the feeling that I must try harder the next time, that I never seem capable enough to paint something as beautifully as it deserves to be painted. If I can just see that my work is simply what it is—that other people's opinions are simply their opinions . . . .

All of it in the end is part of my life, and is only interesting if I can learn something in the process of living it. Right now I am looking forward to the next book that I will illustrate.

Postscript

I noticed that in the first autobiography that I wrote for the Gale series I wrote mostly about the people and events in my life that led to my becoming a children's book illustrator. I would like in this postscript to say something about my personal life after I became an illustrator.

I remember when I was a child (growing up in New York City) my grandmother used to tell me many stories, one in particular about a romantic hero in a series she read in her Armenian newspaper. I asked her one day how I would know when the right person for me would appear. My grandmother answered that he would come from very far away, from the other side of the country, and that he would find me. I didn't question how she knew this nor did I believe or disbelieve her, but the information got stored in that vast information center in my brain where so much is left to be forgotten. Years went by and although I wished very much to marry, it did not seem to happen. Then when I was thirty-eight years old, David Kherdian, a poet and writer, came into my life. I would like to add that he came from California to New York where we met. We were married two months later and moved to Lyme Center, New Hampshire, where we spent the first two years of our marriage. So many strange things happened there that it is hard to relate them all. Briefly, however, we traveled to Armenia (the home of his and my ancestors) for one month, we bought our first home, David was hospitalized with acute arthritis (from which he later fully recovered), I was awarded the Caldecott medal, and I was diagnosed with cancer. The surgery for cancer was a huge shock so early in my marriage; however, it made me realize that there is more to life than this body that we live in, and it opened my world to a spiritual life that I have pursued ever since. So in the first two years of our marriage we experienced the good, the difficult, and the miraculous.

New Hampshire was beautiful and inspiring, but the winters were very cold and long and the spring was in some ways harsher because of mud season. We lived up a very long dirt road and spent an enormous amount of time trying to haul our poor car out of the mud. So we finally sold our house and moved to Columbia County in New York.

David and I have had thirty good years of sharing our life, our cats, our work, and our spiritual quest. In 1977 we moved to Oregon to join a group of people who were studying the ideas of George Ivanovich Gurdjieff, an Armenian/Greek mystic. They had a farm about thirty-five

Book jacket from **The Animal** *written by David Kherdian and illustrated by Nonny Hogrogian, 1984.*

minutes south of Portland, where we lived and worked together to try to raise our level of consciousness. David wished to start a small publishing venture there and, with a crew of people who knew a lot more about building and carpentry than the two of us, we converted an old hop barn into a publishing house with a four-room apartment over it (where the two of us lived). We bought an old proof press, a wonderful book on hand bookbinding by Aldren Watson, some type and type drawers, and we began to learn how to make books by hand. I studied marbling with a few women so that we could put marbled endpapers in our books. We called ourselves Two Rivers Press and soon there were about seven or eight people working together in publishing every Sunday. The books looked and felt beautiful, but we sold them as cheaply as machine-made books, hoping only to raise enough money to pay for the paper and binding supplies for each new project.

We lived on the farm for nine years. During that time, in addition to working on our own books and Two Rivers Press books, we each taught a class at the school (writing and drawing). We often worked out in the gardens where we grew our own food.

In 1986 we returned to New York where we discovered that life had become much more expensive and so for a while we concentrated hard on earning a decent living. We collaborated on many books, including *The Great Fishing Contest, The Cat's Midsummer Jamboree, Right Now, Feathers and Tails, The Golden Bracelet,* and *Lullaby for Emily.* We published a multiethnic literary journal called *Forkroads,* and at the present time we are publishing a small Gurdjieff quarterly journal called *Stopinder.*

We have moved many times in the past thirty years. I suppose some people think we are crazy because moving is

difficult, but I like to think that we move with our lives. As life directs us, so we go, rather than dreaming about lost opportunities. Since 1986 we have lived in upstate New York; Charlottesville, Virginia; Blue Hill, Maine; back to New York, then Northern California, and now, Oregon. Of course, each time we move, we spend several months making the home a permanent place that reflects our lives, never considering that we might move again.

With these moves come new friends and new impressions which seem to present themselves, both in David's work and in mine and in the life of our well-loved and well-traveled cat, Tessie, who is now fifteen years old and believes she has traveled quite enough. Tessie, of course, is the wonderful model for *The Cat Who Loves to Sing* and *The Cat's Midsummer Jamboree.*

As I mentioned in my earlier biography, I often spoke about retiring from illustrating children's books, the main reason being that slowly the publishing world was beginning to change. Large corporations were buying up the small publishing companies and the flavor of working with editors who were also our friends and guides had also changed. The bottom line had become all important and had taken the joy out of working with them. Now for the first time in my experience our work had to have the approval of the publicity and promotion staffs rather than simply of an editor and/or an art director. Nevertheless, one has to eat, so for a while I kept trying to work on one book a year. Finally, in 1997, I decided I *really* would retire from illustrating books.

For a while, after we moved to Sebastopol, California, and remodeled yet another house, I began to paint just for myself. And it was a joy to have that freedom. Many of my paintings contain a feeling of dance in them. And as those recent few years went by as I was painting, a germ of an idea began in my head and finally fell out of me on to the page in the form of a story for young children. The story is about a little tiger who grows up to be a teacher of dancing. It is, of all the books I have worked on, the one that is closest to my heart. And it is, in reality, about someone who has been and continues to be a teacher to me. But when I read the story over—I thought—this is a very special story, but what publisher do I know who would even understand the message that I would like to share with children?

After much pondering about the matter, speaking to friends, and checking publishers' catalogs, I finally sent the manuscript and a couple of illustrations to Hampton Roads, a small publisher in Charlottesville, Virginia, who publishes books that contain truths about life and the spirit. This is what tiger needed, and so, *The Tiger of Turkestan* has found a home and will be published in the fall of 2002. Hampton Roads is also publishing a novel by David this year called *The Revelations of Alvin Tolliver.*

I will, as soon as I complete *Tiger,* retire once again to my painting until it is time to plant the garden or until I receive another inspiration that would bring me out of "retirement" once more. The word "retirement" is quite inaccurately used here since I have probably been busier in retirement than out of it. But it indicates more a time in my life when I need to live as I really wish to live, and work is a large part of what I take joy in doing. So retirement means (for both David and for me) writing and/or painting/illustrating as the inspiration moves us to do so, publishing our journal, and earning supplementary income from buying and selling used books on the net which is almost like a hobby for us. It usually includes driving to an interesting place, discovering wonderful books that have been discarded, having a nice lunch out, and then coming home and cleaning and renewing the books and listing them on the net. It is work and fun together, and it includes preserving what is worth preserving.

I also love to cook and to garden, and David loves to golf, and Tessie loves to sleep for twenty hours a day, knowing that we are near. It is a good life.

Writings

FOR CHILDREN; SELF-ILLUSTRATED

One Fine Day, Macmillan (New York, NY), 1971.
Apples, Macmillan (New York, NY), 1972.

Billy Goat and His Well-Fed Friends, Harper (New York, NY), 1972.
The Hermit and Harry and Me, Little, Brown (Boston, MA), 1972.
Rooster Brother, Macmillan (New York, NY), 1974.
Handmade Secret Hiding Places, Overlook Press (Woodstock, NY), 1975.
(Adaptor) *The Contest,* Greenwillow (New York, NY), 1976.
Carrot Cake, Greenwillow (New York, NY), 1977.
The Pearl: Hymn of the Robe of Glory, Two Rivers, (Aurora, OR), 1979.
(Reteller) *Cinderella,* Greenwillow (New York, NY), 1981.
(Reteller) *The Devil with the Three Golden Hairs,* Knopf (New York, NY), 1983.
(Reteller) *The Glass Mountain,* Knopf (New York, NY), 1985.
(Reteller) *Noah and the Ark,* Knopf (New York, NY), 1986.
The Cat Who Loved to Sing, Knopf (New York, NY), 1988.
The First Christmas, Greenwillow (New York, NY), 1995.

Nonny Hogrogian and husband, David Kherdian, with cat Sossi, in Aurora, Oregon, 1984.

The Tiger of Turkestan, Hampton Roads (Charlottesville, NC), 2002.

ILLUSTRATOR

Nicolete Meredith, *King of the Kerry Fair,* Crowell (New York, NY), 1960.

Henrietta Bancroft, *Down Come the Leaves,* Crowell (New York, NY), 1961.

Sorche Nic Leodhas, *Gaelic Ghosts,* Holt (New York, NY), 1963, published as *Gaelic Ghosts: Tales of the Supernatural from Scotland,* Bodley Head (London England), 1966 (includes *Ghosts Go Haunting*).

Sorche Nic Leodhas, *Always Room for One More,* Holt (New York, NY), 1965.

Aileen L. Fisher, *Arbor Day,* Crowell (New York, NY), 1965.

Sorche Nic Leodhas, *Ghosts Go Haunting,* Holt (New York, NY), 1965.

Robert Burns, *Hand in Hand We'll Go: Ten Poems,* Crowell (New York, NY), 1965.

Barbara Schiller, *The Kitchen Knight,* Holt (New York, NY), 1965.

(Reteller) Virginia A. Tashjian, *Once There Was and Was Not,* Little, Brown (Boston, MA), 1966.

William Shakespeare, *Poems,* Crowell (New York, NY), 1966.

Mary O'Neill, *The White Palace,* Crowell (New York, NY), 1966.

Julie Whitney, *Bears Are Sleeping,* Scribner (New York, NY), 1967.

Beatrice Schenk de Regniers, *The Day Everybody Cried,* Viking (New York, NY), 1967.

Isaac Bashevis Singer, *The Fearsome Inn,* translated by Elizabeth Shub, Scribner (New York, NY), 1967.

The Renowned History of Little Red Riding Hood, Crowell (New York, NY), 1967.

(Translator) Thomas P. Whitney, *The Story of Prince Ivan, the Firebird, and the Gray Wolf,* Scribner (New York, NY), 1968.

The Thirteen Days of Yule, Crowell (New York, NY), 1968.

Christian Morgenstern, *The Three Sparrows and Other Nursery Rhymes,* translated by Max Knight, Scribner (New York, NY), 1968.

Esther Hautzig, *In School: Learning in Four Languages,* Macmillan (New York NY), 1969.

Theodor Fontane, *Sir Ribbeck of Ribbeck of Havelland,* translated by Elizabeth Shub, Macmillan (New York, NY), 1969.

Virginia Hamilton, *The Time-Ago Tales of Jahdu,* Macmillan (New York, NY), 1969.

James Stephens, *Deirdre,* Macmillan (New York, NY), 1970.

(Reteller) Virginia Haviland, *Favorite Fairy Tales Told in Greece,* Little, Brown (Boston, MA), 1970.

(Translator) T. P. Whitney, *Vasilia the Beautiful,* translated from the Russian, Macmillan (New York, NY), 1970.

Jacob Ludwig Karl Grimm, *About Wise Men and Simpletons: Twelve Tales from Grimm,* translated by Elizabeth Shub, Macmillan (New York, NY), 1971.

Rachel Hogrogian, *The Armenian Cookbook,* Atheneum (New York, NY), 1971.

Cheli Durán Ryan, *Paz,* Macmillan (New York, NY), 1971.

(Reteller) V. A. Tashjian, *Three Apples Fell from Heaven,* Little, Brown (Boston, MA), 1971.

David Kherdian, *Looking Over Hills,* Giligia (Aurora, OR), 1972.

One I Love, Two I Love, and Other Loving Mother Goose Rhymes, Dutton (New York, NY), 1972.

(Compiler) David Kherdian, *Visions of America: By the Poets of Our Time,* Macmillan (New York, NY), 1973.

(Editor) David Kherdian, *Poems Here and Now,* Greenwillow (New York, NY), 1976.

(Compiler) David Kherdian, *The Dog Writes on the Window with His Nose, and Other Poems,* Four Winds (New York, NY), 1977.

David Kherdian, *Country Cat, City Cat,* Four Winds (New York, NY), 1978.

Leila Ward, *I Am Eyes, Ni Macho,* Greenwillow (New York, NY), 1978.

(Translator) David Kherdian, *Pigs Never See the Stars,* Two Rivers (Aurora, OR), 1982.

Count Bobrinskoy, *Peacock from Heaven,* Two Rivers (Aurora, OR), 1983.

David Kherdian, *Right Now,* Knopf (New York, NY), 1983.

David Kherdian, *The Animal,* Knopf (New York, NY), 1984.

David Kherdian, *Root River Run,* Carolrhoda (Minneapolis, MN), 1984.

George MacDonald, *The Day Boy and the Night Girl,* Knopf (New York, NY), 1988.

David Kherdian, *A Song for Uncle Harry,* Philomel (New York, NY), 1989.

David Kherdian, *The Cat's Midsummer Jamboree,* Philomel (New York, NY), 1990.

David Kherdian, *The Great Fishing Contest,* Philomel (New York, NY), 1991.

Rumer Godden, *Candy Floss,* Philomel (New York, NY), 1991.

David Kherdian, *Asking the River,* Orchard Books (New York, NY), 1993.

(Reteller), David Kherdian, *Feathers & Tails: Animal Fables from around the World,* Philomel (New York, NY), 1992.

David Kherdian, *Juna's Journey,* Philomel (New York, NY), 1993.

David Kherdian, *By Myself,* Holt (New York, NY), 1993.

David Kherdian, *Lullaby for Emily,* Holt (New York, NY), 1995.

David Kherdian, *The Golden Bracelet,* Holiday House (New York, NY), 1998.

Autobiography Feature

(John) Thacher Hurd

1949-

Imagine a yellow clapboard house just outside a tiny village in northern Vermont. It is below the town road, in a hollow that is a hay field six or eight acres in size. From the field you can see Mount Philo not more than a mile away, and from the top of Mount Philo you can see Lake Champlain, and across the lake, the Adirondacks.

The house sits at the end of a winding driveway. A sprawling lawn goes all the way around, and in summer a vegetable garden blooms on the southern side. In fall the vegetables are harvested and canned, or frozen in a big freezer. The barn, attached directly to the house, has a cupola on top with a big bell from an abandoned schoolhouse.

From the porch the lawn slopes gently down to the banks of a river. It is not a big river, but bigger than a stream. The water in the river flows over granite worn smooth through the eons. Here and there are deep depressions in the smooth granite. Some are just the size of a bathtub and so are called by that name. The boy who lives there loves to swim and play in those bathtubs. The river is gentle and shallow and he is safe there under the watchful eye of his mother. There is a little bench and a table overlooking the river, a place to rest after swimming, or have a picnic on a hot summer day with his parents' friends, who have come up from the big city to talk about art and books. On summer nights there are fireflies in profusion lighting up the dark. The boy sometimes collects them in jars and puts them by his bed for a light as he goes to sleep.

That boy, of course, is me, growing up in Vermont until I was five. I was deeply attached to that house, and I still think of it as my primal home. Its textures and sensations are the deepest in my memory: Running on the lawn in summer, filled with happiness, down towards the river. Or playing in the attic of the barn, discovering treasures hidden there. Life was full of wonders: the fireflies in summer, thunderstorms at night (which terrified me), and visits to the feed store down the road, with its rich smells of corn and other grains.

The house was sturdy but dilapidated, rescued in the depths of the Depression by my father, the illustrator Clement Hurd. Slowly he fixed up the house, putting in electricity and running water, and wide pine boards on the walls in the living room, and papering the walls of the bathroom with proofs of the book he illustrated for Gertrude Stein, called *The World Is Round*.

My parents married in 1939. They had met in New York through mutual friends, my father living in New York working as a freelance illustrator, and my mother already writing children's books and teaching elementary school. After they were married they lived in North Ferrisburg for the next fifteen years.

On the hill above the house there was a small studio, an old building that Clem brought on a truck and placed on a stone foundation. I loved to climb up the hill to the studio, just to sit in the atmosphere of art being made, to smell the smells of paint, to play with the brushes, and to look at the old paintings that Clem collected. This was where he created the pictures for the children's books he and my mother, Edith Thacher Hurd (we called her Posey), created, my mother doing the writing and my father the illustrating.

I think it was out of these experiences as a child, being around my father's studio and inhaling the flavors of his work, that I became an artist myself. It was like growing up with parents who were immersed in music; art was everywhere, and my parents lived lives that were deeply creative.

My parents were friends with Margaret Wise Brown, with whom they both collaborated on books. My father illustrated several of her best books, including *Goodnight Moon* and *The Runaway Bunny,* and my mother co-authored several wonderful, funny Little Golden Books with Margaret, such as *Five Little Firemen* and *Two Little Miners* (the first book Richard Scarry illustrated).

Brownie, as she was called, would arrive at our house in Vermont wrapped in fur, in a big convertible with the top down, with her dog in the back. They would settle in for a weekend of work on books. My father said that if he was working with Brownie, Posey would be the peacemaker; if Posey was working with her, Clem was the mediator. Brownie was intense to work with and could be demanding, but she always got the best out of those she worked with.

She could also be wonderfully ridiculous. One of the photos in this essay shows Brownie holding up a small terrier. The caption in the original photo album says: "Brownie holding Nothing." My mother and Brownie had decided to name a dog Nothing just to see "what psychological effect the name Nothing would have on a dog." Poor creature.

When I was two my parents and I went to visit Brownie at her isolated house ("The Only House"), on the island of Vinalhaven off the coast of Maine. Although I was too young to remember, my parents have told me that it was a tumultuous weekend. Brownie's house was only accessible by water, and she proposed to meet my parents in the middle of Penobscot Bay, us on the ferry to North Haven and Brownie in her sailboat. Brownie assured my parents that the ferry would stop in the middle of the bay, but of course the captain of the ferry had never heard of such a thing, and only agreed at the last minute to stop in the midst of the bay, while I, only two, was handed over the railing and down to Brownie in her tippy sailboat. That night in her little house she prepared an exotic dinner for me. I don't know what was in it, probably a lobster. I loudly rejected it and cried for mush. After dinner I was led to a bedroom which Brownie had furnished all in fur, with a fur bedspread and a bearskin on the floor, jaws wide open. This was too much for a two-year-old, and I burst into tears and was instead tucked into my parents bed.

One of my most treasured possessions is the photograph shown as part of this essay, of Brownie pushing me through the snow in Vermont, both of us wrapped in fur; echoes of her book *The Little Fur Family,* one of my favorites.

Another of my favorites by her is *Sailor Dog,* illustrated by Garth Williams, one of the earliest books I remember from my childhood and still an inspiration to me as I create my own books. It begins: "Born at sea in the teeth of a gale, the sailor was a dog. Scuppers was his name." I have always been entranced with that opening. It gives a tremendous sense of adventure right from the first line, and Garth Williams' illustration is no less dramatic, showing Sailor Dog at the prow of his little sailboat looking bravely into a howling gale. I used the same word pattern in the opening of one of my own books, *Hobo Dog,* published in 1980. The book begins: "Born in a boxcar rolling west, the drifter was a dog, Hobo was his name." My story is of course different from *Sailor Dog,* but I wrote it as an homage to Brownie's book.

In 1986, our family went back to visit the house in North Ferrisburgh, still owned by the woman who had bought it from my parents in 1954. We found it almost unchanged. The bathroom was still wallpapered with proofs of *The World Is Round.* In the hall landing we found first proofs of *Goodnight Moon* covering the walls, and a painting of my father's from *The Little Brass Band* still hung on the bedroom wall. The same curtains hung on the windows and the lawn still sloped down to the river with its bathtubs. We were hypnotized by the experience, and it brought back many deep memories.

My mother wrote more than seventy-five books, from picture books for the youngest child to nonfiction for teenagers. She had a strong sense of rhythm and flow in a story. She loved to read out loud and would seem to hypnotize herself (and me) with the cadences of what she was reading to me as a child. I would sit in bed and she would sit next to it, reading a book she had written, or a Little Golden Book, or *Treasure Island* or *Robin Hood.* It was a very traditional way of reading, flowing out of her with a steady pace. It had a kind of majesty to it, a gravity that would occasionally be punctured by her sense of humor. As a child I couldn't help but be caught in the spell of her reading. She influenced how I write, and how important rhythm is to my own writing.

Once when I was about five or six I painted a still life on construction paper at school. It was all bright colors, oranges and blues and deep blacks. I brought it home and my parents admired it greatly. But then my mother went one step further and got my father to frame it and hang it in our kitchen in a big heavy frame. This amazed me. I was just a kid, and I knew that my picture was nowhere near the level of my father's art. But my parents gave me such a feeling of confidence with that gesture.

When I started on my own writing career, I was hesitant to show my work to my mother. But she was very open to teaching me. She helped me with my first three or four books, until eventually I worked on my own. She would never lecture, but she would show me directly how a children's picture book worked: how important the turning of each page was, how important the characters were, and especially how important the rhythms of the language were. Through her I began to realize the subtleties of writing a book for small children.

When it was time for me to go to kindergarten, in 1954, we moved to California. My parents were tired of the bitterly cold winters in northern Vermont, and the one-room schoolhouse in North Ferrisburg left much to be desired. I think they were also very much affected by the death of Margaret Wise Brown, who had died suddenly in 1952 after an operation in France. I think that Brownie had been a focus for many of the illustrators and writers who worked with her, a center of creativity for many people involved in children's books. Now that center was gone. My parents wanted to move on to something new.

Thacher Hurd

Thacher with his parents, eminent children's author/illustrator team, Clement and Edith Thacher Hurd.

So my father packed everything into an old pickup and he and a friend drove across the country, while my mother and I flew. We settled in Mill Valley, a town just across the Golden Gate Bridge from San Francisco. That was where I really grew up, though our family kept the connection to Vermont. Every summer we return to a farm that my father bought in 1950, not far from our original house in North Ferrisburgh.

In Mill Valley we lived on the side of Mount Tamalpais in a ranch house in the woods. Mill Valley was an odd kind of suburbia in those days, a town of steep canyons with tall redwood trees and rushing streams in the winter, and lots of fog in the summer. In some ways it felt like a typical American suburb, but a suburb filled with artists and oddballs. Our next door neighbor's wife drank twenty cups of coffee a day and vacuumed the house every day, and lived a typical suburban life, except that her husband was the ex-champion boxer of Burma and used to give his son and me boxing lessons in his living room. I would go over to their house for a delicious sandwich of white bread, margarine, and white sugar. My parents wouldn't think of eating white bread or margarine, so for me it was a delicious forbidden treat.

Up the street lived Red Valens and his wife Win and their four children. Red was a writer and a good friend of my father's. One never knew what Red might be up to, always looking dashing in his convertible Mustang, tearing around the narrow winding lanes of our neighborhood in a jaunty tweed cap. He used to irritate my father by calling up and putting on strange, incomprehensible accents, pretending to be people he wasn't. I remember one Halloween when he got all the neighborhood children to come to his house. He read Edgar Allen Poe out loud to us in the dark, all the while passing around peeled grapes,

which he told us were eyeballs, and other slimy items. All deliciously terrifying for an eight-year-old.

My parents had a large circle of friends, many of whom were artists and writers. The children's book author Don Freeman, the creator of *Corduroy* and other wonderful books, was a frequent visitor. Don would arrive for a party dressed like an artist: dark blue overcoat, beret on his large head, carrying a trumpet in its case. He was a large man who loved to talk and act the part of the artist. I was enthralled with him. If he grew bored with the conversation at the party, he would go out on the deck and pull out his trumpet and play into the night, romantic ballads and cool jazz. His books *Norman the Doorman* and *Pet of the Met* are still among my favorites.

My mother had insisted when we moved to California that my father buy a new house—not a fixer-upper, as my parents had spent the last fifteen years in the creative chaos of fixing up their house in Vermont. My father loved to fix up houses. It was another creative outlet for him.

And so our house in Mill Valley was a newly built tract home in the hills, surrounded by trees. I loved the neighborhood and played with a group of kids from our street. We played baseball every afternoon in an improvised field at the junction of two mountain streets, barely big enough for a game. At the edge of the road the hill fell away sharply, and a foul ball was sure to be lost into the redwoods and down the steep mountainside. We learned to buy the cheapest baseballs, as we never kept any ball for long. We played until dark or until there weren't enough kids left for a game.

Being an only child, I of course spent much time alone.

I was sickly with asthma, especially during the winter months. I remember a lot of rainy winter days alone in my room at home. I loved being alone in some ways, and could keep myself occupied with reading or making forts and playing with tin soldiers, but I also think I was lonely much of the time, though I hardly realized it at the time.

I loved to go to Clem's studio in California and watch him work. His work table was made from an old door on top of two sawhorses, his chair was a vinyl fifties model, though he seldom actually sat in it, preferring to stand as he worked. All around were piles of rice paper, driftwood, block printing ink rolled out on sheets of plate glass, dummies, and drawings in profusion. The smell of inks and paints and papers filled the room.

In the middle of it all stood Clem at his table, his hands covered with ink, muttering a tuneless tune, his mind absorbed in the rhythms of working, trying a print over and over until he got it just the way he wanted it. He would give me my own paints and paper, and I would sit on the floor painting, cozy and content in that well-ordered confusion. Out of the corner of my eye I could watch Clem working, never hurrying or looking for the easy way through a picture, but exploring each idea with deliberate steadiness.

His art seemed to grow out of his sense of touch, a feel for the materials he was working with, his strong hands roaming across a piece of driftwood or a branch of eucalyptus leaves he was about to use in a wood-block print.

There was quiet intensity in his studio as the sun streamed in and music poured from a battered old radio. I loved to sit in that atmosphere and watch Clem work.

He was an extraordinary teacher for he never gave me the sense he was teaching at all. And yet I learned much about how a picture book is put together from him. He quietly went about doing what he was doing, and if I peered over his shoulder that was fine with him. He wouldn't say, "This is the way to do it," but rather: "What do you think about this?" or "Do you like this idea?", and then he would actually listen to what I was saying. When I was about seventeen, he gave me a book that my mother had written, *Catfish,* and suggested that I try illustrating it even though I had no formal education in art and no drawing experience other than hanging around his studio. He showed me how to make a dummy, a mock-up of a picture book. I put together the pages and then struggled to make drawings that looked like something recognizable. Though I could hardly draw at all, I enjoyed the process, and began to think up weird costumes and poses for the characters in *Catfish.*

Slowly I plugged away at the dummy. This was my first experience of actually trying to create a picture book. I started with lots of energy, but when the going got rough I shied away, and never could finish that first dummy. I showed my meager efforts to Clem, shyly. He nodded approval, and I think even sent the unfinished dummy to his publisher Harper & Row, and asked them to let me do the illustrations. They politely declined, and told Clem that he should definitely do the pictures. That he did, but in the course of illustrating *Catfish* he used several of the wackier ideas I had put in my dummy.

It was another ten years before my first book was published, but with that gesture Clem had made me feel as if I could do picture books someday.

My mother also involved me in making books from a young age. She would try out books on me, and once asked me when I was about 8 what I thought the worst thing to call someone was. I replied that the worst thing to call someone was a GREEN PIG. She duly noted it and later named their next book *Last One Home Is a Green Pig.* When I was 16 she showed me a book she was working on called *Little Dog Dreaming.* She asked me for my thoughts on it, and I ended up working so much with her on it that she included me as a co-author on the finished book, though I must admit I have completely forgotten what I actually contributed to the book.

When it was time for me to go to high school I once again went East, to a small coed boarding school in southern Vermont, the Putney School. A hard journey for a shy thirteen-year-old. But after the first year I began to enjoy life in the hills of Vermont. I loved to ski, and I loved the radical quality of Putney life. Interesting people sent their kids there, and artists, writers, and musicians often came to speak or perform. My eyes were opened to a new world of the arts, and I grew to appreciate a whole new world of creativity. Though I didn't become interested in art until later, and I think actually avoided it in my high school years, I felt fortunate to be enriched by the experience of Putney. I never did well academically there, and my parents tore their hair out every time my report card came, but the experience was full with creativity. Rudolf Serkin once came to play a concert at the school, in the dining hall, and I sat just behind him, mesmerized by his stubby hands at the keyboard, producing sounds from another world. My own musical abilities were slim, but I took up the guitar my freshman year, and by my junior year I was playing in a band. We were raucous and unruly and I loved it.

After I graduated from high school I went to the University of California at Berkeley, where I intended to be an English major. I diligently took the intro writing classes, and wrote maudlin "deep" stuff. I moved out of my parents' house in Mill Valley and into a funky apartment with a friend, Darius.

Not too long after I moved away from home, I found myself sitting in English class one day, doodling intensely. I realized as the teacher droned on that I was more interested in the doodles than in what the teacher was saying. A light switched on in my brain: ART. I enrolled in an introductory class, charcoal drawing. The still lifes we were supposed to draw were dull and uninteresting, but I immediately found myself caught up in the process. I would get lost in the picture I was working on, and time seemed to take on a new dimension. A whole new world opened up to me: the visual universe. All the art and creativity I had been absorbing from my parents and their friends started to flow out of me. I needed distance from them to allow it to happen. But at last I had found a creative outlet that was completely absorbing.

The next year I transferred from UC-Berkeley to the California College of Arts and Crafts, down the street in Oakland, and plunged full-time into making art. I had no thought at the time of illustrating books; I just wanted to make art and to learn as much as I could. I was happiest in the life-drawing classes. I used very classical drawing mediums, red chalk and charcoal, and I tried as best I could to learn to draw in a classical style. My painting style had started with modern art and geometrical abstractions, and I slowly moved backward through art history, until by my junior year I was studying the paintings of the seventeenth-century Dutch master Jan Vermeer. I learned how to grind my own paints, studied early methods of glazing or painting in layers, and set out to paint realistic still lifes. At the same time that I was doing very classical work, I was

The family farm in Vermont "where we spent summers."

also taking an etching class in which I was doing free, un-classical pictures, more in the style of cartoons than anything else. My teachers were baffled that the same person was on the one hand doing realistic work, and on the other loose, floppy, childlike drawings. At the time I just went ahead and did it. Only later did I realize that I was slowly moving towards the imaginative work of creating children's picture books.

After I graduated from art school, I set about being an "artist." What kind of artist I didn't know. I took a class in color that was taught at a local junior college, based on the color work of the painter Josef Albers, and it opened my eyes wide to the possibilities of color and color combining. I began to see that color could be a way to express emotion, and I began to use more intense colors and color juxtapositions in my art.

I spent a summer learning carpentry and building myself a studio in the back woods of our place in Vermont. I oriented it so that the windows would cast even, cool northern light on the still lifes I planned to paint. But by the time the studio was finished, in the fall of 1972, my mind had gone on to other things. I felt inside that there was something missing from what I was doing in my art, and I couldn't quite figure out what it was. I was doing very restrained, classical pictures, and a year after I graduated from school I had a show at a small gallery in Vermont. I invited a couple who were close friends to choose any of the pictures they liked as a present. They looked at the show, and thought it over, and in an amazing bit of honesty that I will never forget, they said that they didn't want any of the pictures. At first I was hurt, but then they said something interesting: "We just don't see you in these pictures, Thacher. The Thacher we know, with his humorous way of looking at things, isn't there in these quiet pictures." That certainly made me ponder where I was going with art. And made me realize that I needed to bring myself to what I was doing, all of myself, not just a certain technical skill.

Soon after that I started to work on an idea for a children's book. It seemed like the natural thing to do. It was called *Jason's House*, and I labored mightily on that book. I had gotten the idea in my head that the pictures in a children's book needed to be drawn in pen and ink, with a lot of detailed cross-hatching (like Maurice Sendak's early work), not noticing that the story needed a different kind of illustration altogether. My parents' agent, Marilyn Marlow, took the book on and tried valiantly to sell it, sending it to many publishers with no success. And rightly so, I'm afraid. Next, I tackled the idea of writing fairy tales, with syrupy morals attached. I showed them to Marilyn, and she looked them over and said, tactfully: "Maybe you should hold on to these for a while." Good advice. Marilyn has been my agent ever since, and her good advice and thoughtful words have always been a part of creating books for me. I think of her as a friend, and someone who has helped me enormously in my career.

My lack of success discouraged me, so I turned to carpentry to make my living. I bought a pickup truck and had a rubber stamp made that said: "Thacher Hurd, Carpenter." I did remodeling and odd jobs. I enjoyed learning the craft, and seeing something created out of

wood, but I kept feeling drawn to art. I was living in a little cabin high on Mount Tamalpais in Mill Valley at the time, and I had an old chair in my living room, a chair I had owned since college. One spring day I decided that the old chair was old and decrepit enough, and it was time to throw it away. So I took it to the dump on the top of my car and I left it there. But as I drove away I looked back. I saw the old chair sitting there and realized that I had grown attached to it without even knowing it. I didn't go back to save it, but I did think about that chair a lot, and I began to wonder if I might create a book out of something from my own life. I slowly began to work on a book about a boy's attachment to a chair, and what he does about it when his parents want to throw it away. The drawings were difficult for me, and awkward, but the story seemed to have an emotional center that I hadn't found before in my writing. Instead of writing about something "made-up" or imaginary, I was writing about an experience I'd had, and this gave the writing a new sense of grounding and aliveness.

I had been introduced by Marilyn Marlow to Susan Hirschman, the wonderful founder and editor at Greenwillow Books in New York, and so I sent the rough dummy to her. To my amazement she accepted it. I was astonished and thrilled. But then the real work began, as it often does. She thought the story was fine as it was, but the awkward

Baby Thacher in his carriage pushed by Margaret Wise Brown, author and family friend.

illustrations weren't ready for publication. She asked me would I do the dummy over again? Of course I would, and so I did a new dummy with new illustrations, and sent it to her. Shortly thereafter she called me and said she thought the pictures were coming along well, but would I have another try and do a new dummy? And so it went on for about six or seven versions of the book. Each time Susan would be supportive and encouraging, but each time she wanted me to give it another try. And to the end she stayed positive, though *The Old Chair* never amounted to much, quickly sinking after a season or two. But I had learned a lot by having to redo the book over and over.

My next book, *The Quiet Evening*, was another experience altogether. I was very much influenced by Margaret Wise Brown's books at the time, and I think unconsciously I wanted the book to be another *Goodnight Moon,* which my father had illustrated. Of course nothing can approach that book in its subtlety or mystery, but I was innocent enough to try. The words for *The Quiet Evening* came to me day by day, as if they were being parceled out by my subconscious, and all I had to do was to show up at breakfast and the next installment would appear. It was a strange, almost mystical experience and one that has never really been repeated for me, except with the book *Little Mouse's Big Valentine,* which also seemed to fall out with little effort. The pictures for *The Quiet Evening* were also a new experience for me; they fulfilled a desire to bring all that I had learned about color into a picture book.

Susan gave me little direction on this book, in contrast to *The Old Chair.* It was a more complete and fully realized book, and the illustrations seemed richer and fuller.

I began to move away from the influence of my parents. I felt drawn to creating picture book adventures, as exciting and thrilling as possible. The books I remember most from my own childhood have always been adventures. Among my favorites were the Scribner's Classics illustrated by N. C. Wyeth. I loved the excitement of discovering the Wyeth illustrations in the midst of the text, beautifully lit figures on a dashing mission in the night, or archers in the trees of Sherwood forest.

My first try at adventure was *Hobo Dog,* the book I wrote as an homage to Margaret Wise Brown, and then came my first urban adventure, *Axle the Freeway Cat,* which was published by Harper in 1981. It was my attempt to bring a sense of coziness to the big city, and an adventure to the freeway. Axle is a cat who creates a cozy home for himself under the rush of the freeway, but longs for some companionship in the big lonely world of the city. I began to be more confident in my illustrations, though they still seemed awkward to me. In those days illustrations were often done as "preseparated" artwork, with the artist having to create separate pictures for each of the colors in the book. If the colors in a book were to be red, blue, and yellow, one created pictures in black and white for each of those colors. Since the art was done in black and white, one could not see exactly what the colors were going to look like in the finished book, but had to visualize them through the use of special color charts. An exhausting process, but it could also produce interesting, unexpected results. Now books are produced using full color process, which allows one to work in any colors or medium.

Illustration from Axle the Freeway Cat *written and illustrated by Thacher Hurd, published by Harper, 1981.*

In 1976, Olivia Scott and I were married in Vermont. We had been friends for many years, having first met at the California College of Arts and Crafts. She has been my friend, companion, fellow traveler on life's many twists and turns, as well as an astute and caring critic of my work in progress. I always show her whatever I'm working on, and though I don't always agree with her suggestions, I deeply trust her intuitive instincts in looking at children's books. Our older son Manton was born in 1977 and our younger son Nicholas in 1982. It has been a joy to have children in our lives, to see them grow and explore the world around them. People sometimes ask me: "Are you inspired by your children? Do you get ideas from them?" The answer is not simple, because my children are an inspiration to me in many ways, but I think that the books come from something inside me, some inner place of creativity. But I often learned from watching my children read, and observing which books interested them, and which bored them.

Mystery on the Docks came after *Axle* and was my first mystery. I have always loved the old Humphrey Bogart and Jimmy Cagney movies of the '30s and '40s, but the plots baffle me; I can never quite figure out who double-crossed whom. *Mystery on the Docks* was my attempt to write a *noir* children's book (with an understandable plot). The book came to me first as a mood, a vague feeling in the back of my mind. Not a definite plot or character, but just a feeling of the docks at night, the fog rolling in, foghorns blowing. Slowly the character of Ralph, who owns the diner on Pier 36, began to emerge. I imagined Ralph singing to himself in his diner; from that I came to the idea that Ralph played the accordion and loved opera. Ralph's favorite opera singer, Eduardo Bombasto, is kidnapped by

Illustration from **Mystery on the Docks** *written and illustrated by Thacher Hurd, published by HarperCollins, 1983.*

Big Al and his nasty gang of rats, and Ralph gets involved in the mystery that follows. I was working on it one day with Robert Warren, my editor, when one of us, I don't remember which, had the idea to put a question at the end of certain key pages in the book. For example, on the left page it reads:

"Hey, come back here!" Ralph yelled. "Pay up!"

But the pier was empty.

Then on the right hand page:

Or was it?

It was a simple device to lead a child to turn the page and give a sense of suspense to the book. An important part of creating a picture book is the building of suspense from page to page, for to children each page is its own world.

The drawings for *Mystery on the Docks* were also done as preseparated artwork, which was difficult, but I loved drawing rats as gangsters and wharfside lowlifes. I was pleased when it was chosen to be a featured book on the *Reading Rainbow* television program, and loved the dramatic reading by Raul Julia.

Then came *Mama Don't Allow,* a book that came out of my love for music.

After high school I had played in a rock band called the New Tokaloma Swamp Band. It was probably one of the world's worst bands, but it was the '60s and everybody wanted to play in a band. I played guitar loudly and wildly, with little concern for measures, beginnings, or endings of songs. I loved to blast away with the volume on ten, though I would get lost in the music and often miss my cues. It wasn't really my strength, but I've always loved playing music, and consider myself a frustrated musician. So it's natural that music creeps into my books, and I try to make them as rhythmic as possible. For me, rhythm is the basis of writing, and the key to what makes a book work. The rhythm of a text is the rhythm of the book as a whole, what makes it come alive.

Mama Don't Allow grew out of the traditional song of the same name, a jug band tune that has been recorded by all kinds of artists, including Doc Watson and George Lewis, the New Orleans jazz clarinetist. I first heard the song on KPFA, our local listener-sponsored radio station in Berkeley. It was the theme song for a jazz and folk music program, and that first version I heard on the radio was squawky and free form, a chance for all the musicians in a group to play a solo. Although I had never been to New Orleans, the song made me think of jazz bands on hot nights and alligators on the bayou. I couldn't get the idea of the song out of my head; it seemed like the perfect rebellion for a four-year-old. What child wouldn't love to yell out, "Mama don't allow no music playing 'round here! We don't care what mama don't allow, we're gonna play that music anyhow!"

Soon I started working on the story. First, I needed a band, a band of swamp creatures: a bird, a lizard, and a mouse with a bowler hat on his head, and a possum named Miles who played the saxophone. Recalling my band in the '60s, I called it the Swamp Band. The first two pages came easily: "Miles got a saxophone for his birthday." (His mother says: "Oh, how nice!") Then turn the page and: "SQUAWK!" a picture of Miles playing the saxophone very loudly and his mother and father recoiling in horror: "Oh, how awful!" I knew that the band would be called the Swamp Band in homage to my teenage band and that the story had something to do with hungry alligators, but the rest was a jumble. Would the band play for the alligators? Would the alligators eat the band? My story quickly deteriorated into chaos. I worked enthusiastically on the story, tantalized by the energy of the idea, but completely unable to fit the pieces together. Alligators! Swamp Band! Music! Bayous! Everything was there, but nothing would come together. I worked on the story for two months, and finally gave up in frustration. I put the book away, figuring that it probably just wasn't meant to be. We were struggling to get by at that time, so I went back to being a carpenter, and spent the next year building a house, which at the time seemed a lot more straightforward than writing children's books. After a year of lifting plywood and digging foundations my back gave out and I got sick of pounding nails. Carpentry lost its charm. Books once again seemed like a better path.

I had committed to doing a second book about Hobo Dog (*Hobo Dog's Christmas Tree*), which I worked on next, but more importantly I wanted to get back to *Mama Don't Allow.*

I took the dummy out of the drawer and looked at it. It was still a jumble, but somehow the book had worked itself out in the back of my mind while I was nailing shingles and pulling electrical wire through walls. It fell into place, and I was thrilled. I started to create a new dummy, with rough illustrations, a small, sedate version of the book. But then I came to the page where the alligators dance, and the words seemed to be crying out for big colorful pictures. I threw away my small sedate dummy and started over with a big dummy. I began in the heart of the book and worked my way outward, bringing the rest of the book into the same loud style of illustration. The gooier, the gloppier, the thicker the paint the better.

I zoomed through it, more enthusiastic than I had been about any other book. It was bigger and bolder than anything I had done before, and I was pushing color to a brighter level. When it was finished it was wild, and I rushed it into the mail, confident and happy. Surely someone would buy it. But it wasn't yet to be. The book was sent to two or three publishers, but no one liked it. Either it was too loud or the pictures were too crude or the editor was worried that no one knew the song.

I was thoroughly discouraged. Again, I put the book away, and went back to working on other books. But after a few months I started taking the rough dummy with me to school visits, and I discovered that kids loved it, even when I read from a very rough version. I loved reading it to them. It was the first book (and maybe the only one of mine) that I could read to a group of first graders and have them get completely out of hand, laughing and stomping their feet and generally sympathizing with Miles and his Swamp Band. Teachers sometimes felt that they had to step in and restore order, and would even sit facing the students to make sure they didn't step out of line. But I never felt that I couldn't bring them back from the edge of chaos.

I visited a school in Sacramento, and as usual read *Mama Don't Allow* to the students, and as usual they responded with enthusiasm. They asked me when the book would be published and I told them that I hadn't yet found a publisher for it. Unbeknownst to me, the fifth graders at the school later wrote letters to a publisher they thought was my publisher, saying that they thought *Mama Don't Allow* was a good book, and why hadn't they published it yet? Unfortunately they sent the letters to a publisher I wasn't intending to send the book to. Eventually, though, *Mama Don't Allow* found a home at Harper, thanks to Robert Warren, who by then had become my regular editor. I spent a year revising the book, and then five months doing the final artwork. For me, looking back on it now, the finished book looks a little too finished, more polished than my original rough version, and lacking the wild abandon of the original. But the book has continued to find new readers and is probably my best known book. I still love to read it

Wife Olivia stands behind the seated three: father Clem, mother "Posey," and author himself about 1984.

to a raucous group of first graders.

In 1983 Olivia and I started Peaceable Kingdom Press as a way to augment my income from creating books. We started in the back bedroom of our house in Berkeley, and our first product was a poster from my father's illustrations for *Goodnight Moon.* We had mentioned to Clem that we wanted to start publishing posters from children's books, and *Goodnight Moon* would be wonderful to have as our first poster. Before we knew it, Clem arrived on our doorstep in Berkeley with 1000 posters he had had printed. With a smile he offered them to us, and we were off. Soon we had published posters by Maurice Sendak and Chris Van Allsburg and William Steig. We packed posters for shipping in our garage and soon found that we were running out of room both for posters and for the people we hired to work in the company, and so we moved to larger quarters. As time went by, Olivia took over the running of the business, and I continued to do books. I helped out with the computers and other odd jobs. And we always spent much of our time together in the kitchen talking about the ins and outs of the business. By the mid-'80s we had added greeting cards to our line. We loved getting to know many of the illustrators we worked with, artists such as Aliki, Jane Dyer, James Marshall, Rosemary Wells, and Kevin Henkes, among many others who have enriched our lives.

My connection with Vermont appeared in my next book, *The Pea Patch Jig,* which came out in 1986. I was going to illustrate a version of the Uncle Remus stories, a project which eventually fell through, but a song that was going to be included in that book kept rattling around in my head. An old fiddle tune called "The Pea Patch Jig," it was rediscovered by the incomparable musician John Hartford. I kept thinking about it, and created a story which grew out of that title, about Baby Mouse and the mouse family who live in Farmer Clem's garden in the hills of Vermont. Farmer Clem doesn't quite know they are there, but he and they are both a part of the garden. The first page is a picture of our place in Vermont, and the next shows Farmer Clem, looking a lot like my father, working in his garden. It was

the first time I had mixed animal characters with people, and real people with an imaginary story, and somehow it all came together. The book ends on a festive note, with the mouse family dancing the Pea Patch Jig under the midsummer moon. Baby Mouse and her family figured in two other books that came out a few years later, *Blackberry Ramble* and *Tomato Soup.* Usually I don't like to write books in series, as I always feel that the succeeding books are weaker than the first, but Baby Mouse and her mischief cried out for sequels. In *Blackberry Ramble* I worked in Dr. Wainer (changed into a mouse), the country doctor who delivered me in Vermont.

My next book was a slightly different project, a swamp book that involved "paper engineering." I had become fascinated with pop-up books, and began to buy them and take them apart just to see how they worked. The floor of my studio was covered with tiny bits of papers as I cut and pasted endlessly, experimenting with different angles and folds to get creatures to stand up, move, wiggle, and open their jaws. The book I created was *A Night in the Swamp,* a "moveable book" with frogs, rats, alligators, and turtles in a nonsensical story that is really just an excuse for them to move around. When it came time for the book to be printed, my editor Robert called me and said: "The book is being printed in Colombia, and either you or I have to oversee it. I'm not going because last time I went to Colombia I was almost kidnapped!" Robert then told me a hair-raising story of crime in Bogotá, reassuring me at the end: "But don't worry, Thacher, you're going to Cali, and that's much safer." And so I went to Colombia and had a fascinating time seeing how they create pop-up books, which are put together by hand, each piece glued together individually . . . and didn't get kidnapped.

Little Mouse's Big Valentine, published in 1990, was one of the more straightforward books I have worked on, and it was inspired by a small valentine that I made for Olivia one year. The card was a picture of a tiny mouse carrying a big paper valentine, looking forlorn and in need of someone to give it to. I don't remember what the card said on the inside, but one day a few years later I happened to come across the card in a box of pictures. It stuck in my mind and within a few weeks the story just fell out, completely formed. My books seldom happen like that, but *Little Mouse* was a joy to find, and a book that had a very personal meaning for me.

More recently has come *Art Dog,* another book that had a long gestation period. I have come to realize that for me, books that take a long time often come out better. So I just let the books take their course and give them as much time as they need. My publisher has given up giving me deadlines.

Art Dog, oddly, started out as a completely different book. I began in the early '90s to write a book that was about frogs in a pond singing an opera. Slowly I worked on the book, putting it away for months at a time while I worked on other projects. Each time I took it out to work on it, it evolved and transmutated a little, passing through many stages as the story changed and drifted away from the original idea. But I kept working on it, feeling that it was evolving into something that would eventually work. After

Arthur Dog was a guard at the Dogopolis Museum of Art. He liked his job.

Illustration from **Art Dog,** *written and illustrated by* **Thacher Hurd,** *published by HarperCollins, 1996.*

Hurd with his wife, Olivia, at Peaceable Kingdom Press, about 1997.

I had been working on the book sporadically for a few years, I decided that I should create a dummy and move closer to a finished story. By this time the frogs and the pond and the opera were all gone; it had mutated into *Ultra Dog.*

It was a story about a dog singer named Carmen Riviera, Bad Mutt, the president of Bow-Wow Bits Dogfood company, and Biff, the ordinary dog. Biff could turn into Ultra Dog, "a canine of extraordinary abilities." I labored hard on the dummy, creating full-color pictures for the first half of the book. But I couldn't seem to get the second half right, which is always a bad sign. Children's books are easy to begin and hard to finish. I showed the dummy to Olivia and read it to her, and she was not enthusiastic, which bothered me at the time, but I knew that she was right. I put the book away again, and forgot about it. Then one day I was driving down the freeway when suddenly the thought came to me: "What is Ultra backwards?" I thought, "ART!!", and in a flash I realized that the book should be about Art Dog, an adventure based on art and its visual richness. I rewrote it, and set the action in a museum with art thieves and a daring rescue by Art Dog. I did several dummies to further refine the direction of the book. Like a hound dog, I knew I was close on the trail of the book I had been looking for all that time, but there were still a few more steps. I showed the book to a friend, and she suggested that Art Dog needed a place to live and a job and a life, so I added that at the beginning of the book—it made all the difference. Working with my editor Robert Warren further clarified and refined it, and then I started

the process of creating the illustrations. I spent a long time collecting postcards and pictures of famous masterworks. I would take them into my studio and try to turn them into "dog" masterpieces. Some of them easily fell into place, and others didn't seem to work and were discarded. Slowly I collected the pictures I wanted, and worked them into the book, particularly in the Dogopolis Museum. Turning pictures such as Seurat's *Le Grand Jatte* into "dog" pictures was one of the most entertaining aspects of creating the book. I chose an Edward Hopper picture, *Cape Cod Morning,* for the last page in the book, but when it came time to make it into a "dog" picture I found that I had such a feeling of reverence for Hopper I couldn't do it, and so I left it as is, pretty much the only picture in the book that is left untouched.

Since *Art Dog* was published, it has been gratifying to see children's responses to the book. Often at schools I visit, the students have made their own versions of Art Dog pictures, and have transformed other masterpieces into Art Dog pictures. A friend, John LaTronica, who lives in Binghamton, New York, created a full-scale solid wood model of Art Dog's brushmobile for a show at a children's museum in Binghamton, and it was later exhibited at a show of my work at HarperCollins in New York.

HarperCollins started a new program in 1997 called Growing Tree, a series of board books for newborn through three-year-olds, and I have created two board books for that program, the first of which, *Zoom City,* came out in 1998. It is a book for one- to two-year-olds, with just seven double-page spreads, printed on heavy cardboard. For the first time I worked on the computer to do the illustrations. Using the programs Painter and Adobe Photoshop, I scanned photos of old cars and then added color, dogs, and other photos, combining it all in the computer in a kind of digital collage. I found that it took a long time to learn the programs, but once I felt comfortable working in the medium, it became like any other medium and I was able to visualize ideas without having the computer get in the way. It also loosened me up, and I felt energized by the freedom of working on the computer. The book happened quickly as I zipped through the pictures, and I was thrilled when it was chosen as one of the *New York Times* Best Illustrated Books of the Year. My son Nicholas contributed several photos he had taken for background photos. He also contributed two small painted pictures which are incorporated into a picture in *Dinosaur Chase,* a book I illustrated.

I love the bright colors one can achieve when working on the computer, and the flexibility of it. Working on paper, I am limited by the paper itself; too many corrections and layers will start to muddy the paper and produce visual mush. But the computer can save any number of versions of a picture, and one can easily go backwards in the process to earlier versions. I like to call it "pushing light," for that is all it really is, moving around tiny pixels of electronic light. More recently, the second book I have done for Growing Tree is *Cat's Pajamas.* It continues in the same vein of *Zoom City,* except that I created almost all the drawings for the book on paper in black ink, and then scanned them into the computer to add the color. I found that I could be completely free with the drawings on paper, and did many versions of each drawing. Then I would go back and choose the few that I wanted to put in the book. Instead of having to carefully construct

The author with Olivia and their sons Manton (middle) and Nicholas (far right), 2001.

each composition on paper I could play infinitely with them on the computer. But it certainly doesn't seem to go any faster just because it is on the computer; perhaps even a bit slower, as there are always a million choices to make and a million directions to go in.

For many years I visited schools frequently to talk about my books, but I do less of it nowadays; I find it breaks my concentration and I would rather be in my studio working than out on the road staying in a Motel 6. But I still enjoy visiting schools occasionally and seeing kids respond directly to books. Children are refreshingly direct: if they like a book they stay focused, if not they let you know with yawns, squirms, wanderings, and comments like: "When is this book going to be over?" Once I went to a school in northern California to do a visit. I was late, it was a hot Friday afternoon, and the whole school from kindergarten to eighth grade was packed into the auditorium, feeling restless. I started my presentation and then turned to the big pad of paper they had set up for me to draw on. I grabbed a marker and started to draw a picture from *Mystery on the Docks.* Before I was halfway through, a loud voice from the front-row kindergartners said: "Does this guy know what he's doing?" Everyone tittered and I tried to keep my composure and keep drawing. Then again the voice: "Is this guy sure he knows what he's doing?"

Where in the adult world could one find such straightforward honesty?

I think that I try to write the books that I would have liked to read when I was a child—books with strong characters and a sense of mystery. Children identify so completely with the characters they read about in books that they live through these characters and see themselves as the characters. I feel that the main character in a picture book should be strong and full of energy with a spirit of adventure and a sense of his own power to solve whatever comes his way.

A project that was a pure joy to do was *Watercolor for the Artistically Undiscovered,* for Klutz Press. John Cassidy, the head of Klutz, had suggested the idea to me. After talking it over with John I plunged into six months of watercolor play. I would work completely freely, dripping, splattering and smushing the color. Then every two weeks John and the designer, MaryEllen Podgorski, and I would go over what I had created. Our editorial meetings took place over breakfast at Bette's Oceanview Diner in Berkeley where I would lay out a pile of watercolor paper covered with splatters, drips, weird creatures, and doodles. We would look at everything and decide what might work. John let the work I brought to those meetings decide what direction the book would go in, and was always enthusiastic. It evolved in an organic way, which of course is the best way to make a book happen. We wanted it to be a watercolor instruction book that would be the opposite of most art instruction books, whose purpose seems just to show off the skill of the artist, while not encouraging the novice artist to get in there and throw paint around and have fun. The basic message of our watercolor book is that anybody can do it: nobody is lacking in the ability to enjoy themselves with watercolor.

As Peaceable Kingdom Press grew larger over the years, so did the stress of ownership. It became increasingly difficult to manage a successful, growing company. In 1997 Olivia decided to take a break, and I took over as the full-time head. This meant leaving my studio behind for the most part, and throwing myself into managing. From 1997 through 2000 I spent my time guiding the company as best I could, until in 2000 we were able to sell the company. Fortunately, the company continues as before with offices in Berkeley, but Olivia and I play a much smaller role. Our two sons Manton and Nicholas are now grown. Manton has just graduated from college and Nicholas is embarking on his college career at an art school. Another artist in the family!

Happily, I am now able to go back to the studio full-time. Though I expected to plunge right back into creating books, I have found myself in one of those creative detours that is the lifeblood of an artist. Suddenly fascinated with photography, I spend my time shooting pictures and working in a darkroom I constructed in our basement at home. I have always taken many detours in my artistic career, but I feel enriched when I come back to my primary interest, making children's books, and have learned not to worry if a detour comes along, knowing that they sometimes lead to the main route I want to take in my artistic life. I have drawers filled with story ideas; someday they will find life and become finished books. Each book comes in its own time, each book has its own life.

Writings

FOR CHILDREN

(With mother, Edith Hurd) *Little Dog Dreaming,* illustrated by father, Clement G. Hurd, Harper, 1965.

FOR CHILDREN; SELF-ILLUSTRATED

The Old Chair, Greenwillow, 1978.
The Quiet Evening, Greenwillow, 1978, reissued, 1992.
Hobo Dog, Scholastic Book Services, 1980.
Axle the Freeway Cat, Harper, 1981.
Mystery on the Docks, Harper, 1983.
Hobo Dog's Christmas Tree, Scholastic, 1983.
Mama Don't Allow, Harper, 1984.
Hobo Dog in the Ghost Town, Scholastic, 1985.
Pea Patch Jig, Crown, 1986, published with cassette, Random House/McGraw Hill, 1988, HarperCollins, 1995.
A Night in the Swamp (pop-up book), Harper, 1987.
Blackberry Ramble, Crown, 1989, HarperCollins, 1995.
Little Mouse's Big Valentine, Harper, 1990.
Tomato Soup, Crown, 1991.
(Co-author with John Cassidy) *Watercolor for the Artistically Undiscovered,* Klutz, 1992.
Little Mouse's Birthday Cake, HarperCollins, 1992.
Art Dog, HarperCollins, 1996.
Zoom City (board book), HarperCollins, 1998.
Santa Mouse and the Ratdeer, HarperCollins, 1998.
Cat's Pajamas, HarperCollins, 2001.

FOR CHILDREN; ILLUSTRATOR

Ida Luttrell, *Mattie and the Chicken Thief,* Dodd, 1988.
Dayle Ann Dodds, *Wheel Away!,* Harper, 1989.
Carolyn Otto, *Dinosaur Chase,* HarperCollins, 1991.
Leah Komaiko, *Fritzi Fox Flew in from Florida,* HarperCollins, 1995.

ADAPTATIONS

Mystery on the Docks and *Mama Don't Allow* were adapted for television and broadcast on *Reading Rainbow,* Public Broadcasting Service (PBS-TV), 1984. *Mama Don't Allow* was also broadcast on *CBS Storybreak,* Columbia Broadcasting System, Inc. (CBS-TV), 1986; was adapted for videocassette, Random House, 1988; and was adapted for a children's opera, *Muskrat Lullaby,* performed by the Los Angeles City Opera, October 6, 1989. *Art Dog* was adapted into a filmstrip by Live Oak Media in 1999. *Santa Mouse and the Ratdeer* was adapted for television by Sony Wonder and broadcast on Fox Television in 2000.

J–K

JOHNSON, Art 1946-

Personal

Born March 15, 1946, in Lowell, MA; son of Arthur V. and Bessie (Sideris) Johnson; married Juanita Roberts (a teacher), December 26, 1970; children: Alexa Britt, Candace Raven. *Education:* Tufts University, B.A., 1967; University of Massachusetts—Lowell, M.Ed., 1977; Northwestern University, C.A.G.S., 1979; Boston University, Ed.D., 1997. *Religion:* Jehovah's Witness.

Addresses

Home and office—Nipper Enterprises, Inc., 7 Steadman St., Chelmsford, MA 01824. *Agent*—Teachers Idea Press, Box 6633, Englewood, CO 80155-6633. *E-mail*—johnsonart@aol.com.

Career

Author and educator. Nashua School District, Nashua, NH, math teacher, 1967-99; Boston University, Boston, MA, visiting professor, 1999—. Consultant, New Hampshire State Department of Education, 1988-98. Speaker at conferences in the United States, Canada, and Hungary. *Member:* National Council of Teachers of Mathematics, Association of Math Teachers of New Hampshire (representative to Math Teachers in New England, 1981-90).

Awards, Honors

New Hampshire Teacher of the Year, 1992; Presidential Award, 1992, for excellence in Mathematical Teaching; Tandy Prize, 1995.

Writings

Classic Math: History Topics for the Classroom, Dale Seymour (Palo Alto, CA), 1994.
Building Up to Bubbles, Didax, 1997.
Building Geometry, Dale Seymour (Palo Alto, CA), 1997.
Geometry Tools for a Changing World, Prentice-Hall (Upper Saddle River, NJ), 1998.
Famous Problems and Their Mathematicians, Teacher Ideas Press (Englewood, CO), 1999.
(With Susan H. Chapin) *Math Matters: Understanding the Math You Teach, Grades K-6,* Math Solutions (Sausalito, CA), 2000.

Art Johnson

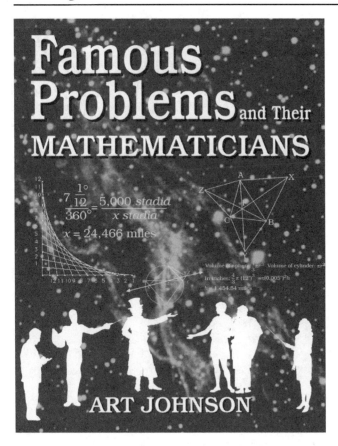

Using historical and biographical facts, Johnson shows students how to find the solutions to more than sixty commonly taught math problems, then apply their newly developed skills to everyday life.

Work in Progress

Research on proportional reasoning in adolescents.

Sidelights

Art Johnson has written several books on mathematics and its history for middle and high school students and their teachers. He told *SATA:* "When I was in elementary school I enjoyed all my school subjects, but I especially liked mathematics. The numbers and shapes obeyed specific rules and never deviated from their relationships to each other. They followed the rules, and you could depend on that. English and history were different. The rules of grammar weren't always true in the great books I read, never mind about poetry, which can seem to follow no form at all. History had a flow through time, but events didn't always turn out as they should have. There were anomalies everywhere I looked. Nothing like the beauty and elegance of mathematics.

"As I grew older I was convinced about the superiority of mathematics to English and history. There was a certain clarity to mathematics that English and history could never have. But here I am, a writer who writes about the history of mathematics, among other topics. What happened? How did I ever get to be a writer, and about mathematics history, no less?

"I think it has to do with having something to say, and being excited about it. I still find many areas of mathematics engaging, and I hope to convey that feeling to others through my writing. While not everyone is going to find mathematics compelling, I hope I can help them appreciate that mathematics matters.

"Sometimes I think I will wake up and it is all a dream. I am actually writing, and about my beloved mathematics. What could be better?"

Johnson's *Famous Problems and Their Mathematicians* presents sixty mathematical conundrums, biographical information about the mathematicians famous for solving them, and brief write-ups for classroom use that are "engaging and are quite suitable as in-class material or homework problems," according to Thomas S. Downey of *Kliatt.* Johnson was praised by reviewers for presenting a broad range of offerings, including information on male and female mathematicians, problems ranging in difficulty from the easiest (appropriate for fifth graders) to the most difficult (which may be useful in high school classrooms), and both obscure and famous problems, such as Fermat's last theorem, Goldbach's conjecture, the four-color map theorem, and Konigsberg bridges. Throughout, Johnson succeeds in sharing "the excitement and mystery of math ... and demonstrates how the discoveries can be applied to everyday situations," remarked a contributor to *Curriculum Review.* Most importantly, Downey commented that Johnson's brief mathematical summaries make it "much easier for teachers to include some interesting historical context into their classes."

Biographical and Critical Sources

PERIODICALS

Curriculum Review, March, 2000, review of *Famous Problems and Their Mathematicians,* p. 12.
Kliatt, March, 2000, Thomas S. Downey, review of *Famous Problems and Their Mathematicians,* p. 34.

* * *

KELLY, Laurene 1954-

Personal

Born December 3, 1954, in Hobart, Tasmania, Australia; daughter of Irene Stubbs Slicer. *Education:* Attended high school. *Politics:* "Environmentalist."

Addresses

Home—Tasmania, Australia. *Agent*—c/o Spinifex Press, PO Box 212, North Melbourne, Victoria 3051, Australia.

Career

Children's worker at a refuge in Sydney, Australia, 1983-87; animal caretaker in Tasmania, Australia, 1987-92; writer, 1992—.

Writings

Australia for Women, Spinifex Press (North Melbourne, Victoria, Australia), 1992.
I Started Crying Monday (young adult fiction), Spinifex Press (North Melbourne, Victoria, Australia), 1999.
The Crowded Beach, Spinifex Press (North Melbourne, Victoria, Australia), 2000.

Contributor to *Australia for Women: Travel and Culture,* edited by Susan Hawthorne and Renate Klein, Spinifex Press (North Melbourne, Victoria, Australia), 1994.

Sidelights

Laurene Kelly told *SATA:* "I spent my early childhood in Tasmania, which instilled a great love of the environment. I worked with abused children and tried to be an advocate for them. I looked after injured and orphaned wildlife. I have a commitment to the environment and would love to see the end of logging old-growth native trees for wood chips in Tasmania.

"I believe in women's rights and children's rights to live in a safe world, free of war and greed. My first political action was organizing anti-Vietnam war protests when I was at high school, and I've maintained political activism on some level ever since.

"I live near the beach, which I find a great solace. It also helps with focusing ideas."

*   *   *

KIRSHNER, David S. 1958-

Personal

Born May 26, 1958, in Winnipeg, Manitoba, Canada; son of Michael and Betty Kirshner. *Education:* University of Manitoba, B.Sc. (zoology; with honors), 1980; University of Sydney, Ph.D., 1985.

Addresses

Home—P.O. Box 1486, North Sydney, New South Wales 2060, Australia. *E-mail*—crocdoc@davidkirshner.com.

Career

Illustrator and consultant in zoology. Parks Canada, worked as a park naturalist and interpreter in the Canadian Rocky Mountains; also worked at zoos in Canada and Australia.

Illustrator

Encyclopedia of Mammals, Weldon Owen, 1990.
Encyclopedia of Birds, Weldon Owen, 1991.
Encyclopedia of Reptiles and Amphibians, Weldon Owen, 1992.
Encyclopedia of Fishes, Weldon Owen, 1994.

David S. Kirshner

My First Pocket Guide: Reptiles and Amphibians, National Geographic, 1996.
Investigate: Snakes, Random House Australia (Milsons Point, Australia), 2000.

Also illustrator of numerous other titles.

Sidelights

David S. Kirshner told *SATA:* "My fascination with animals, and with drawing them, began when I was only a few years of age. As a five-year-old boy, I loved to draw a neighbor's mounted caiman, which she had brought back from Florida as a souvenir. Although interested in all animals, reptiles have always held a particular fascination for me, possibly because there are very few species of reptiles in and around Winnipeg, Canada, where I grew up. Consequently, upon completing my honors degree in zoology at the University of Manitoba, I traveled to Australia to undertake research on Indo-Pacific crocodiles for my doctorate. After a few years spent working in zoos in Australia and Canada, and working as a park naturalist and interpreter for Parks Canada in the Canadian Rockies, I returned to Australia to live. Within a year I began to illustrate full-time, turning a former hobby into a career.

"Currently living in Sydney, Australia, I now specialize as an illustrator of wild and domestic animals of all types, both realistic and caricaturized, for advertising campaigns and for books and magazines. My background in zoology is a great aid, particularly with illustrations of animals that are meant to be realistic and accurate. On occasion I act as the writer and/or scientific consultant on the books I am illustrating, and I would like to expand on consultant/writer/illustrator combinations in future books."

*   *   *

KITT, Tamara
See de REGNIERS, Beatrice Schenk (Freedman)

*   *   *

KRUPP, E(dwin) C(harles) 1944-

Personal

Born November 18, 1944, in Chicago, IL; son of Edwin F. (an engineer) and Florence Ann (Olander) Krupp; married Robin Suzanne Rector (an artist and teacher), December 31, 1968; children: Ethan Hembree. *Education:* Pomona College, B.A., 1966; University of California, Los Angeles, M.A., 1968, Ph.D., 1972. *Hobbies and other interests:* Comic books (especially "Uncle Scrooge" and "Dr. Strange"), reading ghost stories and supernatural tales of terror, running around the block.

Addresses

Office—Griffith Observatory, 2800 East Observatory Rd., Los Angeles, CA 90027.

Career

Astronomer and educator. Griffith Observatory, Los Angeles, CA, curator, 1972-74, director, 1974—. Member of faculty at University of California, El Camino College, and University of Southern California. Host of *Project: Universe* (television series), Public Broadcasting Service (PBS). *Member:* American Astronomical Society (chairman of historical astronomy division,

E. C. Krupp

1984-86), Astronomical Society of the Pacific (board member, 1983-87), Explorers Club (fellow), Sigma Xi.

Awards, Honors

Science writing award, American Institute of Physics/ U.S. Steel Foundation, 1978, for *In Search of Ancient Astronomies;* Science Writing Award, American Institute of Physics, Children's Book of the Year, Child Study Association, and Outstanding Science Trade Book for Children designation, National Science Teachers Association/Children's Book Council, all 1985, and Notable Work of Nonfiction award, Southern California Council on Literature for Children and Young People, 1986, all for *The Comet and You.*

Writings

(Editor and contributor) *In Search of Ancient Astronomies,* Doubleday (Garden City, NY), 1978.

Echoes of the Ancient Skies: The Astronomy of Lost Civilizations, Harper (New York, NY), 1983.

(Editor and contributor) *Archaeoastronomy and the Roots of Science,* Westview Press (Boulder, CO), 1984.

The Comet and You, illustrated by wife, Robin Rector Krupp, Macmillan (New York, NY), 1985.

(With others) *Mapping Spaces,* Peter Blum, 1987.

(With others) *Visions of the Sky,* Coyote Press, 1988.

The Big Dipper and You, illustrated by Robin Rector Krupp, Morrow (New York, NY), 1989.

Beyond the Blue Horizon: Myths and Legends of the Sun, Moon, Stars, and Planets, HarperCollins (New York, NY), 1991, with new introduction, Oxford University Press (New York, NY), 1992.

The Moon and You, illustrated by Robin Rector Krupp, Macmillan (New York, NY), 1993.

Skywatchers, Shamans, & Kings: Astronomy and the Archaeology of Power, Wiley (New York, NY), 1997.

The Rainbow and You, illustrated by Robin Rector Krupp, HarperCollins (New York, NY), 2000.

Contributor to books, including *Fire of Life: Smithsonian Book of the Sun,* edited by Joe Goodwin and others, Smithsonian (Washington, DC), 1981; and *Science and the Paranormal,* edited by George O. Abell and Barry Singer, Scribner (New York, NY), 1981. Also author of sound recordings *Ancient Astronomy,* 1979, and *Archaeoastronomy: Sky and Culture,* 1980, both produced by American Chemical Society. Editor-in-chief, *Griffith Observer,* 1974—.

Sidelights

Combining his interest in ancient civilizations with his knowledge of astronomy, E. C. Krupp has authored a number of thought-provoking books on archaeoastronomy—the study of the astronomy of ancient cultures—for both young people and adults. In addition to such works as 1983's *Echoes of the Ancient Skies: The Astronomy of Lost Civilizations* and 1997's *Skywatchers, Shamans, & Kings: Astronomy and the Archaeology of Power,* Krupp has partnered with his wife, illustrator and educator Robin Rector Krupp, to create several books that interpret the factual wonder of the changing skies for modern young people. Reviewing the couple's 1989 collaboration, *The Big Dipper and You,* for the *Washington Post Book World,* reviewer Elizabeth Ward praised the book's "witty" illustrations and noted that "Krupp's greatest asset as a science writer for children is his clear, relaxed, conversational style." *The Comet and You,* which the couple published in 1985, received similar praise, and was the winner of numerous awards for children's nonfiction because of its engaging approach to a scientific topic.

Krupp was born in Chicago, Illinois, in 1944, and attended Pomona College after graduating from high school. In 1966 he enrolled at the University of California, Los Angeles, where he earned the advanced degree in astronomy that would result in his eventual appointment as director of Los Angeles's Griffith Observatory in 1974. In addition to working at Griffith, Krupp has traveled the world and, as he once explained to *SATA,* has "photographed and studied more than sixteen hundred ancient and prehistoric sites throughout the world, including England, Scotland, Wales, Ireland, France, Italy, Spain, Malta, Corsica, Sardinia, Germany, Poland, Bulgaria, Greece, Egypt, throughout Central America, Mexico, Peru, Colombia, Chile, Bolivia, India, Iran, Indonesia, Cambodia, Thailand, Jordan, Israel, Japan, Turkey, Ukraine, Easter Island, Tibet, Mongolia, Australia, New Zealand, Canada, the United States, and the People's Republic of China."

Krupp's purpose in writing has been to make science "one route to entertainment," as he explained, "and entertainment is for me a vehicle for sharing the experience of science. Rational thought and imaginative thought are tools for survival. Anyone with a Darwinian outlook will recognize that misleading oneself with pseudoscientific notions is a misuse of a valuable tool. It could cost us plenty." Through his editorship of 1978's *In Search of Ancient Astronomies,* Krupp provides readers with a science-based discussion of everything from the origins and purpose of Great Britain's ancient Stonehenge to the pseudo-archaeoastronomy promoted by such writers as Eric von Daniken. And through his contribution to *Science and the Paranormal,* Krupp has sought to draw a distinction between what earlier peoples interpreted as the existence of a ghostly netherworld and the equally unexplained phenomenon of today.

In an effort to present a scholarly, scientifically sound study of the sociological aspects of archaeoastronomy, Krupp published *Skywatchers, Shamans, and Kings.* Calling its author an "astronomer with a Jungian streak," a *Publishers Weekly* contributor praised the work, which focuses on the power accorded to those ancients who could seemingly harness the prophetic properties of the heavens. Surveying the world's great cultures—China, Egypt, Peru, Tibet, Africa, and elsewhere—Krupp contrasts the traditions based on sky gods with those rooted in earth-bound gods and goddesses. He "engagingly explores the historic derivation of political control from the skies" to ancient rulers, the *Publishers Weekly*

contributor explained, while a *Kirkus* reviewer called Krupp's analysis "evocative, absorbing, and informative."

In 1989's *The Big Dipper and You,* Krupp writes for a younger audience. In addition to outlining the facts modern astronomers have been able to glean about Ursa Major, he goes on to discuss the North Star, Polaris, and shows how the well-known Big Dipper constellation has been used by travelers throughout the centuries. His *The Comet and You* was published to coincide with the appearance of Halley's Comet, an event which occurs only once in every seventy-six years. In this book Krupp compares that well-known comet to others that have been visible from Earth, and he explains Halley's path through the solar system and the reason for its regular reappearance.

In *The Moon and You* Krupp presents curious young readers with a wealth of factual information about the Man in the Moon, such as phases, rotation, and effects on the Earth's tides, and also recounts the many myths and legends that have grown up around our planet's moon. Noting that the volume is "packed with information on anything a young reader would ever want to know about the moon," *Appraisal* contributor Sally L. Clutter found her praise of *The Moon and You* augmented by co-reviewer Leonard D. Holmes, who noted, "This book is fun!" before going on to commend Krupp's "clear, accurate" text.

The Krupps again teamed up for *The Rainbow and You,* wherein they reveal the myth, magic, and science behind one of the most colorful phenomena of nature—this time with the help of a brightly clad, bewhiskered leprechaun guide to take young readers from page to page. Noting that Krupp's "clear text" helps curious junior scientists understand rainbow mechanics and predict where and when to look for rainbows, reviewer Patricia Manning commented in her *School Library Journal* appraisal that the greatest strength of *The Rainbow and You* is that it "instructs readers how to make scientific observations when [rainbows] occur."

"The interaction of the brain with the sky is a universal and fundamental human experience," Krupp once explained to *SATA* while describing the fascination people have had with the movement of the heavens throughout history. "What we make of the sky determines how we think of ourselves and how we behave. Traveling to faraway places with strange-sounding names in pursuit of this experience puts one at the heart of human nature. Of course, it's also present back in your own backyard—provided the sky is dark!"

Biographical and Critical Sources

PERIODICALS

Appraisal, fall, 1994, Sally L. Clutter and Leonard D. Holmes, review of *The Moon and You,* pp. 32-33.
Horn Book, spring, 1994, Daniel Brabander, review of *The Moon and You,* p. 117.

Kirkus Reviews, July, 1989, review of *The Big Dipper and You,* pp. 992-993; October, 1996, review of *Skywatchers, Shamans, & Kings,* p. 1447.

Library Journal, October, 15, 1996, Gloria Maxwell, review of *Skywatchers, Shamans, & Kings,* p. 88.

New Scientist, September 13, 1979.

New West, October 8, 1979.

Publishers Weekly, October 14, 1996, review of *Skywatchers, Shamans, & Kings,* p. 72.

School Library Journal, October, 1989, Elaine Fort Weischedel, review of *The Big Dipper and You,* p. 106; February, 1994, Margaret M. Hagel, review of *The Moon and You,* p. 112; May, 2000, Patricia Manning, review of *The Rainbow and You,* p. 162.

Times Literary Supplement, May 16, 1980.

Washington Post Book World, November 5, 1989, Elizabeth Ward, review of *The Big Dipper and You,* p. 20.

L

LANINO, Deborah 1964-

Personal

Born March 3, 1964, in New York, NY; daughter of Peter Geoffry Lanino (a safety engineer) and Ursula Maria Winkler (an accountant); married George Eduardo Esguerra (a creative art director), June 27, 1993; children: Dylan Peter. *Education:* Attended Studio Art Centers International (SACI), 1985; Pratt Institute, B.F.A. (with honors), 1986. *Politics:* Democrat. *Religion:* Catholic.

Addresses

Home—6735 Ridge Blvd., Apt. 6B, Brooklyn, NY 11220.

Career

Illustrator and fine artist. *Exhibitions:* Lanino's work has been exhibited at the Society of Illustrators, New York, NY; Picot Hall, Albany, NY; SACI Gallery, Florence, Italy; and Schafler Gallery, Brooklyn, NY. *Member:* Graphic Artists Guild, Society of Children's Book Writers and Illustrators.

Illustrator

Charles Tazewell, *The Littlest Angel,* Children's Press (New York, NY), 1998.
Deborah Hopkinson, *Maria's Comet,* Atheneum (New York, NY), 1999.
Corinne Demas, *Nina's Waltz,* Orchard (New York, NY), 2000.

Illustrator of young adult book jackets for publishing houses, including Clarion; Henry Holt; Orchard; Greenwillow; Simon & Schuster; Farrar, Straus and Giroux; and Random House; illustrator of Barnes & Noble Classics book covers, including *Wuthering Heights* by Emily Brontë, *Huckleberry Finn* by Mark Twain, and *Heidi* by Johanna Spyri.

Deborah Lanino

Sidelights

Deborah Lanino has contributed her fine art paintings to several picture books for children. Her first, *The Littlest Angel,* is a new edition of Charles Tazewell's classic Christmas story in which a new angel's troubles adjusting to life in heaven are eased when an older angel realizes the child is homesick and arranges for a box of his earthly belongings to be brought to him. Precious as it is to him, the young angel offers the box to the newborn baby Jesus and a grateful Deity transforms the gift into the Star of Bethlehem. First published in 1946, the story has appeared in numerous editions, but Lanino's illustrations "are muted and full of texture, and not at all sentimental," according to a reviewer for *School Library Journal.*

Lanino's next book, *Maria's Comet,* is a fictionalized biographical episode from the life of nineteenth-century astronomer Maria Mitchell which was written by Deborah Hopkinson. Author and illustrator place young Maria in Nantucket in the early 1800s, as one of nine children whose days are spent helping her mother care for her siblings and the house while her heart longs to be up on the roof with her father and his telescope. When brother Andrew runs away to sea, Maria becomes her father's new assistant, and eventually, as the author notes in an epilogue, discovers a comet, teaches astronomy at Vassar College, and helps found the Association for the Advancement of Women. Lanino's acrylic paintings echo the style of the period as well as the poetic language of the text, according to reviewers. "The artist closes the distance between earth and stars with the warmth and softness that permeate each illustration," remarked a reviewer for *Publishers Weekly*. Margaret Bush described Lanino's achievement in similar terms in *School Library Journal:* "Warm, deep tones of brown and midnight blue suffuse the soft-edged, full-page acrylic views of the house, sky, and seaside town."

Lanino has also contributed the illustrations to Corinne Demas's picture book, *Nina's Waltz,* in which a young girl and her father set out to attend a fiddling contest. The father's intention to play "Nina's Waltz," a tune he wrote for his daughter's birthday, is derailed when his hands are stung by wasps on the way to the contest. Little Nina gathers her courage and takes her father's place on stage. Lanino's paintings celebrate both the love of music and the rural setting of the story, according to Kathleen Whalin in *School Library Journal,* who dubbed *Nina's Waltz* "a hymn to the transforming power of music."

Biographical and Critical Sources

PERIODICALS

Booklist, September 15, 1999, Carolyn Phelan, review of *Maria's Comet,* p. 268.
Kirkus Reviews, September 1, 1999, review of *Maria's Comet,* p. 1418.
Publishers Weekly, October 11, 1999, review of *Maria's Comet,* p. 75.
School Library Journal, October, 1998, review of *The Littlest Angel,* p. 46; October, 1999, Margaret Bush, review of *Maria's Comet,* pp. 115-116; November, 2000, Kathleen Whalin, review of *Nina's Waltz,* p. 113.

ON-LINE

Deborah Lanino Web page, http://www.deborahlanino.com/ (April 28, 2001).

*   *   *

LAUGHLIN, Rosemary 1941-

Personal

Born June 20, 1941, in Omaha, NE; daughter of Anton (a railroad clerk) and Adele (a teacher; maiden name, Brumleve) Munch; married Patrick Laughlin (a universi-

ty professor); children: three sons. *Education:* Duchesne College, B.A., 1963; University of Chicago, M.A., 1964, Ph.D., 1968.

Career

Author and high school English teacher.

Writings

Trouble on the Shoshone, Winston-Derek, 1988.
The Great Iron Link: The Building of the Central Pacific Railroad, Morgan Reynolds (Greensboro, NC), 1996.
The Pullman Strike of 1894: American Labor Comes of Age, Morgan Reynolds (Greensboro, NC), 2000.
John D. Rockefeller: Oil Baron and Philanthropist, Morgan Reynolds (Greensboro, NC), 2001.

Sidelights

In her book *The Great Iron Link: The Building of the Central Pacific Railroad,* Rosemary Laughlin profiles the five men who are considered responsible for making the dream of a railroad stretching from one American coast to the other a reality. The planning and surveying for the project was performed by Theodore Judah, while Charlie Crocker, Mark Hopkins, Collis Huntington, and Leland Stanford provided the financial backing. "Their personal contributions help the reader to understand the complexity of this great achievement," observed a reviewer in *Voice of Youth Advocates.* In addition to these men, Laughlin covers the contributions of the countless Chinese emigrants who performed the back-breaking work. As well, the author also discusses the less-than-heroic actions of the owners after the railroad was built, including eliminating competition, driving-up prices, and bribing politicians to look the other way. The book contains a "clearly written and lively text," as well as contemporary black-and-white photographs of the men and the railroad, according to George Gleason of *School Library Journal.*

Biographical and Critical Sources

PERIODICALS

Kirkus Reviews, June 1, 1996, review of *The Great Iron Link,* p. 835.
School Library Journal, April, 1997, George Gleason, review of *The Great Iron Link,* pp. 150-51.
Voice of Youth Advocates, August, 1997, review of *The Great Iron Link,* p. 165.

*   *   *

LEWIS, E. M. (Mary Melwood)

Personal

Born in Carlton in Lindrick, Nottinghamshire, England; daughter of John Burtwistle (an estate trustee) and Mary Agnes (a registrar; maiden name, Justice) Hall; married

Morris Lewis; children: Robert Hall, Roderick Alan. *Education:* Attended schools in England. *Politics:* "Nil." *Religion:* "Nil."

Addresses

Home—5 Hove Lodge Mansions, 16 Hove St., Hove, Sussex, England.

Career

Teacher and author. Formerly worked as an elementary school teacher in England.

Awards, Honors

Arts Council award, 1964, for *The Tingalary Bird,* and 1965, for *Five Minutes to Morning;* prize from London *Observer*/Rank Organization, 1982; Foyle's Book of the Month Selection, for *Nettlewood.*

Writings

FICTION; UNDER PSEUDONYM MARY MELWOOD

Nettlewood (children's novel), Deutsch (London, England), 1974, Seabury Press (New York, NY), 1975.
The Watcher Bee (children's novel), Deutsch (London, England), 1982, second edition, Scholastic (London, England), 1995.
Reflections in Black Glass (adult novel), Deutsch (London, England), 1987.

PLAYS; UNDER PSEUDONYM MARY MELWOOD

The Tingalary Bird (first produced in London, 1964), New Plays (New York, NY), 1964.
Five Minutes to Morning (first produced in London, 1965), New Plays (New York, NY), 1966.
Masquerade, first produced in Nottingham, England at Nottingham Playhouse, 1974.
The Small Blue Hoping Stone, music by Nancy Kelel, first produced in Detroit, MI, 1976.

Plays represented in anthologies, including *All the World's a Stage,* Delacorte (New York, NY).

Sidelights

Better known to readers and playgoers alike by her pseudonym Mary Melwood, British writer E. M. Lewis combined a love for the theater and a sense of fun with her affection for children to produce a number of dramas and fictional works for young people. Her plays, which include 1964's *The Tingalary Bird* and 1976's *The Small Blue Hoping Stone,* were created to appeal to the youthful audience that had developed as a result of the early twentieth-century movement to create a uniquely child-oriented theater. This movement was increasingly embraced by schools and community theater groups throughout the United States and Great Britain.

Born in Nottinghamshire, England, Lewis wrote her first full-length play when she was a pre-teen. Drawn to the stage as a child, she became involved in local theater,

going on to establish a small company in her hometown in 1936 and eventfully writing her own theatrical productions. In 1964 Lewis's play *The Tingalary Bird* was produced for London audiences. Writing in *Twentieth-Century Children's Writers,* Ursula M. Jones called Lewis "a writer for children of the first order."

Like all of Lewis's plays, *The Tingalary Bird* is designed for a young audience; even so, its subject matter has been called disturbing, albeit humorous, by some critics. The play focuses on a childless, married couple: the strong-willed wife dominates her husband, who is seemingly inadequate for any task put to him. One night a severe thunderstorm breaks out, and a strange bird suddenly appears in the couple's home, seeking refuge from the storm. An argument soon takes shape between husband and wife over the exact color of the bird's eyes: Are they golden yellow, as the husband insists, or brilliant green, as the wife stridently proclaims? Like the storm, the argument subsides by morning. The bird has also flown, leaving the couple listless and saddened over their bickering. The wife's need to dominate her husband has been replaced by a tired acquiescence, and the pair's relationship now seems more balanced, although theater goers are left wondering if the bumbling husband will ever be able to reliably shoulder the responsibilities given over to him by his wife. Noting the positive change in the couple's relationship, Jones said that Lewis's "audience leaves ... wiser and well entertained."

The effects of a single evening are also the subject of Lewis's 1965 play, *Five Minutes to Morning,* which was produced in London. In this work, a young boy finds himself in a quandary over the future of a schoolhouse he has recently inherited. Although he would like to sell the property and get some ready money, the boy also feels a sense of obligation to the teacher who is now living on the property. During the night he has a dream that shows the negative effects of selling the property to a buyer who would make the teacher's life miserable by being an obnoxious landlord. Upon waking, the boy knows that the right thing to do is to retain ownership of the property himself and save the teacher from having to deal with a landlord who would be less tolerant of his tenant's quirky personality.

Lewis has also written two children's novels noted for their deeply detailed settings and measured pace. In her first novel, *Nettlewood,* twelve-year-old Lacie is sent to live with her father's cousins in the English Midlands after he is injured. She is befriended by a local girl, Gertie Sprott, and the two become increasingly intrigued by the mysteries surrounding Nettlewood, the local manor where Lacie's cousin Nora works as a nurse. The mystery unravels at a leisurely pace over the course of one summer in the 1920s, and the effect is "somewhat old-fashioned," according to Beryl Robinson in *Horn Book,* "because of the fullness of detail and the natural and unhurried progress of the action." In a *School Library Journal* review, Sarah Law Kennerly remarked upon the unusual pacing of this female coming-of-age novel, calling *Nettlewood* "a complex, sensitively written suspense story which successfully captures the world of a girl just emerging from childhood into adolescence."

In her second children's novel, *The Watcher Bee,* an adolescent girl in rural England cautiously feels her way toward maturity. Here, Kate describes the evolution of her ongoing relationship with Charlie—her former childhood friend as well as her current teenage antagonist—and her determination not to be merely a watcher but someone who actively participates in life. Set in the 1930s, this "leisurely, old-fashioned novel evokes a timeless view of adolescence," as Nancy C. Hammond remarked in *Horn Book.* The mystery Melwood's protagonist must solve in *The Watcher Bee,* concerns the nature of the adult world and what roles the adult Kate and Charlie will take in the troubling years between the two world wars. "This is not a novel with a grand sweep or a dramatic plot," remarked a reviewer in the *Bulletin of the Center for Children's Books,* adding that "it is more like a frieze in needlepoint," with each detail contributing to the overall effect of the whole. To that end, "Melwood has a dramatist's ear for dialogue, and for what is significantly not said," Margaret Meek concluded in *School Librarian.*

Biographical and Critical Sources

BOOKS

Twentieth-Century Children's Writers, St. James (Detroit, MI), 1995.

PERIODICALS

Bulletin of the Center for Children's Books, October, 1975, review of *Nettlewood,* p. 30; January, 1984, review of *The Watcher Bee,* p. 92.

Horn Book, August, 1975, Beryl Robinson, review of *Nettlewood,* p. 382; February, 1984, Nancy C. Hammond, review of *The Watcher Bee,* p. 62.

School Librarian, September, 1982, Margaret Meek, review of *The Watcher Bee,* p. 254.

School Library Journal, May, 1975, Sarah Law Kennerly, review of *Nettlewood,* p. 71.

M

MATHABANE, Mark 1960-

Personal

First name originally Johannes; name changed, 1976; born October 18, 1960, in Alexandra, South Africa; son of Jackson (a laborer) and Magdelene (a washerwoman; maiden name, Mabaso) Mathabane; emigrated to the United States, became U.S. citizen; married Gail Ernsberger (a writer), in 1987; children: Stanley, Arthur, Bianca, Nathan. *Education:* Attended Limestone College, 1978, St. Louis University, 1979, and Quincy College, 1981; Dowling College, B.A., 1983; attended Columbia University, 1984. *Religion:* "Believes in God."

Addresses

Home—341 Barrington Park Lane, Kernersville, NC 27284. *E-mail*—mark@mathabane.com.

Career

Lecturer and writer, 1985—. *Member:* Authors Guild.

Awards, Honors

Christopher Award, 1986; Speaker of the Year, National Association for Campus Activities, 1993; White House Fellow, 1996-97.

Writings

Kaffir Boy: The True Story of a Black Youth's Coming of Age in Apartheid South Africa, Macmillan, 1986, published as *Kaffir Boy: Growing out of Apartheid,* Bodley Head, 1987.
Kaffir Boy in America: An Encounter with Apartheid, Scribner, 1989.
Miriam's Song: A Memoir, Simon & Schuster, 2000.

FOR ADULTS

(With Gail Mathabane) *Love in Black and White: The Triumph of Love over Prejudice and Taboo,* Harper-Collins, 1992.
African Women: Three Generations, HarperCollins, 1994.

Mark Mathabane

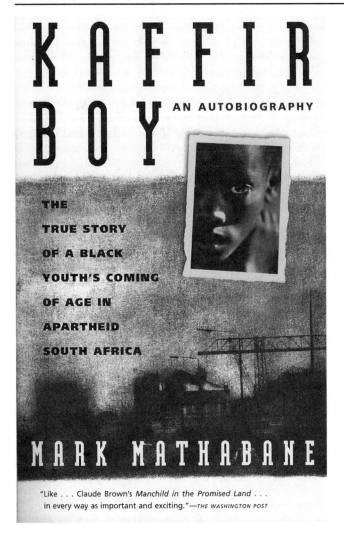

KAFFIR BOY

AN AUTOBIOGRAPHY

THE TRUE STORY OF A BLACK YOUTH'S COMING OF AGE IN APARTHEID SOUTH AFRICA

MARK MATHABANE

"Like . . . Claude Brown's *Manchild in the Promised Land* . . . in every way as important and exciting."—*THE WASHINGTON POST*

Mathabane writes of his poverty-stricken childhood in a South African shantytown under apartheid and his arrival in the United States on a tennis scholarship. (Cover photo by Fred Housel; illustration by Kirsty McLaren.)

Sidelights

"What television newscasts did to expose the horrors of the Vietnam War in the 1960s, books like *Kaffir Boy* may well do for the horrors of apartheid in [the] '80s," Diane Manuel predicted in a 1986 *Chicago Tribune Book World* review of *Kaffir Boy: The True Story of a Black Youth's Coming of Age in Apartheid South Africa.* In that book, author Mark Mathabane's first, he recounts his early life in the black township of Alexandra, outside Johannesburg. The eldest of his parents' seven children, the author lived in dire poverty and constant fear, until he almost miraculously received a scholarship to play tennis at an American college. *Washington Post Book World* critic Charles R. Larson hailed *Kaffir Boy* as "violent and hard-hitting," while Peter Dreyer in the *Los Angeles Times Book Review* described Mathabane's autobiography as "a book full of a young man's clumsy pride and sorrow, full of rage at the hideousness of circumstances, the unending destruction of human beings, [and] the systematic degradation of an entire

society (and not only black South African society) in the name of a fantastic idea."

The Alexandra of *Kaffir Boy* was a place of overwhelming poverty and deprivation, of incessant hunger, of horrific crimes committed by the government and citizen gangs, and of fear and humiliation. It was a township where many of the black residents either spent hours searching in garbage dumps for scraps of food discarded by Johannesburg whites or prostituted themselves for meals. It was a place where "children grow up accepting violence and death as the norm," as Larson reflected. One of Mark Mathabane's childhood memories is of his being startled from sleep, terrified to find police breaking into his family's shanty in search of persons who emigrated illegally—as his parents had—from the "homelands," or tribal reserves. His father, Jackson Mathabane, was imprisoned following one of these raids and was repeatedly jailed after that. Mathabane recalls in *Kaffir Boy* how his parents "lived the lives of perpetual fugitives, fleeing by day and fleeing by night, making sure that they were never caught together under the same roof as husband and wife" because they lacked the paperwork that allowed them to live with their lawful spouses. His father was also imprisoned—at one time for more than a year with no contact with his family—for being unemployed, losing jobs as a laborer because he lacked the "proper documents."

However, those blacks who lived in the urban ghettos near Johannesburg were actually better off than those who were forcibly resettled in the outlying homelands. "Nothing is more pathetic in this book than the author's description of a trip he takes with his father to the tribal reserve, ostensibly so that the boy will identify with the homelands," wrote Larson. "The son, however, sees the land for what it really is—barren, burned out, empty of any meaning for his generation." In *Kaffir Boy* Mathabane depicts the desolation of the Venda tribal reserve as "mountainous, rugged and bone-dry, like a wasteland.... Everywhere I went nothing grew except near lavatories.... Occasionally I sighted a handful of scrawny cattle, goats and pigs grazing on the stubbles of dry brush. The scrawny animals, it turned out, were seldom slaughtered for food because they were being held as the people's wealth. Malnutrition was rampant, especially among the children." Charles Larson noted that the visit to the homeland backfires when the "boy [becomes] determined to give up his father's tribal ways and acquire the white man's education."

Although Mathabane had the opportunity to get at least a primary education, so grim was his life that by age ten he contemplated suicide. "I found the burden of living in a ghetto, poverty-stricken and without hope, too heavy to shoulder," he explained in his memoir. "I was weary of being hungry all the time, weary of being beaten all the time: at school, at home and in the streets.... I felt that life could never, would never, change from how it was for me." But his first encounter with apartheid sparked his determination to overcome the adversities.

Mathabane's grandmother was a gardener for an English-speaking liberal white family in an affluent Johannesburg suburb. One day she took her grandson to work, where he met Clyde Smith, the employer's eleven-year-old son. "My teachers tell us that Kaffirs [blacks] can't read, speak or write English like white people because they have smaller brains, which are already full of tribal things," Smith told Mathabane, the author recalled in *Kaffir Boy.* "My teachers say you're not people like us, because you belong to a jungle civilization. That's why you can't live or go to school with us, but can only be our servants."

Determined to prove young Smith wrong, Mathabane resolved to excel in school. He even taught himself English—although blacks were only allowed to learn tribal languages at the time—through comic books that his grandmother brought home from the Smith household. "I had to believe in myself and not allow apartheid to define my humanity," Mathabane pointed out.

Mrs. Smith also gave Mathabane an old wooden tennis racket. After teaching himself to play, he then sought coaching. As his game improved, he began to fare well at tournaments and gained recognition as a promising young athlete. In 1973 Mathabane attended a tennis tournament in South Africa where the late American tennis player Arthur Ashe publicly condemned apartheid. Ashe became Mathabane's hero, "because he was the first free black man I had ever seen," the author was later quoted as saying by the *New York Times.* After watching Ashe play against other professionals, Mathabane strove to do as well as his hero. Eventually, Mathabane became one of his country's top players, and this gave him opportunities to meet influential white tennis players who did not support apartheid; 1972 Wimbledon winner Stan Smith, another American tennis professional, befriended Mathabane and urged him to apply for tennis scholarships at American schools. When Mathabane did so, he won one; *Kaffir Boy* ends with the author boarding a plane headed for South Carolina.

Lillian Thomas in the *New York Times Book Review* asserted that "it is evident that [Mathabane] wrestled with the decision whether to fight or flee the system" in South Africa. The author was involved in the 1976 township uprisings in Soweto, where more than 600 black people were killed when police opened fire on a peaceful student protest. However, Mathabane continued to be friends with whites whom he had met at his athletic club. He also was the only black in a segregated tournament that was boycotted by the Black Tennis Association, but he participated believing that he would meet people who could help him leave South Africa. Afterward he ran for his life when attacked by a gang of blacks who resented his association with whites.

David Papineau in the *Times Literary Supplement* did not find fault with Mathabane for leaving South Africa. In a 1987 review, the critic contended that Mathabane "does make clear the limited choices facing black youths in South Africa today. One option is political activity, with the attendant risk of detention or being forced underground.... Alternatively you can keep your head down and hope for a steady job. With luck and qualifications you might even end up as a white-collar supervisor with a half-way respectable salary."

Mathabane continued his life story in *Kaffir Boy in America: An Encounter with Apartheid,* which chronicles his experiences in 1978 as a student at Limestone College, South Carolina. Although armed with copies of the Declaration of Independence and the U.S. Constitution, Mathabane learned that the United States was not the promised land after all. *Kaffir Boy in America* is an account of Mathabane's efforts to get a good education and of his early career as a journalist and writer. Along the way, Mathabane struggled to understand American popular culture and racial attitudes. Writing in the *Journal of Modern African Studies,* Mwizenge S. Tembo observed that "*Kaffir Boy in America* shows the extent of the contradictions that exist in the world's leading superpower." A *Library Journal* reviewer stated that *Kaffir Boy in America* was "generally well-written," but "like many sequels, this one lacks the power of the original." Lorna Hahn of the *New York Times Book*

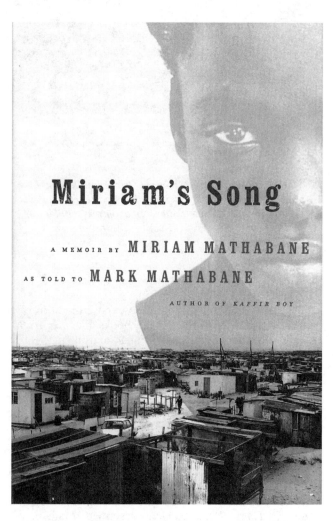

Writing in the voice of his sister, Mathabane tells the story of her coming of age during the time apartheid came to an end in South Africa. (Cover photos by Allan Penn and Gail Mathabane.)

Review praised Mathabane's fairness in his discussion of American attitudes toward South Africa, and she described *Kaffir Boy in America* as "an inspiring account of a young man's self-realization and his commitment to the self-realization of others."

With *Love in Black and White: The Triumph of Love over Prejudice and Taboo,* which Mathabane coauthored with his American wife, Gail Ernsberger, the author responded to people who criticized his decision to marry a white woman. In chapters divided into each spouse's perspective, this 1992 book describes the hostility that interracial marriages still face from both races. *Kirkus Reviews* called *Love in Black and White* "a personal and candid account of what it means to break an intransigent taboo—and a heartwarming affirmation of love and commitment."

In 1994, Mathabane published *African Women: Three Generations,* in which he recounts the life stories of his mother, grandmother, and sister in order to tell the larger tale of what it meant to grow up female and black in South Africa under apartheid and the legacy of colonialism. *African Women* received mixed reviews from critics. While *Booklist* contributor Hazel Rochman noted that "the political is made personal in scenes of daily confrontation," the *New York Times Book Review*'s Veronica Chambers questioned Mathabane's decision to tell the women's stories in what she felt was his own voice rather than theirs. She also found that because Mathabane failed to sketch the larger social and political context in the book, the women's problems seemed to be "boyfriends and cheating husband." Chambers added, "With *African Women: Three Generations,* it feels as though [Mathabane's literary] well is beginning to run dry."

Mathabane's fifth book, *Miriam's Song: A Memoir,* was published in 2000. It uses the same narrative approach to focus on the sorrows that befell his younger sister, born in 1969. Like her brother, Miriam was rescued by an overseas educational opportunity. Again, the story is told in a first-person voice, and the scenes of life in Alexandra—their household's chronic poverty and parents' combative marriage, the cruelty of Miriam's teachers at a township school—are especially vivid when told from a child's perspective. "It is evening. I'm sitting on the kitchen floor in front of a cozy fire from a red-hot *mbawula,* a brazier, watching Mama cook dinner," *Miriam's Song* recalls. "I have no toys to play with, so I often watch Mama do chores. Our house, which overlooks a donga (gully) and a dusty street called Hofmeyer, is in yard number forty-seven on Thirteenth Avenue. It has two small rooms, three small windows with several broken panes, and no running water, electricity, or indoor toilet."

Like Mathabane's other books, *Miriam's Song* provides literary snapshots of daily life under apartheid. Miriam recounts a dinner of porridge and chicken intestines in the midst of reliving a particularly horrific school day, when she had been whacked with a heavy ruler after failing a fingernail inspection. When the crying six-year-

old girl wipes her nose on her sleeve, her enraged teacher smacked her on the head. But Miriam's mother must borrow fingernail clippers from a neighbor, and even a simple handkerchief is beyond their means. After her father disparages a school that would punish so young a child for such an infraction, Miriam explains to readers that such a school was the only education available to her, and harshness was part of the system there. "Black schools had to abide by the strict discipline rules set by the Department of Bantu Education, and corporal punishment was high on the list of those rules," she and Mathabane point out in *Miriam's Song.*

Interwoven into *Miriam's Song* is the gripping story of the end of apartheid in South Africa. During Miriam's teen years, opponents to the system made the black townships the focal point of protest, and places like Alexandra descended into a dangerous spiral of police violence and armed uprisings. Mathabane and his sister also recount the particular obstacle facing black South African women: an economic situation where poverty is nearly insurmountable, and alcoholism and abusive relationships are often the rule rather than the exception. Rape and unplanned pregnancies kill many young women's dreams of finding careers or lives outside the townships. As she entered her teen years, Miriam was determined to finish high school, and she dreamed of becoming a nurse. She found solace in the religion of her mother, a devout Christian, and managed to save a small nest egg for her future. Sadly, these funds are stolen by a family member, then Miriam's boyfriend sexually assaults her and she becomes pregnant. At that point, it appears that her dream is lost. But her brother in America comes to her rescue. *Miriam's Song* ends as his *Kaffir Boy* did, with Miriam leaving South Africa for college.

New York Times Book Review writer Mary Ellen Sullivan praised the book's dramatic account of political activity in Alexandra, which Sullivan asserted "brings a critical chapter of South African history to life." The reviewer also termed the way in which Mathabane let his sister tell her own story one of *Miriam's Song*'s finest attributes: the elder brother, she wrote, "perfectly captures her guileless wisdom."

In the years since its publication, Mark Mathabane's *Kaffir Boy* has become a part of the curriculum in high schools and colleges across the U.S. The author is a popular speaker on college campuses, and in 1996 he was named a White House fellow to the Department of Education. The eighteen fellows conducted research trips to Panama and South Africa as part of this yearlong fellowship. The year concluded with Mathabane and his colleagues submitting educational initiatives they had devised to the Department.

Mark Mathabane, his wife, and their four children, live in North Carolina. In a 1990 interview, Mathabane told Bruce W. Nelan of *Time* that he found the American South markedly different from his college experiences in New York City. The far more segregated urban north is similar to what life was like in South Africa under apartheid—some whites in northern cities, Mathabane said, "seldom set foot in a ghetto. They know nothing about the real life of black people. They react to what they see on television. I know because that is the way they reacted to me." In North Carolina, by contrast, Mathabane saw "that in places in the South where change has occurred, it has been genuine. Many white people go out of their way not to be seen as racists, not to give a racial connotation to any situation."

In his lectures to high school and college students, Mathabane recounts his own story, through it stressing the need to use any opportunity available. He sees education—and even a substandard one, be it in Bantu or a problem-plagued American urban public system—as the salvation. "With education you are made to accept the universality of human beings," he told Nelan in *Time.* "You can see yourself in other people."

Biographical and Critical Sources

BOOKS

Mathabane, Mark, *Kaffir Boy: The True Story of a Black Youth's Coming of Age in Apartheid South Africa,* Macmillan, 1986.

Mathabane, Mark, *Miriam's Song: A Memoir,* Simon & Schuster, 2000.

The Schomburg Center Guide to Black Literature, Gale (Detroit, MI), 1996.

St. James Guide to Young Adult Writers, 2nd edition, St. James Press, 1999.

PERIODICALS

Africa Today, July-September, 1996, Sheldon W. Weeks, review of *African Women: Three Generations,* p. 329.

Booklist, February 15, 1994, Hazel Rochman, review of *African Women: Three Generations,* p. 1034.

Chicago Tribune Book World, April 13, 1986, Diane Manuel, review of *Kaffir Boy.*

Christian Science Monitor, May 2, 1986; April 25, 1994; February 21, 1995.

Journal of Modern African Studies, December, 1990, Mwizenge S. Tembo, review of *Kaffir Boy in America,* p. 723.

Kirkus Reviews, November 15, 1991, review of *Love in Black and White.*

Library Journal, April 15, 1986, Elizabeth Widenmenn, review of *Kaffir Boy,* p. 76; June 1, 1989, review of *Kaffir Boy in America,* p. 116; December, 1991, A.O. Edmonds, review of *Love in Black White,* p. 158; April 1, 1994.

Los Angeles Times Book Review, March 30, 1986, Peter Dreyer, review of *Kaffir Boy.*

New Statesman & Society, March 30, 1995, Victoria Brittain, review of *African Women: Three Generations,* p. 37.

Newsweek, March 9, 1992, Laura Shapiro, review of *Love in Black White,* p. 62.

New York Times, March 2, 1987; September 24, 1987; December 14, 1997.

New York Times Book Review, April 27, 1986; August 13, 1989; February 16, 1992, Andrea Cooper, review of *Love in Black and White;* July 31, 1994, p. 25; August

13, 2000, Mary Ellen Sullivan, review of *Miriam's Song.*

People Weekly, July 7, 1986; February 17, 1992, Susan Shapiro, review of *Love in Black and White,* p. 25.

Publishers Weekly, February 28, 1986, Genevieve Stuttaford, review of *Kaffir Boy,* p. 111; April 28, 1989, review of *Kaffir Boy in America,* p. 66; December 6, 1991, review of *Love in Black and White,* p. 53; March 21, 1994, review of *African Women: Three Generations,* p. 62.

School Library Journal, February, 2001, Jane S. Drabkin, review of *Miriam's Song,* p. 145.

Sage, spring, 1995.

Seventeen, August, 1987, Lesley Poindexter, review of *Kaffir Boy,* pp. 242+.

Time, November 12, 1990, Bruce W. Nelan, "Taking the Measure of American Racism," p. 16.

Times Literary Supplement, August 21, 1987, David Papineau, review of *Kaffir Boy.*

Washington Post Book World, April 20, 1986, Charles R. Larson, review of *Kaffir Boy.*

ON-LINE

Mark Mathabane Web site, located at http://www.mathabane.com (January, 2001).*

*   *   *

McGRAW, Eloise Jarvis 1915-2000

OBITUARY NOTICE—See index for *SATA* sketch: Born December 9, 1915, in Houston, TX; died November 30, 2000, in Portland, OR. Author. McGraw was an award-winning writer of fiction, fantasy, and mysteries for children and young adults. She received her first Newbery Honor Award in 1952, for *Moccasin Trail,* which also received a Lewis Carroll Shelf Award in 1963. Subsequent honors included a 1978 Edgar Award for *A Really Weird Summer,* an L. Frank Baum Award (which she shared with her daughter, Lauren McGraw) for her contributions to the "Oz" saga, and two additional Newbery Honor Awards for *The Golden Goblet* (1962) and *The Moorchild* (1997). An accomplished artist as well as a skilled writer, McGraw created covers for many of her titles, including 1996's *The Moorchild.* Although McGraw worked primarily as an author throughout her life, she cultivated an interest in a diverse range of hobbies, from acting and stagecraft to ceramics and drill-team horseback riding.

OBITUARIES AND OTHER SOURCES:

PERIODICALS

New York Times, December 5, 2000, "Eloise McGraw, Children's Author, 84," p. C23.

Publishers Weekly, December 18, 2000, "Eloise McGraw 1915-2000," p. 29.

Washington Post, December 2, 2000, p. B07.

MEDEARIS, Angela Shelf 1956-

Personal

Surname is pronounced "ma-dare-is"; born November 16, 1956, in Hampton, VA; daughter of Howard Lee (a real estate broker) and Angeline (an interior decorator) Shelf; married Michael Rene Medearis (a funding review specialist), January 25, 1975; children: Deanna Renee. *Education:* Attended Southwest Texas State University, 1974-75. *Religion* Non-denominational.

Addresses

Home and office—P.O. Box 91625, Austin, TX 78709-1625.

Career

Book Boosters, Austin, TX, founder, 1989—; Children's Radio Bookmobile, Austin, producer, 1989-92; author. Consultant/author for Scholastic, Macmillan, and McGraw-Hill. *Member:* Society of Children's Book Writers and Illustrators, Austin Writers' League.

Angela Shelf Medearis

Awards, Honors

Citation, Violet Crown Awards, and Notable Children's Social Studies Book, National Council for the Social Studies/Children's Book Council, 1992, for *Dancing with the Indians;* Pick of the List, American Booksellers Association, for *Zebra Riding Cowboy.*

Writings

FOR CHILDREN

Picking Peas for a Penny, State House, 1990, revised paperback edition, Scholastic (New York, NY), 1993.
Dancing with the Indians, illustrated by Samuel Byrd, Holiday House (New York, NY), 1991.
The Zebra Riding Cowboy, Holt (New York, NY), 1992.
Come This Far to Freedom: A History of African-Americans, illustrated by Terea D. Shaffer, Atheneum (New York, NY), 1993.
(Adaptor) *The Singing Man: Adapted from a West African Folktale,* illustrated by Terea D. Shaffer, Holiday House (New York, NY), 1994.
Our People, illustrated by Michael Bryant, Atheneum (New York, NY), 1994.
Annie's Gifts, illustrated by Anna Rich, Just Us (Orange, NJ), 1994.
Poppa's New Pants, illustrated by John Ward, Holt (New York, NY), 1995.
Treemonisha (from the opera by Scott Joplin), illustrated by Michael Bryant, Holt (New York, NY), 1995.
(Reteller) *The Freedom Riddle,* illustrated by John Ward, Dutton (New York, NY), 1995.
We Play on a Rainy Day, illustrated by Sylvia Walker, Cartwheel (New York, NY), 1995.
Skin Deep and Other Teenage Reflections: Poems, illustrated by Michael Bryant, Macmillan (New York, NY), 1995.
Too Much Talk, illustrated by Stefano Vitale, Candlewick (Cambridge, MA), 1995.
Eat, Babies, Eat!, illustrated by Patrice Aggs, Candlewick (Cambridge, MA), 1995.
Bye-Bye, Babies!, illustrated by Patrice Aggs, Candlewick (Cambridge, MA), 1995.
The Adventures of Sugar and Junior, illustrated by Nancy Poydar, Holiday House (New York, NY), 1995.
Here Comes the Snow, illustrated by Maxie Chambliss, Scholastic (New York, NY), 1996.
We Eat Dinner in the Bathtub, illustrated by Jacqueline Rogers, Scholastic (New York, NY), 1996.
The Friendship Garden, illustrated by Marcy Ramsey, Celebration (Glenview, IL), 1996.
Barry and Bennie, illustrated by Pat Cummings, Celebration (Glenview, IL), 1996.
Kyle's First Kwanzaa, illustrated by Gershom Griffith, Celebration (Glenview, IL), 1996.
The 100th Day of School, illustrated by Joan Holub, Scholastic (New York, NY), 1996.
The Spray-Paint Mystery, illustrated by Richard Williams, Scholastic (New York, NY), 1996.

We hear about our grandpa,
as our wagon creaks along,
living with the Indians
because slavery was wrong.

A black family takes part in a Seminole Indian celebration in Medearis's **Dancing with the Indians.** *(Illustrated by Samuel Byrd.)*

Haunts: Five Hair-Raising Tales, illustrated by Trina Schart Hyman, Holiday House (New York, NY), 1996.

Tailypo: A Newfangled Tall Tale, illustrated by Sterling Brown, Holiday House (New York, NY), 1996.

The Ghost of Sifty-Sifty Sam, illustrated by Jacqueline Rogers, Scholastic (New York, NY), 1997.

Rum-A-Tum-Tum, illustrated by James E. Ransome, Holiday House (New York, NY), 1997.

Poppa's Itchy Christmas, illustrated by John Ward, Holiday House (New York, NY), 1998.

Seeds Grow, illustrated by Jill Dubin, Scholastic (New York, NY), 1999.

Best Friends in the Snow, illustrated by Ken Wilson-Max, Scholastic (New York, NY), 1999.

Seven Spools of Thread: A Kwanzaa Story, illustrated by Daniel Minter, Albert Whitman (Morton Grove, IL), 2000.

(With Michael Medearis) *Daisy and the Doll,* paintings by Larry Johnson, Vermont Folklife Center (Middlebury, VT), 2000.

"RAINBOW BIOGRAPHY" SERIES

Little Louis and the Jazz Band: The Story of Louis "Satchmo" Armstrong, illustrated by Anna Rich, Lodestar, 1994.

Dare to Dream: Coretta Scott King and the Civil Rights Movement, illustrated by Anna Rich, Lodestar, 1994.

Princess of the Press: The Story of Ida B. Wells-Barnett, Lodestar, 1997.

"AFRICAN-AMERICAN ARTS" SERIES; WITH HUSBAND, MICHAEL R. MEDEARIS

Cooking, Twenty-First Century (New York, NY), 1997.

Dance, Twenty-First Century (New York, NY), 1997.

Music, Twenty-First Century (New York, NY), 1997.

FOR ADULTS

The African-American Kitchen: Cooking from Our Heritage, Dutton (New York, NY), 1994.

A Kwanzaa Celebration: Festive Recipes and Homemade Gifts from an African-American Kitchen, Dutton (New York, NY), 1995.

Ideas for Entertaining from the African-American Kitchen, Dutton (New York, NY), 1997.

Contributor of articles on African-American art to *Crisis,* 1987-90. Contributor to *American Way* magazine, 1999-2000.

Sidelights

Angela Shelf Medearis is the author of dozens of titles for young readers, ranging from picture books to folktales to biographies. Many feature memorable African-American characters, whether fictional or real, and critics have praised her ability to give her subjects a sense of depth on the page. Medearis was born in 1956 in Hampton, Virginia, but "moved constantly," as she once said, because of her father's career. "I used books and reading as a way of adjusting to new surroundings. I knew that my favorite books would be waiting for me at the library in whatever new place we were going.

"I've always loved to read but I can't recall ever reading any books by or about African-Americans when I was in elementary school," Medearis continued. "My favorite

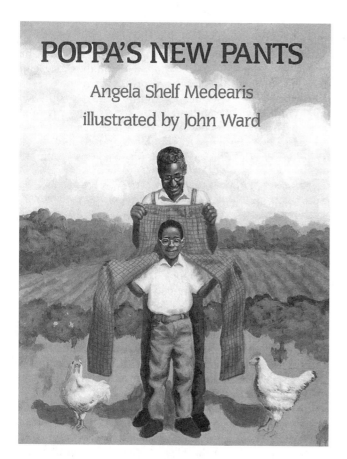

Confusion reigns when Poppa asks Grandma Tiny, Aunt Viney, and Big Mama to hem his new pants before church in Medearis's picture book. (Cover illustration by John Ward.)

author as a child was Laura Ingalls Wilder. I also enjoyed biographies about famous people in history. My tastes in books haven't changed much since I was a child. I still love biographies and ninety percent of the books I read are children's picture books," she admitted. She began writing them herself in 1990, while a mother and wife in Austin, Texas. Her first published work, *Picking Peas for a Penny,* appeared in 1990, while her second, *Dancing with the Indians,* won two children's book awards. In this latter work, an African-American girl recounts her family's trip to a Seminole Indian pow-wow and explains the long ties between the two groups; her grandfather had been a slave and was rescued by a Seminole when he fled. The work describes three important dances the Seminoles perform at such pow-wows.

Medearis's fiction books for young readers continue with *Annie's Gifts,* published in 1994 and based in part, Medearis told *SATA,* on her own childhood. Its heroine is the confused daughter in a music-loving family; both Annie's brother and sister play several instruments well, but she seems tone-deaf and every attempt she makes results in a terrible racket. The distressed youngster writes a poem about her troubles instead, and her father reminds her that her talent for poetry and drawing are very unique gifts. "Annie's family is real and likable, and the message of each person finding his or her own gifts a worthwhile one," noted Susan Dove Lempke in a *Bulletin of the Center for Children's Books* review. Jos N. Holman, writing in *School Library Journal,* also praised Medearis's work. The "writing is gentle and affectionate," Holman noted, "and provides a great example of parental reinforcement and support."

Some of Medearis's books are adaptations of folktales, such as 1994's *The Singing Man.* Based on a Nigerian Yoruba legend, the retelling is a parable about three brothers who must choose occupations; the village elders, however, decree that Banzar's decision to become a musician is unacceptable, and he must leave his village. Away from the village he meets a griot, or storytelling musician, and they decide to travel together. The griot teaches Banzar how to earn a living by song, and Banzar's talents gain him so much renown that he is hired by the king. One day, he sees his brothers in the marketplace and realizes that they are desperate, for his former village has been struck by famine. He arranges both a reunion and help for them. His family's dismissal of his choice of career is forgiven; as one character says, "Yams fill the belly and trade fills the pockets, but music fills the heart." Reviewing *The Singing Man* for *School Library Journal,* Barbara Osborne Williams noted that "the story imparts the subtle bits of wisdom found in traditional African folklore." A *Publishers Weekly* reviewer declared that Medearis "comes to full maturity as a storyteller with this engaging folktale."

Medearis has lived in Austin, Texas, for several years, and the rural parts of the state have served as a backdrop for many of her picture books. In *Poppa's New Pants,* a young boy named George visits his grandparents and aunts in Texas. His grandfather, Poppa, asks the women of the house to shorten his new trousers, but they all claim to be too tired. Then, each of the three feels guilty and wakes in the middle of night to hem them; George, sleeping in the kitchen, is kept awake by these ghostly sewers. In the morning, Poppa discovers his pants now extend only to his knees, so they are given to George. "The full-color paintings show a loving African American family in a rural setting," remarked Karen James in *School Library Journal*. "The story, told from the boy's point of view, radiates warmth and gentle humor," stated *Five Owls* reviewer Marilyn N. Robertson, who called it "a story with charm and with universal appeal."

Poppa and George return for the holiday-themed 1998 picture book, *Poppa's Itchy Christmas*. Wishing for a BB gun, George is disappointed by a scarf instead. Another package reveals a gift of itchy woolen underwear, but then he opens a present from Poppa and finds new ice skates. Realizing he needs all the other gifts in order to enjoy his new skates, George becomes thankful for all of his warm new clothes. "The child's first-person narrative is honest and energizing," noted *School Library Journal* reviewer Mary M. Hopf, who went on to call the book "a warm and fuzzy holiday selection."

Medearis tackled multicultural friendships for her 1995 book, *The Adventures of Sugar and Junior*. The two title characters—African-American Sugar Johnson and Hispanic Santiago "Junior" Ramirez—are ages seven and eight, and the pages reveal the story of their friendship and relate some of their favorite activities. "Medearis has done a fine, understated job of showing what it means to be a friend," remarked *Booklist* reviewer Julie Corsaro. That same year, Medearis also adapted the book *Treemonisha* from a Scott Joplin opera by the same name, a classic of African-American musical culture. She retells the story of the African-American woman in 1880s Arkansas who saves her community from a con artist. *Bulletin of the Center for Children's Books* reviewer Roger Sutton declared that "the adaptation, incorporating pieces of Joplin's libretto, is smooth and lively."

Medearis also wrote *The Freedom Riddle* in 1995, adapting a story that first appeared in a volume by William Faulkner. The work is a picture book aimed at older readers. Set on a plantation during the slavery era, the pages recount the way in which Jim, a wise and proud slave, wins his freedom after betting that his master will not be able to solve a riddle. Jim plans his conundrum for an entire year, and though the reader already knows all the clues to the riddle by the time the master is confounded by it, the story was nevertheless an entertaining one, according to a *School Library Journal* reviewer. "Medearis's text flows easily to provide an interesting view of a troubled time and a satisfying ending," the critic declared.

Medearis published a number of other works in 1995, including *Too Much Talk*, her adaptation of a Ghanaian legend. One day, a farmer thinks the yams he is digging out of the soil are speaking to him—and his dog then concurs. Distraught, he runs away and meets others who

Dogs, cloth, and even the king's throne speak in **Too Much Talk.** *(Written by Medearis and illustrated by Stefano Vitale.)*

claim that this happens to them as well—a weaver hears from his cloth and a fisherman gets an earful from his fish. They visit their chief, who tells them they are being foolish. Much to the king's surprise, when they leave, his throne agrees with his decision. "Medearis retells the tale with particular attention to sound and rhythm," stated *Horn Book* reviewer Maeve Visser Knoth. Corsaro, reviewing the book for *Booklist*, praised its "simple style, strong rhythms and repetition, and zesty humor."

Another work from Medearis set in rural Texas was the 1996 monster tale, *Tailypo: A Newfangled Tall Tale*. Here, Kenny Ray is frightened by the odd varmint that comes into his cabin but leaves its tail behind and then tries to get back in. Finally Kenny Ray shouts, "I don't have it!," which seems to frighten the beast away. "Medearis employs the loose, flamboyant style of many performing storytellers," remarked *Booklist*'s Corsaro. A similar work published that same year was *Haunts: Five Hair-Raising Tales*. Here, Medearis retells a quintet of folk legends for readers aged ten to twelve. The "Fiddler Man" scares two orphaned slaves, but they retaliate by taking cotton from the field and putting it in their ears to stop his music. Corsaro, writing in *Booklist*, called this story "a metaphor for the terrors faced by free blacks during slavery days."

Medearis won praise for her 1997 book *Rum-A-Tum-Tum*. Taking place in New Orleans during the late 1890s, the story follows the activities of a young African-American girl living there. Woken by the shouts of the street vendors in her French Quarter neighborhood every morning, she goes on to tell about the city's vibrant African-American life—its jazz bands, its market place, and the funeral parades whose drums beat out the title. "Medearis's poetic rhyme captures the rhythm of the street cries and the ragtime beat" of such ensembles, noted Hazel Rochman in *Booklist,* while Carol Ann Wilson, writing for *School Library Journal,* called the book "a jubilant excursion through an earlier time in a fascinating place."

Medearis has also written a number of nonfiction books. In 1993's *Come This Far to Freedom: A History of African-Americans,* readers aged ten to twelve learn about heroic moments in black history, from events in Africa to the civil rights era. Medearis discusses a period, then provides a sketch of a person who played a key role in it, such as abolitionist Frederick Douglass or Supreme Court Justice Thurgood Marshall. "The individuals are well chosen," stated Lyn Miller-Lachmann in *School Library Journal,* who commented further that "most are well known, though some could be considered unsung heroes."

Other nonfiction works from Medearis include three in the "Rainbow Biography" series for Lodestar aimed at readers in grades three to five. The first of these was 1994's *Little Louis and the Jazz Band: The Story of Louis "Satchmo" Armstrong.* Here, Medearis recounts the life of jazz legend Louis Armstrong. In *Dare to Dream: Coretta Scott King and the Civil Rights Movement,* Medearis draws upon the autobiography of Dr. Martin Luther King Jr.'s widow to reveal the challenges she faced, all the while interweaving important events in the civil rights movement. *Booklist* reviewer Linda Ward-Callaghan described the work as "a concise, engaging biography for young readers." Medearis also wrote *Princess of the Press: The Story of Ida B. Wells-Barnett* for the series in 1997. Here, she sketches the life of this writer and cofounder of National Association for the Advancement of Colored People (NAACP). Orphaned as a young teen, the future civil rights leader struggled to keep her siblings together. She became a teacher, but a talent for writing developed into a prominent career as a writer and then owner of a number

Medearis teams with her husband, Michael, for this book, based on the true story of a young girl's courageous reading of a poem about her black doll. (Cover illustration by Larry Johnson.)

of African-American publications. "Medearis does a good job of portraying her subject's strong will and passion," declared Katherine Borchert in a review for *School Library Journal.*

With her husband, Michael, Medearis coauthored *Daisy and the Doll,* a story based on an actual event in Vermont in the 1880s. Daisy, the sole African-American student in her class, is dismayed by a school competition in which all the students are given a doll and a poem to memorize. Daisy's doll is a rag doll with a black face, which causes her classmates to snicker, and she dislikes the poem. She is somewhat reassured when she talks with her father about feeling different, but when she takes the stage with her doll to recite the poem, she feels ashamed. Instead she makes up an impromptu new poem, which stuns the audience but wins her first prize. Kate McClelland, in her review for *School Library Journal,* commended the book as "an authentic, child-centered look at the black experience around the turn of the 20th century." A contributor to *Publishers Weekly* praised the heroine's "crisp and amiable voice" and "the narrative's emotion-charged tenor," while *Booklist* critic Denia Hester also commended the coauthors' efforts. "The honest text . . . will give children a deeper sense of what real beauty means," Hester declared.

In 2001, Medearis was invited by the newly elected and fellow Texas resident President George W. Bush to be one of thirteen authors honored during his inauguration. Later that same year, First Lady Laura Bush selected Medearis to accompany her on Mrs. Bush's first school visit in Washington, D.C. Medearis once remarked that "when I was growing up, authors didn't visit the schools I attended. That's why I really enjoy visiting schools now. I know how important it is to tell young people that if they can write well, they're just as gifted as any other type of artist. I try real hard to make my school visits as educational and fun as possible. . . . Most people think I'm funny. I like to make people laugh. I really, really like to make kids laugh. It's one of the happiest sounds in the world."

Biographical and Critical Sources

BOOKS

Medearis, Angela Shelf, adaptor, *The Singing Man: Adapted from a West African Folktale,* Holiday House (New York, NY), 1994.

Medearis, Angela Shelf, *Tailypo: A Newfangled Tall Tale,* Holiday House (New York, NY), 1996.

PERIODICALS

Bloomsbury Review, September-October, 1995, Beth Bahler, review of *Skin Deep,* p. 31.

Booklist, March 1, 1994, Denia Hester, review of *Our People,* p. 1265; January 1, 1995, Linda Ward-Callaghan, review of *Dare to Dream,* p. 819; October 15, 1995, Julie Corsaro, review of *The Adventures of Sugar and Junior,* p. 404, Susan Dove Lempke, review of *Eat, Babies, Eat!,* and *Bye-Bye, Babies!,* p. 412; November 15, 1995, Hazel Rochman, review of *The Freedom Riddle,* p. 556; January 1, 1996, Julie Corsaro, review of *Too Much Talk,* p. 840; August, 1996, Ilene Cooper, review of *Here Comes the Snow,* p. 1910; November 1, 1996, Julie Corsaro, review of *Tailypo,* p. 504; February 1, 1997, Julie Corsaro, review of *Haunts,* p. 941; February 15, 1997, Denia Hester, review of *The Spray-Paint Mystery,* p. 1023; May 1, 1997, Hazel Rochman, review of *Rum-A-Tum-Tum,* p. 1502; December 1, 1997, Helen Rosenberg, review of *Princess of the Press,* p. 634, Susan Dove Lempke, review of *The Ghost of Sifty Sifty Sam,* p. 642; February 1, 1998, Denia Hester, review of *Cooking,* p. 1006; September 15, 2000, Denia Hester, review of *Daisy and the Doll,* p. 242, Gillian Engberg, review of *Seven Spools of Thread,* p. 249.

Bulletin of the Center for Children's Books, May, 1994, Betsy Hearne, review of *Our People,* pp. 295-296; April, 1995, Susan Dove Lempke, review of *Annie's Gifts,* p. 282; February, 1996, Roger Sutton, review of *Treemonisha,* p. 196; February, 1997, Janice M. Del Negro, review of *Haunts,* pp. 214-215; January, 1998, Janice M. Del Negro, review of *The Ghost of Sifty Sifty Sam,* p. 168.

Five Owls, May, 1995, Marilyn N. Robertson, review of *Poppa's New Pants,* p. 105.

Horn Book, spring, 1994, Lois F. Anderson, review of *Come This Far to Freedom,* p. 171; November, 1995, Maeve Visser Knoth, review of *Too Much Talk,* p. 752.

Kirkus Reviews, September, 1994, review of *The African-American Kitchen,* p. 1211; June 15, 1995, review of *Skin Deep,* p. 860; October 1, 1995, review of *The Freedom Riddle,* p. 1434; October 15, 1995, review of *Treemonisha,* p. 1497; September 15, 1997, review of *Princess of the Press,* p. 1460.

Library Journal, August, 1994, Judith C. Sutton, review of *The African-American Kitchen,* p. 118; December, 1995, review of *A Kwanzaa Celebration,* p. 148.

Magpies, March, 1996, review of *Too Much Talk,* p. 27.

Publishers Weekly, December 13, 1993, review of *Our People,* p. 69; September 5, 1994, review of *The Singing Man,* p. 108; December 2, 1996, review of *Haunts,* p. 62; April 14, 1997, review of *Rum-A-Tum-Tum,* p. 74; October 6, 1997, review of *The Ghost of Sifty Sifty Sam,* p. 49; September 28, 1998, review of *Poppa's Itchy Christmas,* p. 58; August 28, 2000, review of *Daisy and the Doll,* p. 83.

School Library Journal, January, 1994, Lyn Miller-Lachmann, review of *Come This Far to Freedom,* p. 126; September, 1994, Barbara Osborne Williams, review of *The Singing Man,* p. 210; November, 1994, La-Vonne Sanborn, review of *Dancing with the Indians,* pp. 66-67, Robin Works Davis, review of *Little Louis,* pp. 115-116; February, 1995, Eunice Weech, review of *Dare to Dream,* p. 109; June, 1995, Karen James, review of *Poppa's New Pants,* p. 92; September, 1995, Jos N. Holman, review of *Annie's Gifts,* pp. 182-183; October, 1995, review of *The Freedom Riddle,* pp. 39-40; December, 1995, Judith Glover, review of *The Adventures of Sugar and Junior,* p. 88; March, 1996, Emily Kutler, review of *Eat, Babies, Eat!* and *Bye-Bye, Babies!,* p. 178; September, 1996, Sharon D. Pearce, review of *Here Comes the Snow,* p. 185; April, 1997, Janet M. Blair, review of *The*

Spray-Paint Mystery, p. 114, Mary Jo Drungil, review of *Haunts,* p. 138; July, 1997, Carol Ann Wilson, review of *Rum-A-Tum-Tum,* p. 71, Renee Steinberg, review of *Music* and *Dance,* p. 109; November, 1997, Joyce Adams Burner, review of *Cooking,* p. 132; December, 1997, Katherine Borchert, review of *Princess of the Press,* p. 113; October, 1998, Mary M. Hopf, review of *Poppa's Itchy Christmas,* p. 42; September, 2000, Kate McClelland, review of *Daisy and the Doll,* p. 205; October, 2000, review of *Seven Spools of Thread,* p. 65.

Voice of Youth Advocates, February, 1994, Karen Hartman, review of *Come This Far to Freedom,* p. 399.

*   *   *

MELWOOD, Mary
See LEWIS, E. M.

*   *   *

MOWAT, Claire (Angel Wheeler) 1933-

Personal

Born February 5, 1933, in Toronto, Ontario, Canada; daughter of Louis Ward and Winifred (Angel) Wheeler; married Farley Mowat (an author), March 29, 1965. *Ethnicity:* "English." *Education:* Ontario College of Art, associate's degree, 1956. *Politics:* New Democrat. *Religion:* Anglican.

Addresses

Home—18 King St., Port Hope, Ontario, Canada L1A 2R4; and R.R.1, River Bourgeois, Nova Scotia, Canada B0E 2X0.

Career

Commercial artist, graphic designer, and writer.

Writings

FOR YOUNG ADULTS

The Girl from Away (first volume of "Andrea Baxter" trilogy), illustrated by Malcolm Cullen, Key Porter (Toronto, Canada), 1992.
The French Isles (second volume of "Andrea Baxter" trilogy), Key Porter (Toronto, Canada), 1994.
Last Summer in Louisbourg (third volume of "Andrea Baxter" trilogy), Key Porter (Toronto, Canada), 1998.

FOR ADULTS

The Outport People (memoir), McClelland & Stewart (Toronto, Canada), 1983.
Pomp and Circumstances (nonfiction), McClelland & Stewart (Toronto, Canada), 1989.

Contributor to radio broadcasts of Canadian Broadcasting Corp. Contributor to periodicals.

Work in Progress

An untitled work.

Sidelights

In addition to her works of nonfiction for adults, Canadian author Claire Mowat has also written three young adult novels comprising the "Andrea Baxter" trilogy. The books chronicle Andrea's adventures in various regions of Canada, beginning in her thirteenth year. The series opens with *The Girl from Away,* in which Andrea is sent to stay with relatives for the Christmas holidays while her newly married mother honeymoons in Florida. Mowat portrays Andrea as a typical teenager—she resents her mother's new husband, Brad, and at first feels like an outsider when her Newfoundland visit begins. She soon becomes involved in community activities, such as mummering (a Christmas tradition in which costumes are worn to fool one's neighbors). Later, she and her cousins help to rescue a beached whale. Andrea returns to her hometown of Toronto with a more positive outlook, and resolves to try and build a relationship with Brad. In his review of the novel for *Canadian Children's Literature,* Raymond E. Jones termed the narrative "well-intentioned, completely positive fiction." He also stated, however, that the plot includes some implausible plot developments and under-developed characters. By contrast, *Quill & Quire*'s Kit Pearson found that "this short novel has much to recommend it." While Pearson also felt that Andrea's characterization could be more fully realized, she summarized Mowat's novel as "a pleasant, easy to read story with an interesting setting."

The Girl from Away proved to be popular with young readers. Mowat delivered more of Andrea's adventures in two additional volumes: *The French Isles,* published in 1994; and 1998's *Last Summer in Louisbourg.* In the trilogy's second installment, Andrea returns to New-foundland to stay with her relatives while her mother and stepfather journey to Sierra Leone on a teacher training expedition. Andrea, her uncle, and her cousin end up on the French island of St. Pierre, after their fishing boat is trapped in a heavy fog. Because of a mishap regarding fishing rights, Andrea's uncle is jailed, and she and her cousin are housed in a guest house run by another family member. Despite her uncle's unfortunate circumstance, Andrea has a pleasant stay on St. Pierre, and acts as a French-English translator at the guest house. Several sections of French dialogue appear in the text without accompanying English translation, although *Quill & Quire* contributor Ken Setterington points out that "it's possible for non-French readers to get a general understanding of the discussions even without a full translation."

In *Last Summer in Louisbourg,* the third volume of the trilogy, Andrea travels to Canada's Cape Breton, after winning her school's essay contest. The prize is summer employment at the Fortress of Louisbourg. In the eighteenth-century setting of this historic location, adults and children recreate life as it was for Louisbourg's original inhabitants. Andrea dresses in period costumes and participates in activities relevant to the time period. She and her roommate Justine are also selected to play small parts in a film being shot at the fort, and Andrea soon has a crush on a member of the film crew. *Canadian Children's Literature* reviewer S. R. MacGillivray commented that "this novel, like the others [in the trilogy], explores the issue of connection." In this case, Mowat is less concerned with family relationships than with the links between the past and the present or what MacGillivray identifies as "the role of the past as it impinges on the present." While a plot twist near the end of the story is not, according to *Quill & Quire*'s Hadley Dyer, fully resolved, MacGillivray felt that Mowat succeeds in narrating "the elements of the life of a typical mid-teen who is gradually learning about life and herself ... and about connectedness at the personal and national levels."

Mowat once said: "The three novels *The Girl from Away, The French Isles,* and *Last Summer in Louisbourg* form a trilogy for young adults. The principal character, Andrea Baxter, is featured in all of them. She becomes one year older with each subsequent novel: thirteen, fourteen, fifteen.

"The stories are set in Atlantic Canada. *The Girl from Away* centers on adventures in Newfoundland during the Christmas season. *The French Isles* is a story that takes place mainly in St. Pierre et Miquelon, a tiny, island territory belonging to France but adjacent to Newfoundland. It is an area where fishing disputes with Canada often occur. *Last Summer in Louisbourg* is set in Cape Breton Island, Nova Scotia, specifically in the Fortress of Louisbourg, a recreation of a French fortified village that actually stood there in the eighteenth century. The story is contemporary because my heroine has a summer job there, but there are many references to real historical events throughout the novel.

"I did not intend originally to become a writer," Mowat continued. "I liked drawing and painting, and so I chose to study at an art college. However, I discovered, somewhat later, that I was far more effective and successful whenever I wrote—letters, journals, articles, and eventually books. I am more fulfilled when I reach people through the written word rather than through the visual arts.

"I enjoy reading books by women who have gone to live amid a human culture in which they did not grow up and who have then reflected upon it and written about it. This, perhaps, led to my first book, *The Outport People.* However, I imagine I have been influenced, to some extent, by every book I have ever read.

"I grew up in a big, industrial city—Toronto. Over the past thirty years or so, I have lived in several rural locations in the Atlantic provinces of Canada where the lives that people live are, to me, more interesting than was my early life in Toronto.

"Generally I write in the afternoons. I work on various old, non-automated typewriters. I have nothing against computers. It's just that I have never found anyone who could teach me how to use one. When it comes to machinery of any kind I am handicapped or challenged, or whatever current buzz words are used to describe a person who has trouble learning to operate even a new radio or toaster or lawnmower. No doubt I write more slowly than a lot of authors, but that's not such a bad thing."

Mowat is also the author of a memoir, *The Outport People,* and the nonfiction title *Pomp and Circumstances.*

Biographical and Critical Sources

PERIODICALS

Canadian Children's Literature, Volume 72, 1993, Raymond E. Jones, review of *The Girl from Away,* pp. 51-51; Volume 25, 2000, S. R. MacGillivray, review of *Last Summer in Louisbourg,* pp. 82-83
Canadian Living, December, 1984.
Canadian Materials, January, 1993, Dave Jenkinson, review of *The Girl from Away,* p. 16; November-December, 1994, Virginia Davis, "The Pick of the Fall Season in Canada," p. 209.
Globe and Mail (Toronto), July 8, 1984; February 7, 1987; March 2, 1998.
Quill & Quire, September, 1992, Kit Pearson, review of *The Girl from Away,* p. 76; November, 1994, Ken Setterington, review of *The French Isles,* p. 37; April, 1998, Hadley Dyer, review of *Last Summer in Louisbourg,* p. 35
Toronto Star, June 7, 1987.

N–O

NOBLE, Trinka Hakes

Personal

Born in Michigan. *Education:* Michigan State University, B.A. (art); studied illustration in New York City with Uri Shulevitz; graduate study at New School for Social Research (now New School University).

Addresses

Home—Upper Montclair, NJ. *Agent*—c/o Dial Books for Young Readers, 345 Hudson St., New York, NY 10014.

Career

Children's author and illustrator. Has taught art in Michigan, Virginia, and Rhode Island.

Awards, Honors

Notable Book designation, American Library Association (ALA), 1980, Golden Sower Award Honor, Nebraska Library Association, and Children's Choice Book designation, Children's Book Council/International Reading Association, both 1981, all for *The Day Jimmy's Boa Ate the Wash;* Junior Literary Guild selection, 1984, for *Apple Tree Christmas.*

Writings

FOR CHILDREN

(And illustrator) *The King's Tea,* Dial (New York, NY), 1979.
The Day Jimmy's Boa Ate the Wash, illustrated by Steven Kellogg, Dial (New York, NY), 1980.
(And illustrator) *Hansy's Mermaid,* Dial (New York, NY), 1983.
Jimmy's Boa Bounces Back, illustrated by Steven Kellogg, Dial (New York, NY), 1984.
(And illustrator) *Apple Tree Christmas,* Dial (New York, NY), 1984.

Meanwhile Back at the Ranch, illustrated by Tony Ross, Dial (New York, NY), 1987.
Jimmy's Boa and the Big Splash Birthday Bash, illustrated by Steven Kellogg, Dial (New York, NY), 1989.

Several of Noble's books have been translated into Spanish.

ILLUSTRATOR

Mary Calhoun, *The Witch Who Lost Her Shadow,* Harper (New York, NY), 1979.
Susan Pearson, *Karin's Christmas Walk,* Dial (New York, NY), 1980.
Marilyn Singer, *Will You Take Me to Town on Strawberry Day?,* Harper (New York, NY), 1981.

Adaptations

Five of Noble's stories were recorded on audiocassette as *The Day Jimmy's Boa Ate the Wash, and Other Stories,* read by Sandy Duncan, Caedmon, 1986.

Sidelights

Trinka Hakes Noble, whose titles include *The King's Tea, Apple Tree Christmas,* and *The Day Jimmy's Boa Ate the Wash,* is an author and illustrator of books for children. Raised on a farm in a rural area of Michigan, Noble was one of seven children. Her early schooling consisted of classes in a one-room schoolhouse that drew children of all ages together from miles around. In the fifth grade, her last year of attending school there, she was the only student working at her grade level. Art, which had been her favorite subject during her early education, continued to fascinate her, and after graduating from high school she worked for a year to save up enough money to attend art classes at Michigan State University. After graduating from college, Noble put her art training to use as a teacher at schools in Michigan, Virginia, and Rhode Island before settling down in the New York City area. In New York, Noble was fortunate to study illustration with artist Uri Shulevitz at his Advanced Workshop in Greenwich Village, and she supplemented that education with classes at the New School for Social Research.

Noble's first published book, *The King's Tea,* which she wrote and illustrated, was praised by a *Publishers Weekly* critic for its incorporation of "the snowballing effects that children love." In the book a cup of tea prepared for the king's breakfast is ruined when soured milk is added; this in turn ruins the king's mood, and the negative effects spread throughout the kingdom as everyone from the tea steward to the milk cows in the field pass along the blame. Fortunately, by lunchtime the problem is solved—a rain shower has sweetened the buttercups eaten by the milk cows, who in turn provide sweeter milk for tea. Reviewers particularly praised Noble's earth-toned watercolor washes. *Horn Book* reviewer Kern M. Klockner noted that in her "gentle" artwork the author/illustrator "captures the rough features and peasant clothing of her characters, giving careful attention to detail." Donnarae MacCann also commented in her review of *The King's Tea* for *Wilson Library Bulletin* that Noble's technique of "radically [varying] the size of objects in her illustrations ... adds a subtly comic aspect to many scenes, without the use of conventional cartoon devices."

Noble's 1983 book, *Hansy's Mermaid,* takes place in Holland and is the story of a mermaid who is stranded in a pool left after a spring flood of the Zuider Zee river. Discovered by the Klumperty family, the mermaid, Seanora, is quickly dressed and taken under the wing of the Klumperty sisters, who decide that the best thing for their new friend would be to become as expert at sewing, butter churning, and cheese making as they are. Kept from her home in the sea, Seanora's unhappiness is detected by the family's young son, Hansy. While he brings her seaweed and helps her to participate in winter sports such as skating despite the fact that she has no legs, Hansy realizes that the landlocked mermaid will never be happy. Ultimately, he helps Seanora return to her home in the sea. Praising Noble's soft pencil drawings and the "fairy tale quality" of her text, Jonni Moore found *Hansy's Mermaid* to be a "thoroughly satisfying fantasy in picture book format" in her *School Library Journal* assessment. *Horn Book* reviewer Ann A. Flowers also praised the book as "sensitive, imaginative, and thoughtful."

In *Apple Tree Christmas,* published in 1984, the joys of a rural childhood are reflected in Noble's prose and illustrations. Taking place in 1881, the story revolves around young Katrina's love for an apple tree near her home that succumbs to the extreme cold of a Michigan winter. After the tree falls, she realizes that her sadness is shared by every person in her family, each of whom loved the tree for different reasons: her sister Josie loved to swing from the tree's branches, while her parents loved the tree's fruit and its shade. On Christmas Day, Katrina's father surprises each of the sisters with gifts from the tree: Josie's swing has been refurbished, while the wood from the tree has been used to make a drawing table for budding artist Katrina. Praising the tale for its evocation of the family-centered holiday spirit of years past, *School Library Journal* reviewer Elizabeth M. Simmons dubbed *Apple Tree Christmas* a "quiet, quaint story that will be enjoyed by children who love a touch of the old-fashioned," while a *Bulletin of the Center for Children's Books* writer praised Noble for her use of "period detail and some evocative watercolor paintings."

Published in 1980, *The Day Jimmy's Boa Ate the Wash* was the first book by Noble to introduce her popular young protagonist and his pet boa constrictor. In this story, a young girl named Meggie quietly relates what happens when Jimmy decided to bring his pet snake along on her class's field trip to a local farm. In typical Noble fashion, confusion and fun are the result: pigs board the school bus and eat everyone's lunch, raw eggs become missiles in the hands of gleeful children, and the hungry snake makes away with the laundry, all of which is highlighted in colorful fashion through the illustrations of Steven Kellogg. Reviewing the work in the *Bulletin of the Center for Children's Books,* a critic dubbed *The Day Jimmy's Boa Ate the Wash* "total nonsense, great fun," and noted that Noble's "bland delivery is in effective contrast with the zany events, each strengthening the other." A *Booklist* contributor echoed this praise, calling the book "a top-notch choice that children will not want to put down."

Jimmy and his boa have appeared in several more collaborations between Noble and Kellogg, each told with what *School Library Journal* contributor Cynthia K. Leibold described as Noble's "now familiar droll ... style." In 1984's *Jimmy's Boa Bounces Back,* the pet snake makes a fussy garden-club party a memorable event through his entrance disguised as a flowery hat on the head of Meggie's mother. Not surprisingly, the genteel mood of the party quickly evaporates after the boa decides to uncurl and go in search of a light lunch. Meggie's mother is ultimately banished from the garden club, while the boa finds a new best friend in Miss Peachtree's pet poodle.

"The return of Jimmy and his boa is reason to cheer," proclaimed *School Library Journal* reviewer Trev Jones on the arrival of *Jimmy's Boa and the Big Splash Birthday Bash,* "for the action is as frenzied, frantic, and wacky as before." This time out, a birthday outing to SeaLand serves as the spark to a host of outrageous events, and by the end everyone in the party has taken a plunge into the whale tank, frolicked with penguins, and dodged hungry sharks. Jones went on to praise Noble for her skill in "captur[ing] the logic of children and the way in which they tell a story" by leaving out the crucial bits until someone directly asks them "why?"

In addition to writing and illustrating her own work, Noble has contributed her artistic talents to the works of other authors, including Marilyn Singer, Susan Pearson, and Mary Calhoun.

Biographical and Critical Sources

PERIODICALS

Booklist, January 1, 1981, review of *The Day Jimmy's Boa Ate the Wash,* p. 625; April 1, 1987, Ilene Cooper, review of *Meanwhile, Back at the Ranch,* p. 1208.

Bulletin of the Center for Children's Books, April, 1981, review of *The Day Jimmy's Boa Ate the Wash,* p. 158; July, 1983, review of *Hansy's Mermaid,* p. 215; October, 1984, review of *Apple Tree Christmas,* p. 33.

Catholic Library World, April, 1981, p. 405.

Horn Book, December, 1979, Kern M. Klockner, review of *The King's Tea,* p. 656; February, 1981, Ann A. Flowers, review of *The Day Jimmy's Boa Ate the Wash,* p. 44; October, 1983, Ann A. Flowers, review of *Hansy's Mermaid,* p. 564; November, 1989, Ethel R. Twichell, review of *Jimmy's Boa and the Big Splash Birthday Bash,* p. 763.

Junior Bookshelf, August, 1987, review of *Meanwhile, Back at the Ranch,* pp. 165-166.

Kirkus Reviews, February 15, 1980, review of *The King's Tea,* p. 212; February 15, 1981, p. 209; February 15, 1987, review of *Meanwhile, Back at the Ranch,* p. 303.

Language Arts, May, 1981, p. 592.

Newsweek, December 1, 1980, p. 103.

New York Times Book Review, January 13, 1985, review of *The Day Jimmy's Boa Ate the Wash,* p. 26.

Publishers Weekly, June 11, 1982, review of *The King's Tea,* p. 63; May 25, 1984, review of *Jimmy's Boa Bounces Back,* p. 60; August 12, 1988, review of *Apple Tree Christmas,* p. 462.

School Library Journal, October, 1979, Carolyn K. Jenks, review of *The King's Tea,* pp. 143-144; January, 1981, p. 54; September, 1983, Jonni Moore, review of *Hansy's Mermaid,* p. 110; September, 1984, Cynthia K. Leibold, review of *Jimmy's Boa Bounces Back,* p. 108; October, 1984, Elizabeth M. Simmons, review of *Apple Tree Christmas,* p. 174; November, 1989, Trev Jones, review of *Jimmy's Boa and the Big Splash Birthday Bash,* p. 91.

Times Literary Supplement, July 24, 1981, Kicki Moxon Browne, review of *The Day Jimmy's Boa Ate the Wash,* p. 840; September 7, 1984, p. 1006.

Wilson Library Bulletin, November, 1979, Donnarae Mac-Cann, review of *The King's Tea,* pp. 183, 205; May, 1981, p. 689.*

*   *   *

OUTCALT, Todd 1960-

Personal

Born October 12, 1960, in Vincennes, IN. *Education:* Indiana State University, B.A.; Duke University, M.Div.

Addresses

E-mail—teoutcalt@aol.com.

Todd Outcalt

Career

United Methodist pastor.

Writings

Before You Say "I Do": Important Questions for Couples to Ask before Marriage, Berkley Publishing (New York City), 1998.

The Best Things in Life Are Free, Health Communications (Deerfield Beach, FL), 1998.

Meeting-Space Ideas for Youth Ministry, Group Publishing (Loveland, CO), 1998.

Seeing Is Believing! Youth Talks for Every Occasion, Abingdon (Nashville, TN), 1998.

The Heat Is On! Cool Ideas for Summertime Youth Events, Abingdon (Nashville, TN), 1998.

Holidays, Holy Days, and Other Big Days for Youth, Abingdon (Nashville, TN), 1999.

Show Me the Way: 50 Bible Study Ideas for Youth, Abingdon (Nashville, TN), 2000.

Last-minute Meetings: 101 Ready-to-go Games & Lessons for Busy Youth Leaders, Abingdon (Nashville, TN), 2001.

Candles in the Dark, Wiley (New York, NY), in press.

Last-Minute Meetings, Abingdon (Nashville, TN), in press.

Author of "Nuptials" and "For the Groom," both regular columns in *Bride;* author of "Midweek Message," a regular feature at the author's web site.

Sidelights

Todd Outcalt told *SATA:* "When I was twelve years old, someone asked me what I wanted to be when I grew up. I said, 'A writer.' There was no way of knowing then, however, what it would take to become a published writer. I just knew I wanted to write. My first published piece was a three-line poem I had written as a high school senior. I was paid five dollars for my effort but didn't have the courage to tell many people about it.

"Since then, I've written mountains of material, for teenagers especially, but I continue to enjoy all types of writing and literature. Over the years I've written several novels (none yet published), hundreds of short stories and humorous pieces, and now a few books. Most of what I write, however, will never see print.

"I believe the simplest definition of a writer still holds: a writer is someone who writes. Some writing finds its way into print, other writing does not. Sometimes payment follows, sometimes not. But a writer can never forget that words still have power, that there are still many avenues of the human experience yet to be explored and recorded. Although I have written but [a] few books, I have received mail from many corners of the earth—letters from people I'll never meet, but who have found something beneficial in my work. That's enough to keep any writer writing."

Biographical and Critical Sources

ON-LINE

Todd Outcalt Web site, http://www.toddoutcalt.com (June 28, 2001).

P

PARK, Barbara 1947-

Personal

Born April 21, 1947, in Mount Holly, NJ; daughter of Brooke (a banker and business owner) and Doris (a school secretary; maiden name, Mickle) Tidswell; married Richard A. Park (a commercial real estate broker), June 28, 1969; children: Steven Allen, David Matthew. *Education:* Attended Rider College, 1965-67; University of Alabama, B.S., 1969.

Barbara Park

Addresses

Home—Scottsdale, AZ. *Office*—c/o Random House, 1540 Broadway, New York, NY 10036.

Career

Author of books for young people. *Member:* PEN International, Authors Guild.

Awards, Honors

Children's Choice Award, International Reading Association/Children's Book Council, 1983, for *Beanpole,* 1987, for *The Kid in the Red Jacket,* and 1997, for *Junie B. Jones and That Meanie Jim's Birthday;* Young Hoosier Award, 1985, for *Operation: Dump the Chump;* Georgia Children's Book Award, Maud Hart Lovelace Book Award, and Texas Bluebonnet Award, all 1985, and Utah Children's Book Award, 1987, all for *Skinnybones;* Parents' Choice Award, 1985, for *Buddies,* 1987, for *The Kid in the Red Jacket,* 1990, for *Maxie, Rosie, and Earl—Partners in Grime,* and 1991, for *Rosie Swanton—Fourth Grade Geek for President;* Milner Award, 1986, for *Operation: Dump the Chump;* Tennessee Children's Choice Book Award, 1986, for *Operation: Dump the Chump,* and 1987, for *Skinnybones;* Best Children's Book of the Year, *School Library Journal,* 1987, for *The Kid in the Red Jacket;* Library of Congress Book of the Year, 1987, for *The Kid in the Red Jacket,* 1990, for *Maxie, Rosie, and Earl—Partners in Grime,* and 1991, for *Rosie Swanton—Fourth Grade Geek for President;* West Virginia Honor Book, 1990, for *The Kid in the Red Jacket,* and 1991, for *My Mother Got Married (And Other Disasters);* Young Adults' Choice, International Reading Association, 1997, for *Mick Harte Was Here.* Park has received numerous children's choice awards from state library associations for her books.

Writings

JUVENILE FICTION

Don't Make Me Smile, Knopf (New York, NY), 1981.

Operation: Dump the Chump, Knopf (New York, NY), 1982.

Skinnybones, Knopf (New York, NY), 1982.

Beanpole, Knopf (New York, NY), 1983.

Buddies, Knopf (New York, NY), 1985.

The Kid in the Red Jacket, Knopf (New York, NY), 1987.

Almost Starring Skinnybones, Knopf (New York, NY), 1988.

My Mother Got Married (And Other Disasters), Knopf (New York, NY), 1989.

Maxie, Rosie, and Earl—Partners in Grime, Knopf (New York, NY), 1990.

Rosie Swanson—Fourth Grade Geek for President, Knopf (New York, NY), 1991.

Dear God, Help!!! Love, Earl, Knopf (New York, NY), 1993.

Mick Harte Was Here, Knopf (New York, NY), 1995.

Psssst! It's Me ... the Bogeyman (picture book), illustrated by Stephen Kroninger, Atheneum, 1998.

The Graduation of Jake Moon, Atheneum, 2000.

"JUNIE B. JONES" SERIES; FOR BEGINNING READERS; ILLUSTRATED BY DENISE BRUNKUS

Junie B. Jones and the Stupid Smelly Bus, Random House (New York, NY), 1992.

Junie B. Jones and a Little Monkey Business, Random House (New York, NY), 1993.

Junie B. Jones and Her Big Fat Mouth, Random House (New York, NY), 1993.

Junie B. Jones and Some Sneaky Peeky Spying, Random House (New York, NY), 1994.

Junie B. Jones and the Yucky Blucky Fruitcake, Random House (New York, NY), 1995.

Junie B. Jones and That Meanie Jim's Birthday, Random House (New York, NY), 1996.

Junie B. Jones Loves Handsome Warren, Random House (New York, NY), 1996.

Junie B. Jones Has a Monster under Her Bed, Random House (New York, NY), 1997.

Junie B. Jones Is Not a Crook, Random House (New York, NY), 1997.

Junie B. Jones Is a Party Animal, Random House (New York, NY), 1997.

Junie B. Jones Is a Beauty Shop Guy, Random House (New York, NY), 1998.

Junie B. Jones Smells Something Fishy, Random House (New York, NY), 1998.

Junie B. Jones Is (Almost) a Flower Girl, Random House (New York, NY), 1999.

Junie B. Jones and the Mushy Gushy Valentine, Random House (New York, NY), 1999.

Junie B. Jones Has a Peep in Her Pocket, Random House (New York, NY), 2000.

Junie B. Jones Is Captain Field Day, Random House (New York, NY), 2000.

Junie B. Jones Is a Graduation Girl, Random House (New York, NY), 2001.

Junie B., First Grader (at Last!), Random House (New York, NY), 2001.

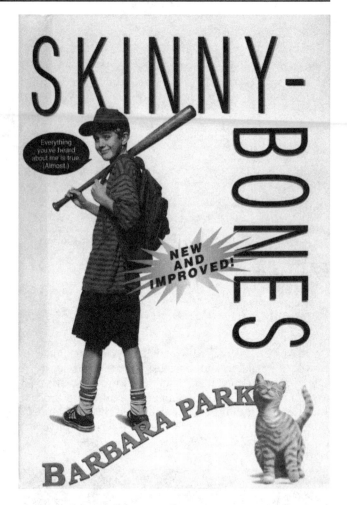

Admittedly a lousy baseball player, "Skinnybones" Alex brags his way into a pitching contest with the best player in school. (Cover illustration by Jeff Walker.)

Sidelights

Dubbed "one of the funniest ... writers around," by *Booklist*'s Ilene Cooper, and an author "who has consistently shown an ability to shed humorous light on potentially dreary situations," by Betsy Hearne in *Bulletin of the Center for Children's Books,* juvenile novelist Barbara Park tackles subjects from peer pressure to divorce to dealing with the death of a sibling to facing the devastation caused by Alzheimer's—all with a distinctly sardonic and light touch. Her award-winning novels, such as *Don't Make Me Smile, The Kid in the Red Jacket, Skinnybones, Maxie, Rosie, and Earl—Partners in Grime, Mick Harte Was Here,* and *The Graduation of Jake Moon,* attest to her winning prose and themes that challenge but do not overwhelm young readers. In her series of chapter books for beginning readers, the "Junie B. Jones" books, she presents a plucky and feisty female protagonist who gets herself involved in adventures from discovering the identity of a secret valentine to learning what to do with a fruitcake won in a school carnival.

Born in Mount Holly, New Jersey, in 1947, Park confessed in her autobiography page for the Random

House Web site that "as a kid I had absolutely no interest in writing whatsoever." She did, however, have a great interest in humor. "I always found myself incredibly amusing," she further commented. "So from the first grade on, whenever a funny thought hit me, I would happily blurt it out for the whole class to hear." By high school she had developed a strong interest in reading. Then, little by little, her feelings about writing began to change, too. Graduating from the University of Alabama in 1969, she married that same summer. Her husband, Richard, was serving in the U.S. Air Force, and suddenly Park thought that writing—which she could do at home while her two boys were growing up—could be a good outlet for her humorous side.

Park began with adult stories and articles, but had limited success. Then one of her sons brought home a book by juvenile author Judy Blume, and everything crystallized for the budding author. She suddenly saw that writing for young readers was exactly the genre for her. Setting herself a two-year deadline in which to get a book published, Park got to work dredging up her own childhood memories as well as focusing on the typical day-to-day problems faced by her own two boys. She wrote diligently and soon had three novels in hand. When *Operation: Dump the Chump* was accepted by Knopf, the editor there was enthusiastic enough to pick up the other two titles as well.

Park's first published book, *Don't Make Me Smile,* features a male protagonist, ten-year-old Charlie Hickle, whose parents are getting a divorce. Charlie does not accept his parents' decision quietly or politely; he acts out in often humorous and poignant ways, as at the picnic for his eleventh birthday which turns into a

Junie decides to be a beautician and practices on her dog, her slippers ... and herself. (From Junie B. Jones Is a Beauty Shop Guy, *written by Park and illustrated by Denise Brunkus.*

disaster. Marsha Hartos, reviewing this debut title in *School Library Journal,* felt that Park's book "achieves a beautiful balance between humor and sadness," while *Booklist*'s Hearne noted that the "[s]cenes and dialogue have a natural bittersweet flavor and move smoothly to the inevitable adjustment." Writing in *Horn Book,* Mary M. Burns concluded, "while divorce is certainly not a humorous subject, the topic is handled in a way which reminds one that tears and laughter are the warp and woof of the human comedy." Charlie makes a reappearance in the 1989 title, *My Mother Got Married (And Other Disasters),* in which his mother marries Ben Russo, a widowed father of two children. The concept of blended family takes on new and humorous meanings in this novel, which "is a delight for all readers, but ... especially appreciated by those in Charlie's position," according to a contributor for *Publishers Weekly.*

Another ten-year-old, Oscar Winkle, is featured in *Operation: Dump the Chump,* in which the chump in question is his younger, bothersome brother, Robert. Oscar's elaborate plans, of course, go awry, but not before providing some chuckles along the way. Though some reviewers felt the plot and ultimate resolution were too obvious, others, including *Booklist*'s Cooper thought that "[k]ids might see the punch line coming, but they'll be laughing out loud all the way there." *Books for Keeps* reviewer Pam Harwood found this story of sibling rivalry to be "a classic."

Skinnybones features another young male protagonist, Alex, who finds his situation as the smallest little league ball player a constant irritation. He gains redemption, however, when he wins a contest to be in a television commercial and becomes a different kind of celebrity. Cooper wrote in *Booklist* that "*Skinnybones* equals tickled funny bones," and Lena Denham Smith, reviewing the same title in *Catholic Library World,* called the middle-grade novel a "funny, irreverent story for every child who has ever been an underdog—and for parents and teachers who sometimes forget it isn't easy to be a kid." Park reprised Alex for the 1988 title, *Almost Starring Skinnybones,* in which Alex stars in a cat commercial which catapults him to school dramatics. "Alex's struggles to reconcile his dreams with the rough realities of middle school are related in a humorous, fast-moving style," concluded a writer for *Publishers Weekly* in a review of the sequel.

With her fourth novel, *Beanpole,* Park began writing from a girl's point of view, realizing that she could have as much fun with feisty female characters as with male ones. Lillian is just turning thirteen and is shaped like the title of her book. Her three wishes for her birthday—to get a bra, to dance with a boy, and to get on the Pom Squad—are partly and disappointingly granted, but along the way Lillian begins to take a humorous view of her problems. "Park continues to depict, amusingly, the imperfection of preteen life," wrote *Booklist*'s Cooper, who further commented, "Park will win readers with her light, bright comedic style." Lisa Lane, reviewing *Beanpole* in the *Christian Science Monitor,* concluded, "Barbara Park is offering her readers encouragement. In this perceptive novel about growing up, she captures the feeling of what it is like to be a seventh-grade 'loser' and shows that a place on the pom-pom squad or dancing with a boy isn't necessarily the way to success."

"Park pulls off a neat trick" with *Buddies,* declared Cooper in *Booklist.* "She has written an absolutely hysterical novel that incorporates a poignant message." The message, left somewhat unresolved at the end, is about peer pressure. Dinah, off to summer camp, wants to create a new popular image for herself, but is not prepared to deal with a tag-along girl who meets her on the bus and threatens to blow her cover. It is up to Dinah to tell Fern, the nerd, that her attentions are not wanted. Guilt-ridden by her actions, Dinah vows thereafter to treat an unpopular school friend with more respect. "Barbara Park has written a breezy, upbeat novel about teenage popularity at summer camp," observed Rita M. Fontinha in *Kliatt.* "An age-old message is given a new look here," concluded Fontinha. "It's refreshing to see that peer pressure doesn't always prevail."

More unwanted attentions are served up in *The Kid in the Red Jacket,* in which ten-year-old Howard Jeeter is having trouble adjusting after his recent move from Arizona to Massachusetts. Things get even worse when six-year-old Molly Vera Thompson, his next door neighbor, decides she's going to be Howard's friend. Hearne, writing in *Bulletin of the Center for Children's Books,* felt that Park handled this novel of adjustment with "her usual humor and child's-eye perspective," and *School Library Journal* critic Linda Wicher joined in the chorus of critical approval in calling the book "[a]nother first-rate addition by this author to the middle-grade popular reading shelf."

In a mini-series known as "The Geek Chronicles," a trio of misfits, Maxie, Rosie, and Earl, parade through three books by Park: *Maxie, Rosie, and Earl—Partners in Grime, Rosie Swanson—Fourth Grade Geek for President,* and *Dear God, Help!!! Love, Earl.* The three kids are meant for each other: Maxie is the top student, resented by all the other kids in his class, while Rosie is a know-it-all tattletale and Earl is something of an overweight wimp. With the first book in the series, Park wrote a book so funny "readers can't help but laugh out loud," according to *Booklist*'s Cooper. The three friendless fourth graders team up when they meet in the principal's office, each sent there for a different offense, and the fun takes off from this chance meeting. "Park's characters are so real, yet so wild, the actual plot hardly matters," wrote Cooper. A writer for *Kirkus Reviews* found that *Maxie, Rosie, and Earl—Partners in Grime* was "[s]ure to be a hit," and that "Park's use of funny-sounding, probably unfamiliar words will elicit belly laughs, as will her characters' outrageous predicaments." The trio's humorous adventures continue in *Rosie Swanson—Fourth Grade Geek for President* and in *Dear God, Help!!! Love, Earl.*

With the 1995 *Mick Harte Was Here,* "Park turns her wry eye on a serious subject," wrote *Booklist*'s Cooper, "the death of a sibling." Thirteen-year-old Phoebe Harte

Fourteen-year-old Jake recalls the tragedy of his grandfather's Alzheimer's disease in Park's 2000 novel. (Cover illustration by Paul Colin.)

describes with "love, wit, and anger," according to Cooper, her brother Mick and how his death in a biking accident has affected her and her family. Cooper concluded that there "is a sea of real emotion here," and that "readers will find themselves touched by this book." A writer for *Publishers Weekly* felt that by making it clear that Mick would have survived the accident had he been wearing a bike helmet, "Park dramatically and convincingly delivers a powerful message."

Another powerful message is presented in *The Graduation of Jake Moon* in which eighth-grade Jake must come to grips with his beloved grandfather's slide into Alzheimer's. Jake feels shame at his grandfather's condition and more shame at his own reaction to the old man's illness, a dramatic tension which is increased even further at Jake's graduation. "This novel takes readers into the uncompromising world of Alzheimer's disease," wrote Betty Carter in *Horn Book,* "allowing them to see it through the eyes of a likable and very human narrator." Trev Jones, writing in *School Library Journal,* found *The Graduation of Jake Moon* to be a "touching, perceptive, and heartening novel enriched by unforgettable characters."

Something of a departure for Park is the 1998 picture book title, *Psssst! It's Me ... the Bogeyman,* "a traditional baddie's not-quite-successful effort to counter press reports," according to *Booklist*'s John Peters. The Bogeyman in question gives readers the inside information on his scary tactics. Park presents a bad old Bogeyman who is a "wisecracking haunt, at once menacing and whiny," Peters noted. Peters concluded that Park "moves into picture books with this hilarious anodyne for nighttime fears." John Sigwald, reviewing the same title in *School Library Journal,* found this Halloween book to by a "year-round panacea for anyone who's ever been afraid of the things that go bump in the night."

Park is also well known for her series of beginning readers featuring the kindergartner Junie B. Jones. These short books each feature a problem to be dealt with, from taking the bus to a visit to the beauty shop. Eighteen titles strong and growing, the series has attracted young readers for its blend of humor and winning characterization. A writer for *Kirkus Reviews* found the first title in the chapter book series, *Junie B. Jones and the Stupid Smelly Bus,* to be "a genuinely funny, easily read story." Junie hides out in the supply closet rather than take the bus home. Reviewing the same title in *School Library Journal,* Gale W. Sherman noted that Park "is truly a funny writer" and that Junie B., though a kindergartner, is "sure to make middle grade readers laugh out loud when they read about her adventures on the first day of school." "Park has a wonderful ear for the dialogue of five-year-olds and an even better grasp of how their minds operate," commented Kay Weisman in a *Booklist* review of the fourth title in the series, *Junie B. Jones and Some Sneaky Peeky Spying.* The book was a "sure bet for beginning chapter-book readers," concluded Weisman. In *Junie B. Jones Is a Beauty Shop Guy,* the irrepressible Junie accompanies her father to a beauty shop to have his hair cut. Deciding she has hit on a profession for herself, she begins practicing the fine art of haircutting, clipping away at her bunny slippers, the family dog's hair, and finally her own locks, with disastrous results. "Readers will find plenty to laugh about as Junie tries to cover up the evidence," wrote *Booklist*'s Carolyn Phelan, who concluded, "this short chapter book will amuse the many fans of the refreshing series." Writing about the same title in *School Library Journal,* Linda Bindner observed that the "honesty and inventiveness of this savvy kindergartner make the Junie B. books accessible and completely enjoyable."

With all of Park's books it is this accessibility and enjoyment factor which proves so successful, according to reviewers. Park deals with problems of all sorts in her books, from the frivolous to the serious, but in the end she lets her own humorous take on life dictate how she presents her story. "I don't write books to try to impart heavy morals or messages," Park once said. "I don't particularly like it when teachers ask students to list what 'lessons' they have learned from one of my stories.... I don't believe that in order to be worthwhile a book must try to teach some weighty lesson in life."

What Park wants from her fiction is to create living, breathing people. After reading J. D. Salinger's *Catcher in the Rye* in high school, Park had a revelation she shared with *SATA:* "It was the first book I saw as a person and not as a book, and that is the way I want my books to feel to my readers. I want my books to feel like people."

Biographical and Critical Sources

BOOKS

Children's Literature Review, Volume 34, Gale (Detroit, MI), 1995.

PERIODICALS

Booklist, September 1, 1981, Betsy Hearne, review of *Don't Make Me Smile,* p. 50; March 1, 1982, Ilene Cooper, review of *Operation: Dump the Chump,* pp. 899-900; September 15, 1982, Ilene Cooper, review of *Skinnybones,* p. 118; October 1, 1983, Ilene Cooper, review of *Beanpole,* p. 300; April 15, 1985, Ilene Cooper, review of *Buddies,* p. 1198; March 1, 1990, Ilene Cooper, review of *Maxie, Rosie, and Earl—Partners in Grime,* p. 1348; December 1, 1992, Ilene Cooper, review of *Junie B. Jones and the Stupid Smelly Bus,* p. 671; March 1, 1993, p. 1230; April 1, 1993, p. 1434; November 15, 1993, p. 626; November 15, 1994, Kay Weisman, review of *Junie B. Jones and Some Sneaky Peeky Spying,* p. 602; March 1, 1995, Ilene Cooper, review of *Mick Harte Was Here,* p. 1242; August, 1998, John Peters, review of *Psssst! It's Me ... the Bogeyman,* p. 2016; November 15, 1998, Carolyn Phelan, review of *Junie B. Jones Is a Beauty Shop Guy,* p. 591; March 15, 1999; June 1, 2000.

Books for Keeps, July, 1990, Pam Harwood, review of *Operation: Dump the Chump,* p. 11.

Bulletin of the Center for Children's Books, November, 1981, p. 53; March, 1982, p. 136; October, 1983, p. 35; May, 1985, pp. 173-174; March, 1987, Betsy Hearne, review of *The Kid in the Red Jacket,* p. 133; March, 1988, p. 143; February, 1989, Betsy Hearne, review of *My Mother Got Married (And Other Disasters),* p. 154.

Catholic Library World, May-June, 1983, Lena Denham Smith, review of *Skinnybones,* p. 425.

Christian Science Monitor, October 7, 1983, Lisa Lane, "7th Grader Becomes a Winner," p. B3.

Horn Book, January-February, 1982, Mary M. Burns, review of *Don't Make Me Smile,* p. 46; November-December, 1997; September-October, 2000, Betty Carter, review of *The Graduation of Jake Moon,* p. 579.

Kirkus Reviews, March 15, 1990, review of *Maxie, Rosie, and Earl—Partners in Grime,* p. 428; September 1, 1991, p. 1168; August 1, 1992, review of *Junie B. Jones and the Stupid Smelly Bus,* p. 993; January 1, 1993, p. 67.

Kliatt, spring, 1986, Rita M. Fontinha, review of *Buddies,* p. 12.

Publishers Weekly, March 18, 1988, review of *Almost Starring Skinnybones,* pp. 87-88; January 20, 1989, review of *My Mother Got Married (And Other*

Disasters), p. 148; April 13, 1990, p. 66; August 30, 1991, p. 83; July 20, 1992, review of *Junie B. Jones and the Stupid Smelly Bus,* p. 250; November 6, 1995, review of *Mick Harte Was Here,* p. 68; September 7, 1998, p. 94; October 9, 2000, p. 41.

School Library Journal, October, 1981, Marsha Hartos, review of *Don't Make Me Smile,* p. 145; March, 1987, Linda Wicher, review of *The Kid in the Red Jacket,* p. 164; August, 1990, p. 149; November, 1992, Gale W. Sherman, review of *Junie B. Jones and the Stupid Smelly Bus,* p. 75; November, 1997, p. 96; February, 1998, p. 89; September, 1998, John Sigwald, review of *Psssst! It's Me ... the Bogeyman,* p. 178; December, 1998, Linda Bindner, review of *Junie B. Jones Is a Beauty Shop Guy,* p. 88; December, 2000, Trev Jones, review of *The Graduation of Jake Moon,* p. 55.

ON-LINE

Barbara Park Page, http://www.randomhouse.com/ (March 24, 2001).

*   *   *

POLACCO, Patricia 1944-

Personal

Born July 11, 1944, in Lansing, MI; daughter of William F. (a traveling salesman and television talk-show host) and Mary Ellen (a teacher; maiden name, Gaw) Barber; first marriage c. 1962 (marriage ended); married Enzo Mario Polacco (a chef and cooking instructor), August 18, 1979; children: (first marriage) Traci Denise, Steven John. *Education:* Attended Ohio State University, California College of Arts and Crafts, and Lancy College; Morash University (Melbourne, Australia), B.F.A., 1974; Royal Melbourne Institute of Technology, M.A., Ph.D., 1978; also studied in England, France, and Russia. *Hobbies and other interests:* Travel, running, pets, painting, sculpture, and egg art.

Addresses

Home—118 Berry St., Union City, MI 49094. *Agent*—Edythea Selman, 14 Washington Pl., New York, NY 10003.

Career

Full-time author and illustrator, 1986—. Consultant to museums on icon restoration; founder of company Babushka, Inc.; creator and promoter of "Stop the Teasing" campaign to remove damaging behavior from American culture; speaker for school and reading organizations. *Member:* Society of Children's Book Writers and Illustrators (SCBWI).

Awards, Honors

International Reading Association Award for younger readers, 1989, for *Rechenka's Eggs;* Sydney Taylor Book Award for picture books, 1989, for *The Keeping Quilt;* Commonwealth Club of California Award, 1990,

Patricia Polacco

for *Babushka's Doll,* and 1992, for *Chicken Sunday;* Golden Kite Award, 1992, for *Chicken Sunday;* Jane Addams Award honor book, 1993 for *Mrs. Katz and Tush;* American Book of the Year Award nomination, 1995, for *Pink and Say;* featured speaker, Virginia Hamilton Conference at Kent State University, 1996. Gold Award, 1999, for *Thank You, Mr. Falker;* Education for Social Responsibility Award.

Writings

Firetalking (autobiography), photographs by Lawrence Migdale, Richard C. Owen (Katonah, NY), 1994.

PICTURE BOOKS; SELF-ILLUSTRATED, EXCEPT AS NOTED

Meteor!, Dodd, Mead (New York, NY), 1987.
Rechenka's Eggs, Philomel (New York, NY), 1988.
Boat Ride with Lillian Two Blossom, Philomel (New York, NY), 1988.
(With Ernest Lawrence Thayer) *Casey at the Bat,* Putnam (New York, NY), 1988.
The Keeping Quilt, Simon & Schuster (New York, NY), 1988, tenth anniversary edition with eight new drawings, 1998.
Uncle Vova's Tree, Philomel (New York, NY), 1989.
Babushka's Doll, Simon & Schuster (New York, NY), 1990.
Just Plain Fancy, Bantam (New York, NY), 1990.
Thunder Cake, Philomel (New York, NY), 1990.
Some Birthday!, Simon & Schuster (New York, NY), 1991.
Appelemando's Dreams, Philomel (New York, NY), 1991.

Chicken Sunday, Philomel (New York, NY), 1992.

Mrs. Katz and Tush, Bantam (New York, NY), 1992.

Picnic at Mudsock Meadow, Putnam (New York, NY), 1992.

The Bee Tree, Putnam (New York, NY), 1993.

Babushka Baba Yaga, Philomel (New York, NY), 1993.

My Rotten Redheaded Older Brother, Simon & Schuster (New York, NY), 1994.

Pink and Say, Philomel (New York, NY), 1994.

Tikvah Means Hope, Doubleday (New York, NY), 1994.

Babushka's Mother Goose (collection of stories and poems), Philomel (New York, NY), 1995.

My Ol' Man, Philomel (New York, NY), 1995.

The Trees of the Dancing Goats, Simon & Schuster (New York, NY), 1996.

Aunt Chip and the Great Triple Creek Dam Affair, Philomel (New York, NY), 1996.

I Can Hear the Sun: A Modern Myth, Philomel (New York, NY), 1996.

In Enzo's Splendid Gardens, Philomel (New York, NY), 1997.

Uncle Isaaco, Philomel (New York, NY), 1997.

Mrs. Mack, Philomel (New York, NY), 1998.

Thank You, Mr. Falker, Philomel (New York, NY), 1998.

Welcome Comfort, Philomel (New York, NY), 1999.

Luba and the Wren, Philomel (New York, NY), 1999.

The Calhoun Club, Philomel (New York, NY), 2000.

The Butterfly, Philomel (New York, NY), 2000.

Betty Doll, Philomel (New York, NY), 2001.

Several of Polacco's works have been translated into Spanish.

Adaptations

Spoken Arts has released a series of videos based on Polacco's books: *Rechenka's Eggs* in 1991, *Chicken*

Twenty years ago I held Traci Denise in the quilt for the first time. Someday she, too, will leave home and she will take the quilt with her.

Polacco traces the history of a cherished family quilt in her popular self-illustrated picture book **The Keeping Quilt.**

Sunday in 1992, *The Keeping Quilt* in 1993, *Aunt Chip and the Great Triple Creek Dam Affair* in 1996, *Pink and Say* in 1996, and *Thank You, Mr. Falker* in 1999; the company has also issued *Rechenka's Eggs* and *Thunder Cake* on video. Sound recordings of several of the author's works have also been issued: *Chicken Sunday,* Scholastic, 1993, *Just Plain Fancy,* Bantam Doubleday Dell Audio, 1994, *Casey at the Bat,* Spoken Arts, 1994, *The Keeping Quilt,* Spoken Arts, 1998, *Meteor!, Thunder Cake,* and *Thank You, Mr. Falker.* Several of Polacco's works have been issued in book/cassette combinations.

Work in Progress

Development of a line of toys, videos, and other items based on Polacco's books for online sale.

Sidelights

Author and illustrator Patricia Polacco is "as natural a storyteller as they come," according to Shannon Maughan of *Publishers Weekly.* The highly praised, award-winning Polacco has over thirty picture books to her credit, quite a feat in light of the fact that she did not start publishing until 1987, at the age of forty-one. A popular writer and artist, Polacco is lauded for transforming childhood memories, favorite episodes from family history, and elements from her Russian, Ukrainian, Jewish, and Irish heritage into works that are noted for their freshness, originality, warmth, panache, and universality. Polacco's books, such as *The Keeping Quilt, Uncle Vova's Tree, Pink and Say, My Ol' Man, In Enzo's Splendid Gardens, Welcome Comfort,* and *The Butterfly,* among others, feature characters of different races, religions, and age groups, and celebrate both diversity and commonality. Several of her works retell family stories that have been handed down for generations. The author's books often include Russian and Jewish customs and folklore, although she has also written about African and Native Americans, the Irish, and the Amish. In works such as *Babushka's Mother Goose, Babushka Baba Yaga,* and *Luba and the Wren,* Polacco retells folktales using a revisionist approach. Her stories are noted for clear, fluid language that makes them suitable for reading aloud. As an illustrator, Polacco often places penciled faces against bright colors, patterned backgrounds, and stark white space in works done in such mediums as watercolor, gouache, charcoal, and collage.

Polacco was born in Lansing, Michigan, in 1944, the daughter of William Barber, a salesman who became a television talk-show host, and Mary Ellen Gaw Barber, a teacher. Her father was of Irish descent and her mother was from a Russian and Ukrainian background. After her parents' divorce when she was three years old, Polacco and her older brother spent their school years with their mother and summers with their father. The author spent her early childhood living on a farm in Union City, Michigan, but when she was five, her Babushka (grandmother) passed away, and the author, her mother, and brother moved to Coral Gables, Florida,

For the next few days we worked very hard. We made almost a dozen "Pysanky" eggs. When people came in, they picked them up and said things like, "Beautiful!" "Splendid!" "Intricate!" "Glorious!" We sold them all in one single day.

To thank her for her Sunday chicken dinners, neighborhood children sell decorated eggs and buy Eula an Easter hat. *(Illustration from* Chicken Sunday, *written and illustrated by Polacco.)*

for three years before settling in Oakland, California. Writing on her Web site, Polacco recalled that living on the farm in Union City "was the most magical time of my life ... and that my Babushka and other grandparents were some of the most inspirational people in my life.... I would say that these relationships with my grandparents have most definitely influenced my life and work.... Personally, I feel that this is the most valuable experience of my life ... having the wonder of knowing both children and elderly people."

Polacco inherited a natural storytelling voice from both sides of the family. Stories, both oral and related from books, became a focus for her as an introspective child, though she had problems reading on her own. At age fourteen she was diagnosed with dyslexia; by this time, however, she had already suffered her classmates' teasing for her poor progress in reading and math. Sketching and illustrating became her twin refuges; her classmates were speechless when confronted with her fluid artwork. The life of her imagination became Polacco's refuge as an adolescent.

Graduating from high school, Polacco received a scholarship to college, but decided to marry at eighteen. She attended Ohio State University for a couple of terms, but eventually dropped out to go to work and have two children, Traci and Steven. After she and her first husband were divorced, Polacco began undergraduate studies in California. She went to Australia for further

education, earning an M.F.A. in painting from Morash University in Melbourne and a Ph.D. in Russian and Greek iconographic history from the Royal Melbourne Institute of Technology. While studying in Australia, Polacco met her second husband, Enzo, an Italian Jew from Trieste, Italy, who is a chef and cooking instructor as well as a Holocaust survivor.

Throughout her life, Polacco has been a maker of books. She told Maughan of *Publishers Weekly,* "I've always made rough dummies, like thick greeting cards, for people in my life to celebrate any occasion." At the insistence of a friend who admired these efforts, Polacco joined her local chapter of the Society of Children's Book Writers and Illustrators and began turning her family stories into picture books. In 1987, Polacco and her mother went to New York to show around her eighty-pound portfolio; the pair saw sixty publishers in a week. Polacco told Maughan, "I was too stupid to be frightened, and I just loved it." The same year, she sold her first book, *Meteor!*

Meteor! is the "mostly true" tale about the events that occur after a fallen star crashes in the backyard of Grampa and Gramma Gaw in Union City, Michigan. After the meteor lands, the news buzzes through town, more detailed with every telling. Soon the farm becomes a carnival ground complete with a circus. When the festivities end, the townspeople who have touched the meteor feel that it has changed their lives. Called "an

A young girl just can't win when she competes with her brother. (Illustration from My Rotten Redheaded Older Brother *written and illustrated by Polacco.)*

affectionate poke at small-town life" by a critic in *Kirkus Reviews, Meteor!* was praised by a reviewer in *Publishers Weekly* as "an enchanting book [that] overwhelmingly expresses the magic that suddenly pervades a small town, from the funny, folksy way the story is told to the imaginative, full-color illustrations." Polacco produced *The Calhoun Club,* a sequel to *Meteor!,* in 2000. In this book, children's author Petra Penwrite sets out to prove that the meteorite in her hometown of Union City is real and that it grants wishes to children.

Polacco's second book, *Rechenka's Eggs,* is a folkloric tale set in Russia before the Revolution. In this work, old Babushka, who lives alone in her small country home, paints beautiful, prize-winning eggs that always win first place at the Easter Festival. Babushka rescues Rechenka, a goose shot by a hunter, nurses her back to health, and in so doing receives the gift of beautifully colored eggs which the goose lays for her. Noting the book's "beauty and authenticity," Shaun Traynor of the *Times Educational Supplement* called *Rechenka's Eggs* "the perfect Easter book for all seasons." Leonard Marcus of the *New York Times Book Review* stated that the book "is as much about friendship and the workmanlike small things of this life as it is about faith," while Marcus Crouch of the *Junior Bookshelf* concluded, "This lovely book introduces a new and outstanding talent to the field of children's books . . . . It is a picture-book of outstanding quality."

The Keeping Quilt, a picture book published in 1988, is one of Polacco's most popular works. In this book, little Patricia narrates the story of a quilt that has been in her family for many years. The quilt ties together four generations of an immigrant Jewish family and becomes a symbol of their love and faith. Writing in *School Library Journal,* Lee Bock called *The Keeping Quilt* a "beautifully conceived book" and a "lovely story," while Denise M. Wilms of *Booklist* concluded, "Useful for the sense of history it presents to young viewers (especially in discussions of genealogy), this tale also carries a warm message on the meaning of family." In 1998, Polacco produced a revised edition of *The Keeping Quilt* to celebrate its tenth anniversary. The first edition ended with a picture of Polacco holding her newborn daughter; the revised edition expands the story with five new pages of text and paintings that depict her two children and their use of the Keeping Quilt.

Polacco has published several other books that deal with her Jewish heritage and the history of Jews in the United States and abroad. In *Tikvah Means Hope,* a Jewish family finds hope after a devastating fire in the hills of Oakland, California. A reviewer for *Publishers Weekly* thought that Polacco's drawings "skillfully and emotionally convey the anguish and suffering of the community, as well as its resilience and hopefulness." In *The Trees of the Dancing Goats,* Polacco once again draws on family memory and stories to tell the tale of how a Jewish family in Michigan helps make their neighbors' Christmas memorable during an outbreak of scarlet fever. "Polacco's brightly colored, detailed paintings in marking pens and pencil show a child in a close, loving

home that is bursting with energy and joy," wrote *Booklist*'s Hazel Rochman in a review of *The Tree of the Dancing Goats.*

With *Uncle Isaaco,* Polacco focused on the events of the Holocaust. In the book she tells of how her husband, Enzo, was expelled from his home in Trieste, Italy, as a little boy by the Nazis and how he missed his beloved uncle most of all. She also details the suffering of the Jews in World War II and the bravery of the French Resistance in *The Butterfly,* a story originally told to her by her Aunt Monique. Monique's mother hides a Jewish family in her basement and tries to help them escape. Wendy Lukehart, writing in *School Library Journal,* felt that the book was a "perfect blend of art and story," while *Booklist*'s Rochman concluded that "what will hold grade-school kids is the truth of the friendship story and the tension of hiding to survive."

Polacco has also dealt with issues of race in several of her books. In *Chicken Sunday,* a picture book published in 1992, neighborhood children help to get Miss Eula an Easter bonnet that she likes and in so doing win over a local Jewish shopkeeper. Carolyn Phelan of *Booklist* wrote, "Though ethnic differences too often divide and even destroy people, this first-person narrative merges various traditions with the innocent acceptance of childhood. In this moving picture book, the hatred sometimes engendered by racial and religious differences is overpowered by the love of people who recognize their common humanity. In strident and divisive times, here is a quiet, confident voice of hope." Calling *Chicken Sunday* "an authentic tale of childhood friendship," Dorothy Houlihan of *School Library Journal* noted that Polacco's tale "resonates with the veracity of a personal recollection and is replete with vivid visual and visceral images."

Polacco blended questions of race with another family tale in one of her most highly regarded books, *Pink and Say.* Published in 1994, this poignant work relates a story set during the Civil War that was told by her great-great-great-grandfather on her father's side. In this book, fifteen-year-old Sheldon Russell Curtis (Say), an Ohio boy left for dead in a Georgia battlefield, is rescued by gravedigger Pinkus Sylee (Pink), an African-American teen who is a fellow Union soldier. Pink drags Say to his home a few miles away. While the boy convalesces, he and Pink become friends and share their secrets: Pink can read—a knowledge forbidden to slaves—and wants to fight slavery, while Say admits that he is a deserter and that he shook the hand of Abraham Lincoln; this becomes a talismanic handshake between Pink and Say. Pink teaches Say to read, and his fervor against slavery inspires Say to rejoin his regiment. However, both boys are taken prisoners by the Confederates, who kill Pink's mother and throw the friends into the Andersonville prison camp. Due to his skin color, Pink is hung a few hours after entering the prison, while Say is released several months later. A reviewer in *Publishers Weekly* noted, "This book stands as a testament to [Pink's] life"; the critic added that Polacco's "gripping story resonates with emotion as she details the chilling and horrible reverberations of war and social injustice." A critic in *Kirkus Reviews* noted that Polacco tells her story "carefully and without melodrama so that it speaks for itself. The stunning illustrations ... are completely heartbreaking. A spectacular achievement." Writing in the *New York Times Book Review,* Henry Mayer concluded that Polacco "has addressed the theme of interracial friendship in previous books with heartfelt sentiment, but *Pink and Say* has a resonance that these contemporary stories lack. It is rare to find a children's book that deals so richly, yet gently, with the sober themes of slavery and freedom, martyrdom, and historical memory."

Thank You, Mr. Falker, a picture book published in 1998, is one of the author's most purely autobiographical works. In this story, ten-year-old Trisha yearns to read, but has been teased constantly by her classmates because she stumbles over words and numbers. Although she has gotten attention because of her art work, Trisha has hidden the fact that she can't read. Her fifth-grade teacher, Mr. Falker, is sympathetic to her difficulty. Using his own money, he pays a reading specialist to work with Trisha until she overcomes her problem. At the end of the story, Trisha finally—and joyfully—reads the words on the page of a book. Rochman, writing in *Booklist* noted, "Trisha isn't idealized; we see her messy and desperate, poring over her books. This will encourage the child who feels like a failure and the teacher who cares."

The eponymous protagonist of *Welcome Comfort* is a lonely, overweight foster child who is taken under the wing—or rather in the sleigh—of a rather plump school custodian. Comfort has never known the joys of Christmas until the mysterious custodian and his wife initiate him. A reviewer for *Publishers Weekly* noted that "this warm blend of fantasy and reality delivers a satisfying surprise ending," and that Polacco's artwork "is even more vibrant than usual." Reviewing the same title in the *Washington Post Book World,* Michael Patrick Hearn called the book "as warm as a down comforter and told with the conviction and cadences of a tall tale."

Whether writing about inter-generational relationships, cross-cultural friendships, Russian witches, or Jewish quilts, Polacco is happily at home in her created worlds and makes such worlds accessible to her readers, as well. As she noted in *Firetalking,* her autobiography, "I am lucky ... so very lucky! I love my life. Can you imagine doing what you love every day? ... My thoughts boil in my head. They catch the air and fly. The images and stories come back with fury and energy.... My heart sings whenever I am drawing."

Biographical and Critical Sources

BOOKS

Children's Literature Review, Volume 40, Gale (Detroit, MI), 1996, pp. 175-201.

Polacco, Patricia, *Firetalking,* Richard C. Owen (Katonah, NY), 1994.

PERIODICALS

Booklist, December 1, 1988, Denise M. Wilms, review of *The Keeping Quilt,* p. 654; March 15, 1992, Carolyn Phelan, review of *Chicken Sunday,* p. 1388; November 1, 1996, Hazel Rochman, review of *The Trees of the Dancing Goats,* p. 509; May 1, 1998, Hazel Rochman, review of *Thank You, Mr. Falker,* p. 1522; November 15, 1998, p. 597; May 15, 1999, p. 1700; April 4, 2000, Hazel Rochman, review of *The Butterfly,* p. 1479; August, 2000, p. 155.

Junior Bookshelf, June, 1988, Marcus Crouch, review of *Rechenka's Eggs,* p. 131.

Kirkus Reviews, April 1, 1987, review of *Meteor!,* p. 557; April 15, 1993, p. 535; June 1, 1994, p. 779; September 15, 1994, review of *Pink and Say,* p. 1279; April 15, 1997, p. 647; May 1, 1999, p. 726.

New York Times Book Review, April 3, 1988, Leonard Marcus, review of *Rechenka's Eggs,* p. 16; November 13, 1994, Henry Mayer, review of *Pink and Say,* p. 42; May 31, 1998, p. 40; December 19, 1999, p. 31; July 18, 1999, p. 24.

Publishers Weekly, April 10, 1987, review of *Meteor!,* p. 95; February 15, 1993, Shannon Maughan, "Patricia Polacco," pp. 179, 185; August 15, 1994, review of *Pink and Say,* p. 95; September 12, 1994, review of *Tikvah Means Hope,* p. 90; September 2, 1996, p. 130; September 30, 1996, p. 87; October 12, 1998, p. 76; September 27, 1999, review of *Welcome Comfort,* p. 56; June 12, 2000, p. 72.

School Library Journal, October, 1988, Lee Bock, review of *The Keeping Quilt,* p. 136; May, 1992, Dorothy Houlihan, review of *Chicken Sunday,* p. 92; August, 1994, p. 150; November, 1996, pp. 90-91; August, 1998, p. 144; December, 1998, p. 89; June, 1999, p. 119; May, 2000, Wendy Lukehart, review of *The Butterfly,* p. 151.

Times Educational Supplement, March 25, 1988, Shaun Traynor, review of *Rechenka's Eggs,* p. 31.

Washington Post Book World, December 12, 1999, Michael Patrick Hearn, "Picturing the Holidays," p. 15.

ON-LINE

Patricia Polacco Web site, www.patriciapolacco.com (March 25, 2001).*

*   *   *

POLLEMA-CAHILL, Phyllis 1958-

Personal

Surname is pronounced Po-*lee*-ma-*Kay*-hill; born November 28, 1958, in Winona, MN; daughter of Cyrus and Ramona Pollema; married Jeff Cahill, 1983. *Education:* Rocky Mountain College of Art and Design, A.A., 1986. *Hobbies and other interests:* Reading, gardening, cooking, studying French.

Addresses

Home—Colorado Springs, CO. *Agent*—Wilkinson Studios, 901 West Jackson Blvd., Suite 201, Chicago, IL 60607. *E-mail*—Ppcahill@aol.com.

Phyllis Pollema-Cahill

Career

Designer and creative director for various design firms, 1976-95; freelance illustrator for children's books and magazines, 1995—. *Member:* Society of Children's Book Writers and Illustrators, Graphic Artists Guild.

Illustrator

Amy Goes to School, Shortland Publications (New Zealand), 1996.

The Talent Show, Shortland Publications (New Zealand), 1996.

The Indigo Jackal, Kumuda Reddy, 1996.

Ingrid Lawrenz, *The Day Mama Played,* Chariot/Victor (Colorado Springs, CO), 1997.

The Lotus Flower, Shortland Publications (New Zealand), 1997.

Helen Bannerman, *Tigers for Supper,* Star Bright Books (New York, NY), 1998.

Bubbles, Shortland Publications (New Zealand), 1998.

(Contributor of illustrations) *Belonging to His Family,* Pacific Press, 1998.

Carol Reinsma, *God's Big Story,* International Bible Society (Colorado Springs, CO), 1999.

Mi Dia, Scott Foresman/Addison-Wesley (Glenview, IL), 1999.

Carol Reinsma, *I Talked to God Today,* International Bible Society (Colorado Springs, CO), 1999.

Great-Great Grandfather's Railroad, Wright Group (San Diego, CA), 1999.

Free to Learn, Perfection Learning, 1999.

Carol Reinsma, *Tell Me the Story of Jesus,* International Bible Society (Colorado Springs, CO), 2000.

Grandma Ellen and Me, Pacific Press, 2000.

Carol Reinsma, *Teach Me to Be Wise,* International Bible Society (Colorado Springs, CO), 2001.

Helen Ketteman, *Carlos Helps Out,* Wright Group (San Diego, CA), 2001.

Contributor of illustrations to magazines, including *Highlights for Children, Guideposts for Kids, Jack and Jill, Story Friends, Pockets, On the Line,* and *Friend.* Also contributor of illustrations to textbooks.

Sidelights

Phyllis Pollema-Cahill told *SATA:* "I grew up in rural Minnesota. As a child I loved to color and paint, yet it wasn't until high school that I realized I had enough ability to become an artist. The summer after my high school graduation, I was offered a position as an assistant artist in a small design studio. At the time, I was signed up to attend an art school in California, but I decided to postpone my college education and soon was learning about camera-ready art, Rapidographs, and rubber cement.

"That was the beginning of a fifteen-year career as a graphic artist. My last position was as creative director

Artwork by Pollema-Cahill.

for one of the McGraw-Hill divisions. What I learned about creating art for printing, meeting deadlines, and working as part of a team is invaluable to what I do now. Graphic design really strengthened my composition skills and introduced me to my Macintosh, which I love but don't use for illustration.

"I later received my degree in illustration from Rocky Mountain College of Art and Design in Denver, Colorado, an excellent school where I learned a tremendous amount about figure drawing, color theory, art history, and more figure drawing.

"I feel very fortunate to have been illustrating full-time since December of 1995. It's a wonderful thing to be able to bring stories to life for children, and it's what I've wanted to do for many years. So far I've illustrated more than a dozen picture books and many magazine stories. I've also illustrated textbooks, activity books, posters, and book covers.

"Strong drawing skills are very important to me. I'm a stickler for correct proportion, perspective, and anatomy. Drawing people is probably my favorite thing. I draw them from my imagination, rather than relying on models or photographs. People's faces, hands, and expressions fascinate me.

"I work in traditional watercolor. I find the clean, transparent washes incredibly beautiful. Color and value are very important to me also. I spend a lot of time and thought organizing the values and choosing the palette for each project.

"One of my favorite parts of illustrating is the research. I've learned about Korean horsehair hats, the nesting habits of puffins, how to make paper, and many other interesting things. I like knowing that my illustrations are as accurate as possible.

"I live in Colorado, at the foot of Pikes Peak, with my husband, Jeff, and our two cats, Mickey and Patches. I have three grown stepchildren and a step-granddaughter. When I'm not illustrating, I like to read young adult novels, garden, and cook. I also speak French, and I help moderate a 'listserv' of children's book illustrators."

Biographical and Critical Sources

ON-LINE

Illustration for Children's Publishing, http://www. phylliscahill.com/ (January 3, 2001).

R

RANSOME, James E. 1961-

Personal

Born September 25, 1961, in Rich Square, NC; married Lesa Cline (a teacher), September 2, 1989; children: Jaime, Maya, Malcolm. *Education:* Pratt Institute, B.F.A. (illustration); studied at Art Students League.

Addresses

Home—Poughkeepsie, NY. *Agent*—c/o William Morrow & Co., 1350 Avenue of the Americas, New York, NY 10019.

Career

Artist and educator. Pratt Institute, Brooklyn, NY, instructor. Speaker at schools and at Virginia Hamilton Conference, Kent State University, 1996. *Exhibitions:* Has shown works in many galleries, including Kimberly Gallery, New York City; Artist's Proof, New England; Society of Illustrators, New York City; Chowan College, NC; Elizabeth Stone Gallery, Birmingham, MI; African-American Museum of Fine Art, CA; Sterling Creations, NJ; Essex Community College, NJ; and Art for Living, NJ. Permanent installations include Charlotte Public Library, Charlotte, NC, and Children's Museum of Indianapolis. *Member:* Society of Illustrators.

Awards, Honors

Parenting Reading Magic Award, 1990, for *Do Like Kyla;* Parent's Choice Foundation annual award, 1990, for *Aunt Flossie's Hats (and Crab Cakes Later);* Coretta Scott King Honor award, and American Library Association (ALA) notable book designation, both 1993, both for *Uncle Jed's Barbershop;* Coretta Scott King Award for illustration, International Board on Books for Young People Honor Award, and ALA notable book designation, all 1994, all for *The Creation;* Simon Wiesenthal Museum of Tolerance Award, 1996, for *The Wagon.*

James E. Ransome's rich paintings reflect the strong characters found in William H. Hooks's Freedom's Fruit.

Illustrator

Elizabeth Fitzgerald Howard, *Aunt Flossie's Hats (and Crab Cakes Later),* Clarion (New York, NY), 1990.

Angela Johnson, *Do Like Kyla,* Orchard Books (New York, NY), 1990.

Arthur A. Levine, *All the Lights in the Night,* Tambourine (New York, NY), 1991.

Katherine Mead, *Does Your Grandpa Say Galoshes?,* Silver Burdett (Morristown, NJ), 1991.

Lenny Hort, *How Many Stars in the Sky?*, Tambourine (New York, NY), 1991.

Denise L. Patrick, *Red Dancing Shoes*, Morrow (New York, NY), 1993.

Angela Johnson, *The Girl Who Wore Snakes*, Orchard Books (New York, NY), 1993.

Margaree King Mitchell, *Uncle Jed's Barbershop*, Simon & Schuster (New York, NY), 1993.

Christine Widman, *The Hummingbird Garden*, Macmillan (New York, NY), 1993.

Deborah Hopkinson, *Sweet Clara and the Freedom Quilt*, Knopf (New York, NY), 1993.

James Weldon Johnson, *The Creation*, Holiday House (New York, NY), 1994.

Eve Feldman, *That Cat!*, Tambourine (New York, NY), 1994.

Marilee R. Burton, *My Best Shoes*, Morrow (New York, NY), 1994.

Sharon M. Draper, *Ziggy and the Black Dinosaurs*, Just Us (East Orange, NJ), 1994.

Michael Rosen, *Bonesy and Isabel*, Harcourt (New York, NY), 1994.

Jan Carr, *Dark Day, Light Night*, Hyperion (New York, NY), 1995.

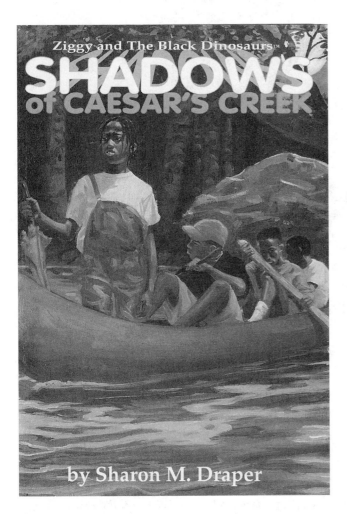

Ransome illustrated the cover of Sharon M. Draper's **Shadows of Caesar's Creek.**

Valerie and Vanessa Flournoy, *Celie and the Harvest Fiddler*, Tambourine (New York, NY), 1995.

Charlotte Zolotow, *The Old Dog*, revised edition, HarperCollins (New York, NY), 1995.

William H. Hooks, *Freedom's Fruit*, Knopf (New York, NY), 1996.

Tony Johnston, *The Wagon*, Tambourine (New York, NY), 1996.

Charlotte Watson Sherman, *Eli and the Swamp Man*, HarperCollins (New York, NY), 1996.

Elisabeth Jane Stewart, *Bimmi Finds a Cat*, Clarion (New York, NY), 1996.

Angela Shelf Medearis, *Rum-a-tum-tum*, Holiday House (New York, NY), 1997.

Donna L. Washington, reteller, *A Pride of African Tales*, HarperCollins (New York, NY), 1997.

Sharon M. Draper, *Shadows of Caesar's Creek* ("Ziggy and the Black Dinosaurs" series), Just Us (East Orange, NJ), 1997.

Eve Bunting, *Your Move*, Harcourt (San Diego, CA), 1998.

Patricia and Frederick McKissack, *Let My People Go: Bible Stories Told by a Freeman of Color to His Daughter, Charlotte, in Charleston, South Carolina, 1806-16*, Atheneum (New York, NY), 1998.

Jacqueline K. Ogburn, *The Jukebox Man*, Dial (New York, NY), 1998.

Eve Bunting, *Peepers*, Harcourt (San Diego, CA), 2000.

Lesa Cline-Ransome, *Satchel Paige*, Simon & Schuster, 2000.

Deborah Hopkinson, *Under the Quilt of Night*, Atheneum (New York, NY), 2000.

Dinah Johnson, *Quinnie Blue*, Holt (New York, NY), 2000.

J. J. Reneaux, reteller, *How Animals Saved the People: Animal Tales from the South*, Morrow (New York, NY), 2000.

Robert D. San Souci, reteller, *The Secret of the Stones: A Folktale*, Phyllis Fogelman (New York, NY), 2000.

James Haskins and Kathleen Benson, *Building a New Land: African Americans in Colonial America*, HarperCollins (New York, NY), 2001.

Jacqueline Woodson, *Visiting Day*, Scholastic (New York, NY), 2001.

Lesa Cline-Ransome, *Quilt Alphabet*, Holiday House (New York, NY), 2001.

Ferida Wolff, *It Is the Wind, I Think*, HarperCollins (New York, NY), in press.

Illustrator of book jackets for young adult books, including *The Middle of Somewhere, Winning Scheherazade, Children of the Fire, Down in the Piney Woods, The Cry of the Wolf,* and *Chevrolet Saturdays.*

Sidelights

The work of artist and illustrator James E. Ransome has been chosen to grace the texts of many well-known authors, among them Patricia McKissack, Charlotte Zolotow, and James Weldon Johnson. Awarded for many of his illustration efforts, Ransome has developed his career along the lines of his mentor, noted illustrator Jerry Pinkney, by specializing in bringing to life stories that reflect the strong ties and traditional history of

Ransome's boldly colored paintings illustrate his wife's biography of legendary pitcher Satchel Paige, the first African American to pitch in a major league World Series game. (Illustration from Satchel Paige, *written by Lesa Cline-Ransome.)*

African-American families: Margaree King Mitchell's *Uncle Jed's Barbershop,* Dinah Johnson's *Quinnie Blue,* and Katherine Mead's *Does Your Granpa Say Galoshes?,* among others. "I am a visual storyteller," Ransome once commented, "and because each book has a special voice, my approach toward each is different as well. Whether it be through my choice of palette, design, or perspective, there is always a desire to experiment and explore what makes each book unique."

Born in rural Rich Square, North Carolina, in 1961, Ransome was raised far away from the urban art galleries and financially well-endowed libraries that would one day provide him with a place to exhibit his art for children to enjoy. His interest in drawing began at an early age; it found its first outlet in pencil sketches of hot-rod cars and comic book characters, and eventually grew into detailed illustrations of the Bible stories he read to his aging grandmother. By elementary school Ransome had come under the influence of television cartoons and *MAD* magazine; he created stories featuring him and his friends and tried to illustrate them in the *MAD* style. He further developing his drawing skills through how-to books on drawing he found at his school library, because his school did not offer art classes.

As a high school sophomore, Ransome moved north to Bergenfield, New Jersey, where he was suddenly exposed to a wealth of creative instruction, not only in drawing but also in photography and film making. Working with film quickly became his new passion; as Ransome recalled in a profile for *Embracing the Child* online: "Through photography, I discovered the power perspective, value, and cropping could have on a single image. Through film making, I discovered the many ways to pace a story with the aid of camera angles and framed images." After completing a number of student films, Ransome began to work in animation. It would be a course in drawing and painting taken as a way of improving his animation skills that rekindled Ransome's childhood interest in illustrating. After high school graduation he moved to Brooklyn, New York, and attended the prestigious Pratt Institute, graduating with a B.F.A. in illustration.

During his years at Pratt Ransome was exposed to the work of a number of artists who would strongly influence his own artistic style. In addition to nineteenth- and early twentieth-century painters such as Mary Cassatt, John Singer Sargent, Winslow Homer, and Edgar Degas, contemporary illustrators Bernie Fuchs, Robert Cunningham, Skip Leipke, and Jerry Pinkney showed Ransome new ways to engage in "visual storytelling." Ransome's relationship with the award-winning Pinkney not only opened the young student's eyes to the fact that there were African-American artists who were highly successful in their field, but it also developed into a close friendship when Pinkney became Ransome's mentor.

In 1989 Ransome received his first illustration assignment that would become a published book for children:

Elizabeth Fitzgerald Howard's *Aunt Flossie's Hats (and Crab Cakes Later).* The book is a tale of two young girls who visit their hat-loving aunt and hear the story about each colorful hat in the older woman's closet. Ransome's oil paintings for *Aunt Flossie's Hats (and Crab Cakes Later)* were praised by reviewers and earned him the first of several illustration awards. His ability to present a poignant, warm-hearted depiction of an African-American family was central to his success with the many illustration projects that followed. In *Uncle Jed's Barbershop,* for example, the story of a favorite older relative and his lifelong dream is enhanced by oil paintings that "present a warm portrait of a loving family in both hard times and good," according to *Horn Book* contributor Hanna B. Zeiger. Equal praise for Ransome's contribution was given by *Booklist* critic Deborah Abbott, who noted that "A real strength [of *Uncle Jed's Barbershop*] is the paintings, which capture memorable characters and family life in the rural South with a warmth and depth that is truly moving."

Ransome also illustrated Dinah Johnson's picture book *Quinnie Blue,* published in 2000. Dealing again with a beloved relative, this story reveals the oral traditions that develop within families, as a young girl learns old stories from her grandmother and namesake, Quinnie Blue, then draws parallels with her own life and makes these stories her own. "Even more than the text," noted a *Publishers Weekly* reviewer, "Ransome's closely focused portraits of girl and grandmother underscore the love shared by them and their close-knit family." Calling *Quinnie Blue* "visually lovely," *School Library Journal* contributor Louise L. Sherman added that the illustrator "beautifully contrasts the present suburban life with the more rural past of the family." *Booklist* contributor Ilene Cooper praised Ransome for his "handsome paintings set against a background of weathered wood [that] are every bit as lyrical as the text."

In addition to his ability to capture the close emotional bond between family members, Ransome has also been successful at portraying the confusing emotions of childhood. In a new edition of Charlotte Zolotow's classic *The Old Dog,* a poignant story about the death of a beloved pet is updated through Ransome's illustrations of a young African-American boy coping with death and loneliness. Praising his technique as "masterful" in portraying emotions, *School Library Journal* contributor Martha Topol added that Ransome's "richly hued illustrations capture the intensity of [the boy's] grief." Other critics commented on the book's design, which incorporates a panel of autumn leaves on each left-facing page that provide "an expressive image for an unsentimental story about connection and loss and renewal," according to *Booklist* reviewer Hazel Rochman.

A different emotion is captured in Ransome's oil paintings for Jan Carr's *Dark Day, Light Night,* wherein a young girl must learn to control her mood after things do not go her way. Noting that the illustrator "pays careful attention to the use of light and shadow" within his illustrations, *Horn Book* contributor Ellen Fader commented favorably on his ability to "extend ... the image implicit in the [book's] title." Susan Dove Lempke noticed the "great expression" within Ransome's artwork, citing his success in portraying young Manda's transformation "from glowering to glowing, and depicting [her aunt] as realistically unglamourous but infused with joy and loving tenderness" in her *Booklist* appraisal of *Dark Day, Light Night.*

During the course of his career, Ransome has been asked to illustrate many books that focus on the history and folklore of African Americans. Several, such as William H. Hooks's *Freedom's Fruit,* take as their subject life as a slave prior to the U.S. Civil War. This 1996 picture book focuses on Mama Marina, a conjure woman who cleverly transforms a request by her master to protect his grape crop from thievery into a means whereby her daughter and her daughter's boyfriend make their escape. Hooks's powerful language "is mirrored in Ransome's evocative illustrations," commented *School Library Journal* reviewer Lisa Dennis, who added that the illustrator's "dark, yet vibrant paintings" bring "the characters to life" and engage the audience. Additional praise was forthcoming from Hazel Rochman, who noted in her *Booklist* review that "Ransome's rich paintings set the dramatic confrontations against the plantation scenes as the seasons change."

Conjure women are joined by tricksters and wise men, as well as by hapless fools, in storyteller J. J. Reneaux's *How Animals Saved the People: Animal Tales from the South.* In this 2000 work, Ransome brings to life eight folk tales via "full-bleed, spry watercolors" that "ably capture the traits of the memorable characters, the rural Southern setting and the pervasive humor" of Reneaux's stories, according to a *Publishers Weekly* contributor. The richness of African-American folklore is again reflected by Ransome's brush within the pages of Robert D. San Souci's *The Secret of the Stones.* This 2000 picture-book tells the story of a childless couple who pick up and pocket two beautiful white stones discovered on the path as they walk home from the cotton fields. In the coming days the pair arrive home to find all the chores done, but the mystery is solved when they discover that the stones are, in fact, two children who have fallen under an evil spell. John Peters commented in *Booklist* that the illustrator portrays San Souci's hardworking young couple "and their verdant rural setting with dignified richly colored, uncluttered realism." Praising the work as a "perfectly magical offering," *School Library Journal* reviewer Ann Welton added that "Ransome's oil-on-paper illustrations are big, bold, and arresting."

In addition to illustrating books for young people, Ransome has completed a number of large artworks and murals. He teaches courses at the Pratt Institute and also travels to schools around the country to speak to budding artists and young fans of his work. "By conveying to young readers the individual traits of characters," he once commented, "I only hope that I am instilling an appreciation for all the wonderfully unique qualities and cultural and racial differences we all possess."

Biographical and Critical Sources

BOOKS

Rollock, Barbara, *Black Authors and Illustrators of Children's Books,* second edition, Garland (New York, NY), 1992.

PERIODICALS

Booklist, September 1, 1993, Deborah Abbott, review of *Uncle Jed's Barbershop,* p. 69; September 1, 1995, Hazel Rochman, review of *The Old Dog,* p. 90; February 15, 1996, Susan Dove Lempke, review of *Dark Day, Light Night,* p. 1025; February 15, 1996, Hazel Rochman, review of *Freedom's Fruit,* p. 1020; September 1, 1996, Susan Dove Lempke, review of *Eli and the Swamp Man,* p. 132; January 1, 2000, John Peters, review of *The Secret of the Stones,* p. 934; February 15, 2000, review of *Satchel Paige,* p. 1109; April 15, 2000, Ilene Cooper, review of *Quinnie Blue,* p. 1552.

Horn Book, September-October, 1991, p. 584; January-February, 1992, p. 65; November-December, 1993, Hanna B. Zeiger, review of *Uncle Jed's Barbershop,* p. 727; November-December, 1995, Martha V. Parravano, review of *The Old Dog,* p. 762; May-June, 1996, Ellen Fader, review of *Dark Day, Light Night,* p. 320.

New Yorker, November 25, 1991, p. 146.

New York Times Book Review, February 21, 1993, p. 22.

Publishers Weekly, March 16, 1990, review of *Do Like Kyla,* p. 68; February 15, 1991, p. 88; April 5, 1991, p. 145; November 1, 1991, p. 80; December 7, 1992, p. 63; April 24, 1995, review of *Bonesy and Isabel,* p. 71; February 23, 1998, review of *Your Move,* p. 77; June 1, 1998, review of *The Jukebox Man,* p. 48; May 29, 2000, review of *Quinnie Blue,* p. 82; December 18, 2000, review of *How Animals Saved the People,* p. 77.

School Library Journal, April, 1990, p. 92; May, 1991, p. 79; March, 1992, p. 216; June, 1993, Karen James, review of *Sweet Clara and the Freedom Quilt,* p. 76; December, 1995, Kevin Wayne Booe, review of *Aunt Flossie's Hats,* p. 62; December, 1995, Martha Topol, review of *The Old Dog,* p. 93; February, 1996, Lisa Dennis, review of *Freedom's Fruit,* pp. 84-85; June, 1996, Carol Schene, review of *Eli and the Swamp Man,* p. 124; May, 1998, Carolyn Noah, review of *The Jukebox Man,* p. 124; February, 2000, Ann Welton, review of *The Secret of the Stones,* p. 115; June, 2000, Louise L. Sherman, review of *Quinnie Blue,* p. 116.

ON-LINE

Embracing the Child, http://www.eyeontomorrow.com/ (April 26, 2001), "James Ransome, Illustrator."*

RIDDEN, Brian (John) 1934-

Personal

Born June 8, 1934, in Sydney, Australia; married Elva Sorensen (a teacher and musician), August 27, 1955; children: Anne Collett, Paul, Jennifer, Geoffrey. *Education:* Sydney Teachers College, diploma of teaching, 1952; Australian National University, B.A., 1962; University of British Columbia, M.Ed., 1972. *Hobbies and other interests:* Tennis, sea, rainforest, theater, symphony orchestra, travel.

Addresses

Home and office—Queensland, Australia.

Career

English teacher, English department head, university lecturer, and education administrator in Australia and British Columbia, Canada, between 1953 and 1987. Writer, 1990—. *Member:* Australian Society of Authors, Queensland Writers Centre.

Awards, Honors

Mentorship, Australian Society of Authors, 1997; literature grant, Australian Council for the Arts, 1999; Notable Australian Children's Book, Children's Book Council of Australia, 2000, for *Whistle Man*.

Writings

FOR YOUNG ADULTS

Outfall, Greater Glider Productions (Melbourne, Australia), 2000.
Whistle Man, Lothian (Melbourne, Australia), 2000.
Blind Fear, Lothian (Melbourne, Australia), 2001.

Work in Progress

Winter Rainbow, "a fictionalized account of a twelve-year-old's experience in a creative-expressive grief counseling program"; two young adult historical novels with Australian settings.

Sidelights

Brian Ridden told *SATA:* "As a child I won prizes in state and Australia-wide writing competitions. I had my first feature published at age fifteen. I tried to combine writing with a career in school-teaching, doing university studies by correspondence and at night, and raising four children. I succeeded in publishing leisure features and reviewing children's books for a capital-city newspaper, but abandoned a children's novel. I became more involved in teaching and administration until my hearing failed. Retirement re-fired my writing, giving me the opportunity to write for children full-time.

Brian Ridden

"I write almost every day and enjoy it immensely. I write what I like to think of as 'serious entertainment.' First and foremost, I tell stories for their own sake because I believe in the value of the imagined world. My stories are often about heroism in ordinary lives; I hope children will explore thoughts and feelings about meeting challenge and managing change in their own lives."

Biographical and Critical Sources

PERIODICALS

Australian Book Review, December 2000-January 2001, Pam Macintyre, review of *Whistle Man,* p. 59.
Reading Time, Volume 45, number 1, review of *Whistle Man.*
Sunday Age, November 5, 2000, review of *Whistle Man,* p. 11.

*   *   *

RUSSELL, Sharman Apt 1954-

Personal

Born July 23, 1954, at Edwards Air Force Base, CA; daughter of Milburn Grant (a test pilot) and Faye Lorrie (a bridge teacher) Apt; married Peter Forsythe Russell (a city planner), January, 1981; children: Maria Hallie, David Grant. *Education:* Attended University of California, San Diego, and University of California, Berkeley, received B.S. (with honors), 1976; University of Montana, M.F.A., 1980. *Politics:* Democrat.

Addresses

Home—1113 West St., Silver City, NM 88061. *Office*—Department of Humanities, Western New Mexico University, Silver City, NM 88062. *E-mail*—sharman@zianet.com.

Career

El Paso Times, Silver City, NM, stringer, 1981; Western New Mexico University, Silver City, instructor in developmental writing, 1981—; Antioch University, faculty member in creative nonfiction for low-residency M.F.A. program, 1997—; writer. *Member:* Society of Children's Book Writers and Illustrators, Poets and Writers, PEN West, Phi Beta Kappa.

Awards, Honors

Fellowship, Writers at Work, 1989; Henry Joseph Jackson Award in nonfiction, 1989; Pushcart Prize, 1990, for "Illegal Aliens"; Booksellers Award, Mountain and Plains, and Zia Award, New Mexico Press Women, both 1992, both for *Songs of the Fluteplayer: Seasons of Life in the Southwest.*

Writings

FOR CHILDREN

Frederick Douglass, Chelsea House (New York, NY), 1987.

Sharman Apt Russell

The Humpbacked Fluteplayer, Knopf (New York, NY), 1994.

FOR ADULTS

(With Susan Berry) *Built to Last: An Architectural History of Silver City, New Mexico,* New Mexico Historical Society (Santa Fe, NM), 1986.
Songs of the Fluteplayer: Seasons of Life in the Southwest, Addison-Wesley (Reading, MA), 1991.
Kill the Cowboy: A Battle of Mythology in the New West, Addison-Wesley (Reading, MA), 1993.
When the Land Was Young: Reflections on American Archaeology, Addison-Wesley (Reading, MA), 1996.
The Last Matriarch (novel), University of New Mexico Press (Albuquerque, NM), 2000.
Anatomy of a Rose: Exploring the Secret Life of Flowers (nonfiction), Perseus Books, 2001.

Also author of *Illegal Aliens.* Coeditor of Western New Mexico University *Alumni Bulletin,* 1981-83 and 1985-87. Contributor to periodicals, including *Missouri Review, Threepenny Review, North American Review, New Mexico Magazine, New York Times,* and *Nature Conservancy.*

Sidelights

Sharman Apt Russell is an educator and writer whose publications include both history and fiction for adults and children. Russell was born at Edwards Air Force Base in 1954, and she earned her undergraduate degree at the University of California in Berkeley. In 1981, after receiving a master's degree from the University of Montana, she worked as a stringer for the *El Paso Times.* Later that year, she became an instructor in developmental writing at Western New Mexico University.

In 1994 Russell released *The Humpbacked Fluteplayer,* her first book of fiction for a younger audience. The novel depicts the adventures of May, who is unhappy about her family's recent move to Arizona, and her classmate Evan. While on a school field trip in the Phoenix desert, the two children are transported to an alternate universe populated by six magical tribes. May and Evan are enslaved by one of the tribes and must work with Wren, a fellow slave, in order to free the slaves, bring peace to the tribal kingdom, and return to their own universe. Along the way, May develops an appreciation for her new home and gains an understanding of the importance of working with others to resolve conflict. While the *School Library Journal*'s Patricia Manning claimed that Russell's characters are "somewhat two-dimensional," a *Publishers Weekly* reviewer found that her "desert landscapes are richly evocative and the cultures of each tribe are suitably distinct." The same reviewer praised Russell as "a fantasist of real potential."

In writing her first book for adults, *Built to Last: An Architectural History of Silver City, New Mexico,* Russell collaborated with Susan Berry. That work, which appeared in 1986, was followed by *Frederick Douglass,* a biography of the American lawyer who became an anti-slavery activist in the mid-nineteenth century. Russell then published *Songs of the Fluteplayer: Seasons of Life in the Southwest,* which received both a Booksellers Award and a Zia Award. In 1993 she produced another adult volume, *Kill the Cowboy: A Battle of Mythology in the New West.*

When the Land Was Young: Reflections on American Archaeology, published in 1996, concerns social changes reflected in American archaeological practices. A *Publishers Weekly* reviewer hailed the book as "an exciting portrait of archeology today," and *Booklist* reviewer Donna Seaman described *When the Land Was Young* as "a lively, confident, and free-flowing history."

When the Land Was Young was followed by 2000's *The Last Matriarch* and *Anatomy of a Rose,* published in 2001. *The Last Matriarch* is a historical novel set in prehistoric North America. In the book, an elderly woman recalls her life, including her encounters with dangerous animals and her interactions with other members of her clan. A *Publishers Weekly* reviewer described *The Last Matriarch* as a "well-researched novel" and affirmed that Russell "authentically recreates the world of ... hunters and gatherers who lived ... more than 1,000 years ago."

Biographical and Critical Sources

PERIODICALS

Booklist, February 1, 1988, review of *Frederick Douglass,* p. 933; March 1, 1994, Mary Harris Veeder, review of *The Humpbacked Fluteplayer,* p. 1262; May 15, 1996, Donna Seaman, review of *When the Land Was Young: Reflections on American Archaeology,* p. 1567; March 1, 2000, Patricia Monaghan, review of *The Last Matriarch,* p. 1195.

Discover, April, 2001, Deborah A. Hudson, review of *Anatomy of a Rose,* p. 82.

Library Journal, March 15, 2000, Susan A. Zappia, review of *The Last Matriarch,* p. 129.

New Scientist, February 17, 2001, Gail Vines, review of *Anatomy of a Rose,* p. 53.

Publishers Weekly, April 4, 1994, review of *The Humpbacked Fluteplayer,* p. 80; April 29, 1996, review of *When the Land Was Young: Reflections on American Archaeology,* p. 61; January 10, 2000, review of *The Last Matriarch;* March 12, 2001, review of *Anatomy of a Rose,* p. 73.

School Library Journal, April, 1994, Patricia Manning, review of *The Humpbacked Fluteplayer,* p. 130.

Whole Earth, summer, 1998, Elizabeth Thompson and Heather Price, review of *When the Land Was Young: Reflections on American Archaeology,* p. 92.

S

SAPORT, Linda 1954-

Personal

Born February 13, 1954, in Denver, CO; daughter of Walter (an optician) and Eileen (a bookkeeper) Saport; married Steve Elder (a poet), May 17, 1999. *Education:* University of Colorado, B.S., 1976, attended art classes, 1993-95; attended Colorado Institute of Arts, 1995.

Addresses

Home—Boulder, CO.

Linda Saport

Career

Has worked in various jobs in advertising, film, and video in Boston, MA, San Francisco, CA, and Denver, CO; has worked in a library and in a book store in Colorado. Illustrator of children's books, 1996—. *Exhibitions:* Society of Illustrators, 1999; Kentucky Derby Museum, 2001. *Member:* Society of Children's Book Writers and Illustrators.

Awards, Honors

Americas Award, Consortium of Latin American Studies Programs, 1997, for *The Face at the Window*.

Writings

ILLUSTRATOR; FOR CHILDREN

Regina Hanson, *The Face at the Window,* Clarion (New York, NY), 1997.

Lynn Joseph, *Jump Up Time: A Trinidad Carnival Story,* Clarion (New York, NY), 1998.

All the Pretty Little Horses: A Traditional Lullaby, Clarion (New York, NY), 1999.

Tololwa M. Mollel, *Subira, Subira,* Clarion (New York, NY), 2000.

Kerry Brown, *Tupag the Dreamer,* Marshall Cavendish (New York, NY), 2001.

Nancy White Carlstrom, *Before You Were Born,* Eerdmans (Grand Rapids, MI), 2001.

Work in Progress

Illustrations for *The Company of Crows,* by Marilyn Singer, expected in 2002.

Sidelights

Linda Saport told *SATA:* "As a child, I would cut pictures of paintings out of calendars and magazines and tape them to the walls of my bedroom—I would pretend I lived inside them. I spent a lot of time playing alone in my room; I liked to rearrange the furniture.

Set in contemporary Jamaica, this 1997 work, which tells of a girl's fear of a mentally ill woman, feature Saport's pastels.
(Illustration from The Face at the Window, *written by Regina Hanson.)*

Tatu must gather three whiskers from a lion to learn how to win her younger brother's love in Tololwa M. Mollel's **Subira Subira**, *illustrated by Saport.*

"One of my favorite Christmas presents was a set of watercolors that came with sponges in all different shapes. I liked to sit at a table in my room and mix up the colors. I loved art in school. I was usually chosen to decorate the bulletin boards. In high school I worked in acrylic and oil paints. The school bought one of my paintings to hang in the principal's office.

"As much as I loved art, I didn't think a person could earn a living at it. In college I studied journalism. But I wasn't very interested. After graduating, I went from job to job looking for something I liked to do. I worked in advertising and film and video and was miserable most of the time. I worked in Boston, San Francisco, and Denver. I've had so many jobs I can't remember them all. After more than ten years, I left the city and moved to the Rocky Mountains. I got a job in a bookstore. At last, I found something I liked! I loved being surrounded by books. I discovered the beautiful artwork in children's books.

"Then I got a job in a library and started to take art classes. When I took a class in children's book illustration, I became inspired. I put together a portfolio and took it to New York. I enjoyed meeting the editors and art directors and seeing their offices. The world of children's publishing seemed very special. I came home, but nothing happened. Then I went back to New York the following year with my portfolio and I was given a chance to illustrate my first book. I was the most excited I've ever been in my life (except for when I met my gorgeous husband, the poet Steve Elder).

"Even though I've now illustrated six books, I still feel like a beginner. I hope to keep developing and improv-ing. I'd like to explore different mediums and to experiment more with book design. My ultimate goal is to create a world in a book that a child or adult can enter into and inhabit. That's why I like to use color so much. I want to create settings where the colors are more vibrant and alive than everyday life.

"Now that I'm an illustrator I spend a lot of time alone in my studio where I cut out reproductions of paintings from magazines and tape them all over the walls, and I still pretend I live inside of them."

Saport's intensely colored pastel illustrations are credited with reflecting and augmenting the emotional content of the stories they accompany. In her first book, *The Face at the Window,* written by Regina Hanson, the author takes on the little-discussed topic of mental illness in a Jamaican setting as three children throwing stones at Miss Nella's mango tree accidentally hit the house, bringing the mysterious woman to the window. The children run away in fear, but Dora's dread only increases as night brings on a terrific rain storm, for one of the girls had told her that disaster will befall the person who looks at Miss Nella's face. "Saport's dense, hazy pastel illustrations are by turns foreboding and washed with relief, vibrantly evoking both setting and mood," remarked a reviewer for *Kirkus Reviews.* When Dora's parents explain that Miss Nella suffers from mental illness, Dora decides to apologize to the woman, and in the process learns to be less frightened of what she does not understand. "Teachers will find this an interesting stepping-stone to discussions of mental illness," concluded Carolyn Phelan in *Booklist.*

Jump Up Time: A Trinidad Carnival Story, written by Lynn Joseph, tells a story critics found universally applicable to younger siblings gazing in envy at an older sibling who is hogging the spotlight. Little sister Lily is consigned to the sidelines while her parents design and create an elaborate costume for older sister Christine to wear in the "jump up time" at the Children's Carnival. When Christine has an attack of stage fright at the last moment, however, Lily steps forward to reassure her and is rewarded in the end with the chance to wear her big sister's headdress.

For her next effort, *All the Pretty Little Horses,* Saport took the lyrics of the traditional lullaby as text for pastel illustrations critics dubbed dreamy and inspired by magic realism. The song may have originated in the American South during slavery times, and Saport depicts an African-American mother gently rocking an infant while cakes and horses float through the luminous sky above. The opening picture of mother and child "[radiates] love and care in an image that is larger than the page can hold," observed Susan M. Moore in *School Library Journal.* The book includes the musical notation for the lullaby at the end. "This is sure to become a favorite version of a beautiful song," predicted Hazel Rochman in *Booklist.*

Saport next teamed up with author Tololwa M. Mollel for *Subira, Subira,* a contemporary rendering of a traditional African folktale about learning patience. Tatu is charged by her father with the after-school care of her younger brother Maulidi after the death of their mother, and after many battles with the willful boy, the girl seeks out the advice of a spirit woman, MaMzuka. The older woman charges Tatu with using her courage and patience to gather three whiskers from a lion in order to learn what to do with her little brother. On her third try, Tatu's song puts the lion to sleep and allows her to gain her prize, which MaMzuka immediately discards, telling the girl to use the same patience to earn her brother's love. Saport's illustrations capture the magic of Mollel's story, "skillfully blend[ing] elements of mystery and everyday life in depictions of a spooky nighttime forest and glowing-eyed lion," remarked a reviewer in *Publishers Weekly. School Library Journal* reviewer Tina Hudak recommended *Subira, Subira* to all libraries with storytelling programs, concluding that the "marriage of a poignantly written tale with sophisticated artwork revitalizes a time-honored story."

Biographical and Critical Sources

PERIODICALS

Booklist, June 1, 1997, Carolyn Phelan, review of *The Face at the Window,* p. 1717; January 1, 1999, Hazel Rochman, review of *All the Pretty Little Horses;* February 15, 2000, Hazel Rochman, review of *Subira, Subira,* p. 1116.

Bulletin of the Center for Children's Books, May, 2000, Janice M. Del Negro, review of *Subira, Subira.*

Kirkus Reviews, April 1, 1997, review of *The Face at the Window,* p. 556; September 1, 1999, review of *All the*

Pretty Little Horses, p. 1421; February 15, 2000, review of *Subira, Subira.*

Publishers Weekly, January 17, 2000, review of *Subira, Subira,* p. 56.

School Library Journal, June, 1997, Betty Teague, review of *The Face at the Window,* pp. 88, 90; November, 1998, Sally Bates Goodroe, review of *Jump Up Time,* p. 87; December, 1999, Susan M. Moore, review of *All the Pretty Little Horses,* pp. 115-116; April, 2000, Tina Hudak, review of *Subira, Subira,* p. 123.

*   *   *

SESCOE, Vincent E. 1938-

Personal

Born July 31, 1938, in Washington, DC; married to Gillian P. (a federal civil servant), February 20, 1970. *Education:* Attended Howard University, 1962-64, and Alliance Français, Paris, 1964-65; University of Maryland, Far East and Europe campuses, A.A., 1975; attended American University, 1978-79. *Hobbies and other interests:* Watercolors, drawing and illustration,

Vincent E. Sescoe

gourmet cooking and dining, fishing, travel, gardening, "rooting for the Washington Redskins."

Addresses

Office—c/o The Brookfield Reader, 137 Peyton Rd., Sterling, VA 20165-5605.

Career

Federal Civil Service, worked as analyst, manager, chief training officer, and chief human resources officer, 1962-96. Northern Virginia Family Service/Training Futures, volunteer, 1997—; past mentor for local public school system. *Military service:* U.S. Air Force, 1956-60. *Member:* Society of Children's Book Writers and Illustrators (associate member).

Awards, Honors

American Legion Citation for Meritorious Service, Post 21, 1959-60, for illustrating and newsletter reporting (U.S. Air Force); four Certificates of Appreciation, two Meritorious Unit Citations, four Exceptional Performance Awards, and the Career Intelligence Medal, all for career as a federal civil servant; Volunteer of the Year, Northern Virginia Family Service/Training Futures, 2000; nomination for Fairfax County Volunteer 2000 Award.

Writings

Double Time, The Brookfield Reader (Sterling, VA), 2001.
Oh No! It's Those Pesky Squirrels Again!, The Brookfield Reader (Sterling, VA), in press.

Work in Progress

After the Ashes, fiction for young adults.

Sidelights

Vincent E. Sescoe told *SATA:* "Writing and travel have been my lifelong companions. As a preteen, I spent many hours writing and illustrating zany newsletters to share with my family. Also I was fascinated with foreign travel to the extent that I collected scores of travel brochures. It was through them that I first visited Rome, Paris, London, Hawaii, and Hong Kong as a daydreamer.

"By the time I reached high school, my skills as an illustrator had progressed to the point where my art teacher encouraged me to study fine arts in college, but the irresistible call of faraway places beckoned, so I joined the Air Force. On Johnston Island Air Base, 700 miles southwest of Honolulu, I volunteered to serve as a reporter and cartoonist for the base newsletter. Later, back in Washington, D.C., I worked the night shift as a civil service employee, while attending Howard University as a fine arts major. I was fortunate to study under Lois Mailou Jones. The formal training was fantastic, and I made the dean's list the first year, but faraway

places beckoned again. My civil service job offered me the opportunity to work in France. It was a 'no-brainer.' If Uncle Sam paid me to live in Paris, what choice did I have?

"Post cards from Paris gave way to travel essays and impressions of life in Paris. I attended art school briefly, then the Alliance Français for six months (to learn French), then I hit the road every chance I got! England, Ireland, Italy, Switzerland, Spain, and Portugal were destinations I had dreamed of as a child. I was the insatiable traveler: the more I saw, the more I needed to see and record. After two years in Paris, I was assigned to Vietnam, from which I traveled to Hong Kong, Bangkok, Tokyo, Taipei, and Sydney, writing travel pieces on every country. Later I served in England and Germany, both of which places I used as launch pads to explore Europe in depth. London holds a special place in my heart, because it was there that I met and married the love of my life, the inspiration for much of my work. After nearly three decades of marriage, Gillian still puts up with me and my crazy ideas.

"Twelve years, twice around the world, and many countries later, I was recalled to Washington. The official reason for my return was to place me in a management development track—I thought it was because I was having too much fun abroad—but that didn't stop me from numerous business and personal trips abroad. Although stuck behind a desk, I found plenty of time to write for in-house newsletters and journals, and I encouraged others to write for the newsletter as a means of improving their skills. In addition to being a manager, I developed a reputation as the 'go-to' guy for special writing projects. That gave me a false sense of security, because I thought it would be easy to make the transition from government wordsmith to real writer. Was I in for a big surprise!

"With retirement only ten years away, I started taking writing courses. My adventurous past led me to believe I would write travel and other feature articles, but I was attracted to children's literature because my first book, *Double Time,* evolved from course-work with the Institute of Children's Literature. *Double Time* is a time-travel, search-and-rescue story that takes place between the Battles of Brandy Station and Gettysburg. I did the artwork on the inside back cover, including the drawings of Generals Lee and Meade. History offers countless story leads. I love writing middle-grade and young adult fiction because I try to see and capture life from my readers' perspective. Also, I am still a kid at heart, according to my wife. With an overactive imagination and a rich background from which to draw, I have enough themes, outlines, and sketches for my next six projects.

"I don't have idols or heroes, but there are many people I admire. In the genre, those who have influenced me are Gary Paulsen, Christopher Paul Curtis, Julius Lester, Jerry Pinkney, J. K. Rowling, Robert San Souci, and Laurence Pringle. Also Susan K. Baggette, publisher of *The Brookfield Reader,* deserves tremendous credit for believing in me and for snatching clarity out of the jaws of chaos with my manuscript. As I continue to learn and practice the craft of children's literature, I hope to motivate another kid who likes writing, drawing, and daydreaming about travel."

* * *

SMITH, Rebecca 1946-

Personal

Born August 30, 1946, in Riverdale, MD; daughter of Homer Thawley and Victorine (Lafferty) Hopkins; married Dunham Hayes Smith, April, 1969; children: Kara Smith Rappaport, Daniel Hopkins. *Education:* Gettysburg College, B.A., 1968; University of Maryland, teacher certification, 1969. *Hobbies and other interests:* Hiking, biking, travel, sketching.

Addresses

Home—31 High Rock Rd., Sandy Hook, CT 06482.

Career

Art teacher at public schools in Maryland and Connecticut, 1969-73; art teacher in workshops and in private instruction, 1991-98. Independent Beauty Consultant, Mary Kay, Inc., 1999—. Newtown Meals on Wheels, president, 1995-1999, copresident, 2000-01; Visiting Nurses Association, Newtown, member of board of directors, 1998—.

Rebecca Smith

Writings

Crabbing Time, Richard C. Owen Publishers (Katonah, NY), 1999.

Work in Progress

Vernal pool research on salamanders.

Sidelights

Rebecca Smith told *SATA:* "*Crabbing Time* is my first children's book. It was inspired by a childhood activity that was shared with my cousins every summer. My interest in writing was really inspired by my desire to illustrate. I was fortunate to have the opportunity to attend an ongoing writing workshop led by a well-known children's author for four years. I could visualize the step-by-step story of *Crabbing Time,* and from this I completed the text. Although I did not illustrate my first book, I look forward to doing both the text and illustrations for a future book."

* * *

SPAULDING, Douglas
See BRADBURY, Ray

* * *

SPAULDING, Leonard
See BRADBURY, Ray

* * *

STEADMAN, Ralph 1936-

Personal

Born May 15, 1936, in Wallasey, Cheshire, England; son of Lionel Raphael (a commercial traveler) and Gwendoline (Welsh) Steadman; married Sheila Thwaite, September 5, 1959 (divorced, 1972); married Anna Deverson (a teacher), December 8, 1972; children: (first marriage) Suzannah, Genevieve, Theo, Henry; (second marriage) Sadie. *Education:* Attended East Ham Technical College, 1957-64, and London College of Printing and Graphic Arts, 1958-64. *Politics:* "Apolitical." *Religion:* Church of England. *Hobbies and other interests:* Gardening, collecting, writing, fishing, sculpture, astronomy.

Addresses

Agent—Sobel Weber Associates, Inc., 146 East 19th St., New York, NY 10003.

Career

Freelance cartoonist and illustrator. Early in career worked at odd jobs, including a manager trainee with F.

Ralph Steadman

W. Woolworth Co., Colwyn Bay, North Wales, a pool attendant in Rhyl, North Wales, and an apprentice aircraft engineer for de Havilland Aircraft Co., Broughton, England, 1952. Kemsley (Thomson) Newspapers, London, England, cartoonist, 1956-59; did freelance work for *Punch, Private Eye,* and *Telegraph* during the 1960s; *New Statesman,* London, political cartoonist, 1978-80. Artist-in-residence, Exeter Cathedral and Festival, 1989, and Cheltenham Festival, 1994. *Exhibitions:* Work exhibited at the National Theatre, 1977, Royal Festival Hall, 1984, Royal Albert Hall, 1997, Les Invalides, 1997, and Warrington Museum, 1998. *Military Service:* Royal Air Force, 1954-56. *Member:* Chelsea Arts Club.

Awards, Honors

Francis Williams Book Illustration Award, 1972, for *Lewis Carroll's Alice in Wonderland;* gold award, Designers and Art Directors Association, 1977, for outstanding contributions to illustration; silver award, Designers and Art Directors Association, 1977, for outstanding editorial illustration; recipient of merit award and voted illustrator of the year, American Institute of Graphic Arts, 1979; Silver Pencil Award (Holland) for children's book illustrations, 1982, for *Inspector Mouse;* Black Humour Award, France, 1986;

W. H. Smith Illustration Award for Best Illustrated Book, and First Prize, Bologna Children's Book Fair, both 1987, both for *I, Leonardo;* BBC Design Award, 1987, for Halley's Comet postage stamps; Critici in Erba Prize, Bologna Children's Book Fair, 1987, for *That's My Dad;* D.Litt., University of Kent (Canterbury, England).

Writings

FOR ADULTS

Still Life with Raspberry; or, the Bumper Book of Steadman, Rapp & Whiting (London, England), 1969.

Dogs Bodies, Abelard-Schuman, 1970, Paddington (New York, NY), 1977.

Zwei Esel und eine Bruecke, Nord Sued Verlag (Hamburg, Germany), 1972, published as *Two Donkeys and a Bridge,* Andersen (London, England), 1983.

Bumper Book of Boobs, Deutsch, 1973.

America, Straight Arrow (London, England), 1974, revised edition, Fantagraphics (Seattle, WA), 1989.

Flowers for the Moon, Nord Sued Verlag (Hamburg, Germany), 1974 (originally published as *Blumen fuer den Mond,* 1974).

Sigmund Freud, Paddington (New York, NY), 1979, Simon & Schuster (New York, NY), 1980.

A Leg in the Wind and Other Canine Curses, Putnam (New York, NY), 1982.

No Good Dogs, Perigee, 1982, Putnam (New York, NY), 1983.

I, Leonardo, Cape (London, England), 1983, Summit (New York, NY), 1983.

Between the Eyes, Cape (London, England), 1984, Summit (New York, NY), 1986.

Paranoids: From Socrates to Joan Collins, Harrap (London, England), 1986.

Who? Me? No! Why?, Steam, 1986.

Scar Strangled Banger, Salem (Topsfield, MA), 1988.

The Big I Am, Cape (London, England), 1988, Summit (New York, NY), 1988.

Visagen und Visionen: Karikaturen, kritische Grafik, Illustrationen, Wilhem-Busch-Gesellschaft (Hannover, Germany), 1988.

Near the Bone, Arrow, 1990.

Tales of the Weird, Cape (London, England), 1990.

The Grapes of Ralph: Wine According to Ralph Steadman, Ebury (London, England), Harcourt (New York, NY), 1992.

Still Life with Bottle: Whiskey According to Ralph Steadman, Ebury (London, England), 1994, Harcourt (New York, NY), 1997.

Jones of Colorado, Ebury (London, England), 1995.

The Book of Jones, Harcourt (New York, NY), 1997.

Gonzo: The Art, Weidenfeld & Nicholson (London, England), 1998, Harcourt (New York, NY), 1998.

Untrodden Grapes: New Wines of the World, According to Ralph Steadman, Ebury (London, England), 1998.

FOR CHILDREN

Ralph Steadman's Jelly Book, Dobson, 1967, published as *Jelly Book,* Scroll (New York, NY), 1970.

(With Fiona Saint) *The Yellow Flowers,* Dobson, 1968, Southwest Book Service, 1974.

(With Richard Ingrams) *The Tale of Driver Grope,* Dobson, 1969.

The Little Red Computer, McGraw, 1969.

The Bridge, Collins (London, England), 1972, Collins & World (Cleveland, OH), 1975.

Ralph Steadman's Bumper to Bumper Book for Children, Pan, 1973.

Cherrywood Cannon (based on a story told by Dimitri Sidjanski), Paddington (New York, NY), 1978.

That's My Dad, Andersen (London, England), 1986, David & Charles, 1987.

No Room to Swing a Cat, Andersen (London, England), 1989.

Teddy! Where Are You?, Andersen (London, England), 1994.

ILLUSTRATOR

Frank Dickens, *Fly Away Peter,* Dobson, 1963, Scroll, 1970.

Mischa Damjan, *Das Eichhorn und das Nashoernchen,* Nord Sued Verlag (Hamburg, Germany), 1964, published as *The Big Squirrel and the Little Rhinoceros,* Norton, 1965.

Daisy Ashford and Angela Ashford, *Love and Marriage: Three Stories,* Hart-Davis (London, England), 1965, reprinted, Oxford University Press (New York, NY), 1982.

Daisy Ashford, *Where Love Lies Deepest,* Hart-Davis, 1966.

Mischa Damjan, *Die Falschen Flamingos,* Nord Sued Verlag (Hamburg, Germany), 1967, published as *The False Flamingoes,* Dobson, 1968, Scroll, 1970.

Charles L. Dodgson, *Lewis Carroll's Alice in Wonderland* (also see below), Dobson, 1967, C. N. Potter (New York, NY), 1973.

Harold Wilson, *The Thoughts of Chairman Harold,* compiled by Tariq Ali, Gnome, 1967.

Mischa Damjan, *The Little Prince and the Tiger Cat,* Dobson, McGraw-Hill (New York, NY), 1968 (originally published as *Der kleine Prinz und sein Kater*).

Randolph Stow, *Midnite: The Story of a Wild Colonial Boy,* Penguin, 1969, reprinted, Bodley Head, 1984.

Tony Palmer, *Born under a Bad Sign,* Kimber, 1970.

Mischa Damjan, *Zwei Katzen in Amerika,* Nord Sued Verlag (Hamburg, Germany), published as *Two Cats in America,* Longman Young Books, 1970.

Patricia Mann, *150 Careers in Advertising: With Equal Opportunity for Men and Women,* Longman, 1971.

Brian Patten, *And Sometimes It Happens,* Steam, 1972.

John Fuller, *Boys in a Pie,* Bernard Stone, 1972.

Charles Causley, *Contemporary Poets Set to Music,* Turret, 1972.

Kurt Baumann, *Der Schlafhund und der Wachlund,* Nord Sued Verlag (Hamburg, Germany), 1972, published as *Dozy and Hawkeye,* Hutchinson, 1974.

Hunter S. Thompson, *Fear and Loathing in Las Vegas: A Savage Journey to the Heart of the American Dream,* Paladin, 1972, reissued, HarperCollins, 1998.

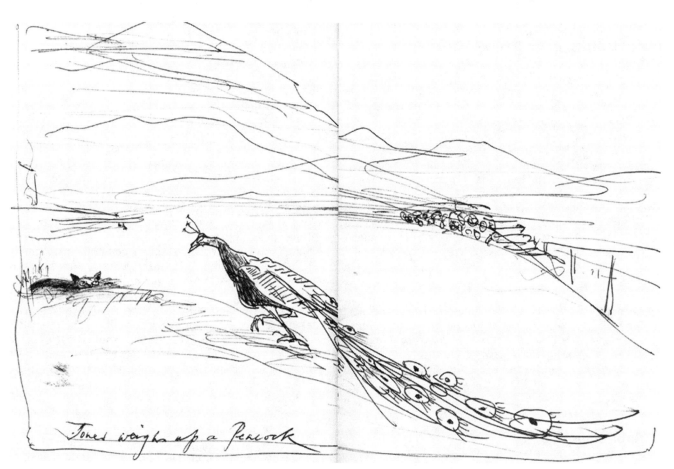

Steadman's self-illustrated **The Book of Jones** *is based on a friend's "mercurial, manic, and utterly seductive" cat.*

Ted Hughes, *In the Little Girl's Angel Gaze,* Steam, 1972.

Charles L. Dodgson, *Lewis Carroll's Through the Looking Glass, and What Alice Found There* (also see below), MacGibbon & Kee (London, England), 1972, C. N. Potter, 1973.

Edward Lucie-Smith, *Two Poems of Night,* Turret, 1972.

Edward Lucie-Smith, *The Rabbit,* Turret, 1973.

John Letts, compiler, *A Little Treasury of Limericks Fair and Foul,* Deutsch, 1973.

Jane Deverson, *Night Edge,* Bettiscombe, 1973.

Flann O'Brien, *The Poor Mouth—an Beal Bacht: A Bad Story about the Hard Life,* Hart-Davis/MacGibbon, 1973, Viking, 1974.

Hunter S. Thompson, *Fear and Loathing: On the Campaign Trail,* Allison & Busby, 1974.

Charles L. Dodgson, *The Hunting of the Snark: An Agony in Eight Fits* (also see below), Michael Dempsey (London, England), 1975, C. N. Potter, 1976.

Bernard Stone, *Emergency Mouse: A Story,* Andersen (London, England), 1978, Prentice-Hall, 1978.

Ted Hughes, *The Threshold,* Steam, 1979.

Bernard Stone, *Inspector Mouse,* Andersen (London, England), 1980, Holt, 1981.

Hunter S. Thompson, *The Great Shark Hunt,* Paladin, 1980.

Adrian Mitchell, *For Beauty Douglas: Adrian Mitchell's Collected Poems, 1953-79,* Allison & Busby, 1982.

Alan Sillitoe, *Israel Sketchbook,* Steam, 1983.

Hunter S. Thompson, *The Curse of Lono,* Bantam (New York, NY), 1983.

Bernard Stone, *Quasimodo Mouse,* Andersen (London, England), 1984.

Robert Louis Stevenson, *Treasure Island,* Harrap (London, England), 1985.

Charles L. Dodgson, *The Complete Alice and Hunting of the Snark* (contains *Lewis Carroll's Alice in Wonderland, Lewis Carroll's Through the Looking Glass, and What Alice Found There,* and *The Hunting of the Snark: An Agony in Eight Fits*), Cape (London, England), 1986, Salem (Topsfield, MA), 1986.

George Orwell, *Animal Farm: A Fairy Story,* Secker & Warburg (London, England), Harcourt (New York, NY), 1995.

Adrian Mitchell, *Who Killed Dylan Thomas?,* Ty Llên (Swansea, Wales), 1998.

Roald Dahl, *The Mildenhall Treasure,* Cape (London, England), 1999, Knopf (New York, NY), 2000.

OTHER

Also author of *Friends Echo* (poetry), 1990, and *My After-Dinner Speech on the Occasion of the Centenary Dinner at Christ Church, Oxford on the 14th January, 1998, to Celebrate the Life of Lewis Carroll,* White Stone, 1998. Contributor of a libretto to Richard Harvey's *Plague and the Moonflowers: An Oratorio,* Altus Records, 1999.

Adaptations

The Bridge was made into a filmstrip with cassette by Listening Library, 1976.

Sidelights

Ralph Steadman is both author and artist of a diverse array of books, nearly all of them humorous in some vein. Beginning his career as a political cartoonist in his native England, Steadman made a name for himself skewering American culture in the 1970s, and has written and illustrated several books for children. Steadman's visual imagery was described by Patrick Skene Catling in the *Spectator* as "a crescendo of angry screams demanding reason and of almost apoplectic howls protesting that the world is failing to behave reasonably."

Steadman was born in 1936 near Liverpool, and was sent to a rigorous boarding school where he was treated cruelly; he eventually dropped out of school to work at a number of odd jobs, including ratcatcher. After a stint in the Royal Air Force, he began cartooning and enrolled in drawing classes. His career was launched when well-known British humor magazines began accepting his submissions. On a visit to New York, Steadman landed an assignment to illustrate a story on the Kentucky Derby, and while there he met Hunter S. Thompson. The two became fast friends, and the article with its vicious illustrations caused somewhat of a stir. Steadman and Thompson collaborated on many other critical assessments of American culture—Thompson wrote with verve and frankness about the seamy underside of life in America, while Steadman's images became indelibly associated with it. The relationship culminated in the publication of Thompson's best-known work, *Fear and Loathing in Las Vegas,* illustrated by Steadman and first published in 1972.

By this time Steadman had also illustrated a number of books written by others, including a 1967 edition titled *Lewis Carroll's Alice in Wonderland* that won the Francis Williams Book Illustration Award. Steadman also began writing his own works, his first in the children's genre was another title from 1967, *Ralph Steadman's Jelly Book. The Little Red Computer, Ralph Steadman's Bumper to Bumper Book for Children,* and several more followed. In 1986, he wrote and illustrated *That's My Dad,* which featured two children talking about their fathers, describing them in increasingly outrageous terms; the illustrations depict their imaginarily monstrous parents. In *No Room to Swing a Cat,* published in 1989, a minuscule little boy dwarfed by his surroundings, complains that his bedroom is too small. He shows his mother that it is too small even to swing the proverbial cat, demonstrating with a variety of other animals to further drive home his point. Reviewing the work in *Books for Keeps,* Pam Harwood commended Steadman's "brilliantly funny and perceptive drawings."

Teddy! Where Are You? was inspired by Steadman's own grandchildren. Surprised when he realized that his granddaughters did not know what a teddy bear was, Steadman depicts the search for the beloved stuffed toy of his own childhood. He discovers a used-toy shopkeeper who bears an uncanny resemblance to his teddy. Steadman's "familiar scratchy drawings exactly match

Steadman illustrated the true story of a British plowman's discovery of the greatest treasure ever found in the British Isles and how he was cheated out of his fortune. *(Illustration from* The Mildenhall Treasure, *written by Roald Dahl.)*

this story, which is funny, tender, wise," claimed Marcus Crouch of *Junior Bookshelf.*

Steadman has also illustrated a few unusual biographies, beginning with *Sigmund Freud* in 1979 and *I, Leonardo* four years later. The latter title features Steadman's illustrations of the famed Italian Renaissance artist Leonardo da Vinci at work near some of his best-known images. A 1984 autobiography *Between the Eyes* was followed by one of Steadman's more controversial works to date, *The Big I Am.* A mock-autobiography of God in conversation form, its pages feature the author's irreverent interpretations of the creation story and criticisms of organized religion. "The whole thing is illustrated (or constituted by) brilliant drawings of explosions with signs of nearly-human faces and forms, agonies, primal chaos, primal fire, emerging figures, devils and angles, demagogues being foul, cities going wrong, and endless deserts with skeletons," noted D. E. Jenkins in *The Listener.*

Steadman lives in a Georgian manor home near Kent, England, with wife and daughter, and has four children by a previous marriage as well. He keeps sheep there and plays the trumpet for a hobby. He has also illustrated a series of popular children's books by Bernard Stone, beginning with *Emergency Mouse.* The 1980 work *Inspector Mouse* won Holland's Silver Pencil Award for children's book illustrating. In 2000, Knopf published *The Mildenhall Treasure* by Roald Dahl, which featured Steadman's illustrations. The work recounted the true story of a English farm worker who found a trove of Roman-era silver and was denied compensation for it.

Biographical and Critical Sources

PERIODICALS

Bloomsbury Review, November-December, 1997, R. K. Dickson, review of *Still Life with Bottle,* p. 35.

Booklist, February 1, 1984, Alan Moores, review of *I, Leonardo,* p. 783; October 15, 1998, Ray Olson, review of *Gonzo,* p. 386.

Books, September-October, 1996, review of *That's My Dad,* p. 24.

Books for Keeps, May, 1991, Pam Harwood, review of *No Room to Swing a Cat,* p. 13; May, 1994, Trevor Dickinson, review of *Teddy!,* p. 35.

Books for Your Children, autumn, 1985, Margaret Carter, review of *I, Leonardo,* p. 5.

Growing Point, September, 1989, Margery Fisher, review of *No Room to Swing a Cat,* p. 5224.

Junior Bookshelf, October 10, 1986, Marcus Crouch, review of *That's My Dad,* p. 181; October, 1989, review of *No Room to Swing a Cat,* p. 220; June, 1994, Marcus Crouch, review of *Teddy!,* p. 98.

Kirkus Review, July 1, 1996, review of *The Grapes of Ralph,* p. 960.

Listener, December 1, 1988, D. E. Jenkins, "On the Edge of the Abyss," pp. 30-31.

Los Angeles Times Book Review, March 13, 1988.

Macleans, December 12, 1983.

Newsweek, December 10, 1979.

New York Times Book Review, December 14, 1980; January 11, 1987, Draper Hill, review of *Between the Eyes,* p. 19; May 14, 1989, Michael Cart, review of *The Big I Am,* p. 22.

New York Times Magazine, October 9, 1983.

Observer (London), December 4, 1983, William Weaver, "Classical Revivals," p. 31; July 19, 1998, Chris Riddell, review of *Gonzo,* p. 15.

Publishers Weekly, August 12, 1996, review of *The Grapes of Ralph,* p. 78; November 2, 1998, review of *Gonzo,* p. 66.

Rolling Stone, December 11, 1980, Greil Marcus, review of *Sigmund Freud,* p. 30.

School Library Journal, December, 2000, Patricia A. Dollish, review of *The Mildenhall Treasure,* p. 157.

Spectator, October 13, 1984, Patrick Skene Catling, "Gonzo Art," p. 33; December 12, 1987, Richard Ingrams, "Humour Books," p. 33.

Times Literary Supplement, January 20, 1984.

Village Voice, January 7, 1980.

Washington Post Book World, September 21, 1980, review of *Sigmund Freud,* p. 12.

*   *   *

STERLING, Brett
See BRADBURY, Ray

*   *   *

SULLIVAN, Sue
See SULLIVAN, Susan E.

*   *   *

SULLIVAN, Susan E. 1962-
(Sue Sullivan)

Personal

Born December 29, 1962; married Tom Sullivan; children: Kerry, Clare. *Education:* University of Massachusetts, B.F.A.; Lesley University, M.A.

Addresses

Home—36 Chatanika Ave., Worcester, MA 01602.

Career

Illustrator.

Illustrator

Cindy Abdelsayed, *Connection to the Heart,* Press-Tige Publishing (Catskill, NY).

Sidelights

Susan E. Sullivan told *SATA:* "Unfortunately our culture tries to discourage us from discussing death openly with our children. As a result, well-intentioned care-givers often fear that bringing the subject up will upset and hurt a grieving child. Whenever I hear about a child whose parent has died, I hear that the care-giver is so relieved that the child is happy (behaving as if the death never occurred) that he or she fears that broaching the subject would spoil the happy mood of the surviving child.

"How sad! Contrary to our cultural belief, I feel that the death of our loved ones can (and should) be discussed as fluidly as any other milestone in life. Teaching our children that the spirits of our beloved ancestors live on in the form of our thoughts and feelings helps them to integrate the concept of death into their experience in a gentle, non-threatening manner.

"When my twin sister Cindy asked me to create *Connection to the Heart* with her, I was thrilled to receive this opportunity. Cindy and I lost our mother to a sudden, unexpected death when we were six years old. My hope is that *Connection to the Heart* will help children who have lost a special person (or animal) to achieve the same spiritual intimacy with their loved ones that I enjoy with my mother to this day." *[For information on Sullivan's work, see entry on Cindy Abdelsayed in this volume].*

T

TACKACH, James 1953-

Personal

Born June 15, 1953, in Passaic, NJ; son of George (a salesman) and Loretta (a saleswoman; maiden name, Rys) Tackach. *Education:* Montclair State College, B.A. (English), 1976; University of Rhode Island, M.A. (English), 1978, Ph.D. (English), 1986. *Politics:* "Registered Democrat." *Hobbies and other interests:* Baseball, fly fishing.

James Tackach describes the life of political activist and author James Baldwin in this biography for middle-schoolers. (Cover photo by Walter Duran.)

Addresses

Office—English Department, Roger Williams University, One Old Ferry Rd., Bristol, RI 02809.

Career

University of Rhode Island, teaching assistant, 1976-78; part-time positions as adjunct instructor at Community College of Rhode Island, University of Rhode Island-Providence, and Rhode Island College, 1978-89; freelance communications consultant, 1979-88; Roger Williams University, Bristol, RI, director of the Writing Center, 1981-87, professor of English, 1991—. *Member:* National Council of Teachers of English, National Education Association, Society for Technical Communication, American Literature Association, Hemingway Society, Society for American Baseball Research, Trout Unlimited, Sigma Tau Delta, Phi Kappa Phi.

Awards, Honors

Humanity Award, Office of Multicultural Affairs, Roger Williams University, 1996.

Writings

YOUNG ADULT NONFICTION

Baseball Legends: Roy Campanella, Chelsea House (New York, NY), 1991.
Baseball Legends: Hank Aaron, Chelsea House (New York, NY), 1992.
The Importance of James Baldwin, Lucent Books (San Diego, CA), 1997.
Brown v. Board of Education, Lucent Books (San Diego, CA), 1998.
The Trial of John Brown: Radical Abolitionist, Lucent Books (San Diego, CA), 1998.
The Emancipation Proclamation: Abolishing Slavery in the South, Lucent Books (San Diego, CA), 1999.
Uncle Tom's Cabin: Indictment of Slavery, Lucent Books (San Diego, CA), 2000.

OTHER

Historic Homes of America, Portland House (New York, NY), 1990.

Great American Hotels, Smithmark (New York, NY), 1991.

(With Joshua B. Stein) *The Fields of Summer: America's Great Ballparks and the Players Who Triumphed in Them,* Crescent Books (New York, NY), 1992.

Slave Narratives, Greenhaven Press, 2000.

The Civil Rights Movement, Greenhaven Press, 2001.

Also contributor to books, including *The African American Encyclopedia,* Marshall Cavendish (Tarrytown, NJ), 1993; *Strategies for Technical Communication: A Collection of Teaching Tips,* edited by Meg Morgan, John McNair, and Deborah S. Bosley, Society for Technical Communication (Arlington, VA), 1994; *Teaching a "New Canon"?: Students, Teachers, and Texts in the College Literature,* edited by Bruce A. Goebel and James C. Hall, NCTE (Urbana, IL), 1995; *The African American Encyclopedia, Supplement,* Marshall Cavendish (Tarrytown, NJ), 1996; *Masterplots: Revised Second Edition,* edited by Frank N. Magill, Salem Press (Pasadena, CA), 1996; *Masterplots II: Juvenile and Young Adult Series,* edited by Frank N. Magill, Salem Press (Pasadena, CA), 1997; *Great Events from History: North American Series, Revised Edition,* edited by Frank N. Magill, Salem Press (Pasadena, CA), 1997; *Cyclopedia of World Authors, Revised Edition,* edited by Frank N. Magill, Salem Press (Pasadena, CA), 1997; *Identities and Issues in Literature,* edited by David Peck, Salem Press (Pasadena, CA), 1997; *The Encyclopedia of Civil Rights in America,* edited by David Bradley and Shelley Fisher Fishkin, Sharpe Reference (New York, NY), 1998; *Masterplots II: Poetry Series Supplement,* edited by John Wilson and Philip K. Jason, Salem Press (Pasadena, CA), 1998; *Short Stories in the Classroom,* edited by Carole L. Hamilton and Peter Kratzke, NCTE (Urbana, IL), 1999; *The Sixties in America,* Salem Press (Pasadena, CA), 1999; *Encyclopedia of North American History,* Marshall Cavendish (Tarrytown, NJ), 1999; *Dictionary of World Biography,* edited by Frank N. Magill, Salem Press (Pasadena, CA), 2000. Fiction published in *Spitball: The Literary Baseball Magazine;* poetry published in *National Pastime* and *Baseball Research Journal.*

Contributor to periodicals, including *Intercom: The Magazine of the Society for Technical Communication, ADE Bulletin, Technical Communication, Writing Center Journal, Saul Bellow Journal, Writing Program Administration, Providence Journal, America's Civil War, New York Times, Baseball Research Journal, Americana, Old Mill News, Sports History,* and *Narragansett Times.*

Work in Progress

Research on Abraham Lincoln's second inaugural address.

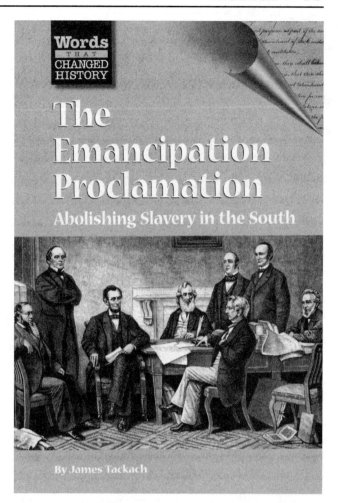

In this work, Tackach discusses slavery as a cause of the Civil War and the impact the Emancipation Proclamation had on the course of the war. (Cover illustration by Northwind Picture Archive.)

Sidelights

"Teaching in a university English department is my primary occupation," James Tackach told *SATA.* "Writing is, for the most part, a summer activity, after I have emptied my briefcase of student papers and cleared my desk of university-related reports and memos. I write very quickly—during a productive day I can generate more than four thousand words—but I need large chunks of time for writing, something that a busy academic schedule of class sessions, class preparation, paper-grading, and committee meetings simply does not allow.

"My writing interests are varied. I have published in many genres (travel, history, sports, humor, short fiction, poetry, literary criticism, personal narrative) and for a variety of audiences (young adults, general readers, academics).

"I have been writing professionally for more than twenty years. My first published article resulted from a call from the deputy sports editor of the *New York Times,* who was interested in a point that I had made in a letter to the editor. To get my work into print, I search for columns open to freelancers in publications that I read, and I have also used *Writer's Market.* Some of my assignments come through word of mouth—an editor calls after hearing from another editor that I might be willing to tackle a certain project.

"For the first time in my writing career, I am now working on a major project—a book or monograph-length study of Abraham Lincoln's second inaugural address—without having a publisher lined up in advance."

As the author of several short historical monographs for young people, Tackach is credited with presenting a wealth of information in a clear and interesting style that is useful for students writing reports as well as for general interest readers. In *Brown v. Board of Education,* for example, Tackach surveys the history of the civil rights movement in the United States beginning with the passage of the Thirteenth Amendment of the Constitution in 1865, and emphasizing the rise of the National Association for the Advancement of Colored People (NAACP) and the work of lawyer (later Supreme Court justice) Thurgood Marshall. The author then discusses how the courts were able to eventually win the battle against educational injustice. "Tackach gives a compelling account of the *Brown* decision," and makes effective use of sidebars to provide additional information, according to Randy Meyer in *Booklist.* In a similar vein, Tackach's *Emancipation Proclamation: Abolishing Slavery in the South* focuses on an important moment in the history of civil rights in the United States, offering background information on slavery and the American Civil War and discussing the legacy of the Proclamation.

Tackach's *The Trial of John Brown: Radical Abolitionist* provides another piece in the puzzle of the history of the American civil rights movement. John Brown was a radical abolitionist whose raid on Harper's Ferry is considered to have launched the Civil War. Brown was eventually tried and executed for his crimes. Tackach puts Brown's ideas in the context of mid eighteenth-century America and discusses the man's upbringing and religious beliefs as they impacted his passion for the abolitionist movement. Allison Trent Bernstein praised *The Trial of John Brown* in a *School Library Journal* review as "a concise, organized look" at Brown, the circumstances that gave rise to his historic raid, and its aftermath.

Tackach is also the author of *The Importance of James Baldwin,* a biographical treatment of the twentieth-century African-American author best known for his novel *Go Tell It on the Mountain* and the autobiographical essays collected in *The Fire Next Time.* A leader in the civil rights movement of the middle of the twentieth century, Baldwin's impact on the arts and society is assessed "with honesty and integrity," according to Peter O. Sieruta in *Horn Book.*

Biographical and Critical Sources

PERIODICALS

Booklist, October 15, 1997, Randy Meyer, review of *Brown v. Board of Education,* p. 396; June 1, 1999, Carolyn Phelan, review of *The Emancipation Proclamation,* p. 1805.
Horn Book, spring, 1997, Peter O. Sieruta, review of *The Importance of James Baldwin,* p. 157.
School Library Journal, February, 1997, Carrol McCarthy, review of *The Importance of James Baldwin,* p. 123; August, 1998, Allison Trent Bernstein, review of *The Trial of John Brown,* p. 184.

* * *

THOMAS, Joyce Carol 1938-

Personal

Born May 25, 1938, in Ponca City, OK; daughter of Floyd David (a bricklayer) and Leona (a housekeeper and hair stylist; maiden name, Thompson) Haynes; married Gettis L. Withers (a chemist), May 31, 1959 (divorced, 1968); married Roy T. Thomas, Jr., (a professor), September 7, 1968 (divorced, 1979); children: Monica Pecot, Gregory Withers, Michael Withers, Roy T. Thomas III. *Education:* Attended San Francisco City College, 1957-58, and University of San Francisco, 1957-58; College of San Mateo, A.A., 1964; San Jose State College (now University), B.A., 1966; Stanford University, M.A., 1967.

Addresses

Home—Berkeley, CA. *Agent*—Anna Ghosh, Scovil-Chichak-Galen Literary Agency, Inc., 381 Park Ave. S., Suite 1020, New York, NY 10016. *E-mail*—author@joycecarolthomas.com.

Career

Worked as a telephone operator in San Francisco, CA, 1957-58; Ravenwood School District, East Palo Alto, CA, teacher of French and Spanish, 1968-70; San Jose State College (now University), San Jose, CA, assistant professor of black studies, 1969-72; Contra Costa College, San Pablo, CA, teacher of drama and English, 1973-75; St. Mary's College, Moraga, CA, professor of English, 1975-77; San Jose State University, San Jose, reading program director, 1979-82, associate professor of English, 1982-83; University of Tennessee, Knoxville, associate professor of English, 1989-92, full professor, 1992-95. Visiting associate professor of English at Purdue University, spring, 1983. *Member:* Dramatists Guild, Inc., Authors Guild, Authors League of America.

Awards, Honors

Danforth Graduate Fellow, University of California at Berkeley, 1973-75; Stanford University scholar, 1979-80, and Djerassi Fellow, 1982 and 1983; *New York*

Times outstanding book of the year citation, American Library Association (ALA) best book citation, and Before Columbus American Book Award, Before Columbus Foundation (Berkeley, CA), all 1982, and American Book Award for children's fiction (National Book Award), Association of American Publishers, 1983, all for *Marked by Fire;* Coretta Scott King Award, ALA, 1984, for *Bright Shadow;* named Outstanding Woman of the Twentieth Century, Sigma Gamma Rho, 1986; Pick of the Lists, American Booksellers, 1986, and Oklahoma Sequoyah Young Adult Book Award Masterlist, 1988-89, both for *The Golden Pasture;* Arkansas Traveler Award, presented by Governor Bill Clinton, 1987; Oklahoma Senate and House of Representatives Citations, 1989; Chancellor's Award for Research and Creativity, University of Tennessee, and Selected Title for Children and Young Adults, National Conference of Christians and Jews, both 1991, both for *A Gathering of Flowers;* Proclamation, City of Berkeley, 1992, and Kentucky Blue Grass Award Masterlist, 1995, both for *When the Nightingale Sings;* 100 Children's Books list, New York Public Library, 1993, Coretta Scott King Honor Book, ALA, Notable Children's Books, National Council of Teachers of English, and Mirrors and Windows: Seeing the Human Family Award, National Conference of Christians and Jews, all 1994, all for *Brown Honey in Broomwheat Tea;* Poet Laureate Award, Oklahoma State University Center for Poets and Writers at the Oklahoma State University, 1996-2000; Governor's Award, presented by the Honorable Frank Keating, Governor of Oklahoma, 1998; Celebrated Storyteller Award, *People* magazine, 1999, for *Gingerbread Days;* Notable Children's Book Award, ALA, Notable Children's Trade Book in Social Studies Award, National Council for the Social Studies/Children's Book Council, Teacher's Choice Award, International Reading Association, and Coretta Scott King Illustrator Honor Book, ALA, all 1999, all for *I Have Heard of a Land;* Parents' Choice Award, 2000, and Oklahoma Book Award, 2001, both for *Hush Songs;* Arrell Gibson Lifetime Achievement Award, Oklahoma Center for the Book, 2001, for body of work.

Writings

YOUNG ADULT NOVELS, EXCEPT AS NOTED

Marked by Fire, Avon, 1982.
Bright Shadow, (sequel to *Marked by Fire*), Avon, 1983.
Water Girl, Avon, 1986.
The Golden Pasture, Scholastic, 1986.
Journey, Scholastic, 1988.
When the Nightingale Sings, HarperCollins, 1992.
House of Light (adult novel; sequel to *Marked by Fire* and *Bright Shadow*), Hyperion, 2001.

FOR CHILDREN

Cherish Me (picture book), illustrated by Nneka Bennett, HarperCollins, 1998.
You Are My Perfect Baby (board book), illustrated by Nneka Bennett, HarperCollins, 1999.
The Gospel Cinderella (picture book), illustrated by David Diaz, HarperCollins, 2000.

Joyce Carol Thomas

The Bowlegged Rooster and Other Tales That Signify (short stories), HarperCollins, 2000.
Hush Songs: African American Lullabies (picture book), illustrated by Brenda Joysmith, Hyperion, 2000.
Joy! (board book), illustrated by Pamela Johnson, Hyperion, 2001.
Angel's Lullaby (board book), illustrated by Pamela Johnson, Hyperion, 2001.

POETRY

Bittersweet, Firesign Press, 1973.
Crystal Breezes, Firesign Press, 1974.
Blessing, Jocato Press, 1975.
Black Child, illustrated by Tom Feelings, Zamani Productions, 1981.
Inside the Rainbow, Zikawana Press, 1982.
Brown Honey in Broomwheat Tea, illustrated by Floyd Cooper, HarperCollins, 1993.
Gingerbread Days, illustrated by Floyd Cooper, HarperCollins, 1995.
The Blacker the Berry: Poems, illustrated by Brenda Joysmith, HarperCollins, 1997.
I Have Heard of a Land, illustrated by Floyd Cooper, HarperCollins, 1998.
A Mother's Heart, A Daughter's Love, HarperCollins, 2001.
Crowning Glory: Poems, illustrated by Brenda Joysmith, HarperCollins, 2002.

PLAYS

(And producer) *A Song in the Sky* (two-act), produced in San Francisco at the Montgomery Theater, 1976.

Look! What a Wonder! (two-act), produced in Berkeley at the Berkeley Community Theatre, 1976.

(And producer) *Magnolia* (two-act), produced in San Francisco at the Old San Francisco Opera House, 1977.

(And producer) *Ambrosia* (two-act), produced in San Francisco at the Little Fox Theatre, 1978.

Gospel Roots (two-act), produced in Carson, CA, at California State University, 1981.

I Have Heard of a Land, produced in Oklahoma City, OK, at the Claussen Theatre, 1989.

When the Nightingale Sings, produced in Knoxville, TN, at the Clarence Brown Theatre, 1991.

(And director) *A Mother's Heart* (two-act), produced in San Francisco, CA, at the Marsh Theater, 2001.

OTHER

(Editor and contributor) *A Gathering of Flowers: Stories about Being Young in America* (includes Thomas's short story "Young Reverend Zelma Lee Moses"), HarperCollins, 1990.

Contributor of short story, "Handling Snakes," to *I Believe in Water,* edited by Marilyn Singer, HarperCollins, 2000. Contributor to periodicals, including *American Poetry Review, Black Scholar, Calafia, Drum Voices, Giant Talk,* and *Yardbird Reader.* Editor of *Ambrosia* (women's newsletter), 1980.

Sidelights

Joyce Carol Thomas is a celebrated author of young adult novels, poetry, and picture books, as well as fiction and poetry for adults. The winner of the American (now National) Book Award for her first novel, *Marked by Fire,* and the Coretta Scott King Award for her second, *Bright Shadow,* Thomas hit the ground running with her writing career and has never looked back. Using her own unique rural background of Oklahoma and California, she has created a lyrical world of childhood—portraying not only its joys but also its gross injustices—that resonates across the racial lines. In both poetry and fiction, Thomas conjures up stories of African-American heritage, family history, and universal truths. Her language is a compilation of the sounds, imagery, and rhythms of her Oklahoma roots, church-going days, and California connections where she worked side-by-side with Hispanics in the fields. Thomas's background as a migrant farm worker in rural Oklahoma and California thus supplies her with the prolific stock of characters and situations that fill her novels while her love affair with language began with the words and songs she heard in church.

Thomas grew up in Ponca City, Oklahoma, a small, dusty town where she lived across from the school. This place has found a permanent home in Thomas's mind. "Although now I live half a continent away from my hometown," Thomas related in *Something about the Author Autobiography Series* (*SAAS*), "when it comes to my writing I find that I am often still there." She has set several of her novels in her hometown, including *Marked by Fire, Bright Shadow, The Golden Pasture,*

and *House of Light.* Thomas loved school as a child and became anxious whenever it appeared she might be late—she didn't want to miss anything. However, she usually missed the first month of school in order to finish up work on her family's farm. Times were lean for Thomas's family, but they always made do. This she attributes partly to her mother's genius at making healthy foods that weren't expensive; she has memories of huge spreads being laid out for Sunday dinners. These scenes of food have stuck with Thomas, for she finds food is one of the focuses in her novels. "Because in such a home food was another language for love, my books are redolent of sugar and spice, kale and collards," Thomas commented in *SAAS.*

When Thomas was ten years old, the family moved to rural Tracy, California. There Thomas learned to milk cows, fish for minnows, and harvest tomatoes and grapes. She also became intimately acquainted with black widow spiders—there was a nest of them under her bed. She was later to use this experience in her novel *Journey.* Likewise, she had a similar experience with wasps when her brother locked her in a closet containing a nest of them; *Marked by Fire* contains some frightening scenes with these insects.

In Tracy, California, Thomas continued spending long summers harvesting crops. She worked beside many Mexicans and began a long-lasting fascination with their language. "When the Spanish speakers talked they seemed to sing," Thomas remarked in *SAAS.* When she went to college, she majored in Spanish and French. "From this base of languages I taught myself much that I know about writing," she related in *SAAS.* She went on to earn a master's degree from Stanford University, and then taught foreign languages in public school.

From 1973 to 1978, Thomas wrote poetry and plays for adults, taught in various colleges and universities, and traveled to conferences and festivals all over the world, including Lagos, Nigeria. In 1982, Thomas's career took a turn when she published *Marked by Fire,* a novel for a young adult audience. Steeped in the setting and traditions of her hometown, the novel focused on Abyssinia Jackson, a girl who was born in a cotton field during harvest time. The title refers to the fact that she received a burn on her face from a brush fire during her birth. This leaves her "marked for unbearable pain and unspeakable joy," according to the local healer. The child shows a remarkable talent for singing until she is raped by a member of the church. The story of how she heals from this tragedy fills the rest of the novel.

The book was critically acclaimed and placed on required reading lists at many high schools and universities. Writing in *Black Scholar,* critic Dorothy Randall-Tsuruta noted that Thomas's "poetic tone gives this work what scents give the roses already so pleasing in color." Reviewing this debut novel in *School Library Journal,* Hazel Rochman felt that while the "lack of a fast-paced narrative line and the mythical overtones may present obstacles to some readers, many will be moved" by the story of Abyssinia. *Best Sellers* reviewer Wendell

Wray noted that Thomas "captures the flavor of black folk life in Oklahoma." Wray further observed that though she "has set for herself a challenging task ... Thomas' book works." Commenting about her stormy novel, Thomas once stated that "as a writer I work to create books filled with conflict.... I address this quest in part by matching the pitiful absurdities and heady contradictions of life itself, in part by leading the heroine to twin fountains of magic and the macabre, and evoking the holy and the horrible in the same breath. Nor is it ever enough to match these. Through the character of Abyssinia, I strive for what is beyond these, seeking to find newer worlds."

Bright Shadow, a sequel to *Marked by Fire,* was published in 1983. In this work, Abyssinia goes to college and ends up falling in love with Carl Lee Jefferson. The couple work through many problems in order to find their own kind of love. The winner of the Coretta Scott King Award, *Bright Shadow* was called a "love story" and "appealing" by Zena Sutherland, writing in *Bulletin of the Center for Children's Books.* However, as with many of Thomas's books, some critics faulted her for the use of overly epic language. Sutherland for one felt that "the often-ornate phraseology" sometimes weakens the story.

Several of Thomas's later books also feature these popular characters from her first two books, including *The Golden Pasture,* which journeys back to Carl Lee's earlier life on his grandfather's ranch, and *Water Girl,* which tells the story of Abyssinia's teenage daughter Amber, given up for adoption. Amber only learns of her biological mother when, after an earthquake, she finds an old letter that speaks of the adoption. Reviewing *The Golden Pasture* in *Publishers Weekly,* a contributor called the book "a spirited, lyrical tale with a memorable cast of characters."

With her imagination and ability to bring authenticity to her novels, Thomas has been highly praised and often compared to other achieved black women authors, including Maya Angelou, Toni Morrison, and Alice Walker. Thomas takes scenes and characters from her youth and crafts them into powerful fiction. "If I had to give advice to young people," Thomas commented in her autobiographical essay, "it would be that whatever your career choice, prepare yourself to do it well. Quality takes talent and time. Believe in your dreams. Have faith in yourself. Keep working and enjoying today even as you reach for tomorrow. If you choose to write, value your experiences. And color them in the indelible ink of your own background."

With *Journey,* her fifth novel, Thomas broke new literary ground for herself, mixing fantasy and mystery to come up with a story of crime and family history. Meggie Alexander, "blessed" at birth by a tarantula, has uncommon powers. Reaching adolescence, she investigates the disappearance of several of her friends in the woods, discovering that some of them have been murdered. Meggie herself is soon kidnaped and thrust into horrible danger. Less well received than many of

House of Light

a novel

Joyce Carol Thomas

The strength of African American women and the power to heal are messages that Thomas seeks to convey in this work.

her other novels, *Journey* did earn accolades from a writer for *Kirkus Reviews* who felt that Thomas "dramatically juxtaposes her story's horror with the joy of existence." Other reviewers, such as Starr LaTronica of *School Library Journal,* were less enthusiastic. "This discordant mixture of fantasy and mystery ... never blend[s] successfully," LaTronica wrote.

With *When the Nightingale Sings,* Thomas created a sort of Cinderella story about young Marigold who is discovered in a swamp and lives with her foster mother, Ruby, and twin stepsisters. As in the fairy tale, this family treats the young girl as a servant rather than a relative. Finally, Marigold turns her attentions away from this abusive foster family and to the local Baptist Church. It is there she finds real salvation, discovering the gift of music in gospel songs. Reviewing this and other books by Thomas in *St. James Guide to Young Adult Writers,* a contributor noted that Thomas's use of language "is exquisite; this craftsmanship provides words that are of music, voice, and song. Her characters are often musical, and the church—the gospel music, rhythm, movement, and harmony—provides not only a backdrop, but a language that expresses the spirit of the community." The same critic went on to observe,

"Proverbs, folk wisdom, scripture, and prophecy are liberally scattered among the voices of the characters."

Thomas employs all these techniques and sources in her first adult novel, *House of Light,* which furthers the story of Abyssinia Jackson begun in *Marked by Fire* and continued in *Bright Shadow.* Now a doctor and healer, Abby Jackson-Jefferson is the main narrator of these tales which relate the lives of a myriad of patients in Ponca City, Oklahoma. Reviewing the title in *Booklist,* Hazel Rochman felt that this title "is sure to be popular for the lively dialogue, the sense of community, and yes, the hopeful message." A *Publishers Weekly* contributor called the book "moving" and "marred only by unsubtle repetition, a rhetorical device Thomas relies on too frequently." However, a *Kirkus Reviews* critic offered a different opinion, writing that "Lyrical, earthy prose gives this deceptively simple story depth and richness."

Much of Thomas's talent, energy, and output has been focused on poetry for young readers and on picture books for the very young. Teaming up with illustrator Floyd Cooper, Thomas has created a trio of poetry books aimed at the five-to nine-year-old reading audience. In the award-winning *Brown Honey in Broomwheat Tea,* Thomas gathers a dozen poems dealing with the family, home, and the African-American experience in a "highly readable and attractive picture book," according to a reviewer for *Booklist.* A *Publishers Weekly* contributor called the poems "lyrical" evocations of the African-American heritage. The title poem recalls Thomas's own childhood when broomwheat tea was used as an elixir for anything that ailed the young girl.

Thomas and Cooper again teamed up for *Gingerbread Days,* a picture book of a dozen poems that "celebrates the passage of a year within the circle of an extended African American family," as Meg Stackpole noted in a *School Library Journal* review. "Like food stored away for winter, this rich harvest of poems contains enough sustenance to last throughout the year," wrote a *Publishers Weekly* reviewer of the same book. "Thomas's simple but touching language describes a hopeful world ... where love is as wonderful as gingerbread, warm and spicy from the oven," the same reviewer concluded. *Horn Book*'s Martha V. Parravano concluded that *Gingerbread Days* was a "worthy companion" to *Brown Honey in Broomwheat Tea,* "made even stronger by Floyd Cooper's glowing, golden illustrations." *I Have Heard of a Land* continues the Thomas-Cooper collaboration, an illustrated book of poems which celebrates the role of African-American women pioneers in the nineteenth-century frontier, largely in Oklahoma. A writer for *Publishers Weekly* called the book a "moving poetic account of a brave black woman," while *Booklist*'s Ilene Cooper dubbed it a "lyrical tribute to the pioneer spirit."

Thomas has also worked with illustrator Nneka Bennett on two books for very young children, *Cherish Me* and *You Are My Perfect Baby.* Reviewing the first title in *Booklist,* Kathy Broderick called Thomas's poem "compelling" and described the book as a "winning offering." Another title for the very young is *Hush Songs,* a book designed for adults to sing to babies and preschoolers, collecting ten African-American lullabies, including three written by Thomas, under one cover. Claiming that "the songs themselves are timeless," *Booklist* reviewer Rochman wrote that the lullabies "touch all of us." With *A Mother's Heart, A Daughter's Love,* Thomas honors the bond between those two family member with poems from the point of view of each. In the *Bowlegged Rooster and Other Tales That Signify,* she serves up five short stories for young readers featuring Papa Rooster and his chick, all set in Possum Neck, Mississippi. "Although the plots are not always terrifically involving," wrote Steven Engelfried in *School Library Journal,* "the animals' personalities and the bustling atmosphere of the barnyard make these tales appealing." Shelley Townsend-Hudson, writing in *Booklist,* felt these tales are "a joy to hear as well as to read."

"I work for authenticity of voice," Thomas commented in *SAAS,* "fidelity to detail, and naturalness of developments." It is this authenticity that critics say sings out in all of Thomas's work, and that allows her fiction and poetry to transcend race, gender, and geography. "I treasure and value the experiences that include us all as people." Thomas concluded in *SAAS.* "I don't pay any attention to boundaries."

Biographical and Critical Sources

BOOKS

Children's Literature Review, Volume 19, Gale, 1990.
Contemporary Literary Criticism, Volume 35, Gale, 1985.
Dictionary of Literary Biography, Volume 33: *Afro-American Fiction Writers after 1955,* Gale, 1984.
St. James Guide to Young Adult Writers, 2nd edition, edited by Tom Pendergast and Sara Pendergast, St. James, 1999.
Thomas, Joyce Carol, *Marked by Fire,* Avon, 1982.
Thomas, Joyce Carol, essay in *Something about the Author Autobiography Series,* Volume 7, Gale, 1989, pp. 299-311.

PERIODICALS

African American Review, spring, 1998, pp. 139-147.
Best Sellers, June, 1982, Wendell Wray, review of *Marked by Fire,* pp. 123-124.
Black Scholar, summer, 1982, Dorothy Randall-Tsuruta, review of *Marked by Fire,* p. 48.
Booklist, February 15, 1986, pp. 861-862; February 15, 1994, review of *Brown Honey in Broomwheat Tea,* p. 1081; September 15, 1995, p. 176; March 15, 1997, p. 1249; February 15, 1998, Ilene Cooper, review of *I Have Heard of a Land,* p. 1009; January 1, 1999, Kathy Broderick, review of *Cherish Me,* p. 891; October 1, 2000, Shelley Townsend-Hudson, review of *The Bowlegged Rooster and Other Tales That Signify,* p. 342; December 15, 2000, Hazel Rochman, review of *Hush Songs,* p. 823; February 15, 2001, Hazel Rochman, review of *House of Light,* p. 1101.
Bulletin of the Center for Children's Books, February, 1984, Zena Sutherland, review of *Bright Shadow,* p. 119; June, 1998, pp. 376-377.
English Journal, April, 1991, p. 83; October, 1993, p. 81.

I work on the illustrations of fairy tales. I first make one picture—which later will be the central 'high point' of the story—the picture I receive like a vision or like a dream. Then I look for the reasons for this impression, the things that have led into such a feeling—this will be the beginning of the story. After, I try to work in my mind to get a good solution for the central expression (aiming at a happy end). This will be the final part of the book.

"I believe that all kinds of art are keys to our subconscious," Vainio concluded. Her musical inspirations include Mozart, Bach, Mahler, Bizet, and Puccini. "With my illustrations I pretend that they move something in the children's minds—for I consider illustration work as any other form of art; maybe it is only the most fortunate one to have such a pure and innocent public as the children are."

Vainio has become known for her dreamy picture books featuring cooly colored watercolor illustrations and plots in which magic is an everyday event. In *The Snow Goose,* her first story to appear in English translation, a little girl builds a snow goose in the snow that melts overnight, and in the spring, when her grandfather brings home a wounded goose, Anna is certain it is her snow goose. The bird dies, but leaves an egg that Anna nurtures until it hatches; then she raises it with love. In the fall, the bird joins a flock of geese and flies away. "Pale watercolors, soft and dreamlike, reinforce the story's subtle mood," observed Harriett Fargnoli in *School Library Journal.* A critic for *Publishers Weekly* faulted the text translation as "choppy" and concluded that the illustrations "impart a dreamy quality and are more effective than the story at conveying the importance of the goose in the girl's world." *School Librarian* contributor Cathy Sutton, however, proclaimed that the illustrations and the text work well together to convey "strong, difficult emotions" associated with the theme of death and loss, which are "dealt with very simply and tenderly."

Don't Be Scared, Scarecrow concerns a friendly looking scarecrow who fails to scare away the birds and is put away in the shed by the farmer, where his friend the dog barks at him. The scarecrow runs away and by virtue of a new hat is able to scare some children and is given a job in a new field. When he himself gets a fright by the strange look of some laundry waving in the night breeze, the scarecrow begins to understand that the dog barked because he did not recognize him, and the scarecrow returns home. While a reviewer for *Publishers Weekly* and Lisa S. Murphy in *School Library Journal* felt that the scarecrow's transformation into a scary creature was not borne out in the illustrations, a critic for *Kirkus Reviews* dubbed Vainio's watercolors "unusually disarming," and described *Don't Be Scared, Scarecrow* as "a gentle tale, with a quiet message of acceptance."

The Christmas Angel is another tale of transformation. Here, a little girl helping her mother and grandmother with preparations for Christmas discovers a music box with a figure on top that she imagines is an angel without wings. When Maria's grandmother tells her that

Lucas is lonely in his tall tower until a storm turns it into a bridge for children from the mainland. (Illustration from The Dream House, *written and illustrated by Vainio.)*

it takes a good deed to earn angel wings, Maria decides to deliver some Christmas cookies to the homeless man she has seen in the neighborhood. When she opens her own Christmas presents, Maria finds the music box among them, an angel complete with wings atop the box. "Vainio's soft, dreamlike watercolors mesh nicely with the gentle story," observed Kay Weisman in *Booklist.* While a critic for *School Library Journal* felt that the author's approach to the issue of homelessness was too simplistic to be satisfactory, *Horn Book* contributor Martha Sibert dubbed *The Christmas Angel* a "touching holiday tale."

Vainio's whimsy takes the forefront in *The Dream House,* in which a man builds his fantasy home on an island. Each room is placed on top of the one before it because of space constraints. At the top is a room entirely for wind chimes. When the wind blows over the tower of the house, it becomes a bridge to the mainland and a group of children travel across to the island to keep the lonely man company. *School Library Journal* reviewer Virginia Opocensky praised Vainio's watercolors, which "perfectly portray the sea, the slightly eccentric builder, and the joyous ending."

Horn Book, March-April, 1996, Martha V. Parravano, review of *Gingerbread Days,* pp. 219-220.
Kirkus Reviews, September 15, 1988, review of *Journey,* p. 1410; February 1, 2001, review of *House of Light.*
Publishers Weekly, July 25, 1986, review of *The Golden Pasture,* p. 191; September 9, 1988, p. 140; October 11, 1993, p. 87; September 25, 1995, review of *Gingerbread Days,* p. 57; January 8, 1996, review of *Brown Honey in Broomwheat Tea,* p. 70; April 6, 1998, review of *I Have Heard of a Land,* p. 77; October 19, 1998, p. 83; February 19, 2001, review of *House of Light,* p. 69.
School Library Journal, March, 1982, Hazel Rochman, review of *Marked by Fire,* p. 162; January, 1984, pp. 89-90; August, 1986, p. 107; October, 1988, Starr LaTronica, review of *Journey,* p. 165; October, 1990, p. 145; February, 1993, pp. 106-107; November, 1993, p. 103; January, 1996, Meg Stackpole, review of *Gingerbread Days,* p. 107; December, 1998, p. 116; August, 1999, p. 132; November, 2000, Steven Engelfried, review of *The Bowlegged Rooster and Other Tales That Signify,* p. 135.
Variety, September 9, 1987, p. 75.

ON-LINE

Joyce Carol Thomas, http://www.joycecarolthomas.com/ (April 3, 2001).

—*Sketch by J. Sydney Jones*

*   *   *

TROUT, Richard E.

Richard E. Trout

Personal

Born in Oklahoma City, OK; married; wife's name, Mavis (a teacher); children: two daughters. *Education:* Oklahoma Christian University, B.S., 1971; Oklahoma State University, M.S., 1973. *Hobbies and other interests:* Scuba diving, outdoor activities.

Addresses

Home and office—8232 Northwest 115th St., Oklahoma City, OK 73162. *E-mail*—caymantrout@aol.com.

Career

Oklahoma City Community College, professor of biology.

Writings

Cayman Gold, LangMarc Publishing (San Antonio, TX), 1999.
Elephant Tears: Mask of the Elephant, LangMarc Publishing (San Antonio, TX), 2000.
Falcon of Abydos: Oracle of the Nile, LangMarc Publishing (San Antonio, TX), 2001.

Biographical and Critical Sources

PERIODICALS

Kliatt Young Adult Paperback Book Guide, May, 2000, Sherri Forgash Ginsberg, review of *Cayman Gold.*

V

VAINIO, Pirkko 1957-

Personal

Born September 24, 1957, in Jamsankoski, Finland; daughter of Olavi and Annikki (Kettinen) Vainio; married Andrea Baldini (a printer), May 7, 1983; children: Irina Baldini. *Education:* Attended Academy of Fine Arts (Helsinki, Finland), 1978-81, 1983. *Religion:* Lutheran.

Addresses

Home—via Metastasio, 19, 51024 Firenze, Italy.

Career

Writer and illustrator of children's books, 1984—. *Exhibitions:* Participated in illustrators' exhibitions at Bologna Book Fair and Itabashi Art Museum (Tokyo, Japan), both 1991. *Member:* Icograda (International Council of Graphics), Grafia (Finnish graphic artists association), Nordiska Tecknare.

Writings

(Illustrator) I. Salo, *Junalla Arikspaaniin,* Sanoma Book Publishing (Finland), 1984.
(Illustrator) A. Savisaari, *Hemppa,* Sanoma Book Publishing (Finland), 1989.

SELF-ILLUSTRATED; IN ENGLISH TRANSLATION

Die Schneegans, Nord-Sud Verlag (Switzerland), 1993, translation by J. Alison published as *The Snow Goose,* James, North-South Books (New York, NY), 1993.
Don't Be Scared, Scarecrow (originally published as *Vogelscheuche Fridolin*), North-South Books (New York, NY), 1994.
The Christmas Angel (originally published as *Weihnachtsengel*), translated by Anthea Bell, North-South Books (New York, NY), 1995.
The Dream House (originally published as *Wir bauen eine Haus-Turm-Bruecke*), translated by J. Alison James, North-South Books (New York, NY), 1997.

The Best of Friends (originally published as *Freunde*), translated by J. Alison James, North-South Books (New York, NY), 2000.

ILLUSTRATOR; IN ENGLISH TRANSLATION; "JOSIE SMITH" SERIES

Magdalen Nabb, *Josie Smith,* HarperCollins (London, England), 1988.
Magdalen Nabb, *Josie Smith at the Seashore,* M. K. McElderry Books, 1990.
Magdalen Nabb, *Josie Smith and Eileen,* M. K. McElderry Books, 1991.
Magdalen Nabb, *Josie Smith at School,* M. K. McElderry Books, 1991.
Magdalen Nabb, *Josie Smith at Christmas,* HarperCollins (London, England), 1992.

Also illustrator of *Josie Smith in Hospital,* by Magdalen Nabb, HarperCollins.

SELF-ILLUSTRATED PICTURE BOOKS; UNTRANSLATED

Kuplamatka Kukkarantaan, Sanoma Book Publishing (Finland), 1988.
Kleiner Vogel flieg ganz hoch, Nord-Sud Verlag (Switzerland), 1990.
Tattivaaran Hattuvaras, Sanoma Book Publishing (Finland), 1992.

Also author and illustrator of *Pieni Kaalimato,* Sanoma Book Publishing (Finland).

Sidelights

After attending the Academy of Fine Arts in Helsinki, Finland, Pirkko Vainio became interested in graphic art, especially black-and-white expression. She told *SATA* that she felt the simplicity of black and white to be "more near to the world of dreams and our subconscious life."

Now an accomplished illustrator, Vainio described for *SATA* her early attempts at illustration: "I saw that every etching I made had a story around it and this brought me to invent stories around the pictures. This is still the way

Maria performs a good deed to help an angel earn her wings in **The Christmas Angel,** *written and illustrated by Pirkko Vainio.*

The whimsy in *The Best of Friends,* Vainio's next book to appear in English, lies in the contrast between the two friends, Hare and Bear, the one small and vegetarian, the other large and carnivorous. Vainio takes the friends through the seasons as they play in summer, hibernate in winter, and wake together to anticipate the spring to come. Reviewers noted the many points at which preschoolers could learn from this book, including lessons about size, seasons, and friendship. "Most importantly they learn that differences can actually enhance a friendship," concluded Lauren Peterson in *Booklist.*

Biographical and Critical Sources

PERIODICALS

Booklist, December 15, 1995, Kay Weisman, review of *The Christmas Angel,* p. 710; June 1, 2000, Lauren Peterson, review of *The Best of Friends,* p. 1911.

Horn Book, spring, 1996, Martha Sibert, review of *The Christmas Angel,* p. 47.

Kirkus Reviews, June 15, 1994, review of *Don't Be Scared, Scarecrow,* p. 853.

Publishers Weekly, October 18, 1993, review of *The Snow Goose,* p. 72; June 13, 1994, review of *Don't Be Scared, Scarecrow,* p. 64.

School Librarian, August, 1993, Cathy Sutton, review of *The Snow Goose,* p. 106.

School Library Journal, January, 1994, Harriett Fargnoli, review of *The Snow Goose,* p. 100; December, 1994, Lisa S. Murphy, review of *Don't Be Scared, Scarecrow,* p. 88; October, 1995, review of *The Christmas Angel,* p. 43; January, 1998, Virginia Opocensky, review of *The Dream House,* p. 94; June, 2000, Judith Constantinides, review of *The Best of Friends,* p. 126.*

Autobiography Feature

Janice VanCleave

1942-

I was born in Houston, Texas, on January 27, 1942, and was an only child until I was almost five years old. There always seemed to be adults, such as aunts and uncles, that periodically lived with us, so I was treated like a fairy princess. One of my younger unmarried aunts often had me entertaining her friends. She would play the piano, and I would sing and dance. She even curled my hair in "Shirley Temple" curls. I really thought I was talented. But why shouldn't I? My adult audience gave me nothing but praise. I did take tap and ballet from preschool through the fifth grade. I danced on stages in theaters as well as on a local television program, but I finally lost interest.

I was four years and ten months old when my mother gave birth to twins, my brother, Dennis and my sister, Dianne. It had not been an easy pregnancy, and on several occasions Mom had to be taken to the hospital. The first time was when I was at school. I was used to my mom being at home when I came in from school, and I was not a happy camper when I discovered she was missing. I did not listen to anyone and looked through the entire house for her. I actually was frightened but appeared to be a spoiled, out-of-control kid. Well, maybe I did have a touch of that. My "other" grandmother had ideas about what should be done to make me behave, and they all involved a board and my bottom. But my aunt was sure that she could console

me by allowing me to roller-skate around in the house. That must have really messed up the floors! I do remember how much fun it was but only for a time. When the skating was over, and Mom had not shown up I was an unhappy camper again. But Dad appeared, and all was at least partly well. Mom soon returned home, and life was rosy again.

Mom and I discussed how my life would change when the new baby came. She told me that I probably would be unhappy about it getting into my stuff. Now where did this lady with a tenth-grade education pick up on this trick of reverse psychology? Must just be a mom thing. I assured her that I was going to love the baby. I was so excited about the new baby that I dreamed about it. It was my live doll, and I had so much fun playing with it.

No one knew that it was going to be two babies instead of one. If you think twins disrupt a household now, think how it was in the late forties. All those diapers to wash and hang on the line. There were no clothes dryers, and the washing machine was one of those types with the rollers. Washing was a full day's job. Guess who got to watch the babies while mom did her household chores? I can't say it was all work. I created ways to entertain the babies, such as pulling them around the yard on a blanket. Mom did get a bit excited about this activity since the babies were bumping their heads as I raced across the lawn pulling the blanket as fast as I could. I had to go back to the mental drawing board and create another way to keep both of them corralled and entertained. That was not an easy assignment once they were crawling.

Unlike in my dream, I didn't want to play with the live babies all the time. So, most of my memories are of things that I did by myself. I had different creative periods as a child as I do as an adult. There was the paper doll period when I spent hours designing clothes for paper dolls. I would lay paper over a paper doll and draw a dress around her, adding tabs to bend over her shoulders and around her waist. I colored and cut out these designs. I had cigar boxes full of paper dolls and clothes. It wasn't that my parents couldn't purchase more dolls and clothes for me—I preferred my own designs.

The marble period was also short. During this time I collected marbles; some I bought, others I traded for or won from neighborhood boys in marble shooting contests. Most girls did not play marble games. Boys seemed to have had the idea that girls were not good at "boy" games, so I found it exciting to beat them if I could. Not because they were boys, but because they said I couldn't. I won a lot of their marbles and stored them in a large cigar box. As with other things, I soon tired of playing marbles and either read about or saw a movie about hidden treasure. So, I buried my box of marbles in the woods adjacent to my house and covered the ground with leaves and limbs. I made a treasure map so that I could later find the box. After some time had passed I looked for the treasure but never found it. I periodically searched for that box of marbles but finally decided that some pirate must have seen me bury it and dug it up after I left. Some kid is probably still telling the story of finding a box of beautiful marbles in the woods.

Adult creative periods have included ceramics, oil painting, and writing. When I say I had a ceramic period, I don't mean I did a few ceramic items. I started with a ceramic cup, and in a short time had my husband build shelves across one wall of our bedroom so that I could store the ceramic pieces in their different stages of production. I prepared chess sets, canister sets, bowls, cups, etc. Every friend and relative received ceramic pieces as presents for birthdays and Christmas. This period lasted for about one year, but the oil painting period was longer—it took a bit of time to take lessons. But once I had a few lessons, I took off painting. Of course, like the ceramic period, friends and relatives received paintings whether they wanted them or not. It may have been easy to display a piece of pottery for a while just to be nice, but it never occurred to me that a painting is a personal item that one selects. No matter, I was off and running, turning out art. I do mean turning out art. I even bought a miter box, which is a special type of saw apparatus used to cut angles. I needed this to cut the angles for picture frames. Yes, not only did I paint pictures, I framed them. I got good at framing but can't really say my art was that great. I enjoyed most doing things for kids. I would purchase a fun storybook and paint one of the scenes. The child not only had a book, they had a picture from Aunt Jane. That is what my nieces and nephews have always called me.

Television and video games were nonexistent when I was a young child. This admission makes me seem

Janice VanCleave

very old, but the truth is that so much technology has developed during my lifetime. Without television, one way that kids entertained themselves was by listening to the radio. I personally hated music programs and waited anxiously for story programs. Radio was a time of imagination. When you listen to a story being acted out via the radio you have to visualize the scenes in your mind. It is true that a picture is worth a thousand words, and without the pictures, careful attention to the words and sounds of the radio program were absolutely necessary. Evenings were a time of quiet family togetherness as we grouped near the radio hanging on every word of the Cisco Kid or the Lone Ranger. Kids didn't have to be reminded to be quiet, they were as engrossed with the story as the adults. Besides, if you were noisy you might be sent to your room. This was a real punishment because there wasn't much you could do there if you were not allowed to take a book to read.

Reading was another activity that I enjoyed, and I read all kinds of books, from Davy Crockett's adventures and Nancy Drew mysteries to Bible stories. There were no wonderful bookstores as there are today, and while my parents were good providers, buying books was not in our budget. Comics and magazines were another story. I often walked the five blocks to our local store to purchase comics for my dad and myself. He loved monster stuff, and I of course wanted romance. There must have been something lacking in my body chemistry because I craved lemons my entire childhood and long into my adult life. I'd buy a dozen lemons and as many comics and spend the day eating the lemons, peel and all, and reading. I've eaten so many lemons during my life that the acid has etched my teeth. While the lemons were inexpensive, the bonding on my teeth to repair the damage was not.

While I had a steady diet of comics, they did not satisfy my hunger to read. We lived on the outskirts of Houston, which would be considered a very rural area today. There were a few houses around, but mostly we were surrounded by wooded lots and traveled on dirt roads. During the first four years of school, I rode a bus to school. Later an elementary school was built about half a mile away. It was on a dirt road, and I enjoyed walking to school. These rural schools did not have much of a library, but there was always the Book Mobile. As a child I never thought much about the Book Mobile. It came every week, so I just expected it to be there. I now appreciate the workers that took the time to provide the opportunity for me to read. I had no special topic that I was interested in. Sometimes I would read a book because I liked the picture on the cover. I don't remember anything about the author or titles of the books, but I once read a series of books that

As a young ballet dancer.

involved the blue willow pattern on china. I still like this pattern.

I was an imaginative child and fantasized by acting out scenes in my mind. To this day I can still feel the excitement of reading about a character preparing to visit a distant relative and how she selected hair ribbons to match her clothes. I thought that was such a neat thing to do. I really wanted to be like the characters that I read about, but the desire for buttons and bows usually was short-lived. In reality I was a tomboy. In one of the stories I read, the female character tied a black satin ribbon around her neck and pinned a cameo to the front of the ribbon. I was so caught up in the plot that I wanted to look elegant like the girl in the book. I didn't have a black satin ribbon, but Mom kept all kinds of things in her sewing cabinet. Maybe there was a ribbon. I was almost correct. There was a black brassiere with black straps. My thought was that the garment was most likely not any good if it was in the sewing drawer, so I cut off one of the straps. It was just the right size to fit around my neck. Now for the cameo. Mom had a collection of jewelry that I'd purchased for her for different events and there was a pin—not a cameo but it would do. About that jewelry—at the time I never questioned the fact that Mom never wore any of it, but then Dad never wore any of the ties I bought him either. Guess a truck driver didn't have much use for ties, but he was always so happy with my present that I continued to buy them. Holiday presents are another story.

I must admit that I had second thoughts about not asking permission to cut off the brassiere strap. This was just one of many times that I got so excited about my project that I didn't stop to ask permission. It wasn't that I was a disobedient child, I was generally finished with the project before realizing that I had not gotten permission. I immediately regretted my actions and sincerely promised myself that I'd not do it again, and I meant it. The problem was that when the creative juices started flowing I was like a runaway train that couldn't be stopped. This behavior plagues me even as an adult.

Yes, I went to school wearing the black bra strap around my neck with the attached pin drawing attention to it. I don't recall any particular comments from anyone, but my teacher may have added the event to stories she shared with other teachers. While school was relatively uneventful that day, my mother's reaction when I returned home was not. I'd gotten used to the "ribbon" around my neck and forgot to remove it. Imagine my surprise when my mother asked if I had gone to school with a brassiere strap tied around my neck. Now, how did she know it was a brassiere strap? I thought it looked like a ribbon. She was more upset that I'd embarrassed her by wearing a brassiere strap in public than by the fact that I'd destroyed the garment.

Movies were a regular Saturday event. By the time I was in the fifth grade, I was allowed to catch a bus and go to the movie theater. It cost me nine cents to get in the theater, and popcorn, sodas, and candy bars were five cents each. Bus fare was four cents, and I often walked the three miles to save the four cents. After all, one more penny would buy a candy bar.

Sunday was a time for church. I liked Sunday school best and loved getting a sticker placed on my attendance picture. I still have one of the pictures somewhere. While I liked attending Bible classes, I liked teaching better and taught my first class at the age of eleven. Well, I thought I was the teacher. Actually I was the helper, but I came to class with things for the little kids to do and even attended training classes with the adults. I still like working with children at church, and I am the official Bible school craft teacher each summer. Summer Bible school is a short, condensed day camp designed to introduce children to the excitement of a relationship with Jesus. The adult workers are drained when it is over and whine a bit about being tired, but we all sign up to do it again. Being a scientist, my Bible craft classes are mostly about science. Science has always been my passion, and I've never found being a Christian and a scientist to be contradictory. I think God staged creation with just enough mystery to keep inquiring minds busy. It is my desire at some time in the near future to publish a fun Christian craft book with the ideas that I use in summer Bible school.

Reading, going to the movies, and working at church had a great influence on my life. But it was my natural curiosity that led me to acting out the plots and discovering for myself the scientific wonders around me. My first real scientific investigation involved the movies, and the results of my studies disclosed that movies were make-believe. This was a discouraging yet eye-opening revelation. My first real hero was Tarzan. I was most envious of his ability to swim any time he wanted to, and what fun it appeared to catch a vine and travel through the jungle. It occurred to me one day that there were grapevines on the trees near my house. I was amazed that I'd not thought about this before. I could have been swinging through the trees all along. I didn't waste any time pulling a vine away from a tree, and even though I had no particular knowledge of the effects of gravity, I was smart enough to cautiously apply my weight to make sure the vine would support me. Yes, the vine selected would do. So I backed off and then ran toward the tree and grabbed the vine. I was shocked that I did not rise and swing forward. I tried it again—obviously repeating the experiment as any good scientist would do. Same results. My thoughts were that I must have done something wrong. Evaluation and a need to do further research was determined (although I did not think in these terms then). I thought I must have remembered the scene incorrectly and decided I'd have to see another Tarzan movie to see what I had done wrong. Looking back on the scene, I am aware that children practice the scientific method all the time. We just don't give them credit for doing it.

Saturday finally came, and I was back at the movies. I was probably the most attentive child in the movie theater that day and the most anxious to leave when the movie was finished. I intensely studied the vines in the movie, how Tarzan ran, where the vines were when he grabbed them, and how they moved. It looked like the vines were hanging straight down and went up when Tarzan grabbed them. Seems that was the way I did it. I went home with a renewed faith that if I ran faster it would work. But alas, I failed again. I did give lots of thought to the problem before determining the Tarzan movie was a fake. Little did I know that I was doing my first physics investigations and had used all the steps of the inquiry approach without anyone making me memorize the steps. This was real hands-on science.

Imagination was a big part of my childhood. Each day was a new adventure—each day of weekends, holidays or time after school, that is. I attended public schools and don't recall having much fun in elementary school except during recess. Upper grade experiences were not much more exciting for me. In the first grade, my memories are of wishing I hadn't forgotten to do my homework. It wasn't that I didn't want to learn, it just seemed that my mind was going in so many different directions that I just forgot the school stuff. I was always so disappointed with myself for forgetting. But how could I have been concentrating on schoolwork the day a man led a small pony into our yard? Second only to swimming, I loved riding horses. The only ones I'd ever ridden had been at a carnival, and they were hitched to a pole and went around in a circle. Now I had the opportunity to actually sit on a horse that wasn't attached to a pole. The man even had a cowgirl outfit for me to wear. Surely my mother would not deprive me of this experience. All she had to do was let the man take my picture. OK, she also had to buy the picture. I really begged, and it worked. While sitting on the horse the bright idea of kicking the horse so that he would walk came to me. As the man prepared his camera, I used my foot on the side of the horse opposite the man to kick the horse, just a little bit. After a couple of taps the horse took a few steps forward. I was riding! The man was so mad at the horse that I felt a bit guilty for getting the animal in trouble, but I would have done it again if I could have gotten away with it.

Second grade happened but I have few memories except the one time that I talked without permission and

Janice posing as a cowgirl on a real live pony.

had to stand in the corner with my arms raised over my head. In my mind I was there for hours, but it had to have been only a short but agonizing time. I wish I'd had understood more about gravity then, and I might have pointed out to the teacher that my hands and arms were changing colors. They were getting lighter in color as the blood drained from them. You can try this with one arm held up and the other down for a few minutes, then compare their color. But I don't think this teacher would have been interested in my scientific observations.

The second grade also held one of my nightmare school experiences. All the kids were lined up to receive a shot. At this time, the county health department gave free vaccinations at school. One by one each child was taken by a nurse behind "the white screen." We had no idea what or who was back there, but children that entered screamed and came out crying and holding their arms. I was so terrified as I approached the screen that when my name was called to be the next victim, I bolted and ran as fast as I could. The nurse and teachers tried to stop me, but I was too determined to escape. I got away and hid in my bus. I stayed crouched between the bus seats until the kids started entering to go home. I doubt that I was hidden for long, and surely my teacher knew where I was and just decided to let my mom handle the affair. Oops! Mom had not entered my mind, but when I got home I knew that she had received a call from my teacher because she gave me the "look." Could whatever she would do to me be worse than being dragged behind the white screen? I tried to explain how I felt, but Mom was not interested. She was more concerned about how she was going to pay the doctor for the shot. Yes, I was going to get the shot after all, so we were off to the doctor's office. But I was a much wiser person now and watched for my chance to make my break. When the doctor and my mom were talking, I very quietly slid off the examining table. I had my hand on the doorknob when my mom grabbed me. It did take several to hold me, and I made every effort to bring help with my screams, but no one came to my rescue and I was given the dreaded shot.

Surprisingly, after the infamous "school shot" experience, I became more interested in showing just how brave I was, and I never again blinked at being given shots. My interest in science increased, and as a teen I once opted for a local anesthetic so I could sit and watch the doctor operate on my wrist to remove a cyst. I'd still prefer to do that if the operation is necessary. I certainly don't like pain, but if I have to be cut on, I'd like to ask questions to make sure the doc is paying attention to what he is doing. Besides, I find that kind of stuff interesting, even more so if it is someone else's blood.

I missed a great deal of third grade due to having bad tonsils. But when I returned I was sure that school was going to be wonderful from then on. The teacher sent home a note requesting money to purchase a coloring book. It was just too wonderful anticipating coloring in a real color book at school. When the books were passed out, I never thought much about the fact that each child had the same coloring book. I was a bit disturbed when the teacher asked us all to turn to the same page, but the reality of the situation finally struck home when she instructed us to pick up a red crayon and color the balloon. We may have

With Dr. Leon Lederman, 1988 Nobel Prize winner in Physics, taken in 1996.

colored in that book after that day, but I have no memory of it. It wasn't fun, and I no longer cared about the coloring book. But I learned from the coloring book experience, one thing being to appreciate the creativity of a child. While I can't say that I was always understanding when my own children and grandchildren made creative messes, I made an effort to understand.

Because of these and other miscellaneous events, I just didn't have a great deal of interest in school. While my parents were interested in my getting an education, they were never involved in school functions and neither was I. They had both had unusual childhoods, something paralleling *The Grapes of Wrath.* I can say that they were both intelligent enough to overcome their lack of formal education and through the years had many successful businesses. My dad was involved with driving or the trucking business most of his life. He had the ability to earn money but was not as skilled at saving it. In retrospect, we lived a rags-to-riches life, but as a child I was never particularly aware of the hard times. Unlike Dad, Mom could stretch every dime, and we never did without. That is not to say that we wore fashionable clothes or lived in a wealthy part of town, but neither did any of the kids at my school. It was a country school, and we were all of the same socioeconomic status—slightly poor. Actually, I considered my family wealthier than others in our neighborhood. This is because having a nice car was first on my dad's list of necessities. If our car wasn't new, it was at least very big and shiny. We were the only family within many blocks that had brick on their house; the lower part of the front of our house was bricked. I was so proud when that brick was put on our house. But it wasn't a pride that made me feel a cut above others, it was a pride for my dad. As a child, I really did think he was the greatest. How wonderful of him to make our home pretty. Mom was a bit more concerned about paying the bills next month. Dad had more of a "bird in hand" philosophy, and he'd worry about tomorrow when it came. He was a wheeler-dealer and often got himself in unusual situations. Once he bought a whole truckload of peaches, but his buyer backed out on the deal. To keep from losing his investment, the peaches had to be sold and sold quickly before they went bad. Dad's idea was that I would sell the peaches while he continued to work. So he set me up a peach stand on the corner of a busy street, and I sold peaches. At twelve years of age, I was not that interested in selling peaches on a corner, but whatever Dad said was what I did. Not because he was strict and would punish me but because from the time I could remember, I would walk fast just to keep in step with him. I really thought he was wonderful.

I didn't get paid for selling the peaches, so the peach selling business began to tarnish Dad's halo. Later, there was a used car lot. I washed the cars, did secretarial work, sold cars, etc. I was only fourteen but managed to get special permission to receive a driver's license. I drove the cars and had money for gas and entertainment, but again I did not receive payment for the work that I did. Dad never paid me for any job that I did for him, even though he had me working instead of hiring someone else. I guess he just didn't think he should have to pay his own kid. I am very careful about this and try to be fair about paying what I owe.

I may not have received a salary for my work, but Dad was very generous with me, and he certainly taught me how to how to sell stuff. I inherited my overachiever, workaholic personality from him. Thankfully I also received a conservative "Let's save for tomorrow" attitude from my mom.

Mom was never comfortable with Dad's lifestyle, so when I was fourteen, she enrolled in cosmetology school, although up until this time she had never expressed a desire to be a beautician, which was the term for the profession at that time. I couldn't wait for her to graduate, because she promised that she would bleach my hair. I eventually was a platinum blond as well as a redhead, raven black, etc. Mom soon opened her own beauty salon and had the personality to work with the public. Unlike Dad's business adventures, she was able to manage her business and made a lasting success of it.

With both parents working, I had a bit more freedom than was good for me, and I stayed home from school at every opportunity. It is interesting that I disliked school so much at that time but spent twenty-seven years teaching. I facetiously have said that I had to make up for all the days that I was absent. The one thing I tried to do as a teacher was to make my classes fun. Fun is not to be equated with "There's nothing educational going on in this class." Rather, fun science just means there's hands-on stuff going on in the class.

My boredom at school can be summed up as total uninvolvement on my part. This was my own fault. I could have been part of the band or athletic programs. I chose not to. By the time I reached the eighth grade I had no doubts that I wanted out of school as soon as possible. That is not to say that I disliked learning, I just disliked school. My feeling intensified each year, and by the tenth grade I asked my dad to please let me drop out of school and go to cosmetology school and work with my mom. While Dad was generally very lenient with me, he was firm about this. Since neither he nor my mom had finished high school (in fact Dad had a sixth-grade education), he was determined that his children would graduate. He informed

"In 1997, I helped promote a national science contest sponsored by Lanocane for teachers and students with Bill Nye, the Science Guy."

me that I would finish school, and if I had other thoughts he would personally escort me to school. Was this the same man who gave me money to go to the movies when I just got fed up with school and stayed home? Of course when I was at the movies, Mom thought I was slaving away at school in my classes. I guess Dad's thoughts were that missing school now and then was not so bad as long as I could keep my grades up, and I did. His adamant response about my dropping out certainly was a surprise, but I got the message loud and clear. OK, so I had to graduate, but that didn't mean that I had to go for twelve years. During the summer after I finished the tenth grade, I took classes in summer school. With these credits, I was able to enter the twelfth grade when school started. I skipped the eleventh grade and graduated a year early. In age I always had been younger than the kids in my class. Because of my January birthday, Mom started me in kindergarten when I was four. That made me fifteen when I started my senior year and sixteen when I graduated in May. My plans were to get that high school diploma and with it secure a good job, get an apartment, a new car, etc. First of all, no one wanted to hire a sixteen-year-old for any job except making and selling hamburgers. Second, unmarried girls couldn't easily get an apartment at this time.

Now what? College? More boring school? Maybe it would be different. I enrolled in college. Surprise, surprise, I loved it. I couldn't get enough of it. I can't say my grades were all A's; after all, I had missed a lot of instruction during my high school years, and even though I made relatively good grades, I was not as educated as I should have or could have been. What a waste of time. If I do nothing else in my life, I hope to encourage young people to get involved in school events and find the fun that is there for them. Life is as boring as one makes it.

While my grades were B's and C's the first year, I truly adapted to the college environment quickly. I attended the University of Houston, which was across town from my home, but I wanted to be a real college student and live in the dorms. My dad fussed about this idea but finally gave in. He drove me to the dorms and discovered how very strict the dorm rules were. He was not allowed in the dorm. The only man ever in the building was someone from maintenance, and he had to announce his presence loud and clear. Actually, the rules for the girls' dorms at that time were much stricter than those in my home, but there were choices that I made on my own. One decision was not a healthy choice. I chose to skimp on food and save my food allowance to purchase shoes. I did lose weight but gained thirty plus pairs of very beautiful shoes. My dad was shocked when he moved me home for the summer.

I never returned to the dorms because I married in August of 1959 before school started. My marriage was to Wade Russell VanCleave, a very handsome young man that I had been dating for two years. Wade had recently returned home from Marine boot camp and planned to work and fulfill the remainder of his military obligation in the Marine Reserves. My intentions were to continue college, but my mother became ill, and I dropped out of the fall semester. Mom recovered from her illness, and I returned to school in the spring of 1960. The only problem was that I returned to school married and pregnant. Being married was great, but I had classic morning sickness, and it was difficult to attend classes. I often sipped on a Coke during a class and threw it up afterwards. I persevered and made it through the semester, passing all my classes with good grades. My first child was born August 6, 1960. She was a beautiful redheaded girl, and my mother named her Rajene Diane. When we brought this bright bundle of joy home from the hospital, my mom looked at her and decided that her name didn't fit. So she called her Ginger, and she is called Ginger to this day.

With a baby to take care of and the expense of college and a baby-sitter, I did not return to college in the fall. During the next two and one-half years, I had two more children, Russell Eugene and David Wade. While I loved my family, I began to feel that my brain needed a bit more stimulation. When David was two years old, I returned to college taking night classes. Wade worked at

At the geographic South Pole in 1997.

the post office as a postal carrier and kept the children for me at night. I had entered college with a desire to be a medical laboratory technician, but I changed my major to education when I returned as a wife and mother. It was my thought that as a homemaker, teaching would allow me to pursue my desire to study science and have quality time with my family. It was a good choice.

My husband was a good provider, but my teaching salary allowed us to have a few extras, such as a modest fishing cabin for weekend retreats. I can't say that the post office paid him a large salary, but we lived within our means. He has always managed our finances, and that has also been with my blessing. I don't care to know how much the telephone or electric bill is. Since my six grandchildren have been born, I just want to know how much money I have to play with. So that I make my grandchildren happy, let me include their names and ages in 2001: Kimberly (19), Jennifer (16), Davin (15), Lauren (13), Lacey (11), David (6).

Teaching school was a sweet and sour job. Sweet in the excitement of knowing that I offered kids the key to a treasure of wonderful knowledge. Sour in the fact that all students were not as obedient and respectful as they should have been, and then there was all that paper work. When I got fed up with it all, I would simply move to another school and start over. I always entered the new school with the idea that I was at Mayberry High and all would be absolutely wonderful. The first year at any job is usually the honeymoon period, and I loved it. The second year I was ready to pack up and go. Actually, I think it may have been me more than the schools. I just had wandering fever and a family with ties that kept me from moving too far. But then my husband had back surgery and retired. It didn't take me long to figure out that we were free to leave.

Our first move was back to his hometown of Marlin, Texas. Of course I had to have a job for the move, but as a science teacher, jobs were plentiful. The only problem was that the school wanted me to teach physics. I was not certified to teach physics, so I checked out one of the last colleges at which I'd taken graduate work and was told that I had the qualifications but needed more hours in their college. It has always been fun for me to know that I took six hours of elementary education so that I could receive a certificate to teach high school physics. I liked Marlin High School. It was there that I sponsored several clubs, one in charge of the homecoming parade. You haven't experienced stress until you direct a parade. There is so much involved, one being the placement of the horses and who is to follow them.

While in Marlin, we lived on a small farm, and for a city gal it was an exciting time. Two and one-half acres is very small, but coming from the suburbs of Houston, it looked very large to me. It was a bit stressful for Wade since he was not able to do the work that he had in the past and was home alone. But he learned what he could and couldn't do. Our two sons, Russell and David, raised animals for class projects. They both earned money hauling hay during the summer, and Ginger tried to drive us crazy wanting to go back to Houston. But two years of farm life was enough for all of us. We literally got out a map and searched for places we might like to move to. We selected Lufkin, Texas, because of the great fishing lakes there. I got a job, and away we went, but this was a very short visit.

I wasn't as happy with the school as I thought I would be, so Ginger got her wish and we returned to Houston. I taught for two years in Houston, and then we were off again. My mom died before we left Houston, and I had even fewer ties to hold me. My dad was as much of a wanderer as I, and I knew that I'd see him periodically no matter where I moved. So, we decided to stretch our boundaries and go out of state. Since Wade was retired, he could search for just the right place. I packed his suitcase, and he set off to find us a home. In a few days he called from Arkansas and said he had found a beautiful piece of land. He put a deposit on it and returned home. Later we returned together and purchased the land. It took a year for me to find a job. Russell was only eighteen but had decided to marry and did. So, our family had increased by one, and we all took off for Arkansas. We had cars and rented trucks. What a sight we were. Since we only had land, we had to rent a place to live. The only available housing were tiny one-family houses, so we rented two houses. This allowed us to be close enough to the land to do our building. I drew the house plans in a spiral notebook, and Wade was the contractor and foreman. Our sons were the main laborers, but I did my share of hauling boards and was one of the main roofers. This was no small task since it was a two-story house. A neighbor that was mentally challenged joined our working team. We paid him for his service as well as invited him to join us for meals. He had no local family and was happy to be part of ours. He did present one problem and that is the fact that he rarely bathed or washed his clothes. He was a bit aromatic, so I encouraged him to bathe and even provided soap and washed his clothes. It wasn't so much that I was being nice as it was survival.

Building the Arkansas house was hard work, but it certainly had its fun times. We started the project in the summer of 1980 with temperatures reaching 110 degrees at times. We had fans in the bedrooms, but the only air-conditioning was in the small living room where we had the

Meeting President George W. Bush, Sr., at a breakfast in 1998 at the Texas Governor's mansion.

television. The prized sleeping accommodation was on a mattress in the back of our pickup. I had never before or since seen so many shooting stars. It was so spectacular to watch these natural fireworks. Guests were treated to a night in the pickup under the stars. They didn't have to wash their faces in the morning because they were usually covered with dew. "Kissed with dew" sounds more poetic. (The seventh-grade teacher who assigned the class to write a poem and then told me that my poem was stupid didn't know what she was talking about. I am poetic.)

It was while teaching chemistry and physics in Ft. Smith, Arkansas, that a local community college offered me the opportunity to design an enrichment class for elementary kids. I wrote the following description for the class, and it was printed in a catalog that was mailed out to the surrounding community:

The Magic of Science

The excitement of science is all around us. In this course, students entering grades 3, 4, 5, & 6 in the fall, will have the opportunity to increase their knowledge of science by having fun. Learn why popcorn explodes; how to boil water with ice; and how to silver plate a penny. The science aspect of everyday life will be brought out through student experiments and teacher demonstrations.

The class was held for one and one-half hours each week for six weeks. The kids had a great time, and my friends told me I was crazy to teach all day and entertain kids after school. Maybe, but a few weeks after the class ended I received a letter from a New York book publisher. She had seen the catalog and the description of my class. She was looking for writers for a special science series. Was I interested in writing? Actually, I wasn't sure at first because I thought she might be from one of the companies that wants you to pay to have your work published. No, I would not be interested in that. But she truly did represent a very reputable company, Prentice-Hall, Inc., so the answer was a definite yes!

Now what? I had never written a book and didn't have a clue about where to start. I had to be mailed instructions on how to write a prospectus so I could send one in for evaluation. My ideas were accepted, and I received a contract to write my first book. There were several problems. I thought I was to write the book and have the art in place and then it would be printed. Art? I have limited drawing skills. Had I gotten myself involved in another project without counting the costs? I asked the publisher so many questions that she finally mailed me a book on how to write a book and arranged to have the artwork done, at my expense of course. The advance I was offered to write the book and the art fee were all to come out of future royalties. The book was published in 1985, and I received my copy while living in Germany. Getting to Germany took a few steps.

We left our home in Arkansas in June of 1984 and returned to Houston because all of our children and our two-year-old granddaughter had returned there. All of a sudden I lost my desire to be in Arkansas. Our stay in Houston was only one year, and during this time Wade's father died. We decided to move back to Marlin and live in

With the then Governor of Texas, George W. Bush, Jr., discussing educational testing in Texas.

his dad's place. Prior to making this decision, I had interviewed with the Department of Defense Dependent Schools hoping for a position to teach on a U.S. military base in Europe. It sounded like an exciting time, and my idea was that my children would come for short holidays in Europe. Maybe Wade and I would move from one base to the next all over the world! Soon after getting unpacked in our farmhouse in Marlin, the offer to teach on a military base in Germany came. We went, but I didn't do well so far from my family. It was one thing to move to another state, but in Germany I couldn't visit my family on weekends. It was even hard for me to make phone calls with the time difference, and I didn't speak German. We made plans to leave at the end of the school year, but during that year we did a great deal of traveling in Europe until finally Wade said he was not visiting one more castle.

As previously stated, I did receive a copy of my first published book in the fall of 1985. It was a most exciting event. I had dreams of grandeur. Wade and I had a great time dreaming about how my writing career would change our lives. We decided that if a book provided even a modest income and I could write enough books, then I could retire from teaching and stay home and write. So, I started researching for a second book. The first one was titled *Teaching the Fun of Physics*. The second would be about chemistry. During some of the many bus tours that we took through Europe during that year, I scribbled out ideas for experiments on writing pads.

We returned to our farm in Marlin in the summer of 1986. After getting settled, I put together a prospectus for the chemistry book and sent it off to Prentice-Hall. Was I surprised to receive such a negative response. Mary Kennan, the editor of my first book, had left the company and the new editor saw no value in my work. My thoughts were that the first book had been a fluke, my writing career was over, and that I'd use the chemistry material in my classroom, but my fairy godmother soon reappeared and provided me the opportunity to write again. I received a form letter from Mary, announcing that she was now at Dodd Mead Publishing and asking if I had any book ideas. I sent her the chemistry material and soon received a

contract. The format of the book was changed some from the one at Prentice-Hall, but it was basically the same style—mine.

My writing career just might happen after all. But it certainly was not going to be financed by the royalty payments from the first book. It took almost seven years for that book to get out of the red. No matter. I was teaching and writing the chemistry book in my spare time. The book was near the stage of being printed when I received the letter telling me that Dodd Mead was in Chapter 11! This on-and-off writing career didn't seem like much fun anymore, but Mary came through again and managed to get another publisher to pick up the chemistry book. Little did I know that this publisher didn't have a children's section and that it was all an experiment. But it was an experiment that was most successful for me as well as the publishing house. My new editor, David Sobel, worked at John Wiley and Sons in New York. The chemistry book, *Chemistry for Every Kid,* that had been given such a bad review by Prentice-Hall was published by Wiley in 1989 and to date has sold more than two hundred thousand copies. Not bad. It certainly let me know that a bad review on a manuscript doesn't mean the work is bad. I have shared this with many new authors.

During the first six months on the market, *Chemistry for Every Kid* sold enough to pay off the advance and the artist's fees with a little extra for me. The book was in the black. The first book was still in the red. Just for fun, I took a picture of me in front of an old rundown farmhouse that was used to store hay. I sent this picture to David with a note thanking him for the royalty check and that with it we were now able to purchase a "fixer-upper" house. David never responded. In fact, during the time I worked with David I sent him lots of goofy pictures and notes, and he never responded. But I later discovered he shared the fun with others.

Even before the sales report on the chemistry book came in, David offered me a contract for a second book. This one would be about biology. He later told me that after the report there had been a staff meeting and the thought was that just maybe the VanCleave books would be very successful. I was invited to come to New York and meet with some of the Wiley staff. Even though I had been to Europe, that was all very protected travel. I was always with a government group. I was a bit apprehensive about the trip and had to confess to David that it terrified me just to think about being in New York. He had to promise to meet me at the airport and that I would not be unescorted at any time during my stay. David met me at the airport in a car. I never gave it much thought. Texans travel everywhere in cars, so why would I think that David had gone to a great deal of trouble to escort me in a car? Discovering this made the trip and David even more special.

My first trip to New York was fun and magical. Some of the fun was the response of the publicist. She was concerned about what I was going to wear on a scheduled television interview. She had every right to be. After all, David had been sharing my fun pictures and notes, and I had sent another about preparing for the New York trip. Our kitchen was being remodeled and while the window was torn out, Wade took a picture of me sitting in the opening with a cup of coffee in my hand. I was wearing a long housecoat and big fluffy house shoes. The note

By the Arctic Ocean, along the beach of Barrow, Alaska, 1998.

accompanying the picture indicated that I was wondering which pair of overalls I should wear to New York, the one with or without lace.

A special friend and clothes designer, Sue Dunham, had insisted that I have a Texas look for the New York trip. She created the most fantastic skirt and coat made of denim. Wade said I looked liked a buffalo hunter in it, but what does he know about fashion? I wore this costume along with fashion boots (I didn't have cowboy boots) to the first meeting. I felt very confident that I looked great, but the publicist immediately asked if she could see the clothes I had brought for the television interview. I guess she felt she still had time to take me shopping. She was happy that I had a black dress with pearls. I wore this bland outfit, but it wasn't the real me. I'd have been more comfortable in my buffalo hunting gear. I've since adopted a style created by Sue Dunham—denim vests with large pockets and science designs. Some of the vests depict a topic from one of my books, such as *Oceans for Every Kid.*

Sue and I along with another friend, Sella Cathey, took a trip to Hawaii. There we visited a Wyland art gallery. Sue studied the art and designed a new vest for me. It is blue with a painted scene of breaching whales. The fun part is that she lost her pattern and made the vest to fit her. Well, Sue is at least five inches taller than me, so my fingers only reached the top of the pockets on the vest. She made an adjustment, but the pockets were still too low. I did not let her change this. I use the vest to demonstrate inertia: if I am

quick enough, I can get my hands in the pockets before the vest moves. Wearing this vest is like wearing a piece of art. I've been stopped on the street by admirers. I wish I had had that vest during my New York trip.

The trip to New York resulted in contracts for four books. The plan was to add to the "Science for Every Kid" series, and we did. The books continued to be successful, and I no longer had to pay for the art. This was helpful, but not enough for me to give up my day job—teaching. Before I finished the contracts, I was invited back to New York to discuss a new series. Soon after this David left the company. It was a sad day for me, but his assistant, Kate Bradford, and I had worked on several books together. David left me in great hands. Kate has been absolutely wonderful.

Later, Wiley offered a multibook contract for ten books, which I accepted. This contract did not specify a book to be written, so Kate and I had lots of freedom. We talked about science topics, and she checked the market to determine how well the book might be accepted. Sometimes ideas came from others in the publishing house. One of the vice presidents asked if I could write a geography book. That was a laughable request for me because I am part of the group that the news media describes as the ignorant Americans who have no clue where geographical locations are. I'd be hard pressed to put a puzzle of the United States together. But, I rarely turn down a challenge and accepted this one. It was a shock to me to discover that geography is much more than map skills. It is basically the location of different science events. What a fun time I had writing that book, and did I ever learn a lot. In fact, the best part of writing is that I learn so much with every book that I write.

There were other multibook contracts offered by Wiley, and I've accepted them all. To date, I have forty-five Wiley books in print and several in various stages of production. Sales hit a remarkable two million in the year 2000. Some of the books have been translated into a total of fourteen foreign languages. I am still having fun writing and still have books to write on the current Wiley contract.

Most of the information in the earlier books came from years of research while teaching as well as any current publications on the topics. In the past few years I've included travel in my research, and one of the most exotic places that I've visited was the geographical South Pole. I actually stood at the South Pole, and there is an actual metal pole stuck in the ice to mark the spot. I walked around the pole, crossing every longitude line. So, I can officially say that I have walked around the earth. I traveled with Randy Landsberg, the education coordinator from CARA (Center for Astrophysical Research in Antarctica) at the University of Chicago. Educators were invited to be part of the adventure while it was happening by keeping up with the project via an active Web site. I sent information about the experiments that we performed via e-mail from different locations during our journey, including the South Pole, which has science facilities as well as living accommodations for about 195 people.

The South Pole trip was sponsored by the National Science Foundation with the objective to encourage student interest in science and Antarctica, one of the last frontiers on Earth. The research done in Antarctica is the foundation for my book *203 Icy, Freezing, Frosty, Cool and Wild Experiments.* It was an awesome experience, and the journals of my travels are still online. A link to this information can be found on my Web site: http://Janice-VanCleave.com.

Having gone to one end of the earth, I had a burning desire to go to the opposite end, but to date I have only made it as far as Barrow, Alaska. It was here that I touched the Arctic Ocean and researched the Arctic tundra. Traveling to and from Barrow was as exciting as being there. I was accompanied by Laura Roberts, an elementary teacher from Louisville, Kentucky, and an associate who field tests many of my books. Laura and I traveled in the direction of Barrow by cruising the Alaska coast. Each port provided exciting opportunities for adventure, including helicopter rides to ice fields for dog sled rides, researching the tops of glaciers, as well as studying the movement of whales. On returning from Barrow we stopped off at Denali National Park and studied many animals in the wild, including moose, eagles, and grizzly bear.

Other travels include various trips to the Hawaiian Islands, but traveling hasn't been the only exciting adventure. In April of 2000, I flew with students from different Texas colleges in NASA's KC-135 plane, which is often called the vomit comet. This plane is used to train astronauts to perform at zero gravity. The effect of zero gravity is achieved by a parabolic flight path, which is an arched path. During the twenty-five seconds it takes the plane to make one parabola, those in the plane experience 0 g to 2 g (twice Earth's gravity). Twenty-five seconds seems a short time, but it can be a very long time if you have twisting camera cords around your neck. Note that I said twisting cords, because when the motion of the plane achieved an effect of zero gravity, the plane dropped down and anything not secured to the craft remained afloat. I was holding to straps on the floor, so I went down with the plane, but the cameras hanging by cords around my neck stayed in midair. I must have tapped the floating cameras because they started rotating and thus twisting the cords. We had been instructed to try to keep our heads still and eyes focused on one spot the first couple of parabolas to

Meeting Dr. William Phillips, 1997 Nobel Prize winner in Physics, at a Baylor University program in 2000.

help with the nausea problem created by the change of forces on the body. But when one is being strangled, nausea is not a top priority. The flight crew saved me from being strangled but couldn't help my nausea. I vomited during twenty-six of the thirty-two parabolas, but I did not let that stop me from experimenting. I dropped stuff with one hand and held the barf bag over my mouth with the other. Even though I spent the flight personally researching the negative effects that a decrease or an increase of gravity has on the human body, it was an awesome experience, and I'd do it again.

My travels also include presenting programs at schools for kids and/or teachers as well as at conventions. I greatly enjoy working with kids and presenting teacher workshops. Conventions allow me to meet so many different librarians, teachers, and people in different professions. As one of the authors invited to the Texas Book Festival in 1998, I was invited to join the other authors at the Texas governor's mansion for breakfast. Laura Bush was the director of the festival, and she and her husband, Governor George W. Bush, were hosting the breakfast. It was a very elegant affair, and I had the pleasure not only to meet Governor Bush but to actually have a conversation with him about education in Texas. Little did I know that in only two short years he would become the president of the United States. At the same breakfast, I also briefly met former president George Bush, Sr. In November of 2000, I was the speaker at a Texas teacher's conference where George Bush, Sr., made a cameo appearance. I managed to meet him again and gave him an autographed copy of one of my books. Meeting a president once is rare, but twice is phenomenal.

Add to this the great honor of meeting two Nobel Prize winners. I met Dr. Leon Max Lederman, American physicist and co-winner of the 1988 Nobel Prize in physics, at a teacher conference where he and I presented programs. Dr. Lederman was the keynote speaker, and I was amazed at how fun and easy his explanations were. A picture of the two of us was sent to Dr. Lederman, and his response was that his grandchildren would be so excited that he had met a famous author. How gracious. I was the one who was in the presence of a celebrity.

Dr. William D. Phillips, American physicist and co-winner of the 1997 Nobel Prize in physics, presented a program at Baylor University, which I attended. Afterwards I asked if he would pose for a picture and commented that I was collecting pictures with Nobel Prize winners and this was my second picture. I told him the first was with Leon Lederman. "Oh! Leon," he said and went on to tell a story of the Judds, the singing stars, and how Naomi Judd had written "Big Bang Boogie" just for Leon.

I squeeze time into my traveling schedule to write more fun science books for kids. My office is now a building a few yards from my home, but that is not to say that the two are not often overflowing with some new idea that I am working on. My husband is in and out of my office during the day, but I spend most of each day by myself. Our home is in a rural area. While we are on a main highway, there are no close houses, only fields of land. I have acres of land and three ponds and my neighbors' land that have provided research materials including a neighbor's buffalo. I must admit that I had not properly researched the behavior of the buffalo before setting up my typewriter inside the fence. Thankfully the animal was only curious about my presence and not violent as I later discovered that they could be. I'll certainly do more research before I get up close and personal while studying another animal.

As to entertainment, I prefer to stay home when I am not professionally traveling. In the spring my fields are covered with wildflowers. A fun pastime this last spring was riding in a trailer pulled by the tractor driven by my husband. Now it wasn't the bumpy trailer ride that I found fun, but at the end of the ride we collected and ate the blackberries that grow wild in our pastureland. This trip was made each evening near dusk for a week or so. Once I had my fill of berries, I would sit on the trailer and watch the water in the pond change colors as the sun set. I greatly enjoyed this experience, but reflecting on it as I write this autobiography is even more enjoyable. Writing is a wonderful experience, and I think everyone should experience its pleasures, even if there is no plan for publication. In fact, I encourage you to write your autobiography and update it periodically. It gives you the opportunity to reflect on the past and to consider the factors that went into your becoming the person you are.

Writings

Teaching the Fun of Physics: 101 Activities to Make Science Education Easy and Enjoyable, Prentice-Hall, 1985.
Janice VanCleave's Guide of the Best Science Fair Projects, Wiley, 1997.
Janice VanCleave's Reproducible Science Experiment Sourcebook, Wiley, 1997.
Janice VanCleave's Science around the Year, Wiley, 2000.
Janice VanCleave's Guide to More of the Best Science Fair Projects, Wiley, 2000.
Janice VanCleave's Teaching the Fun of Science, Wiley, 2001.

"JANICE VanCLEAVE'S SCIENCE FOR EVERY KID" SERIES, AGES 8-12

Astronomy, Wiley, 1989.
Chemistry, Wiley, 1989.
Biology, Wiley, 1990.
Earth Science, Wiley, 1991.
Math, Wiley, 1991.
Physics, Wiley, 1991.
Geography, Wiley, 1993.
Microscopes, Wiley, 1993.
Dinosaurs, Wiley, 1994.
Geometry, Wiley, 1994.

The Human Body, Wiley, 1995.
Ecology, Wiley, 1996.
Oceans, Wiley, 1996.
Constellations, Wiley, 1997.
Food and Nutrition, Wiley, 1999.

"JANICE VanCLEAVE'S SPECTACULAR SCIENCE FAIR PROJECTS" SERIES, AGES 8-12

Animals, Wiley, 1992.
Gravity, Wiley, 1992.
Molecules, Wiley, 1992.
Magnets, Wiley, 1993.
Earthquakes, Wiley, 1993.
Machines, Wiley, 1993.
Microscopes and Magnifying Lenses, Wiley, 1993.
Volcanoes, Wiley, 1994.
Electricity, Wiley, 1995.
Weather, Wiley, 1995.
Rocks and Minerals, Wiley, 1996.
Plants, Wiley, 1997.
Insects and Spiders, Wiley, 1998.
Solar System, Wiley, 2000.

"THE BEST OF JANICE VanCLEAVE" SERIES, AGES 8-12

200 Gooey, Slippery, Slimy, Weird and Fun Experiments, Wiley, 1993.
201 Awesome, Magical, Bizarre and Incredible Experiments, Wiley, 1994.
202 Oozing, Bubbling, Dripping and Bouncing Experiments, Wiley, 1996.
203 Icy, Freezing, Frosty, Cool and Wild Experiments, Wiley, 1999.

"JANICE VanCLEAVE'S A+ PROJECT" SERIES, AGES 13 AND UP

A+ Biology, Wiley, 1993.
A+ Chemistry, Wiley, 1993.
A+ Earth Science, Wiley, 1999.

"JANICE VanCLEAVE'S PLAY AND FIND OUT: EASY EXPERIMENTS FOR YOUNG CHILDREN" SERIES, AGES 4-7

Science, Wiley, 1996.
Nature, Wiley, 1997.
Math, Wiley, 1997.
Human Body, Wiley, 1998.
Bugs, Wiley, 1999.

Work in Progress

Habitats for the "Science for Every Kid" series; *A+ Physics* for the "A+" series; *Energy* for the "Spectacular Science Project" series; *Science Through the Ages* and *Help! My Science Project Is Due Tomorrow* for ages 8-12; *Guide to the Best A+ Science Projects for Kids 13+.*

VESEY, Mark (David) 1958-

Personal

Surname is pronounced *vee*-zee; born February 26, 1958, in New Zealand; son of George Patrick and Joyce (Wollstoncoft) Vesey; married Marise Thorby; children: Spencer Thorby. *Education:* Attended Auckland Technical Institute. *Religion:* Presbyterian.

Addresses

Home—25 Devonshire St., Crowsnest, Sydney, New South Wales 2065, Australia. *Office*—Images Everything, 77 Berry St., Suite 403, North Sydney, New South Wales 2060, Australia. *Agent*—Drawing Book Studio, 283 Alfred St., North Sydney, New South Wales 1060, Australia.

Career

Commercial illustrator and artist, with paintings exhibited in New Zealand and Japan.

Illustrator

(With Spike Wademan and David Carroll) Judith Simpson, *Racing Cars,* Random House (Milsons Point, Australia), 1999.

Felicia James, *The Adventures of Sorry Teddy,* Elephant Publishing (Terrigal, Australia), 2000.

Contributor to periodicals.

Work in Progress

Illustrations for *Anatomica.*

Sidelights

Mark Vesey told *SATA:* "I have been a commercial illustrator in the advertising industry for nearly twenty years. I originally worked in advertising in New Zealand, and exhibited paintings there and in Japan before moving to Sydney in 1986. Since then I have produced thousands of illustrations and have seen my work reproduced in everything from magazines to billboards.

"I have always had an interest in children's book illustration, and since the birth of my son I have been exposed to many different books and styles. My first foray into children's book illustration was the book on racing cars. I have always had a keen interest in cars and found it challenging to produce illustrations for a whole book. It proved to be a rewarding experience, and it was good to gain some recognition in a new area.

"I have since gone on to illustrate a second book aimed at younger children. *The Adventures of Sorry Teddy* is designed to show children how to say 'sorry.' I was allowed a lot of input and creative freedom and enjoyed the process very much. I have also completed a first-aid section for an illustrated *Anatomica,* which has not yet been published.

"I am currently working on illustrations for a book that I have written myself, and this is going well. I hope this will be successful, as I would like to remain working in this area. At present I also continue to paint large canvases. This creates a good balance between commercial demands and creative freedom. It has always been my first love and wellspring for new ideas and inspiration."

*   *   *

VIORST, Judith 1931-

Personal

Surname pronounced "*vee*-orst"; born February 2, 1931, in Newark, NJ; daughter of Martin Leonard (an accountant) and Ruth June (Ehrenkranz) Stahl; married Milton Viorst (a writer), January 30, 1960; children: Anthony Jacob, Nicholas Nathan, Alexander Noah. *Education:* Rutgers University, B.A. (with honors), 1952; Washington Psychoanalytic Institute, graduate, 1981. *Religion:* Jewish.

Addresses

Home—3432 Ashley Terrace N.W., Washington, DC 20008. *Agent*—Robert Lescher, Lescher & Lescher, 47 East 19th St., New York, NY 10003.

Career

Poet, journalist, and writer of books for adults and children. *True Confessions,* New York, NY, secretary, 1953-55; *Women's Wear Daily,* New York, NY, secretary, 1955-57; William Morrow (publisher), New York, NY, children's book editor, 1957-60; Science Service, Washington, DC, science book editor and writer, 1960-63. *Member:* Phi Beta Kappa, American Psychological Association.

Awards, Honors

New Jersey Institute of Technology awards, 1969, for *Sunday Morning,* and 1970, for *I'll Fix Anthony;* Emmy Award (with others) for writing for a comedy, variety, or music program, 1970, for *Annie: The Women in the Life of a Man;* Best Books of the Year citation, *School Library Journal,* 1972, and Georgia Picture Book Award, 1977, both for *Alexander and the Terrible, Horrible, No Good, Very Bad Day;* Silver Pencil Award, 1973, for *The Tenth Good Thing about Barney;* Penney-Missouri Award, 1974, for article in *Redbook;* Albert Einstein College of Medicine Award, 1975; American Academy of Pediatrics Award, 1977, for article in *Redbook;* American Association of University Women Award, 1980, for article in *Redbook;* Christopher Award, 1988, for *The Good-bye Book.*

Writings

FICTION; FOR CHILDREN

Sunday Morning, illustrated by Hilary Knight, Harper, 1968.

I'll Fix Anthony, illustrated by Arnold Lobel, Harper, 1969.

Try It Again, Sam: Safety When You Walk, illustrated by Paul Galdone, Lothrop, 1970.

The Tenth Good Thing about Barney (Junior Literary Guild selection), illustrated by Erik Blegvad, Atheneum, 1971.

Alexander and the Terrible, Horrible, No Good, Very Bad Day (Junior Literary Guild selection; also see below), illustrated by Ray Cruz, Atheneum, 1972.

My Mama Says There Aren't Any Zombies, Ghosts, Vampires, Creatures, Demons, Monsters, Fiends, Goblins, or Things, illustrated by Kay Chorao, Atheneum, 1973.

Rosie and Michael, illustrated by Lorna Tomei, Atheneum, 1974.

Alexander, Who Used to Be Rich Last Sunday (also see below), illustrated by Ray Cruz, Atheneum, 1978.

If I Were in Charge of the World and Other Worries: Poems for Children and Their Parents, illustrated by Lynne Cherry, Atheneum, 1981.

The Good-bye Book, illustrated by Kay Chorao, Atheneum, 1988.

Earrings!, illustrated by Nola Langner Malone, Atheneum, 1990.

The Alphabet from Z to A: With Much Confusion on the Way, illustrated by Richard Hull, Macmillan, 1994.

Alexander, Who's Not (Do You Hear Me? I Mean It!) Going to Move (also see below), illustrated by Robin Preiss-Glasser, Simon & Schuster, 1995.

Sad Underwear and Other Complications: More Poems for Children and Their Parents, illustrated by Richard Hull, Macmillan, 1995.

Absolutely Positively Alexander: The Complete Stories (includes *Alexander and the Terrible, Horrible, No Good, Very Bad Day, Alexander, Who Used to Be Rich Last Sunday,* and *Alexander, Who's Not (Do You Hear Me? I Mean It!) Going to Move*), illustrated by Ray Cruz and Robin Preiss-Glasser, Simon & Schuster, 1997.

Super-Completely and Totally the Messiest, illustrated by Robin Preiss-Glasser, Atheneum, 2000.

Some of Viorst's stories for children have been translated into Dutch, French, German, Japanese, and Spanish. *Alexander and the Terrible, No Good, Very Bad Day, and Other Stories* has been recorded on audiocassette by Blythe Danner for Harper Audio, 1996, and has been made into a musical (lyrics by Viorst and music by Shelly Markham) originally commissioned by the Kennedy Center.

NONFICTION; FOR CHILDREN

(Editor, with Shirley Moore) *Wonderful World of Science,* illustrated by Don Trawin, Bantam, 1961.

Projects: Space, Washington Square Press, 1962.

One Hundred and Fifty Science Experiments, Step-by-Step, illustrated by Dennis Telesford, Bantam, 1963.

Judith Viorst

The Natural World: A Guide to North American Wildlife, Bantam, 1965.

The Changing Earth, illustrated by Feodor Rimsky, Bantam, 1967.

OTHER

The Village Square (poems), illustrated by Tom Ballenger, Coward, 1965.

It's Hard to Be Hip over Thirty and Other Tragedies of Married Life (poems), illustrated by John Alcorn, World, 1968.

(With husband, Milton Viorst) *The Washington, D.C., Underground Gourmet,* Simon & Schuster, 1970.

(With Gary Belkin, Peter Bellwood, Herb Sargent, and Thomas Meehan) *Annie: The Women in the Life of a Man* (television special), Columbia Broadcasting System, 1970.

People and Other Aggravations (poems), illustrated by John Alcorn, World, 1971.

Yes, Married: A Saga of Love and Complaint (collected prose pieces), Saturday Review Press, 1972.

How Did I Get to Be Forty ... and Other Atrocities (poems), illustrated by John Alcorn, Simon & Schuster, 1976.

A Visit from St. Nicholas (to a Liberated Household): From the Original Written in 1823 by Clement Clarke Moore, Simon & Schuster, 1976.

Love and Guilt and the Meaning of Life, Etc., illustrated by John Alcorn, Simon & Schuster, 1979.

Necessary Losses, Simon & Schuster, 1986.

When Did I Stop Being Twenty and Other Injustices: Selected Poems from Single to Mid-Life, illustrated by John Alcorn, Simon & Schuster, 1987.

Love and Guilt and the Meaning of Life (musical play; also produced as *Love and Shrimp*), music by Shelly Markham, produced at Pasadena Playhouse, 1989.

Forever Fifty and Other Negotiations (poems), illustrated by John Alcorn, Simon & Schuster, 1989.

Murdering Mr. Monti: A Merry Little Tale of Sex and Violence (novel), Simon & Schuster, 1994.

Imperfect Control: Our Lifelong Struggle with Power and Surrender, Simon and Schuster, 1998.

You're Officially a Grown-Up; The Graduate's Guide to Freedom, Responsibility, Happiness, Personal Hygiene, and the Conquest of Fear, illustrated by Robin Preiss-Glasser, Simon & Schuster, 1999.

Suddenly Sixty and Other Shocks of Later Life (poems), illustrated by Laurie Rosenwald, Simon & Schuster, 2000.

Author of regular column for *Redbook,* 1968-96, and of syndicated column for *Washington Star Syndicate,* 1970-72. Author of poetic monologues for television. Work represented in anthologies *Don't Bet on the Prince: Contemporary Feminist Fairy Tales in North America and England,* edited by Jack Zipes, Methuen, 1986, and *Turning Points: When Everything Changes,* Troll, 1996. Contributor of poems and articles to periodicals, including *Holiday, New York, New York Times, Venture, Washingtonian,* and *Writer. How Did I Get to Be Forty ... and Other Atrocities* was recorded on audiocassette by Caedmon, 1978.

Everything goes wrong for Alexander in Viorst's classic picture book **Alexander and the Terrible, Horrible, No Good, Very Bad Day.** *(Illustrated by Ray Cruz.)*

No I won't have fun with the baby-sitter.
I hate baby-sitters. They could make you
eat vegetables.

A little boy begs and bargains with his parents not to leave him with a baby-sitter. (Illustration from The Good-bye Book, *written by Viorst and illustrated by Kay Chorao.*)

Sidelights

Poet and fiction author Judith Viorst has blended wry humor and deft self analysis to create a score of entertaining and revealing books for both children and adults. Widely known for her humorous books based on her own family life, Viorst "has shown herself to be a writer of talent and insight who has successfully combined entertainment and enrichment in her creations for the child audience," asserted Douglas Street in the *Dictionary of Literary Biography*. She frankly addresses both children's naughtiness and their serious concerns, writing about such everyday subjects as sibling rivalry, the death of a pet, and a messy little sister with both witty verve and compelling insight. "In her children's books," wrote *Publishers Weekly* contributor Tracy Cochran, "Viorst demonstrates her sensitivity to the sometimes hard truths of childhood." Sometimes her inspiration comes directly from her own sons. She once commented in *Writer* magazine: "Four of the books that I've written for children I consciously sat down and wrote because one child or another of mine had a problem.... And while I was surely not foolish enough to expect that any book I wrote would solve these problems, I hoped it might help my boys to laugh at their problems, or look at them in less troubled, less hopeless ways."

Born in Newark, New Jersey, in 1931, Viorst knew from the second grade that she wanted to be a writer. "I like to take all my feelings and thoughts and put them down in different ways on paper," she commented in an online interview with *Bookreporter.* "I liked having other people read them, too. So I wrote them down, and I sent them out, hoping to have them published." However, it would be many years before her first writing attempts were finally published. Her first real break came when she was working in Washington, D.C., for Science Service and was offered the job to write a science book on NASA's space program when another writer backed out of the project. This led to her first published book, *Projects: Space.* A few science books later, Viorst, who

is married to another writer, Milton Viorst, began submitting poems to magazines and getting them published. Then came her first collection of poems, *The Village Square,* which led to a promotional appearance on a television show seen, in turn, by legendary children's book editor, Charlotte Zolotow, who thought Viorst would be a natural as a children's author. In 1968, Viorst inaugurated this part of her career, but has also continued her writings for adults, especially in her now near-famous, tongue-in-cheek poetry collections that deal with the vicissitudes of getting older: *It's Hard to Be Hip over Thirty and Other Tragedies from Married Life, How Did I Get to Be Forty ... and Other Atrocities, When Did I Stop Being Twenty and Other Injustices, Forever Fifty and Other Negotiations,* and *Suddenly Sixty and Other Shocks of Later Life.* "These iconoclastic works demonstrate the author's refusal to be depressed by, and her ability to work around, the domestic responsibilities that have done in many women hankering after their own careers," wrote Gay Sibley in a critical appraisal of Viorst in *Encyclopedia of American Literature.* Until 1996, Viorst also wrote a regular column for *Redbook* that earned awards and a loyal readership. Her nonfiction books for adults such as *Necessary Losses* and *Imperfect Control* have also been widely praised.

Viorst's work for children combines all the best of the skills she employs in her adult work. From the beginning Viorst presented her young characters realistically, with all their faults, instead of as the paragons of virtue that appear in some children's stories. Her first picture book, *Sunday Morning,* describes the predawn mischief of a pair of young brothers, Anthony and Nick (named after Viorst's older sons), whose parents are trying to sleep in after a late night out. Reviewing this debut title in *School Library Journal,* Elinor S. Cullen thought "[m]ost parents will find the book very funny indeed, and sophisticated children may enjoy seeing themselves as others hear them." In Viorst's next book, *I'll Fix Anthony,* young Nick promises to get revenge, when he's a little older, for all the mean things his older brother has done to him. To some adults, Viorst's unruly characters seemed unsuitable role models for children. Viorst, however, argued in *Writer* that "kids need to encounter kids like themselves—kids who can sometimes be crabby and fresh and rebellious, kids who talk back and disobey, tell fibs and get into trouble, and are nonetheless still likable and redeemable." Her third children's book, *Try It Again, Sam: Safety When You Walk,* is a "cautionary tale," according to a contributor for *Kirkus Reviews,* but an "uncommonly unstuffy" one. In this book young Sam is given the opportunity to go to his friend's house alone, but returns each time he begins to lose his way.

After her first few lighthearted books, Viorst turned to a more subdued topic in *The Tenth Good Thing about Barney.* A young narrator opens the story by stating that his cat, Barney, died recently. The boy's mother asks him to think of ten good things he can say about Barney for the funeral, but he can only come up with nine at

Viorst's witty poetry examines the trials of childhood.
(Cover illustration by Richard Hull.)

Sophie says I should tell you that she didn't MEAN to drown the kitchen in water, even though she left the faucets running.

Neatnik Olivia is sure her sloppy sister Sophie will never be perfect like herself. *(Illustration from* Super-Completely and Totally the Messiest, *written by Viorst and illustrated by Robin Preiss-Glasser.)*

first. Later, after the family has buried Barney and the boy helps his father begin planting a garden, father and son talk about a tenth good thing: that Barney's death and burial will give new life to the grass and flowers. By the end of the book, the boy has adopted his father's view that helping the flowers grow is "a pretty nice job for a cat." Written to help Viorst's sons deal with death, *The Tenth Good Thing about Barney* was "widely praised," according to Street. Writing in the *New York Times Book Review,* Sheila R. Cole noted that Viorst "diffuses the strong emotions surrounding death with a gentle, bittersweet humor." Cole further commented that the book was "charming and sympathetic" though perhaps best suited for a child "for whom death's sorrow is quite distant." *Horn Book*'s Sheryl B. Andrews felt that Viorst "succinctly and honestly handles both the emotions stemming from the loss of a beloved pet and the questions about the finality of death."

Viorst followed *Barney* with the lighter, more humorous *Alexander and the Terrible, Horrible, No Good, Very Bad Day,* which Street proclaimed "without a doubt Viorst's most successful book." From the moment he wakes up with chewing gum in his hair, Alexander— younger brother to Nick and Anthony from *Sunday Morning*—has a day filled with misfortune. By bedtime so much has gone wrong that he wants to move to Australia, but as his mother sympathetically yet astutely notes, "Some days are like that. Even in Australia." Viorst won lasting popularity both in the United States and in England for the book, which a *Times Literary Supplement* writer found "funny but not heartless." The same reviewer observed that Viorst is an author "who can enter imaginatively into a child's difficulties without being either tactless or disablingly sympathetic." Wondering if the "ubiquitous Judith Viorst" would ever run out of "zany anecdotes" from her all-male household, Michael J. Bandler of the *Washington Post Book World* emphatically answered his own question: "We hope not!" Bandler went on to call *Alexander* a "thrilling installment" in tales from the Viorst household. "Small listeners can enjoy the litany of disaster," wrote Zena Sutherland in *Bulletin of the Center for Children's Books.*

Viorst has reprised Alexander for two further tales, *Alexander, Who Used to Be Rich Last Sunday,* and *Alexander Who's Not (Do You Hear Me? I Mean It!) Going to Move.* In the latter volume, Alexander refuses to budge when his father announces the family is moving to a new job 1,000 miles away. He refuses to pack or lift a finger to help out. His brothers give him a hard time, but he refuses to join in the moving frenzy— until his father bribes him with a new dog. "Kids will laugh at the wild exaggeration even as they recognize [Alexander's] heartfelt grief," wrote Hazel Rochman in a *Booklist* review. A writer for *Publishers Weekly* called the same book a "gratifying return" for Alexander and could only hope after all was said and done that "Alexander finds a new complaint." Reviewing the omnibus Alexander volume, *Absolutely Positively Alexander: The Complete Stories,* a contributor for *Publish-*

ers Weekly commented that Viorst "captures the vocal cadences and stubborn, sometimes cranky viewpoint of a young boy."

Other early popular picture books from Viorst include *My Mama Says There Aren't Any Zombies, Ghosts, Vampires, Creatures, Demons, Monsters, Fiends, Goblins, or Things* and the more economically titled *Rosie and Michael.* The former title deals with the sometimes unreliable statements of mothers, and the latter title tells of an undying friendship and especially when a good friend comes in handiest. Reviewing *My Mama Says* in *School Library Journal,* Alice H. Yucht reported that "Viorst presents a marvelous catalogue of monsters that could terrorize an imaginative child as well as a compendium of all the mistakes that mamas make." In a *Publishers Weekly* review of *Rosie and Michael,* a critic claimed that author Viorst and illustrator Lorna Tomei "could make Genghis Khan and Attila the Hun recognize the value of friendship" with their "droll, pointed book."

Having written several verse volumes for adults, Viorst also produced one aimed mostly at children. Published in 1981, *If I Were in Charge of the World and Other Worries* touches on the difficulties of having a girlfriend who is much taller than oneself, the need for "healthier hamsters" and lower basketball hoops, and a mother's decision not to let her son have a dog: "She's making a mistake / because more than a dog, I think / she will not want this snake." In the same volume Viorst also revised a few traditional fairy tales; in her version of "Cinderella," the prince seems less appealing after the glamorous evening has passed, so Cinderella pretends the glass slipper he brings does not fit her after all. Reviewers found the collection amusing and perceptive. Observed Street, "The overall effect achieved is more than satisfying." Another book of poetry geared for both parents and kids is the silly *Sad Underwear and Other Complications.* Reviewing that collection, *Horn Book*'s Nancy Vasilakis noted that the poems "take the same pleasure in the ridiculous that makes the children's poetry of Shel Silverstein and Jack Prelutsky so popular." Vasilakis concluded that the collection "is clearly meant to be chuckled over." *Booklist*'s Mary Harris Veeder declared that "children will ... like the snap and clarity of the poems and have fun with the language."

In 1988 Viorst returned to the picture-book format with *The Good-bye Book,* which describes a little boy's various attempts to prevent his parents from going out for the evening and leaving him home with a babysitter. Persuasion, guilt, pretended illness, and even anger have little effect. Finally left alone with the baby-sitter, who proves much more appealing than he had imagined, the little boy finds his evening surprisingly enjoyable. When she first conceived the story, Viorst was amazed that such a book had not yet been written. As she explained in a *Publishers Weekly* article, "It's probably one of the most common experiences that occurs between a child and his parents ... that tussle when you're going out and your child doesn't want you to leave." Her honest and humorous treatment "will help children and parents alike trying to work through the complex issue of separation," asserted Frances Wells Burck in the *New York Times Book Review*.

With *Earrings!*, "Viorst proves once and for all that she understands little girls as thoroughly as she fathoms the Anthonys and Alexanders of [the] world," observed Vasilakis in a *Horn Book* review. In this story a young girl uses various arguments to convince her parents to let her have her ears pierced. Jane Saliers, writing in *School Library Journal*, felt that while *Earrings!* was "not Viorst at her best," still "she does capture the immediacy of young demands." Vasilakis, however, thought that "Viorst homes in on minor childhood crises with the perfect blend of humor and insight." Another female protagonist is presented in *Super-Completely and Totally the Messiest*, in which Olivia, who is a neatnik and perfectionist, despairs at her sister Sophia who is a complete mess-maker in whatever she does. Sophie, it soon becomes apparent is, in addition to being messy, also very creative, smart, and funny. "It's all pure fun," wrote Susan Hepler in a *School Library Journal* review, "with an undertone of acceptance that's positively reassuring." *Booklist* GraceAnne DiCandido characterized the book as a "comical, if oddly distant, character portrait," while a reviewer for *Publishers Weekly* concluded that Sophie's "antics will surely elicit grins—and perhaps even giggles—from young readers."

Identifying herself as a lover of children's books, Viorst believes that "at their best their language, their art, their seriousness of intent measure up to any standards of excellence," she wrote in *Writer*. "And the beauties and truths and delights that they can offer to our children can meet the deepest needs of the heart and the mind." In seeking to meet the specific needs of her own children Viorst has created a body of work that pleases many and has won a number of awards. She has earned praise for tackling difficult subjects, challenging sexist stereotypes, and honestly presenting both children and their parents in all their flawed humanity. Concluded Street in his *Dictionary of Literary Biography* assessment, "Her place in the annals of postwar American children's fiction is justifiably assured." "To read Judith Viorst is to know her," observed a contributor to *Contemporary Popular Writers*, "and to know her is good fun because she writes about the things that touch us where we live, both figuratively and literally.... Viorst allows us to laugh at ourselves."

Biographical and Critical Sources

BOOKS

Children's Literature Review, Volume 3, Gale (Detroit, MI), 1978.

Contemporary Popular Writers, St. James Press, 1997.

Dictionary of Literary Biography, Volume 52: *American Writers for Children since 1960: Fiction,* Gale (Detroit, MI), 1986.

Encyclopedia of American Literature, edited by Steven R. Serafin, Continuum, 1999.

Viorst, Judith, *The Tenth Good Thing about Barney,* Atheneum, 1971.

Viorst, Judith, *Alexander and the Terrible, Horrible, No Good, Very Bad Day,* Atheneum, 1972.

Viorst, Judith, *If I Were in Charge of the World and Other Worries: Poems for Children and Their Parents,* Atheneum, 1981.

Wheeler, Jill C., *Judith Viorst,* ABDO & Daughters, 1997.

PERIODICALS

Booklist, September 1, 1989, p. 6; December 15, 1993, p. 739; March 1, 1994, p. 1266; April 1, 1995, Mary Harris Veeder, review of *Sad Underwear and Other Complications,* p. 1391; August, 1995, Hazel Rochman, review of *Alexander, Who's Not (Do You Hear Me? I Meant It!) Going to Move,* p. 1949; December 15, 1997, p. 668; February 1, 2001, GraceAnne DiCandido, review of *Super-Completely and Totally the Messiest,* p. 1058.

Bulletin of the Center for Children's Books, December, 1972, Zena Sutherland, review of *Alexander and the Terrible, Horrible, No Good Very Bad Day.*

Horn Book, March-April, 1972, Sheryl B. Andrews, review of *The Tenth Good Thing about Barney;* November-December, 1990, Nancy Vasilakis, review of *Earrings!,* p. 741; May-June, 1994, p. 322; January-February, 1996, Nancy Vasilakis, review of *Sad Underwear and Other Complications,* p. 89.

Kirkus Reviews, July 15, 1970, review of *Try It Again, Sam: Safety When You Walk;* January 1, 1988, p. 60; October 15, 1993, p. 1292; November 15, 1997, p. 1698.

New York Times Book Review, September 26, 1971, Sheila R. Cole, review of *The Tenth Good Thing about Barney;* May 8, 1988, Frances Wells Burck, "'No, I Won't Have Fun with the Baby-Sitter,'" p. 25; January 23, 1994, p. 16; August 13, 1995, p. 23.

Publishers Weekly, October 21, 1974, review of *Rosie and Michael;* February 26, 1988, p. 116; July 7, 1989, pp. 45-46; August 10, 1990, review of *Earrings!,* p. 444; September 11, 1995, review of *Alexander, Who's Not (Do You Hear Me? I Meant It!) Going to Move,* p. 85; October 20, 1997, review of *Absolutely Positively Alexander,* p. 78; December 8, 1997, Tracy Cochran, "Judith Viorst: From the Skin to the Pith," pp. 51-52; April 23, 2000, p. 83; January 22, 2001, review of *Super-Completely and Totally the Messiest,* p. 323.

School Library Journal, January, 1969, Elinor S. Cullen, review of *Sunday Morning;* September, 1973, Alice H. Yucht, review of *My Mama Says There Aren't Any Zombies, Ghosts, Vampires, Creatures, Demons, Monsters, Fiends, Goblins, or Things;* November, 1990, Jane Saliers, review of *Earrings!,* p. 100; April, 1994, p. 123; May, 1995, pp. 116-117; August, 1996, p. 179; March, 2001, Susan Hepler, review of *Super-Completely and Totally the Messiest,* p. 224.

Times Literary Supplement, November 23, 1973, review of *Alexander and the Terrible, Horrible, No Good, Very Bad Day,* p. 1437.

Washingtonian, January, 1998, pp. 41-45.

Washington Post Book World, November 5, 1972, Michael J. Bandler, review of *Alexander and the Terrible, Horrible, No Good Very Bad Day;* January 16, 1994, p. 2.

Writer, April, 1976, Judith Viorst, "The Books Children Love Most," pp. 20-22.

ON-LINE

Bookreporter, http://www.bookreporter.com/ (April 6, 2001), interview with Judith Viorst.

—Sketch by J. Sydney Jones

WALLENTA, Adam 1974-

Personal

Born February 19, 1974, in Bridgeport, CT; son of Alan and Linda (Sherwood) Wallenta. *Education:* Pratt Institute, B.F.A. (with honors). *Politics:* Democrat.

Addresses

Home—22-61 42nd St., Suite D1, Astoria, NY 11105. *E-mail*—Adam@AmericanMule.com.

Career

American Mule Entertainment, owner, art director, artist, and writer.

Illustrator

JoAnn A. Grote, *The American Revolution,* Barbour Publishing (Uhrichsville, OH), 1997.

Norma Jean Lutz, *Escape from Slavery,* Barbour Publishing (Uhrichsville, OH), 1997.

JoAnn A. Grote, *The American Victory,* Barbour Publishing (Uhrichsville, OH), 1997.

Norma Jean Lutz, *Smallpox Strikes!,* Barbour Publishing (Uhrichsville, OH), 1997.

Norma Jean Lutz, *Trouble on the Ohio River,* Barbour Publishing (Uhrichsville, OH), 1997.

Susan Martins Miller, *Boston Revolts!,* Barbour Publishing (Uhrichsville, OH), 1997.

Susan Martins Miller, *Lights for Minneapolis,* Barbour Publishing (Uhrichsville, OH), 1998.

Susan Martins Miller, *The Streetcar Riots,* Barbour Publishing (Uhrichsville, OH), 1998.

JoAnn A. Grote, *Chicago World's Fair,* Barbour Publishing (Uhrichsville, OH), 1998.

JoAnn A. Grote, *The Great Depression,* Barbour Publishing (Uhrichsville, OH), 1998.

JoAnn A. Grote, *The Great Mill Explosion,* Barbour Publishing (Uhrichsville, OH), 1998.

X-Files *characters Dana Scully and Fox Mulder, by artist Adam Wallenta.*

JoAnn A. Grote, *Women Win the Vote,* Barbour Publishing (Uhrichsville, OH), 1998.

Norma Jean Lutz, *The Rebel Spy,* Barbour Publishing (Uhrichsville, OH), 1998.

Norma Jean Lutz, *War Strikes,* Barbour Publishing (Uhrichsville, OH), 1998.

Norma Jean Lutz, *War's End,* Barbour Publishing (Uhrichsville, OH), 1998.

Bonnie Hinman, *Earthquake in Cincinnati,* Chelsea House (Philadelphia, PA), 1999.

Susan Martins Miller, *The Boston Massacre,* Chelsea House (Philadelphia, PA), 1999.

Veda Boyd Jones, *Adventure in the Wilderness,* Chelsea House (Philadelphia, PA), 1999.

Black Tuesday, Barbour Publishing (Uhrichsville, OH), 1999.

Creator of the monthly comic series "The True Adventures of Adam and Bryon," 1998, and "Imagine: The Comic of Adventure, Fantasy, and Fun," 1999—, both for American Mule Entertainment; also illustrator for Marvel Comics. Creator of book covers for romance novels published by Barbour Publishing. Contributor to periodicals, including *Princeton Review.*

Work in Progress

Soulan.

Sidelights

Adam Wallenta told *SATA:* "*Soulan* is a multi-media project that began as a comic book short story in 'Imagine: Comic of Adventure, Fantasy, and Fun,' published by American Mule Entertainment. I am currently writing a three-part screenplay, a novelization, and an ongoing monthly comic series based on the original story. It is a science fiction/fantasy epic adventure that features predominantly African-American characters and revolves around spirituality and peace and knowledge. Exclusive online stories and movie updates can be seen at the Web site http://www.AmericanMule.com."

Wallenta added: "I have been drawing for my entire life. As a child my major influences were comic books and science fiction/adventure movies. I was influenced by the art of John Romita, Jack Kirby, George Perez, and countless other great comic book artists as well as legendary movie poster artist Drew Struzan.

"Both my mother and father encouraged me as an artist. They would always help buy me comics and art supplies and helped to feed my hunger for art however they could. To this day they are my biggest supporters and I thank them for everything. Because of this I try to help and inspire any young artist I meet.

"While attending Pratt Institute new doors were open to me in the world of illustration. I became more aware of artists such as Bob Peak, N. C. Wyeth, Howard Pyle, J. C. Lyenedecker, Alfons Mucha, Frank Frazetta, and more, including one very influential professor, Peter Fiore, who put me on the path which I still follow. I love all art, but my specialty is watercolor and oil, as well as pen and ink.

"While attending Pratt I worked first as an intern and then as a freelancer for Marvel Comics. There I learned the ins and outs of the comic book publishing business and gained many insights into the art. After graduating

from Pratt, I landed several illustrating jobs for various magazines and gaming companies, including *True West/ Old West, America* magazine, and Last Unicorn Games. While working at a part-time job at a book store, I met a well established illustrator named Chris Coccoza. He became a major influence on my life, giving me a lot of insight into the business, and he put me in contact with Barbour Publishing. Little did I know that Barbour would become one of my best clients and help me define my style and career. I illustrated a series of children's books for them, as well as numerous romance covers, and I continue to do work for them.

"I am also the owner of a small publishing and film production company called American Mule Entertainment. We specialize in humor-oriented comics and have recently branched off into the world of science fiction and fantasy. Our first book, 'The True Adventures of Adam and Bryon,' is based on me and my best friend Bryon. I draw it and we write it together. American Mule Entertainment also published 'Imagine: The Comic of Adventure, Fantasy, and Fun.' It is an anthology that includes some of the best new talent in the industry. I wrote several stories and created the art for two of them. I was also the art director and designer. All of our books have a solid, underground fan base and have gathered the attention of Hollywood. Several studios have expressed interest in our characters, and we hope to turn them into feature movies or animated television pieces."

*   *   *

WEISS, Mitch 1951-

Personal

Born May 8, 1951, in New York, NY; son of Sidney (a businessman) and Janet (a psychiatric social worker) Weiss; married Martha Hamilton (a storyteller), June 18, 1983. *Education:* Cornell University, B.A., 1973. *Politics:* Democrat. *Hobbies and other interests:* Tennis, biking, running, hiking, gardening, travel, reading, golf, sports.

Addresses

Home and office—954 Coddington Rd., Ithaca, NY 14850.

Career

Author, storyteller. Somadhara Bakery, Ithaca, NY, co-owner, 1973-75; Moosewood Restaurant, Ithaca, collective co-owner, 1976-84; professional storyteller, 1980—. *Member:* National Storytelling Network.

Awards, Honors

Anne Izard Storytellers' Choice Award, 1992, for *Children Tell Stories;* Storytelling World Gold Award, 1997, for *Stories in My Pocket;* Parents' Choice Recommendation, and National Parenting Publications

Mitch Weiss

Gold Award, both 1998, both for *Stories in My Pocket* (audiocassette); Storytelling World Gold Award, and Parents' Choice Approved Award, both 2000, both for *How and Why Stories;* National Parenting Publications Gold Award, 2000, for *How and Why Stories* (audio recording); Notable Social Studies Trade Book for Young People, National Council for the Social Studies/ Children's Book Council, 2001, for *Noodlehead Stories: World Tales Kids Can Read and Tell.*

Writings

WITH WIFE, MARTHA HAMILTON

Tell Me a Story: Beauty and the Beast (videocassette), Kartes Video Communications, 1986.

Children Tell Stories: A Teaching Guide, R. C. Owen (Katonah, NY), 1990.

Stories in My Pocket: Tales Kids Can Tell, illustrated by Annie Campbell, Fulcrum (Golden, CO), 1996.

How & Why Stories: World Tales Kids Can Read and Tell, illustrated by Carol Lyon, August House (Little Rock, AR), 1999.

Noodlehead Stories: World Tales Kids Can Read and Tell, illustrated by Ariane Elsammak, August House (Little Rock, AR), 2000.

Through the Grapevine: World Tales Kids Can Read and Tell, illustrated by Carol Lyon, August House (Little Rock, AR), 2001.

Adaptations

Stories in My Pocket: Tales Kids Can Tell was adapted by Hamilton and Weiss as an audio recording on cassette, Fulcrum, 1998; *How & Why Stories: World Tales Kids Can Read and Tell* was adapted by Hamilton and Weiss as an audio recording on cassette and compact disc, August House, 2000.

Sidelights

Mitch Weiss and his wife, Martha Hamilton, work together as a storytelling team. Please refer to Martha Hamilton's sketch in this volume for their Sidelights essay.

Weiss and coauthor Martha Hamilton offer thirty original tales and plenty of helpful hints for aspiring young storytellers. (Cover illustration by Annie Campbell.)

Biographical and Critical Sources

PERIODICALS

Booklist, January 1, 1997, Karen Morgan, review of *Stories in My Pocket,* p. 850; November 15, 1998, John Sigwald, review of *Stories in My Pocket* (audiocassette), p. 604; May 15, 2000, Hazel Rochman, review of *How and Why Stories,* pp. 1755-1756; October 15, 2000, Paul Shackman, review of *How and Why Stories* (audiocassette and compact disc), p. 470; February 15, 2001, John Peters, review of *Noodlehead Stories: World Tales Kids Can Read and Tell.*

Bulletin of the Center for Children's Books, March, 1997, Janice M. Del Negro, review of *Stories in My Pocket,* p. 263, February, 2000, Janice M. Del Negro, review of *How and Why Stories.*

Horn Book, July-December, 1999, review of *How and Why Stories.*

Library Talk, January-February, 2000, Dorothy B. Bickley, review of *How and Why Stories,* p. 52.

School Library Journal, May, 1987, Constance Dyckman, review of *Tell Me a Story,* p. 53; August, 1998, Nancy L. Chu, review of *Stories in My Pocket* (audiocassette), pp. 78-79; January, 2000, Elizabeth Maggio, review of *How and Why Stories,* p. 146; July, 2000, Kirsten Martindale, review of *How and Why Stories,* p. 54; January 2001, Marlyn K. Roberts, review of *Noodlehead Stories,* p. 146.

ON-LINE

Beauty and the Beast Storytellers, http://www.people.clarityconnect.com/webpages3/bnb (April 28, 2001).

*　　　*　　　*

WHITWORTH, John 1945-

Personal

Born December 11, 1945, in Nasik, India; son of Hugh (a civil servant) and Elizabeth (Boyes) Whitworth; married Doreen Roberts (a university lecturer); children: Eleanor, Katie. *Education:* Merton College, Oxford, M.A., 1967, B.Phil., 1970. *Politics:* "Few." *Religion:* "Remnants of an Anglican upbringing."

Addresses

Home—20 Lovell Rd., Rough Common, Canterbury, Kent CT2 9D9, England.

Career

Teacher of English as a second language in the south of England, 1969-84; literary journalist and reviewer, 1984—; creative writing teacher, 1990—.

Awards, Honors

Alice Hunt Bartlett Prize, Poetry Society, 1981, for *Unhistorical Fragments;* Cholmondeley Award, 1988.

Writings

Unhistorical Fragments, Secker & Warburg (London, England), 1980.

Poor Butterflies, Secker & Warburg (London, England), 1982.

Lovely Day for a Wedding, Secker and Warburg (London, England), 1985.

Tennis and Sex and Death, Peterloo Poets (Calstock, England), 1989.

(Editor) *The Faber Book of Blue Verse,* Faber and Faber (London, England, and Boston, MA), 1990.

Landscape with Small Humans, Peterloo Poets (Calstock, England), 1993.

The Complete Poetical Works of Phoebe Flood, illustrated by Lauren Child, Hodder Children's (London, England), 1997.

From the Sonnet History of Modern Poetry: Poems, illustrated by Gerald Mangan, Peterloo Poets (Calstock, England), 1999.

Work in Progress

The Whitworth Gun, for Peterloo Poets, and *How to Write Poetry* (nonfiction), for A & C Black.

Sidelights

John Whitworth once commented: "Why do I write? That's a difficult one. I do like getting paid, but of course that's not the primary reason for doing it. I think I started in my late teens with an inflated, romantic notion of the poet's role as unacknowledged legislator and so forth. Now I try to amuse myself and other people.

"I was greatly influenced by the English poets Larkin, Betjeman, and Auden. Now I read Wallace Stevens, Shakespeare, and Keats aloud to myself, though you probably wouldn't guess that from my work. Other influences? Robert Browning and Lewis Carroll; contemporary English poets like Wendy Cope, Sophie Hannah; Roger McGough and Kit Wright; Gavin Ewart, of course. Do Americans know him? Lately I am rather inclined to letting the words do what they like and not worrying too much about the sense. Would that be Ashberry? I can't make much of him, I'm afraid, but the *idea* seems okay.

"How do I write? Directly onto my word processor, making great use of my Roget, my Penguin rhyming dictionary, my *Complete Oxford* with the magnifying glass, and various other reference books, tracking down words and associations. I tend to wake up at four in the morning and do a couple of hours then. Nothing much useful happens after lunch. The great thing about a word processor is that you can have lots of poetic torsos, as it were, littered around your files, and you're not going to lose any of them, unlike bits of paper.... Of course, sometimes I don't know the name of the file I'm looking for, and I find another one. Hurray for serendipity!

"Lately I've written for children. That's a useful discipline. You can't rely on allusion and 'all that.'

Children know what they like, not what they ought to like.

"I've started writing stories of about 2000 words, no more. I don't know yet if they are any good, but I think some are. It's not so different from poetry, or I don't find it so different. Without a word processor, though, I wouldn't do it—all those retyped drafts...."

A British poet, Whitworth has established a reputation for humorous, sometimes satirical, jabs at pretension in its many manifestations, often written in traditional verse forms. Thus his early *Poor Butterflies* was described by London *Observer* reviewer Peter Porter as falling under the rubric of "'good, not-so-clean fun.'" But, Porter quickly added, "there is more to Whitworth than fun and bum: with him the virtuosity of light verse can seem close to high art," citing "I Wish You a Wave of the Sea" and "The True Confessions" as two poems in which the author achieves startling comic effects that ring of authenticity despite their strict rhyme scheme. In a different *Observer* review, Porter called *Lovely Day for a Wedding,* Whitworth's next collection, "even dirtier and funnier this time," but noted a darkening in the poet's tone. With the publication of *Lovely Day, Listener* contributor Dick Davis noted the similarities between Whitworth and the poet Wendy Cope in subject and approach, but added that Whitworth "is a more aggressive, less sly, poet than Ms. Cope." Davis also commented upon a darkening of tone in this work, in which Whitworth's anger at the targets of his satire is barely balanced by the tenderness of poems about his daughter: "In most poems fury seems to have got the better of John Whitworth, and the book's predominant mode is splenetic satire on contemporary British mores." On the other hand, *New Statesman* reviewer John Lucas praised Whitworth's effective use of the demotic in breaking through the pretensions of his satirical targets. But, Lucas added, the poet's attempts at common language do occasionally fail: "*Lovely Day for a Wedding* is an enjoyable read, even though the street language sometimes turns out to smell of the study," Lucas concluded.

Whitworth is right on target again in *Tennis and Sex and Death,* according to Lucas in *New Statesman and Society.* The subject here, as outlined in the volume's title, is what Lucas calls "last as well as middle and middle-aged things," along with Whitworth's usual targets of pretentious literary figures. Here, for example, the poet rhymes *Shelley* with *vermicelli,* "which doubles the insult and doubles you up with helpless laughter," Lucas contended. *Times Literary Supplement* contributor Glyn Maxwell, however, condemned Whitworth's pointed jibes at his literary forebears (and some contemporaries). In his light verse, Whitworth "spends most of his time parenthesizing, confiding, attacking poets whose reputations he can't possibly dent, or defending himself and heroes of his (Ewart, Larkin, Betjeman, Cope) who don't need defending," Maxwell stated. However, this critic continued with surprise, Whitworth's "serious" poetry is something much more interesting. At his best, in poems such as "The Middle-Sized Poem" and "The

John Whitworth

Way It Was ...," "Whitworth allows his poetry to breathe, actually trusts that there are unsaid, suggested feelings or effects that need not be shrugged off or sealed off by a joke or rider, a gloss or an apology." Likewise, Peter Forbes in the *Listener* dubbed the sequence in *Tennis and Sex and Death* on the poet's daughter its most successful: "For a grizzled veteran of interminable tussles with the spirit of the age, little Ellie and her ways are just what the poet needs to bring in a note of reconciliation."

Landscape with Small Humans is an autobiographical treatment of Whitworth's youth in verse. "It's a kind of *Songs of Innocence and Experience* filtered through a Fifties world of Fairy Soap and Ex-Lax, Ike and the King's death," remarked Adam Thorpe in the *Observer.* And, according to Thorpe, through a "perfect fusion of technical adroitness and absolute candour," Whitworth pulls off the tricky business of recounting incidents of childhood bullying and his mother's death both with emotional authenticity. "This is a small human speaking in a vast and suddenly wasted landscape," Thorpe concluded. Whitworth again attempted a child's voice in *The Complete Poetical Works of Phoebe Flood,* a humorous survey of contemporary childhood in which the word "knickers," a British term for underwear, is often a pivotal rhyme.

Biographical and Critical Sources

PERIODICALS

Books for Keeps, March, 1997, Morag Styles, review of *The Complete Poetical Works of Phoebe Flood,* p. 23.
Listener, April 10, 1986, Dick Davis, "Poetry and laughs," pp. 27-28; January 18, 1990, Peter Forbes, "Alchemical hoovering," pp. 28-29.
London Review of Books, February 21, 1991, Blake Morrison, "Sex'n'Love," pp. 14-15.
New Statesman, May 2, 1986, John Lucas, "More to it than saying 'bollocks,'" pp. 24-25.
New Statesman & Society, November 24, 1989, John Lucas, "The pleasure principle," pp. 36, 38.
Observer, October 3, 1982, Peter Porter, "The human face of Mars," p. 32; November 17, 1985, Peter Porter, "Songs from another country," p. 31; April 3, 1994, Adam Thorpe, "Unpack sorrow's suitcase," p. 18.
Times Literary Supplement, April 25, 1980; May 27, 1983; November 3, 1989, Glyn Maxwell, "Farming the unfenced field," p. 1216.

*   *   *

WILLIAMS, Cynthia G. 1958-

Personal

Born May 8, 1958, in Mobile, AL; daughter of Leonard Fred (a truck driver) and Hattie Mae Williams. *Education:* University of South Alabama, B.A. *Religion:* Christian.

Addresses

Office—Channel 4 News, WSMV-Television, P.O. Box 4, Nashville, TN 37202. *E-mail*—cwilliams@wsmv.com.

Career

WKRG-Television, Mobile, AL, began as part-time employee, became news reporter; WMC-Television, Memphis, TN, worked as a reporter; WSMV-Television, Nashville, TN, news anchor and reporter for *Channel 4 News,* 1990—.

Writings

Enid and the Dangerous Discovery, Broadman & Holman (Nashville, TN), 1999.
Enid and the Church Fire, Broadman & Holman (Nashville, TN), 1999.
Enid and the Great Idea, Broadman & Holman (Nashville, TN), 2000.
Enid and the Homecoming, Broadman & Holman (Nashville, TN), 2000.

Sidelights

Cynthia G. Williams told *SATA:* "They say 'man plans and God laughs,' and if that's the case, God must be having a good laugh on me!

"I 'fell' into television news in much the same way that I fell into becoming an author. I never planned a career in television. Coming from the inner city of Mobile, Alabama, I simply always knew I wanted to do something with my life. I worked part-time at the local television station to help pay for college expenses, and the rest is history.

"In 1993 my book writing career began after I was diagnosed with a polyp on my vocal chord. Ever since moving to Nashville, I'd spent many of my days off reading books to children at area schools. My favorites were *Oh the Places You'll Go* by Dr. Seuss, and *The Velveteen Rabbit* by Margery Williams. One day, God spoke to me and said, 'Cynthia, you can write a children's book,' but I promptly dismissed the notion because of my hectic schedule covering the local news and anchoring at the National Broadcasting Company affiliate where I'm presently employed. The polyp diagnosis forced me into surgery to remove it, and it forced me off work, resting and silent for two-and-a-half weeks. The story of an inner-city girl named Enid and her leadership skills in her community came from a place inside me I never knew existed!

"I'm very accustomed to writing for television news (putting words to pictures) but writing the words and picturing Enid and her friends in my imagination were totally new and different for me. Then, getting the first manuscript published was another big job. It took six

Cynthia G. Williams

years and many rejections before I finally got a publisher to take a chance. Through my research in children's book writing, I knew that picture books were expensive to publish and tough to market in an already flooded landscape, so the task was a daunting one indeed! The story of how it came to be is a whole 'nother story in itself! But suffice it to say, Broadman & Holman asked for a whole series once they agreed to publish my initial story of Enid cleaning up her n'hood, which later became *Enid and the Great Idea.*

"News reporting is a very issue-oriented medium. I feel the [Enid] stories, about a gun, a church fire, adoption, and the environment, reflect the times we live in and don't talk down to young children. I hope the stories are presented in such a way that they can encourage young readers to take personal responsibility for their environment, no matter the circumstances of their lives. I hope these stories help to motivate and encourage young readers in areas of character development and fun. Each story is an adventure. In my experience, life is an adventure, and it's never too early to share that concept with children!"

Biographical and Critical Sources

PERIODICALS

Christian Single, June, 2000, Tam Gordon, "Cynthia Williams: Anchoring Her Life," pp. 12-15.
Today's Christian Woman, January-February, 2000, Jane Johnson Struck, "On the Stories That Changed Her Life."

*   *   *

WILLIS, Jeanne (Mary) 1959-

Personal

Born May 11, 1959, in St. Albans, Hertfordshire, England; daughter of David Alfred (a language teacher) and Dorothy Hilda Celia (a teacher of domestic science; maiden name, Avgers) Willis; married Ian James Wilcock (an animator), May 26, 1989. *Education:* Watford College of Art, Diploma in Advertising Writing, 1979. *Politics:* "I don't support any of the parties." *Religion:* "I have my own beliefs."

Addresses

Home—63 Crouch Hill, London N4, England. *Office*—Creative Department, Young & Rubicam Ltd., Greater London House, Hampstead Rd., London NW1, England.

Career

Doyle, Dane, Berenbach, London, England, advertising copywriter, 1979-81; Young & Rubicam Ltd., London, senior writer, group head, and member of board of directors, 1981—; author, 1981—. *Member:* British Herpetological Association.

Jeanne Willis and Tony Ross
SLOTH'S SHOES

The animals of Thunder Tree prepare for Sloth's birthday party, but how long will they wait for him to arrive? (Cover illustration by Tony Ross.)

Awards, Honors

Top Ten Picture Books, *Redbook* magazine, 1987, for *The Monster Bed;* recipient of several industry awards in advertising.

Writings

The Tale of Georgie Grub, Andersen (London, England), 1981, Holt (New York, NY), 1982.
The Tale of Fearsome Fritz, Andersen (London, England), 1982, Holt (New York, NY), 1983.
The Tale of Mucky Mabel, Andersen (London, England), 1984.
The Monster Bed, illustrated by Susan Varley, Andersen (London, England), 1986, Lothrop, (New York, NY), 1987.
The Long Blue Blazer, illustrated by Varley, Andersen (London, England), 1987, Dutton, 1988.
Dr. Xargle's Book of Earthlets, illustrated by Tony Ross, Andersen (London, England), 1988, published as *Earthlets, As Explained by Professor Xargle,* Dutton, 1989.
Dr. Xargle's Book of Earth Hounds, Translated into Human by Jeanne Willis, illustrated by Tony Ross, Anderson (London, England), 1989, published as

Earth Hounds, As Explained by Professor Xargle, Dutton, 1990.

Dr. Xargle's Book of Earth Tiggers, Translated into Human by Jeanne Willis, illustrated by Tony Ross, Anderson (London, England), 1990, published as *Earth Tigerlets, As Explained by Professor Xargle,* Dutton, 1991.

Dr. Xargle's Book of Earth Mobiles, Translated into Human by Jeanne Willis, illustrated by Tony Ross, Andersen (London, England), 1991, published as *Earth Mobiles, As Explained by Professor Xargle,* Dutton, 1992.

Toffee Pockets (poems), illustrated by George Buchanan, Bodley Head (London, England), 1992.

Dr. Xargle's Book of Earth Weather, Translated into Human by Jeanne Willis, illustrated by Tony Ross, Anderson (London, England), 1992, published as *Earth Weather, As Explained by Professor Xargle,* Dutton, 1993.

Dr. Xargle's Book of Earth Relations, illustrated by Tony Ross, Andersen (London, England), 1993, published as *Relativity, As Explained by Professor Xargle,* Dutton, 1994.

Jeanne Willis shows that a girl who uses a wheelchair has the same emotions as any other child in **Susan Laughs.** *(Illustration by Ross.)*

But before Elephant could stop him, Parrot helped himself to a huge beakful.

Parrot learns a sticky lesson about talking too much in **Be Quiet, Parrot!** *(Written by Willis and illustrated by Mark Birchall.)*

In Search of the Hidden Giant, illustrated by Ruth Brown, Andersen (London, England), 1993, published as *In Search of the Giant,* Dutton, 1994.

The Lion's Roar, illustrated by Derek Collin, Ginn, 1994.

The Rascally Cake, illustrated by Paul Korky, Andersen (London, England), 1994.

Two Sea Songs, Ginn, 1994.

The Monster Storm, illustrated by Susan Varley, Andersen (London, England), Lothrop (New York, NY), 1995.

Dolly Dot, Ginn, 1995.

Flower Pots and Forget-Me-Nots, Ginn, 1995.

Wilbur and Orville Take Off, illustrated by Roger Wade Walker, Macdonald Young (Hemel Hempstead, England), 1995.

The Princess and the Parlour Maid, illustrated by Pauline Hazelwood, Macdonald Young (Hemel Hempstead, England), 1995.

Tom's Lady of the Lamp, illustrated by Amy Burch, Macdonald Young (Hemel Hempstead, England), 1995.

The Pet Person, illustrated by Tony Ross, Andersen (London, England), 1996, Dial (New York, NY), 1996.

The Pink Hare, illustrated by Ken Brown, Andersen (London, England), 1996.

What Do You Want to Be, Brian?, illustrated by Mary Rees, Andersen (London, England), 1996.

Sloth's Shoes, illustrated by Tony Ross, Andersen (London, England), 1997, Kane/Miller (Brooklyn, NY), 1998.

The Wind in the Wallows (poetry), illustrated by Tony Ross, Andersen (London, England), 1998.

The Boy Who Lost His Belly Button, illustrated by Tony Ross, Andersen (London, England), 1999, Dorling Kindersley (New York, NY), 2000.

Tinkerbill, illustrated by Paul Cox, Collins (London, England), 1999.

Susan Laughs, illustrated by Tony Ross, Andersen (London, England), 1999, Henry, 2000.

Take Turns, Penguin!, pictures by Mark Birchall, Carolrhoda (Minneapolis, MN), 2000.

Parrot Goes to Playschool, pictures by Mark Birchall, Andersen (London, England), 2000, published as *Be Quiet, Parrot!,* Carolrhoda (Minneapolis, MN), 2000.

What Did I Look Like When I Was a Baby?, illustrated by Tony Ross, Putnam, 2000.

Do Little Mermaids Wet Their Beds?, pictures by Penelope Jossen, Albert Whitman (Morton Grove, IL), 2001.

No Biting, Panther!, illustrated by Mark Birchall, Carolrhoda (Minneapolis, MN), 2001.

Be Gentle, Python!, illustrated by Mark Birchall, Carolrhoda (Minneapolis, MN), 2001.

Dr. Xargle's Book of Earth Weather and *Dr. Xargle's Book of Earth Mobiles* have been translated into Welsh.

Sidelights

British children's writer Jeanne Willis has penned a number of critically acclaimed picture books that instruct as well as amuse. An advertising executive by day, Willis once said: "I had a very vivid imagination as a child. I think I felt everything deeply, and in many respects that was good. My happiness, my excitements seemed to be bigger emotions than other children felt. The bad side of the coin is obvious: deep hurt, dreadful fears. Fear is the downside of having an active imagination. Because I was not confidently articulate, I exorcised these intense feelings on paper. I still do. One day somebody pointed out that such things were commercially viable, so they found their way into stories. One day I shall publish my poetry—my adult poetry. In the meantime, I have to go and feed my toads. Reptiles and amphibians are dear to my heart."

Born in 1959, in Hertfordshire, England, Willis was the daughter of two teachers. As she once recalled, "I grew up in a very safe, suburban environment. I went to a wonderful school which had a huge wheatfield growing next to our playground. I was a useless mathematician, but was one of the first to read and write creatively . . . .

"I belonged to the World Wildlife Guard (now the Worldwide Guard for Wildlife) and had a bedroom full of strange creatures—locusts, stick insects, newts, caterpillars, etc. The fascination with these beasts has remained with me all my life. Indeed when I got married our blessing was held in the Aquarium at the London Zoo in front of the shark tank."

Willis first won acclaim for her "Professor Xargle" series of science books for early elementary grades. Initially published in England, each of them reappeared under a slightly revised title for American audiences. Their premise is the same throughout: the misinformed alien professor of the title tries to explain the odd life forms on Earth. He takes a scientific tone, but his lectures are full of comical errors. In 1988's *Dr. Xargle's Book of Earthlets,* he strains to enlighten his class of fellow aliens about infant humans. He moves on to *Dr. Xargle's Book of Earth Hounds, Translated into Human by Jeanne Willis,* discussing dogs on the planet and how humans spread newspapers on the floor for their young "houndlets" to read. The professor tackles the subject of cats in 1990's *Dr. Xargle's Book of Earth Tiggers.* He tells the class that these felines exhibit bizarre behavior that includes planting "brown stinkseeds" that never grow and leaving "squishy puddings" on the stairs in which humans then trod. Willis's "writing is fresh and fun, the scope of her imagination limitless," enthused a *Publishers Weekly* critic reviewing *Earth Tigerlets, As Explained by Professor Xargle.*

Willis noted that her "Dr. Xargle's" series is simply the result of realizing how absurd human and animal behavior is, and also a desire to believe in "the alien." "I'm sure they exist. In fact, I'm sure they're here already. I often get the feeling I'm on the wrong planet, so perhaps I'm one." In Willis's 1991 installment *Dr. Xargle's Book of Earth Mobiles, Translated into Human by Jeanne Willis,* Xargle enlightens the class on the various modes of transportation on Earth, such as the very popular "stinkfumer," his term for the automobile. *Dr. Xargle's Book of Earth Weather, Translated into Human by Jeanne Willis* tackles meteorology; humans, the professor explains, cope with wet weather by growing large rubber feet that they then have difficulty removing. During hot weather, they enjoy lying in what appears to be nests of brown sugar. "Subtle as well as slapstick humor will appeal to a wide variety of ages," noted Claudia Cooper in her assessment of *Earth Weather, As Explained by Professor Xargle* for *School Library Journal. Dr. Xargle's Book of Earth Relations,* the last title in the series, was published in the United States in 1994 as *Relativity, As Explained by Professor*

Xargle. Here the alien academic talks about human families, and how they "belong to each other whether they like it or not."

Willis has also written poetry, such as the 1992 volume *Toffee Pockets.* Featuring a number of poems about grandparents and grandchildren, the collection was described by *Books for Keeps* contributor Judith Sharman as "easy to read and comforting to hear." Other titles from Willis have used rhyme to tell a story for young readers, such as 1993's *In Search of the Hidden Giant.* In it, a narrator and his sister trek through a forest determined to find the giant they believe lives there. They find many clues—tree roots, they assume, are strands of his hair, while the crackling of tree branches overhead seem to signify his presence to them. In a review of the United States edition, a *Publishers Weekly* critic noted that *In Search of the Giant* is deliberately vague, but "it often exemplifies a way of seeing that naturally delights children."

In *The Rascally Cake,* Willis presents the rhyming tale of Rufus and his attempt to bake a Christmas cake. He uses so many dreadful ingredients that it turns into a monster and chases him. Wendy Timothy, in her review for *School Librarian,* called it "wonderfully horrid." Willis also used humor in *The Pet Person,* a book about a dog's birthday wish for a "person" of his own. His dog parents try to dissuade him, reminding him that such creatures often develop revolting habits, such as eating at the table. In *Sloth's Shoes,* Willis describes a birthday party in the jungle for Sloth, who is so slow in getting there that he misses it entirely. In her 1999 book *Tinkerbill,* Willis's heroine, Sally, learns her parents are expecting a brother or sister for her. Unhappy about this coming change, she makes a wish and believes it comes true when she begins to suspect that her new infant brother is a fairy. Andrea Rayner, writing in *School Librarian,* called *Tinkerbill* "a funny story about sibling rivalry," and one that "is not censorious about the child's jealousy."

Willis also created an amusing storyline for *What Did I Look Like When I Was a Baby?,* published in 2000. After a little boy asks his mother the title question, she replies that he looked bald and wrinkled like his grandfather; across the subsequent pages, young animals in the jungle posit the same question to their mothers. Only the bullfrog is traumatized by the photograph of himself as a tadpole, and his friends must sing a song to get him to come out of hiding. "Ross's cartoonlike illustrations complement the puns and double entendres in the text," noted a *Publishers Weekly* reviewer.

The Boy Who Lost His Belly Button was termed "another whimsical offering from Willis," according to *School Library Journal* reviewer Carolyn Janssen. The youngster wakes up one day, realizes that his navel has disappeared, and ventures into the jungle to look for it. He asks various animals, including a gorilla, lion, elephant, and even a mouse, each of whom display their own belly buttons. He finally learns that a crocodile has stolen his navel and bravely enters a swamp to retrieve

"I've got a teeny one," squeaked the mouse.

"I've got a warty one," grunted the warthog.

A boy questions the jungle animals in the search for his missing belly button and gets a surprise from a crocodile in Willis's **The Boy Who Lost His Belly Button.** *(Illustration by Ross.)*

it—a scene that, possesses "a cinematic-like tension," according to a *Publishers Weekly* critic. Another title from Willis published in 1999 was *Susan Laughs,* a rhyming tale about a little girl and her everyday activities and various moods. Only on the last page is she shown in her wheelchair, but the text reminds readers that she is "just like me, just like you." Hazel Rochman, writing in *Booklist,* praised a message conveyed "without being condescending or preachy."

Willis also penned a series of picture books for very young readers about to embark on the preschool adventure to help them learn the rules of the classroom. *Parrot Goes to Playschool* features a parrot who talks incessantly, but finally eats his Elephant classmate's caramels, which seals his beak temporarily. In *Take Turns, Penguin!,* the ostrich teacher does not seem to notice Penguin's self-centeredness, but the other animal classmates step in to solve the problem themselves. Other titles in the series include *No Biting, Panther!* and *Be Gentle, Python!*

Willis once remarked that her "books arrive in my head when they're ready, sometimes they write themselves. I did start a novel, but suddenly the characters started to misbehave and I lost control of them. It was quite frightening, it was a little like dabbling with the occult. If they were alter-egos, then they were better destroyed. I didn't want to be a part of their world."

Biographical and Critical Sources

BOOKS

Willis, Jeanne, *Dr. Xargle's Book of Earth Relations,* illustrated by Tony Ross, Andersen (London, England), 1993, published as *Relativity, As Explained by Professor Xargle,* Dutton, 1994.

PERIODICALS

Booklist, July, 1994, Julie Corsaro, review of *In Search of the Giant,* p. 1956; June 1, 1998, Annie Ayres, review of *Sloth's Shoes,* p. 1785; August, 2000, Hazel Rochman, review of *Susan Laughs,* p. 2151; December 1, 2000, Gillian Engberg, review of *Be Quiet, Parrot!,* and *Take Turns, Penguin!,* p. 727; December 15, 2000, Connie Fletcher, review of *What Did I Look Like When I Was a Baby?,* p. 829.

Books, April-May, 1996, review of *The Pet Person,* p. 26; summer, 1998, review of *The Wind in the Wallows,* p. 19.

Books for Keeps, March, 1993, Gill Roberts, review of *Dr. Xargle's Book of Earth Tiggers, Translated into Human by Jeanne Willis,* p. 11; May, 1993, Jeff Hynds, review of *In Search of the Hidden Giant,* p. 36; November, 1993, Judith Sharman, review of

Toffee Pockets, p. 11, and Jessica Yates, review of *The Long Blue Blazer,* p. 26; May, 1994, Jill Bennett, review of *Dr. Xargle's Book of Earth Weather, Translated into Human by Jeanne Willis,* p. 12; July, 1995, Bennett, review of *Dr. Xargle's Book of Earth Relations,* p. 11; July, 1999, Margaret Mallett, review of *Tom's Lady of the Lamp,* p. 3.

Books for Your Children, summer, 1991, Leonie Bennett, review of *The Tale of Mucky Mabel,* p. 5.

Horn Book, September, 1994, Hanna B. Zeiger, review of *In Search of the Giant,* p. 582.

Junior Bookshelf, December, 1994, review of *The Rascally Cake,* p. 209; April, 1995, review of *In Search of the Hidden Giant,* p. 69.

Kirkus Reviews, June 1, 1991, review of *Earth Tigerlets, As Explained by Professor Xargle,* p. 738; December 1, 1991, review of *Earth Mobiles, As Explained by Professor Xargle,* p. 1541.

Observer (London), July 21, 1996, Kate Kellaway, "Down with Cuddly Toys," p. 17; August 22, 1999, James Shaw, "Mary Has a Little Lamb," p. 14.

Publishers Weekly, June 7, 1991, review of *Earth Tigerlets, As Explained by Professor Xargle,* p. 64; May 30, 1994, review of *In Search of the Giant,* p. 56; February 23, 1998, review of *Sloth's Shoes,* p. 76; May 22, 2000, review of *The Boy Who Lost His Belly Button,* p. 91; October 2, 2000, review of *What Did I Look Like When I Was a Baby?,* p. 81.

Reading Today, August, 2000, Lynne T. Burke, review of *Susan Laughs,* p. 32.

School Librarian, August, 1992, Margaret Banerjee, review of *Toffee Pockets,* p. 111; April, 1994, Wendy Timothy, review of *The Rascally Cake,* p. 154; February, 1996, Teresa Scragg, review of *The Monster Storm,* p. 17; February, 1997, Trevor Dickinson, review of *The Pink Hare,* p. 22; April, 1999, Andrea Rayner, review of *Tinkerbill,* p. 201.

School Library Journal, April, 1991, John Peters, review of *Earth Hounds, As Explained by Professor Xargle,* p. 106; August, 1991, Rachel S. Fox, review of *Earth Tigerlets, As Explained by Professor Xargle,* p. 157; March, 1992, Joan McGrath, review of *Earth Mobiles, As Explained by Professor Xargle,* p. 226; April, 1993, Claudia Cooper, review of *Earth Weather, As Explained by Professor Xargle,* p. 104; March, 1995, Ronald Jobe, review of *Relativity, As Explained by Professor Xargle,* p. 195; August, 1998, Christy Norris Blanchette, review of *Sloth's Shoes,* p. 147; April, 1999, Carol Schene, review of *What Do You Want to Be, Brian?,* p. 110; May, 2000, Carolyn Janssen, review of *The Boy Who Lost His Belly Button,* p. 158; November, 2000, Linda M. Kenton, review of *Susan Laughs,* p. 137; January, 2001, Kathy M. Newby, review of *Be Quiet, Parrot!* and *Take Turns, Penguin!,* p. 112.*

Y

YEP, Laurence Michael 1948-

Personal

Born June 14, 1948, in San Francisco, CA; son of Thomas Gim (a postal clerk) and Franche (a homemaker; maiden name, Lee) Yep. *Education:* Attended Marquette University, 1966-68; University of California, Santa Cruz, B.A., 1970; State University of New York at Buffalo, Ph.D., 1975.

Addresses

Home—921 Populus Place, Sunnyvale, CA 94086. *Agent*—Maureen Walters, Curtis Brown Agency, 10 Astor Place, New York, NY 10003.

Career

Writer. Part-time instructor of English, Foothill College, Mountain View, CA, 1975, and San Jose City College, San Jose, CA, 1975-76; University of California, Berkeley, visiting lecturer in Asian-American studies, 1987-89, University of California, Santa Barbara, writer-in-residence, 1990. *Member:* Science Fiction Writers of America, Society of Children's Book Writers.

Awards, Honors

Newbery Honor Book award, Children's Book Award, American Library Association, International Reading Association award, and Carter A. Woodson Award, National Council of Social Studies, all 1976, Lewis Carroll Shelf Award, 1979, and Friend of Children and Literature award, 1984, all for *Dragonwings; Boston Globe-Horn Book* awards, 1977, for *Child of the Owl,* and 1989, for *The Rainbow People;* Jane Addams Award, Women's International League for Peace and Freedom, 1978, for *Child of the Owl;* Silver Medal, Commonwealth Club of California, 1979, for *Sea Glass;* National Endowment for the Arts fellowship, 1990.

Writings

FOR CHILDREN AND YOUNG ADULTS

Sweetwater, illustrated by Julia Noonan, Harper (New York, NY), 1973.

Dragonwings, Harper (New York, NY), 1975.

Child of the Owl, Harper (New York, NY), 1977.

Sea Glass, Harper (New York, NY), 1979.

Kind Hearts and Gentle Monsters, Harper (New York, NY), 1982.

The Mark Twain Murders, Four Winds Press (New York, NY), 1982.

Dragon of the Lost Sea (part of "Dragon" series), Harper (New York, NY), 1982.

Liar, Liar, Morrow (New York, NY), 1983.

The Serpent's Children, Harper (New York, NY), 1984.

The Tom Sawyer Fires, Morrow (New York, NY), 1984.

Dragon Steel (part of "Dragon" series), Harper (New York, NY), 1985.

Mountain Light (sequel to *The Serpent's Children*), Harper (New York, NY), 1985.

The Curse of the Squirrel, illustrated by Dirk Zimmer, Random House (New York, NY), 1987.

Age of Wonders (play), produced in San Francisco, 1987.

(Reteller) *The Rainbow People* (Chinese-American folk tales), illustrated by David Wiesner, Harper (New York, NY), 1989.

Dragon Cauldron (part of "Dragon" series), HarperCollins (New York, NY), 1991.

The Lost Garden, Messner (Englewood Cliffs, NJ), 1991.

The Star Fisher, Morrow (New York, NY), 1991.

(Reteller) *Tongues of Jade* (short stories), illustrated by David Wiesner, HarperCollins (New York, NY), 1991.

Dragon War (part of "Dragon" series), HarperCollins (New York, NY), 1992.

(Editor) *American Dragons: A Collection of Asian American Voices,* HarperCollins (New York, NY), 1992.

Butterfly Boy, illustrated by Jeanne M. Lee, Farrar, Strauss (New York, NY), 1993.

Dragon's Gate (sequel to *Mountain Light*), HarperCollins (New York, NY), 1993.

The Shell Woman and the King, illustrated by Yang Ming-Yi, Dial Books (New York, NY), 1993.

The Man Who Tricked a Ghost, illustrated by Isadore Seltzer, Troll (Mahwah, NJ), 1993.

Ghost Fox, illustrated by Jean and Mou-Sien Tseng, Scholastic (New York, NY), 1994.

The Tiger Woman, illustrated by Robert Roth, Troll (Mahwah, NJ), 1994.

The Boy Who Swallowed Snakes, illustrated by Jean and Mou-Sien Tseng, Scholastic (New York, NY), 1994.

The Junior Thunder Lord, illustrated by Robert Van Nutt, Troll (Mahwah, NJ), 1994.

Hiroshima: A Novella, Scholastic (New York, NY), 1995.

Later, Gator, Hyperion (New York, NY), 1995.

Tree of Dreams: Ten Tales from the Garden of Night, illustrated by Isadore Seltzer, BridgeWater Books (Mahwah, NJ), 1995.

Thief of Hearts (sequel to *Child of the Owl*), HarperCollins (New York, NY), 1995.

The City of Dragons, illustrated by Jean and Mou-Sien Tseng, Scholastic (New York, NY), 1995.

Ribbons, Putnam (New York, NY), 1996.

(Reteller) *The Khan's Daughter: A Mongolian Folktale,* illustrated by Jean and Mou-Sien Tseng, Scholastic (New York, NY), 1997.

(Reteller) *The Dragon Prince: A Chinese Beauty and the Beast Tale,* illustrated by Kam Mak, HarperCollins (New York, NY), 1997.

The Imp That Ate My Homework, illustrated by Benrei Huang, HarperCollins (New York, NY), 1998.

The Cook's Family (sequel to *Ribbons*), Putnam (New York, NY), 1998.

The Amah, Putnam (New York, NY), 1999.

The Journal of Wong Ming-Chung: A Chinese Miner: California, 1852, Scholastic (New York, NY), 2000.

The Magic Paintbrush, illustrated by Suling Wang, HarperCollins (New York, NY), 2000.

Cockroach Cooties (sequel to *Later, Gator*), Hyperion (New York, NY), 2000.

Dream Soul (sequel to *The Star Fisher*), HarperCollins (New York, NY), 2000.

The House of Light, Putnam (New York, NY), 2001.

Lady Ch'iao Kuo: The Red Bird of the South, Scholastic (New York, NY), 2001.

"CHINATOWN MYSTERY" SERIES; FOR CHILDREN

The Case of the Goblin Pearls, HarperCollins (New York, NY), 1997.

The Case of the Lion Dance, HarperCollins (New York, NY), 1998.

The Case of the Firecrackers, HarperCollins (New York, NY), 1999.

FOR ADULTS

Seademons, Harper (New York, NY), 1977.

Shadow Lord, Harper (New York, NY), 1985.

Monster Makers, Inc., Arbor House (New York, NY), 1986.

Pay the Chinaman (one-act play; produced in San Francisco, 1987), in *Between Worlds,* edited by M. Berson, Theatre Communications Group (New York, NY), 1990.

Fairy Bones (one-act play), produced in San Francisco, 1987.

Writer of software, *Alice in Wonderland,* Spinnaker, 1985, and *Jungle Book,* Spinnaker, 1986.

Work represented in anthologies, including *World's Best Science Fiction of 1969,* edited by Donald A. Wollheim and Terry Carr, Ace, 1969; *Quark #2,* edited by Samuel Delaney and Marilyn Hacker, Paperback Library, 1971; *Protostars,* edited by David Gerrold, Ballantine, 1971; *The Demon Children,* Avon, 1973; *Strange Bedfellows: Sex and Science Fiction,* edited by Thomas N. Scortia, Random House, 1973; *Last Dangerous Visions,* edited by Harlan Ellison, Harper, 1975; and *Between Worlds,* Theater Communication Group, 1990.

Contributor of short stories to periodicals, including *Worlds of If* and *Galaxy.* Also author of theatrical adaptation of *Dragonwings,* 1991.

Adaptations

Dragonwings was produced as a filmstrip with record or cassette, Miller-Brody, 1979; *The Curse of the Squirrel* was recorded on audiocassette, Random House, 1989. *Sweetwater* is available in braille and on audiocassette.

Sidelights

Novelist, short-story writer, and reteller of folktales, Laurence Michael Yep is the author of fifty works of fiction, mostly for young readers. His award-winning novels include *Dragonwings, Child of the Owl,* and *Sea Glass,* works which chronicle the Chinese-American experience from California to West Virginia and across several generations. Noted for creating fiction that brings the history and culture of Chinese Americans into realistic view, "Yep provides the reader with a new way of viewing Chinese-Americans, not as yellow men [and women] living in white society but as ordinary as well as extraordinary people," according to Joe Stines in the *Dictionary of Literary Biography.*

Born in San Francisco, California, in 1948, Yep balanced the cultures of China and America all through his adolescence. He also learned the trick of watching at an early age. "Working in our family store," Yep noted in a *Publishers Weekly* interview with Leonard S. Marcus, "and getting to know our customers, I learned early on how to observe and listen to people. It was a good training for a writer." But as a child he gave little thought to becoming a writer. He thought of himself instead as a future scientist and was fascinated by machines. And foremost he was an assimilated child. "I was an *American* child," he told Marcus, "so relentlessly that my grandmother became hesitant to talk about Chinese things with me, even about the gods she kept on her bedroom bureau. I regretted this later, when I wanted to know more about my Chinese heritage."

In high school Yep discovered science fiction, and he began writing stories in the genre and submitting them to magazines. A published sci-fi author by the time he was eighteen years old, Yep attended Marquette University from 1966 to 1968, finished his bachelor's degree at the

University of California at Santa Cruz in 1970, and went on to earn a Ph.D. at the State University of New York at Buffalo in 1975. While still a graduate student, he wrote his first novel, the science fiction, *Sweetwater,* published in 1973. Two years later he published *Dragonwings,* and he was on his way as a professional writer.

Dragonwings tells the story of eight-year-old Moon Shadow, a young boy who leaves his mother in China's Middle Kingdom to join his father in the bachelor society of turn-of-the-century San Francisco. Moon Shadow's father, Windrider, a kite-builder, came to the United States to earn money for his family, but also to explore unknown frontiers. Together father and son fulfill Windrider's dream of flying his own plane. Recounting the adventures and discoveries of father and son, Yep reveals a slice of Chinese-American history, for the story parallels that of Fung Joe Guey who flew a biplane in 1909, a footnote to history that Yep came across in his research. Critics applauded Yep's second novel. Ruth H. Pelmas, writing in the *New York Times Book Review,* declared that, "as an exquisitely written poem of praise to the courage and industry of the Chinese-American people, [*Dragonwings*] is a triumph." *Dragonwings* won Yep a Newbery Honor Book award and secured his writing career.

A winner of the *Boston Globe-Horn Book* Award, Yep's 1977 work *Child of the Owl* is, like *Dragonwings,* set in San Francisco's Chinatown, but this time the year is 1960, and a young girl raised by a gambling father and then a suburban uncle is confused by her dual American and Chinese heritage. Having been exposed only to American ways and therefore having no means by which to identify with her Chinese background, Casey discovers new options for living when she is sent to live with her grandmother, Paw-Paw, in Chinatown. The 1995 sequel, *Thief of Hearts,* "focuses on a different generation and different problems," according to Mary M. Burns writing in *Horn Book.* In this tale, young Stacy, daughter of Casey, is paired with a Chinese girl at school and, when the girl is accused of theft, Stacy must come to terms with her own mixed Chinese and American heritage. "Told with candor and controlled emotion, this first-person narrative presents a difficult topic in a manner accessible to a wide audience," Burns concluded. Kathleen M. Campbell, writing in *Voice of Youth Advocates,* found *Thief of Hearts* to be a "poignant story, challenging issues that plague our diverse culture with sensitivity and honesty ...."

Much of Yep's realistic fiction deals with similar themes exploring the Asian-American racial divide. *Sea Glass,* published in 1979, focuses on Craig Chin, a boy whose search for acceptance by both whites and Chinese Americans ends in rejection. Another work with its roots in Yep's personal history is *The Star Fisher,* which the author published in 1991. Based on his parents' life, the novel finds fifteen-year-old Joan Chen moving from the Midwest to a small Southern town in the late 1920s and trying to build bridges for her family, the only Chinese-American family in town. "Joan's story will appeal to

any reader who has ever felt excluded," noted *School Library Journal* contributor Carla Kozak, who added that the "resilience and humor" of Yep's mother and her family "shine through." Alice Phoebe Naylor concluded in her *New York Times Book Review* appraisal that *The Star Fisher* "is a thought-provoking, engaging novel about a fundamental human drama—immigration and cultural isolation." Yep continues the story of *The Star Fisher* in *Dream Soul,* in which Joan wants to celebrate a Western Christmas, an urge which causes a rift between the family's old-world Chinese heritage and the customs of America. *Booklist*'s Linda Perkins commented that the "Lees' first Christmas celebration, though secular, radiates the warmth and spirit of the season," and that Joan's "yearning to be 'American' ... ring[s] painfully true." In her *Horn Book* review, Burns called the book "an appealing family story, blending humor with charm ...."

Similar themes are served up in *Ribbons, The Cook's Family,* and *The Amah,* all dealing with cultural and personal conflicts that arise between the various generations in a Chinese-American family. In *Ribbons,* a promising young ballet student, Robin Lee, is forced to give up her dancing lessons when her grandmother emigrates from Hong Kong. A connection is finally formed between the two when Robin, whose feet have begun to be misshapen with her dancing, one day sees her grandmother's own misshapen feet, bound when she was young. "Yep creates an elegant tale of love and understanding with an upbeat resolution that will please the most demanding readers," wrote a contributor for *Kirkus Reviews.* In *The Cook's Family,* Robin and her grandmother grow increasingly close as Robin's parents begin to argue more and more. Visits with her grandmother to Chinatown, where they are pressed into playing the part of a cook's long-lost family, become a welcome respite from Robin's turbulent home life. Slowly Robin begins to learn about Chinese history and customs, and it is this growth "that is the most intriguing part of the story," according to *Booklist*'s Stephanie Zvirin. *The Amah* tells another story of a hopeful dancer. Young Amy Chin finds her family responsibilities exploding and threatening to interfere with her ballet lessons when her mother takes a job as a nanny or amah for another family. Helen Foster James, reviewing the title in *School Library Journal,* felt that it was a "realistic story of a contemporary Chinese-American family with flaws and strengths."

Many of Yep's books provide readers with a window into both Chinese and Chinese-American history. His 1984 book, *The Serpent's Children,* is set in nineteenth-century China amid the Taiping Rebellion. In its pages readers meet Cassia, a young girl who, along with her family, joins a revolutionary Brotherhood working to eliminate the corruption within the ruling Manchu dynasty. In the novel's sequel, 1985's *Mountain Light,* Cassia and her father, who are returning from a trip through China's Middle Kingdom, meet up with a young man named Squeaky Lau during their journey. On the eventful trip, taken on behalf of the revolution, the clownish Squeaky finds that he possesses his own inner strength and is able to bring out good in others. Although he and Cassia fall in love, Squeaky joins the mass migration to the western United States, where he faces the chaos brought about by the California Gold Rush. And in 1993's *Dragon's Gate,* the story of the revolutionary family continues with Otter, Cassia's fourteen-year-old adopted son, as he too travels to America and works on the Transcontinental Railroad as part of a Chinese work crew carving a tunnel through a portion of the Sierra Nevada mountain range during the 1860s. Readers experience firsthand this often-overlooked period in history, as Otter "must struggle to survive racial prejudice, cold, starvation, the foreman's whip, and the dangers of frostbite and avalanche while trying to reconcile his ideals and dreams with harsh reality," according to Margaret A. Chang in her appraisal of *Dragon's Gate* for *School Library Journal.* Although some reviewers found the storyline of the series less compelling than in *Dragonwings, Booklist* contributor Ilene Cooper praised *Mountain Light* in particular as containing "a rich blend of action, moral lessons, and complex characterizations."

Other historical novels by Yep include *Hiroshima: A Novella,* a fictional portrait of the events surrounding the U.S. decision to drop an atomic bomb on Hiroshima, Japan, on August 6, 1945, thus accelerating the end of World War II. Focusing on one of the "Hiroshima Maidens"—girls and women who survived the bombing and who were eventually sent to the United States for reconstructive surgery—Yep describes both the actual bombing and its tragic and devastating long-term aftermath. Praising Yep for composing his factual story using "unadorned prose suiting its somber subject matter," *Washington Post Book World* contributor Elizabeth Hand wrote that Hiroshima "should be required reading in every classroom in [the United States] and beyond." In *The Journal of Wong Ming-Chung,* Yep tells the story of a Chinese boy named Runt who travels from southern China to join his uncle during the California Gold Rush of 1852. Narrated in the voice of Runt as he writes in his journal, the book is a "solid historical fiction choice," according to *Booklist*'s Carolyn Phelan. Reviewing the title in *School Library Journal,* Mercedes Smith described *The Journal of Wong Ming-Chung* as an "engaging book with strong characters that successfully weaves fact with fiction."

Yep has also written several mysteries, including *The Mark Twain Murders* and *The Tom Sawyer Fires*—featuring nineteenth-century writer Mark Twain as a young reporter in San Francisco—as well as a series of books featuring a group of preteens who solve mysteries within their Chinese-American communities while also learning about their varied cultural heritage. In *The Case of the Goblin Pearls,* Lily Lew and her flamboyant actress-aunt go in search of a set of priceless pearls stolen from a local sweatshop owner by a masked robber. Praising the novel's "snappy dialogue, realistic characterizations and a plot with lots of action," a *Publishers Weekly* contributor added that Yep's spunky

protagonist gains a "growing realization of the complexities of her Chinese heritage." *The Case of the Lion Dance* furthers these adventures when an explosion and robbery serve as a dramatic finale to a competition celebrating the opening of a new restaurant, and Lily and her aunt once again go into action. "Yep makes San Francisco's Chinatown more than a simple backdrop here," noted *Booklist*'s Zvirin, "working in some sense of cultural conflicts within a diverse community as he guides readers through a twisting plot ...." *The Case of the Firecrackers* is the third installment featuring Lily and her aunt. This time they are on the trail of a shooter who tries to kill a teen star at a television show. Cathy Coffman, reviewing the book in *School Library Journal,* contended that both "fans of the series and those new to it will enjoy this well-written mystery." *Booklist*'s Kay Weisman recommended the book "to mystery buffs as well as children fascinated by Chinatown."

Younger audiences are entertained by Yep in books like *Later, Gator,* where Teddy's prank gift of a creepy-looking alligator for his younger brother backfires when he realizes that eight-year-old Bobby has actually taken a shine to his new pet, unaware that it will not live long in captivity. "The story may be a slender one," wrote a contributor for *Publishers Weekly,* "but the insights here are generous." In a sequel, *Cockroach Cooties,* the brothers make a reappearance, this time teaming up to use bugs to defeat the school bully. "Readers will either be instantly attracted to *Cockroach Cooties* or completely repelled by it," wrote Elizabeth Maggio in a *School Library Journal* review, "but those who can stomach the idea of crushed crickets in their chocolate-chip cookies will eat it up." In another humorous novel aimed at younger readers, *The Imp That Ate My Homework,* Yep tells the story of young Jim who teams up with his grandfather—thought to be the meanest man in Chinatown—to do battle with a powerful demon. The tale revolves around a four-armed trickster from Chinese myth who pops up in San Francisco to torment Jim. "Fast-paced action drives the tale with mystical elements only hinted at," noted Elizabeth S. Watson in a *Horn Book* review. More magic and fantasy are mixed in *The Magic Paintbrush,* in which another young boy and his grandfather discover one another and a new way of seeing. Steve goes to live with his immigrant grandfather after the death of his parents. His new life in Chinatown seems incredibly drab until his grandfather's magic paintbrush suddenly transports them beyond the walls of their tenement. "As always," observed a writer for *Publishers Weekly,* "Yep's crisp style keeps the pages turning, and he leavens his story with snappy dialogue, realistic characters and plenty of wise humor." *School Library Journal*'s Sharon McNeil, reviewing the same title, observed that Yep "weaves a tale of alienation turning into affection, and of good prevailing over meanness."

In addition to full-length fiction, Yep has also compiled several volumes of short stories and picture books based on folktales and legends of China. These include *The Rainbow People* and *Tongues of Jade.* His picture books for very young readers include *The Tiger Woman, The City of Dragons, The Khan's Daughter,* and *The Dragon Prince,* retellings of folktales from all over China that introduce young readers to old wisdom. Reviewing Yep's retelling of a Mongolian folktale, *The Khan's Daughter,* for example, a contributor for *Publishers Weekly* noted that the "story embraces human foibles with both the ageless charm of a traditional tale and the informal breeziness of a modern sensibility." Yep is also the author of a four-volume fantasy series, the "Dragon" books—*Dragon of the Lost Sea, Dragon Steel, Dragon Cauldron,* and *Dragon War*—which uses Chinese rather than European legend and myth as its source.

Whether writing historical fiction, fantasy, contemporary tales of life in Chinatown, or retelling the myths and folklore of China, Yep blends well-plotted action with three-dimensional characters and language that does not talk down to young readers. His books provide a window into the Chinese-American experience. "I see myself now as someone who will always be on the border between two cultures," he commented to Marcus. "That works to my benefit as a writer because not quite fitting in helps me be a better observer."

Biographical and Critical Sources

BOOKS

Children's Literature Review, Gale (Detroit, MI), Volume 3, 1978, Volume 17, 1989.
Contemporary Literary Criticism, Volume 35, Gale (Detroit, MI), 1985.
Huck, Charlotte S., *Children's Literature in the Elementary School,* 3rd edition, Holt (New York, NY), 1979.
Dictionary of Literary Biography, Volume 52: *American Writers for Children since 1960: Fiction,* Gale (Detroit, MI), 1986, pp. 392-398.
Johnson-Feelings, Dianne, *Presenting Laurence Yep,* Twayne (New York, NY), 1995.
Nilsen, Alleen Pace, and Kenneth L. Donelson, editors, *Literature for Today's Young Adults,* 2nd edition, Scott, Foresman (Glenview, IL), 1985.
Norton, Donna E., *Through the Eyes of a Child: An Introduction to Children's Literature,* 2nd edition, Merrill (Columbus, OH), 1987.
St. James Guide to Fantasy Writers, St. James Press, 1996, pp. 637-638.
Twentieth-Century Children's Writers, 5th edition, St. James Press, 1999.
Twentieth-Century Science-Fiction Writers, 3rd edition, St. James Press, 1992.
Twentieth-Century Young Adult Writers, 2nd edition, St. James Press, 1999.

PERIODICALS

Booklist, September 15, 1985, Ilene Cooper, review of *Mountain Light,* p. 141; April 15, 1992, p. 1524; January 15, 1995, p. 927; July, 1995, p. 1880; November 15, 1995, p. 566; January 1, 1996, p. 836; January 1, 1997, pp. 846-847; February 1, 1997, p. 940; July, 1997, p. 1817; January 1, 1998, Stephanie Zvirin, review of *The Cook's Family,* p. 817;

October 15, 1998, Stephanie Zvirin, review of *The Case of the Lion Dance,* p. 423; May 15, 1999, p. 1698; September 15, 1999, Kay Weisman, review of *The Case of the Firecrackers,* p. 262; February 1, 2000, p. 1024; April 1, 2000, Carolyn Phelan, review of *The Journal of Wong Ming-Chung,* p. 1473; May 1, 2000, p. 1671; December 1, 2000, Linda Perkins, review of *Dream Soul,* p. 714.
Bulletin of the Center for Children's Books, April, 1989, p. 211; March, 1991, p. 182; July-August, 1991, p. 279; June, 1995, p. 365; September, 1995, p. 34; February, 1996, p. 210; May, 1997, p. 339; December, 1997, p. 144; April, 1998, p. 302; May, 1998, pp. 344-345.
Christian Science Monitor, November 5, 1975, p. B7; May 4, 1977, p. 29; October 15, 1979, p. B11.
English Journal, March, 1982, pp. 81-82.
Horn Book, April, 1978; May-June, 1989, "The Green Chord," pp. 318-322; March-April, 1994, p. 208; July-August, 1995, p. 463; September-October, 1995, Mary M. Burns, review of *Thief of Hearts,* pp. 610-611; September-October, 1995, p. 635; November-December, 1995, p. 752; March-April, 1997, pp. 208-209; September-October, 1997, pp. 594-595; May-June, 1998, Elizabeth S. Watson, review of *The Imp That Ate My Homework,* p. 351; January-February, 2001, Mary M. Burns, review of *Dream Soul,* p. 99.
Interracial Books for Children Bulletin, Volume 7, numbers 2 & 3, 1976; Volume 11, number 6, 1980, p. 16.
Junior Bookshelf, February, 1977, p. 48.
Kirkus Reviews, June 15, 1993, p. 794; April 15, 1995, p. 564; May 1, 1995, p. 642; December 15, 1995, review of *Ribbons,* p. 1778; January 15, 1997, p. 148; December 15, 1997, p. 1844; May 15, 1999, p. 807; December 1, 1999, p. 1893.
Kliatt, September, 1995, p. 16; November, 1995, p. 23.
Lion and the Unicorn, Volume 5, 1981, pp. 4-18.
Locus, March, 1992, p. 64.
New York Times Book Review, November 16, Ruth H. Pelmas, review of *Dragonwings,* 1975; May 22, 1977; January 20, 1980, p. 30; May 23, 1982, p. 37; November 6, 1983, p. 44; July 23, 1989, p. 29; October 13, 1991, Alice Phoebe Naylor, review of *The Star Fisher,* p. 31.
Publishers Weekly, September 20, 1991, p. 135; May 18, 1992, p. 71; June 14, 1993, p. 72; March, 20, 1995, p. 62; May 8, 1995, review of *Later, Gator,* p. 296; May 8, 1995, p. 297; July 24, 1995, p. 64; October, 1995, p. 74; March 4, 1996, pp. 66-67; December 16, 1996, review of *The Khan's Daughter,* p. 59; December 16, 1996, review of *The Case of the Goblin Pearls,* pp. 59-60; August 25, 1997, p. 71; February 14, 2000, Leonard S. Marcus, "Talking with Authors," p.101; March 13, 2000, review of *The Magic Paintbrush,* p. 85.
Reading Teacher, January, 1977, pp. 359-363.
School Library Journal, May, 1991, Carla Kozak, review of *The Star Fisher,* p. 113; June, 1991, p. 114; December, 1991, p. 132; June, 1992, p. 144; January, 1994, Margaret A. Chang, review of *Dragon's Gate,* p. 135; February, 1996, p. 99; March, 1997, pp. 194-195; October, 1997, p. 125; March, 1998, p. 190;

November, 1998, p. 132; July, 1999, Helen Foster James, review of *The Amah,* p. 102; September, 1999, Cathy Coffman, review of *The Case of the Firecrackers,* p. 230; March, 2000, Sharon McNeil, review of *The Magic Paintbrush,* p. 220; April, 2000, Mercedes Smith, review of *The Journal of Wong Ming-Chung,* p. 143; May, 2000, Elizabeth Maggio, review of *Cockroach Cooties,* p. 159; October, 2000, p. 175; June, 2001, Marlyn K. Roberts, review of *Angelfish,* p. 160.

Voice of Youth Advocates, August, 1985, Frank Perry, review of *Dragon Steel,* p. 195; December, 1985, p. 323; June, 1991, p. 116; December, 1991, p. 320; February, 1996, Kathleen M. Campbell, review of *Thief of Hearts,* p. 380; August, 1997, p. 173; December, 1998, p. 362.

Washington Post Book World, May 1, 1977, pp. E1, E8; January 9, 1983, pp. 11, 13; November 6, 1983, pp. 17, 22; May 12, 1985, pp. 13-14; November 10, 1985, p. 20; May 7, 1995, Elizabeth Hand, review of *Hiroshima: A Novella,* p. 14.

Wilson Library Bulletin, June, 1995, p. 120.*

—Sketch by J. Sydney Jones

Z

ZIMMERMAN, Andrea Griffing 1950-

Personal

Born December 2, 1950, in Akron, OH; daughter of Leland (a business consultant) and Mignon (an auditor; maiden name, Griffing) Zimmerman; married David J. Clemesha, 1973; children: Alex, Christian, Chase. *Education:* California State University, Los Angeles, B.A., 1979; University of California, Los Angeles, D.D.S., 1988. *Hobbies and other interests:* Boy Scouts leadership, gardening, travel.

Addresses

Home—San Diego, CA. *E-mail*—dclem@ sdcoe.k12.ca.us.

Career

Part-time dentist. *Member:* Society of Children's Book Writers and Illustrators.

Awards, Honors

Bulletin Blue Ribbon selection, *Bulletin of the Center for Children's Books,* 1999, and Notable Book, American Library Association, 2000, both for *Trashy Town;* Oppenheim Toy Portfolio Gold Award, 2000, and Best Children's Books of 2000, Bank Street College of Education, both for *My Dog Toby.*

Writings

FOR CHILDREN

Yetta the Trickster, illustrated by Harold Berson, Clarion Books (Boston, MA), 1978.

The Riddle Zoo, illustrated by Giulio Maestro, Dutton (New York, NY), 1981.

FOR CHILDREN; WITH HUSBAND, DAVID CLEMESHA

Rattle Your Bones: Skeleton Drawing Fun, Scholastic (New York, NY), 1991.

The Cow Buzzed, illustrated by Paul Meisel, HarperCollins (New York, NY), 1993.

Applesauce and Cottage Cheese, illustrated by Paul Meisel, HarperCollins (New York, NY), 1995.

Trashy Town, illustrated by Dan Yaccarino, HarperCollins (New York, NY), 1999.

My Dog Toby, illustrated by True Kelley, Harcourt (San Diego, CA), 2000.

Sidelights

Andrea Griffing Zimmerman is the author of the children's books *Yetta the Trickster* and *The Riddle Zoo.* In addition, she has collaborated with her husband, David Clemesha, on several more titles for young readers. In *Yetta,* Zimmerman's first story for children, the title protagonist enjoys playing practical jokes so much that she does not care if she is the player or the victim. Set in an eastern European village, the narrative follows Yetta through numerous pranks, including one in which the village turns the tables on the young jokester. *Booklist* reviewer Barbara Elleman commented that each of the book's "four short chapters ... ripple with spirit and humor." Mary I. Purucker, writing in the *School Library Journal,* praised illustrator Harold Berson's "pen-and-ink wit and humor," and found Zimmerman's depiction of Yetta's adventures to be "human, childlike, and universal."

In *The Cow Buzzed,* the second title Zimmerman coauthored with Clemesha, farm animals pass a cold from one creature to the next—along with each animal's signature noise. Thus the cow catches not only the bee's cold, but his buzz as well. The confusion is made worse when the farmer feeds each animal according to his/her noise, so that they all end up with the wrong food. In the end, the cold is stopped by a rabbit who covers his mouth when he sneezes, and the animals ultimately discover the origins of the illness when the bee unexpectedly roars. A *Kirkus Reviews* contributor called this tale "deliciously silly" with "clever new rhymes worked into each repetition of the tricky, catchy rhythm." A *Publishers Weekly* critic noted that "the book's humor is even more infectious than the bee's cold."

Trashy Town, released in 1999, offers readers a glimpse of a day in the life of Mr. Gilly, the trashman, as he and his two rat sidekicks clean up the town's trash with the cheerful refrain: "Dump it in, smash it down, drive around the Trashy Town!" At the end of his day, Mr. Gilly unloads the trash at the dump, then goes home for a bath. Writing in *Horn Book,* Nancy Vasilakis complimented Zimmerman, Clemesha, and illustrator Dan Yaccarino for creating a "well-designed picture book that does a lot with a simple concept." Calling the narrative "an overdue salute to an unsung hero," a *Publishers Weekly* reviewer remarked that "despite the smelly and slimy aspects of garbage collecting, Zimmerman and Clemesha make Mr. Gilly's job seem satisfying." Comparing *Trashy Town* to "Margaret Wise Brown's best work," *Booklist*'s Linda Perkins praised the book as "right on the mark for young children."

Zimmerman and Clemesha's next effort, 2000's *My Dog Toby,* earned similarly positive reviews. In this story, a young girl is convinced of her basset hound's intelligence, despite his inability to learn tricks. Even though the girl's brother suggests that the dog might be "dumb," she perseveres and eventually teaches her pet to sit, leading her brother to conclude that "he's a smart dog" after all. Commenting in *Booklist,* Carolyn Phelan commented on "the understated humor of the text," and summarized the work as "a warm, witty picture book celebrating the mutual devotion of dogs and their owners." *New York Times Book Review* critic Adam Liptak observed that "[Zimmerman and Clemesha] infuse the story with some gentle lessons about appreciating dogs—and people—for what they are."

Zimmerman once commented: "I enjoy making books to amuse young children. I try to place myself in the mind of a child to see the world as children do and to write about what interests them in a way they will find most entertaining. My husband, David, and I work together, inspired by our own children, our own childhoods, and the other children we meet. We are now illustrating some of our books, as well as writing them. We love the thirty-two-page format of picture books for its simplicity and wide potential."

Biographical and Critical Sources

PERIODICALS

Booklist, December 1, 1978, Barbara Elleman, review of *Yetta the Trickster,* p. 621; January 15, 1982, Ilene Cooper, review of *The Riddle Zoo,* p. 656; May 1, 1993, Ilene Cooper, review of *The Cow Buzzed,* p. 1606; August, 1999, Linda Perkins, review of *Trashy Town,* p. 2067; May 1, 2000, Carolyn Phelan, review of *My Dog Toby,* p. 1666.

Horn Book, March, 1999, Nancy Vasilakis, review of *Trashy Town,* p. 204.

Kirkus Reviews, June 1, 1993, review of *The Cow Buzzed,* p. 730.

New York Times Book Review, May 14, 2000, Adam Liptak, "It's a Dog's Life," p. 29.

Publishers Weekly, May 24, 1993, review of *The Cow Buzzed,* p. 84; April 26, 1999, review of *Trashy Town,* p. 82.

School Library Journal, January, 1979, Mary I. Purucker, review of *Yetta the Trickster,* p. 49; February, 1982, Lois Kimmelman, review of *The Riddle Zoo,* p. 72; May, 1999, Lisa Dennis, review of *Trashy Town,* p. 102; May, 2000, Holly Belli, review of *My Dog Toby,* p. 159.

Cumulative Indexes

Illustrations Index

(In the following index, the number of the *volume* in which an illustrator's work appears is given *before* the colon, and the *page number* on which it appears is given *after* the colon. For example, a drawing by Adams, Adrienne appears in Volume 2 on page 6, another drawing by her appears in Volume 3 on page 80, another drawing in Volume 8 on page 1, and so on and so on . . . .)

YABC

Index references to *YABC* refer to listings appearing in the two-volume *Yesterday's Authors of Books for Children,* also published by The Gale Group. *YABC* covers prominent authors and illustrators who died prior to 1960.

X

Y

Yakovetic, Joe *59:* 202; *75:* 85
Yalowitz, Paul *93:* 33
Yamaguchi, Marianne *85:* 118
Yang, Jay *1:* 8; *12:* 239
Yap, Weda *6:* 176
Yaroslava *See* Mills, Yaroslava Surmach
Yashima, Taro *14:* 84
Yates, John *74:* 249, 250
Yee, Wong Herbert *115:* 216, 217
Ylla *See* Koffler, Camilla
Yohn, F. C. *23:* 128; *YABC 1:* 269
Yorke, David *80:* 178
Yoshida, Toshi *77:* 231
Youll, Paul *91:* 218
Youll, Stephen *92:* 227; *118:* 136, 137
Young, Ed *7:* 205; *10:* 206; *40:* 124; *63:* 142; *74:* 250, 251, 252, 253; *75:* 227; *81:* 159; *83:* 98; *94:* 154; *115:* 160; *YABC 2:* 242
Young, Mary O'Keefe *77:* 95; *80:* 247
Young, Noela *8:* 221; *89:* 231; *97:* 195
Yun, Cheng Mung *60:* 143

Z

Zacharow, Christopher *88:* 98
Zacks, Lewis *10:* 161
Zadig *50:* 58
Zaffo, George *42:* 208
Zaid, Barry *50:* 127; *51:* 201
Zaidenberg, Arthur *34:* 218, 219, 220
Zalben, Jane Breskin *7:* 211; *79:* 230, 231, 233
Zallinger, Jean *4:* 192; *8:* 8, 129; *14:* 273; *68:* 36; *80:* 254; *115:* 219, 220, 222
Zallinger, Rudolph F. *3:* 245
Zebot, George *83:* 214
Zeck, Gerry *40:* 232
Zeiring, Bob *42:* 130
Zeldich, Arieh *49:* 124; *62:* 120
Zeldis, Malcah *86:* 239; *94:* 198
Zelinsky, Paul O. *14:* 269; *43:* 56; *49:* 218, 219, 220, 221, 222-223; *53:* 111; *68:* 195; *102:* 219, 220, 221, 222
Zelvin, Diana *72:* 190; *76:* 101; *93:* 207

Zemach, Margot *3:* 270; *8:* 201; *21:* 210-211; *27:* 204, 205, 210; *28:* 185; *49:* 22, 183, 224; *53:* 151; *56:* 146; *70:* 245, 246; *92:* 74
Zemsky, Jessica *10:* 62
Zepelinsky, Paul *35:* 93
Zhang, Ange *101:* 190
Ziegler, Jack *84:* 134
Zimic, Tricia *72:* 95
Zimmer, Dirk *38:* 195; *49:* 71; *56:* 151; *65:* 214; *84:* 159; *89:* 26
Zimmermann, H. Werner *101:* 223; *112:* 197
Zimnik, Reiner *36:* 224
Zinkeisen, Anna *13:* 106
Zinn, David *97:* 97
Zoellick, Scott *33:* 231
Zonia, Dhimitri *20:* 234-235
Zudeck, Darryl *58:* 129; *63:* 98; *80:* 52
Zug, Mark *88:* 131
Zuma *99:* 36
Zvorykin, Boris *61:* 155
Zweifel, Francis *14:* 274; *28:* 187
Zwerger, Lisbeth *54:* 176, 178; *66:* 246, 247, 248
Zwinger, Herman H. *46:* 227
Zwolak, Paul *67:* 69, 71, 73, 74

Illustrations Index

Author Index

The following index gives the number of the volume in which an author's biographical sketch, Autobiography Feature, Brief Entry, or Obituary appears.

This index includes references to all entries in the following series, which are also published by The Gale Group.

YABC—*Yesterday's Authors of Books for Children: Facts and Pictures about Authors and Illustrators of Books for Young People from Early Times to 1960*

CLR—*Children's Literature Review: Excerpts from Reviews, Criticism, and Commentary on Books for Children*

SAAS—*Something about the Author Autobiography Series*

Author Index

Author Index